ce

UTH(

W

Reeftown elite

Reeftown elite

Social mobility in a
black African community
on the Johannesberg Reef

Mia Brandel-Syrier

AFRICANA PUBLISHING CORPORATION · NEW YORK

First published
in the United States of America 1971
by Africana Publishing Corporation
101 Fifth Avenue
New York, N.Y. 10003
© Mia Brandel-Syrier 1971
All Rights Reserved
Library of Congress catalog card no. 70–151 968
ISBN 0 8419 0072 8

Printed in Great Britain

This book is dedicated to Mina Mabombo, brilliant, lovable, poor little Mina, who died from a final fit in a lonely hut in Botswana, abandoned by her family, next to her third fatherless child – and through her to all African women who, as women always do, carry the whole burden of a rapid, all too rapid change.

'It is a lonely man who is not taken seriously by his own people, yet cannot keep aloof from them and their daily miseries.'

Ezekiel Mphahlele
The African Image

Contents

List of tables and figures

Figures

Foreword

by Professor M. G. Marwick

The Reef, or more properly the Main Reef, is the band of gold-bearing conglomerate, a part of the Witwatersrand geological system, whose outcrop runs east and west along the southern Transvaal with Johannesburg at its centre. In human terms 'the Reef' has come to mean the lateral extensions, east and west, of the conurbation that has sprung up on the basis of gold mining and, in those places where maximum workable depths have been reached, has continued on the foundation of the secondary industries that have succeeded it.

In this, South Africa's largest conurbation, there is, in accordance with colonial tradition and more recent legislation, a clear zoning of the residential areas of black and white. In Johannesburg itself, for instance, Africans, who make up some sixty per cent of the city's million or more inhabitants, live in a cluster of townships, i.e. subsidized municipal housing estates, known collectively as Soweto, which are tucked over the south-western horizon out of sight and largely out of mind of the city centre and of most of the white suburbs.

The mining settlements along the Reef east and west of Johannesburg have their own African townships similarly segregated. This book is about the leading residents of one of these townships. It provides a detailed and unusual view of a small but important cranny in the massive edifice of the South African social system. The starker outlines of this system are, of course, well known, since they are the subject of unending debate between critics in the outside world who attack it and those in power within the country who cherish and defend it. To outsiders the system is simply an extension into the twentieth century of the more blatant form of colonialism that was widespread in the nineteenth, a system originally developed for the effective short-term exploitation of a colony's resources, both material and human. Though the countries of most of the critics are nowadays themselves involved in a subtler form of predatory activity, sometimes referred to as 'neo-colonialism', which achieves equally profit-able economic objectives without using the obvious political trappings that seemed essential to them in the nineteenth century and that now linger on with an artificially revived resilience in the Republic of South Africa, they are embarrassed by the unsubtle South African methods of exploiting their 'colonized' indigenous peoples and other ethnic divisions of minority status.

As outside critics see them, South African whites resort to the outdated, though convenient, device of dressing their subjugated second-class citizens in what Hilda Kuper has called 'the uniform of colour'. This time-honoured method involves the socio-political elaboration of genetic categories in such a way that those with recognizable and undisputed traces of non-Caucasoid ancestry are conveniently placed in separate, easily identifiable categories over which, by discriminatory customs and laws, control may be exercised. Outsiders regard the control that is exercised over second-class citizens as a means of their short-term exploitation; for, they point out, it usually involves preventing them from acquiring and exer-cising skills that would be competitive with those of first-class citizens.

To the latter, viewing the system from within, the controls are applied to the indigenous and associated non-white categories of the population 'for their own good' – a phrase interpreted in a variety of ways, including 'for their protection against the effects of too rapid change,' 'to preserve pride in their own culture,' 'to prevent the [believed] adverse effects of intermarriage and miscegenation,' and so on.

Thus, while opponents and supporters of the South African social system perceive it in the same way, they differ in their interpretations of its rationale. The political debate between them has tended to obscure the basic facts that human life everywhere is never totally a matter of politics; that people have other interests; that, even where political activity is forcibly suppressed, life still goes on in its rich variety; and that under a rigid system of control people preserve their sanity – though, to some critics perhaps, postpone their ultimate relief – by busying themselves with their non-political interests.

Mrs Brandel-Syrier tells us a great deal about the non-political activities of the social elite of the African township that she calls Reeftown. Rather than attempt to present the totality of urban African social stratification on some strained Weberian or Warnerian model, the author has wisely confined her attention to the social elite of Reeftown, i.e. those whose social status is pre-eminent and whose claims to social superiority are generally recognized among other residents. She is careful to point out that, while most studies of elites refer to national ones, the subjects of this study constitute a local elite, having characteristics, especially those relating to behaving in a 'polished', 'cultured' way, that bring them together and cause them to be treated as a [Warnerian] local upper class. Particularly interesting is her insistence that the essence of elite qualification is something that has to be displayed: 'Like the proverbial justice which must be seen to be done, so also social status must be seen by the people. It must be "shown" or "displayed", as it was said' (p. 96). While this aspect of Reeftown elite behaviour makes it reminiscent of what Veblen called 'conspicuous consumption', the author's suggestion that it also has a link with a traditional emphasis on ritual display is well worth consideration. The emphasis by Reeftowners on the *style* of behaviour leads to an interesting anomaly. The status of the otherwise humble domestic servant is enhanced by her being a carrier of culture (in the popular rather than the social-science sense) from high-status white homes to African suburbs.

Mrs Brandel-Syrier's personal credentials and the methods she used emerge from various parts of the book, especially the Introduction and the Fieldwork (p. 297). Briefly these can be summarized by saying that she took full advantage of her 'stranger value'; that she undertook some strenuous and conscientious, yet natural and unsimulated, participant observation; and that she made detailed studies of the lives and career histories and the present circumstances of Reeftown's 'top sixty' men.

Though white, and inevitably thus identified by Reeftowners, the author's recent Dutch origin made both her English and Afrikaans 'as ungrammatical and foreign-accented as that of the subjects of her study', something she rightly describes as 'a very great advantage' (p. 299); for it gave her a neutrality which facilitated her collecting some fascinating material on African attitudes to the two ethnic divisions of white South Africans; and the conflict between these results, impressive in their authenticity, and MacCrone's pioneering use in South Africa of the Bogardus social distance test will call for a more careful definition of 'social distance'. Furthermore, Mrs Brandel-Syrier's status as a European (and, if I may say so from personal acquaintance, a cultivated European), as opposed to a locally born white, gave her the additional advantage of being able to excel in, and be helpful about passing on, the very graces of living that the Reeftown elite respected as genuine importations from the fountain-head of civilization rather than the local whites' imitations.

The book's most useful features are its richness of detail, its closeness to the people it describes and the objectivity of its analysis. These qualities must be attributed to the author's intellectual and social skills, her untiring participant observation and her comparative reading. She achieved a close empathy with her subjects, yet it was a controlled empathy that makes many of her passages reminiscent of

Veblen, though fortunately they are garnished with a kindlier wit. One need not extol the virtue of Mrs Brandel-Syrier's years of energetic application to the task of getting to know urban Africans in general and Reeftown and its elite in particular; for at every point it is abundantly clear that she enjoyed her participation in their life and that what might well have been a chore to many a research worker was an enthralling pursuit to her. In getting on equally well with the elite and the township administrators, she was of course fortunate as well as tactful. I had the privilege of knowing the township manager whom she calls 'Mr Jones', and I share her regard for him. It is sometimes said that it is the inefficiency of a Police State that makes it bearable. It is equally true that the rigours of an extended colonial system are sometimes mitigated by the humanity and resourcefulness of an administrator who, confronted by inadequate resources and largely restrictive legislation, develops a consummate skill in extracting from an array of mainly negative conditions every possible advantage that he can win for those in his care. Mr Jones played this part with a quiet, unassuming brilliance, and Mrs Brandel-Syrier's tributes to him are well deserved.

The worth of the book rests on its author's close-up, penetrating, intuitive perception and her comparative analysis rather than on the experimental design or the statistical significance of the research it presents. Although the author has commendably set herself the modest target of providing a qualitative rather than a statistical analysis, she has not neglected similar studies both in South Africa and overseas, and her account of the elite of Reeftown is enhanced by her frequent comparisons of them with the subjects of other studies. These are constant reminders of the fact that, however enthralling the particularity and peculiarity of African townsmen may be, they are townsmen as well as Africans, sharing many of their problems and characteristics with recently urbanized or 'suburbanized' peoples all over the world. In this sense Mrs Brandel-Syrier is *au fait* with sociological theory relevant to her task. Yet one can say with no disrespect to her or to her scholarship that she herself fits the description she gives of her African assistant, the late Miss Mina Mabombo, a description that adds to the sense of poignancy one feels at the loss of Miss Mabombo to social science: 'With her natural powers of observation unimpaired by sociological training, she had an unusually enquiring mind . . .' (Preface).

The kernel of the author's research material consists of the life and career histories of the sixty most socially pre-eminent Reeftowners, and she makes many verbatim references to her detailed records of these, which in some measure she standardized for comparability. These records describe the paths that the elite have taken to their present local pre-eminence and cover their occupational, educational, economic, religious and ethnic characteristics, their domestic circumstances and their relationships with the community in which they lived at the time of the research. Interestingly enough, they show many of the characteristics of the residents of overseas suburban housing estates, such as having greater status anxiety than inner-city dwellers and, among those of highest rank, a tendency to withdraw from community life and to acquire an immunity from the sanctions that normally sustain middle-class respectability. The author takes pains to show how they came to be what they are, climbing educational and occupational ladders, often in a curiously unambitious, unenthusiastic way, though frequently inspired and helped by various 'figures in the background', such as parents (especially mothers), siblings, other relatives, fellow Africans and, in some instances, whites, not forgetting the Afrikaner who 'is now kicking us into growing up' (p. 277) and who, contrary to widely held belief among whites, is preferred, at least by this African elite, to the English-speaking white South African (pp. 267 ff.).

The rise of the Reeftown elite illustrates one of the interesting paradoxes of a plural society. The impenetrable division between black and white acts as a ceiling to upward social mobility; and we are reminded of this by the set-backs some members of the Reeftown elite encountered on their way up. Yet, so massive and forceful is the system of black-white stratification that it creates not merely directly opposed social currents, but also some minor eddies with associated low-pressure areas which help to draw a small fraction of the black population into elite status. As Myrdal noted of the American South, 'while the caste order has held the Negro worker down, it has at the same time created petty monopolies for a tiny Negro middle and upper class' in professions, some service occupations and certain kinds of business.* Under the more articulated system of segregation enmeshing Reeftown, the range of opportunities – similarly for a small proportion of the residents – is even wider, certainly wide enough to justify the author's statement that, though the elite encountered a few set-backs because of colour, 'their colour had rather favoured their careers' in that 'separate development [the officially preferred translation of *apartheid*] gave them opportunities which they might not otherwise have had . . . . The elite arose in a vacuum and naturally filled it' (p. 290).

The book contains a rich assortment, yet a well ordered one, of some of the detailed records Mrs Brandel-Syrier has made of Reeftowners' attitudes, opinions, self-recriminations and aspirations. Her frequent use of verbatim quotations gives the work an unmistakable authenticity and attests to the excellence of the rapport she established with the Reeftowners. One can look forward to this book's sequel in

*Gunnar Myrdal, *An American Dilemma*, New York: Harper, 1944, pp. 693–4.

which she proposes to analyse the social, as against the more personal, factors in the rise to elite status.

In the Introduction Mrs Brandel-Syrier makes this claim: 'The concentration on only a few individuals and the use of the life-history technique have made possible a penetration in depth as yet rarely attained in urban African research; areas have been reached as yet seldom touched by sociological investigation. These open up new fields of study and indicate a number of new questions which can meaningfully be asked. This will probably prove the main value of this research.' By British standards this may not be a modest claim, but it is far from being an extravagant one.

University of Stirling

Preface

This book is based on material collected during the period of a Nuffield Research Fellowship; and I must begin by expressing my thanks to the Nuffield Foundation in London and to the Nuffield Committee of South Africa.

A research project of this nature owes much to the assistance and information given by others. Among these I want to thank most warmly the European Administrators of the Reef township where my research was conducted and who, perforce, cannot be mentioned by name. These include the Manager and Assistant Manager of the Non-European Affairs Department; the two Senior and the four Junior Superintendents, and, particularly, the Township Manager himself. I want to thank these persons not only for their permission to enter the township freely whenever I wished but even more for their confidence in my bona fides and for their patience with my many demands upon their time. This township was more than usually blessed in having a local authority that was at once able, well informed and devoted to a task which was of a magnitude and complexity of which too few people in South Africa, and even fewer in other lands, are aware. I hope I have not betrayed their trust.

I also want to thank the officials of the Department of Bantu Education in Johannesburg, particularly Mr A. S. Bosman, and those of the office of the Chief Bantu Affairs Commissioner, particularly Mr M. Smuts and Mr F. H. Cronjé, for permission to interview their employees during office hours and for much general information.

I owe a debt to the late Professor J. D. Krige, at the time Head of the Department of Social Anthropology at the University of Natal, who supervised and guided the collection of the earliest data for this research. I want to put on record here that, at a stage when I was still expecting the contrary, he predicted that I would find that the elite 'almost automatically fitted into their niches' and 'did not have to begin from scratch'. I also acknowledge the assistance and criticism of Professor M. G. Marwick, at the time Head of the Department of Social Anthropology at the University of the Witwatersrand, during the first period of the interpretation and the patterning of the material.

I also wish to acknowledge the general information so readily given by Miss Giesela Feldman, at one time Head of the Research Department of the Non-European Affairs Department of Johannesburg, as well as by her successor, Miss Joan Verster.

I am further indebted to Professor J. E. Kerrich for statistical advice; to Mr Douglas Hawkins for statistical calculations; to Miss Annabel Goad for drawing some graphs; and to Miss Maryanne Liackman for typing the script. Special thanks are due to Mrs Roy Macfarlane and Mrs A. Prath-Nickels, who helped to correct and improve my English. I am, however, conscious that in spite of their efforts, my English is and remains essentially foreign, the English of someone born and schooled in Holland and for whom English was only a fourth language.

Most of all I probably benefited from the help of Miss Mina Mabombo, my research assistant, who went to live for a while in the township among its residents. Persevering in spite of heavy odds, she assisted me not only in collecting but also in interpreting the data. To facilitate our co-operation, she found a room with my (then) next-door neighbours, and after all the material had been gathered, she worked daily for more than a year with me in my house analysing and classifying, counting and explaining. Exceptionally intelligent, she brought to the task an unusual frankness and a healthy curiosity about her own people. With her natural powers of observation unimpaired by sociological training, she had an unusually enquiring mind and a keen sense of humour. But best of all, she was and dared to be African.

With deep gratitude I finally wish to acknowledge the suggestions and criticism received from Professor Eileen Jensen Krige, Professor of Social Anthropology and Head of the Department of African Studies at the University of Natal; from Professor A. van Selms, Professor of Semitic Languages and Head of the Department of Semitic Studies at the University of Pretoria; and from Mr K. B. Hartshorne, formerly Circuit Inspector of Bantu Education, Johannesburg, and at present Education Planner at the Head Office of the Department, Pretoria. Their willingness to read through the final draft and to give me the benefit of their expertise has been a great encouragement to me.

Last but not least, the people of Reeftown have to be thanked: the elite for their friendship, their confidence and hospitality; the other residents for the kindness with which they tolerated my presence, invited me to their homes, and allowed me to participate in their social lives. Countless people gave me long hours of their time, and bore willingly with my many questions which often dealt with subjects far beyond the immediate requirements of the investigation.

The period of the field research was a disturbed time. There were political upheavals, while further unpopular legislation was enacted. Among others the following occurred: the Treason Trial, the Sharpeville as well as the Langa disturbances; the declaration of the state of emergency and the detention of the leaders; the investigation into the financial affairs of the African businessmen with a view to taxation; the survey among the entire urban population to determine adherence to Chiefs so as to prepare the way for the 'tribal' ambassadors and Urban Bantu Councils; the introduction of passes for women; the passing of the 'Locations in the Sky' Act, etc.

Such events could have threatened the continuation of a research which relied so much on *rapport* between investigator and investigated. Fortunately they did not. For three months in 1960, the township manager asked me to stay away from the area, and for some time thereafter I was still not allowed entry after dusk. But interviews were not too severely curtailed, because my subjects were kind enough to come to me. Contact was maintained and the work continued in my own home in a Johannesburg suburb and in a friend's office in the centre of the city.

If I have understood something of these people in between two cultures, this is due to the explanations so freely and generously given by those among my informants who became my friends and whose friendships continue to this day.

Introduction

The aim of this book is to present an analytical description of the life and career histories of sixty African male individuals who, in the early sixties, constituted the entire social elite of a Bantu township on the Reef of the White Waters in the Transvaal – a township which we called Reeftown. The aim was to discover some of the circumstances which contributed to their upward social mobility.

In recent years, a large volume of literature has arisen around the term 'elite' but, in spite of all controversies, it has been generally accepted as useful in the study of the new social differentiations arising in African societies. The term 'elite' has come to stand for pre-eminence in a particular field of activity, in any one domain of social action.[1] By defining the field of human activity, and the degree of skill or talent required for pre-eminence in that field, the problem of the identification of those to whom this concept applies is solved. In certain applications of the word, this field of activity itself does not even need to be socially highly valued. Therefore, there may be as many elites as there are institutional or occupational hierarchies. But in general usage in social surveys of modern Africans, the particular segment of society in which the elite occupies the top positions ranks high in functional significance.

The objects of this study are not just what would be more properly called a 'sectional' or an 'occupational' elite,[2] but they are a 'social' elite. They occupy positions at the top of the social pyramid in Reeftown. They can claim a position of social superiority in the social life of the township. They enjoy not only a high occupational, educational or financial status but a status more properly called 'social'; what Nadel calls a status of a 'generalized nature',[3] defined as a 'broad pre-eminence extending beyond any one particular domain of activity'.[4] It is this 'social' status, which is not entirely separated from, nor necessarily connected with, the other more specific statuses,[5] which is the common characteristic of a 'social' elite, and in the same way as social status is related to any one of the sectional statuses, so a 'social' elite is related to any one of the sectional elites. Briefly, the term refers solely to position in the social structure and not to any particular behaviour patterns or domestic habits, social styles or moral values.

They are, moreover, an 'educated' elite, a more particularly African concept which they themselves variously describe as 'enlightened', 'polished', 'cultured', 'advanced', 'progressive', 'refined' or 'elevated' – in fact by any other word but 'western' or 'European'.[6] It is by virtue of this characteristic that these individuals can and do associate in a number of socially significant ways, and thus perform the functions of a local upper class.

Most definitions of elite and most elite studies refer to national elites, whereas the subjects of this study form a local elite. A full explanation of the differences between a local and a national elite cannot be given here; but it must be made clear that the findings of this study of a local elite may, but need not necessarily apply to a national elite.[7] Like any other, the African social stratification differs according to the point of view adopted, and the prestige stratification differs according to whether the local scene is viewed from the local point of view, the African national point of view or the European point of view.

Figure 1 The African social stratification as seen from three different points of view:
The national (European), the national (African) and the local African points of view

The European national point of view	The African national point of view	The African local point of view
The African Middle Class[8]	Upper Upper Ordinary Upper Upper Middle	Upper Upper Middle Upper Lower Upper
(An in-between group)	Ordinary Middle	Upper Middle Ordinary Middle
Labourers	Lower	Upper Lower Ordinary Lower

In this schematic representation, the sizes of the cells bear no relationship to the sizes of the population strata.

First of all, much finer distinctions are made locally between the different social strata on the basis of more detailed personal knowledge and actual frequent communication; and this applies particularly to the local upper class, which is quite clearly divided in an upper-upper, a middle-upper and a lower-upper stratum.[9] This type of prestige evaluation becomes more difficult when the personality recedes into the further distance of the nationwide African level. From this national point of view, the same group which in the community is divided into two distinct strata, an upper-upper and a middle-upper stratum, does not appear to be differentiated at all. In addition, this is not considered to be the highest social stratum in South African Bantu society. Similarly, two strata which are clearly distinguishable on the local level, that is the local upper-middle and the ordinary middle class, appear as one ordinary middle class from the African national point of view. Moreover, the local lower-upper stratum, seen nationally, does not even belong to the upper class, but corresponds to the national upper-middle class.[10] In the national upper class, a very small, more exclusive top stratum can be distinguished;[11] but this national upper-upper stratum may have no representatives in the community at all, and in fact did not have any in Reeftown.

Again, from the European point of view, the differentiations between the Africans are even less clearly marked, which results in their designating as 'the African middle class', groups of Africans which are clearly distinguished from the national African point of view and even more so from the local point of view.

Therefore, as and when the field of observation becomes larger and the perspective widens, certain social-class distinctions become progressively blurred.[12] But this is not all – a further result of distance is that the relative importance of certain indicators of social status changes. For instance, residential or marital circumstances, which are of such importance for status on the local level, become less important on the national level, whereas the status importance of occupation increases proportionately.

Even entirely new dimensions of social class can appear in the shift from one point of view to another. When looked at from the African national point of view, real political or socio-religious power becomes an important class criterion. And again, on the interracial level the entirely new determinant of skin colour and race becomes a most important class symbol. This may, however, need some further elaboration.

When racial or cultural antagonisms run high in a country, individuals of each group will be forced to identify themselves with their own racial or cultural group rather than with any other reference group. In such a situation, ethnic consciousness becomes a more important locus of identification than social-class consciousness. This can be observed every day among the different white groups in South Africa, where the situation is similar to that in other heterogeneous countries, for instance, Canada and Belgium or even Finland. In these countries there are, within one 'white' context, two or more different ethnic groups whose linguistic and cultural differences are generally, but not always, reinforced by religious differences, and these differences become major factors in social grouping, to the extent that in certain situations social-status differences within each group become less important for social intercourse than the cultural differences between the groups.

As such a situation, Rosenberg cites war.[13] It is well known that war erases social-class differences within one country in favour of a national patriotism, even if only temporarily.

Such a situation also exists in the South African interracial relationships, in which linguistic and cultural differences between the ethnic groups are aggravated not only by religious differences but also by physical differences, such as skin colour, i.e. differences which no cultural assimilation can wipe out. In these circumstances, such differences cannot be seen in terms of social class. It is not that social-class consciousness in interracial intercourse disappears entirely but that it simply becomes located further down in the hierarchy of possible reference groupings. It becomes less important or even unimportant as a focus of group identification.[14]

Some Europeans do distinguish certain broad social-status differences among Africans, just as some Africans distinguish certain very broad social-class distinctions among the Europeans. But inevitably, there is a far greater awareness of the physical than of the social differences, and the one awareness tends to blot out the other. Only familiarity with these colour differences can gradually have the effect of raising the importance of social differences; but I still believe that it is probably valid to say that at present there is hardly a sense of social equality between the black and the white members of the equivalent social strata in black and white society. It is doubtful, therefore, whether social contact between the two main population groups, the black and the white can, in any meaningful way, be considered in terms of social class at all.

This is the reason why, in my opinion, the term 'African middle class' can have no meaning in terms of association and social interaction with the European middle class. However, it is not meant to have such an associative meaning. It stands for the appearance of certain occupations and a certain so-called 'European' style of life among some Africans in the African sector of South African society.

But, besides the difficulties of defining this 'European' style of life,[15] there is the even more salient objection that (as the Smythes also discovered about their Nigerian social elite)[16] because certain Africans seem to possess certain characteristics which are considered typical of a 'European' middle class, these Africans do not, therefore, occupy the position of a middle class in their own society. In some other aspects, perhaps not so easily observable, these same Africans possess certain characteristics which in western society have sometimes been associated with 'the lower classes', but this does not make these Africans 'lower class' in their own society. Again, in other respects, some of these same, so-called 'middle-class' Africans have the status and perform the roles characteristic of certain upper classes in historical and present-day Europe.[17] Such, for instance, were the subjects of this study, who were fully aware of this fact! To call them middle class places them, moreover, in an unfavourable position towards their occupational/educational/economic peers in the African independent states, where these latter are in their own communities definitely considered as an upper class.

Not only does this group of Africans not enmesh associatively with the European middle class in South Africa, but to consider them in terms of 'European' class patterns – especially in terms of the patterns which western European society manifested in one particular period of its development[18] – raises expectations about these Bantu individuals which they cannot possibly fulfil.

Consequently, it is preferable to approach the subject-matter in terms of 'elite'. The notion of elite does not imply any particular pattern of domestic or kinship relations, specific values and behavioural norms, particular tastes and recreational preferences, or specific ideals and aspirations. It refers exclusively to position in a particular social structure. The concept of 'social' elite refers to position in the prestige structure and to function in the social situations and public events of Reeftown.

Although the definition of a local and a social elite might now be agreed upon, the basic problem still remained: how to identify the elements in a given locality to whom it can be applied by means of valid, reliable and unequivocal measures which also make sense within a theoretical fabric.

In view of the fact that the local elite was also the local upper class, the sample was chosen by using a combination of two different methods. Later these appeared to resemble closely those used in the compilation of two different publications in America[19] and can, therefore, best be described by reference to them.

Who's Who in America is 'a nationally recognized listing . . . of the leading men and women in contemporary American life'.[20] These persons are individuals of high functional class position: they form the top of the major segments of American society. Their status is of the type termed 'achieved', and the selection is made on the basis of certain objective criteria by a board or panel appointed for this task by the publishers.

The *Social Register* is a type of publication compiled independently in some twelve leading American cities. It contains a listing of families of high social-class position; this position is of the type termed 'ascribed', and the election is on the basis of association. From time to time new members are added; they are proposed by persons already listed in earlier publications. An application form is completed and a number of families who have personal and more or less intimate social contacts with the proposed new members are required as seconders to provide all the necessary information. The procedure is similar to the manner in which members are admitted to certain social clubs.

Note that in *Who's Who* those included are individuals, whereas in the *Social Register* they are families. Furthermore, the former publication is of national scope, whereas the second applies only to local communities.

The first selective method could be applied without much difficulty. Reeftown society was still so uncomplex in its structure that the main institutions stood out clearly and unmistakably. They were Education and Administration; Law and Order, as well as Health and Hygiene (including Social Welfare); Trade, Commerce, Banking, and last, but not least, Religion and Politics. While in this selective method, objective criteria could determine inclusion, in the other, the associative method, personal recommendation by knowledgeable informants had to be added to the evidence from our participant observation of the township's affairs.

In our selection we made good use of the findings from the collective and individual ranking tests done over a period of three years, and during earlier investigations, as well as from careful observations of deference behaviour and social groupings.[21]

However, membership in the elite group was anything but a clearly defined and traditionally recognized status. There was no knife-edge borderline between this upper-class group of residents and what can be termed the upper-middle class of Reeftowners. It was difficult, therefore, to delineate the boundaries of the elite downwards and a certain arbitrariness could not be avoided.[22]

Final support for the validity of our selection came from unexpected quarters, when some recognized members of 'High Society' planned to start a new Cultural Club which would be 'very exclusive'. Membership was to be by invitation only, and the first round of invitations carried only the names of those in the 'Top Drawer'. But many of these, and particularly 'the Stiffs', did not even answer, let alone attend the opening meeting. Subsequently, membership was widened to the 'lesser people', but still to 'only the most enlightened', only 'Top Society', and a further round of invitations was sent out to individuals considered to be still among 'the Top people', though less so. We had the satisfaction of seeing all those who received invitations in our sample.

The main sociological tool employed has been the life and family history, which has been used as a means of learning about the socio-cultural milieu, and the past experiences of the individual.[23] Since these people were considered, by themselves and their community, as the most successful persons in the township, a study of their social origins and their careers becomes a study of social mobility.

Mobility is, again, one of those terms which, once introduced into social research, have subsequently been used with a great many different meanings; and, on the assumption that everyone knows what mobility is, it has seldom been defined.[24] Nevertheless, it has been used, often not without a certain vagueness, to describe events and situations which should have been distinguished.

First, it stands for 'change' (more precisely, 'changeability'). In this meaning researchers speak of job mobility, school mobility, geographical or residential mobility.[25] These terms simply denote job changes, school changes, residential changes, changeability or movements. In this meaning of change, the term 'social mobility' has sometimes been used in the sense of 'social change'.[26] As 'elite mobility', for instance, it means that positions at the top are open and accessible to everyone and that, therefore, changes of elite occur.[27]

Secondly, however, the term 'mobility' has been reserved for a particular type of social change, namely, for those changes which refer only to social class and social status. When used in this meaning it is coupled with various adjectival specifications, such as occupational mobility, educational mobility or residential mobility, and indicates that these changes were co-extensive with, or coincidental to, changes in social class and social status. It is in this more special sense of change that the term 'social mobility' is generally, but certainly not always, used. In order to ensure correct understanding, despite this confusion and vagueness, sociologists often write about 'social mobility upwards' or 'social mobility downwards'.

There is a further difficulty. 'Social mobility' as social change with reference to social class and social status, has also been used for some distinct levels of analysis.[28] The one deals with structural changes, i.e. changes in the basis and social structure of a society, with particular reference to changes in social-class relationships and particular class criteria. The study of 'social mobility' in this sense would imply the study of the rise and fall of social classes in the social structure[29] or the rise and fall of certain characteristics in their significance as class criteria.[30] In this sense, a study of 'occupational mobility' would refer to changes in our western social structure, with particular reference to the changing social-status importance of occupations.

On the other level of analysis, certain changes in social status have been studied over two or three successive generations of individuals, or in the lifetime of one individual, and these have also been called studies in 'social mobility'. If one investigates 'occupational mobility' on this level of analysis[31] the term refers to occupational changes over some generations or in the life of one individual, which were co-incidental with changes in the social status of these generations or individuals.[32]

Reissman[33] believes, rightly, that these two dimensions of social mobility – the structural and the individual generational – have not always been, yet should be, distinguished. Obviously, and with regard to this investigation, the social mobility of the African individuals dealt with in this book and that of the ascending generations to be dealt with in a later book are related to the changes in the structure of African society as a whole. These changes are, in their turn, again related to the changing function of the African sector in the European economy. But this will be taken for granted: we shall accept as given that the individuals who raised themselves so successfully in general social prestige as to occupy the highest social positions in Reeftown did so, not only because they were desirous and capable but also because in their changing society the opportunities arose.

Briefly then, the mode of social change studied here is social mobility on the level of the individual career, and certain more specific changes will be related to the same referent. For this reason these will be termed residential, educational and occupational mobility to distinguish them from home changes, school changes and job changes.

However, in so far as the social mobility of these individuals took place within the framework of a different culture, and probably by virtue of their successful acceptance of this culture in at least some of its values and institutions, this can also be viewed as cultural mobility. Hence we shall frequently use the qualification 'socio-cultural' to indicate the twofold changes, mobilities or processes in which our elite were engaged: the one in terms of cultural, the other in terms of social-status criteria.

Leaving the cultural aspect for a later publication, we intend in this book to emphasize rather the social-mobility aspect of the double process. Here we shall investigate more particularly the elite's social positions and roles in their community as well as the careers which have led up to these.

The data are presented in three parts.

Part One will describe the general setting within which the elite must be understood. While, as has already been mentioned, it must be taken for granted, generally, that the social mobility upwards of the individuals studied could not have taken place had their society not offered them the opportunities, we shall in 'The Historical Setting' give a thumbnail sketch of specific changes in the social structure of African society which have been producing and supporting this elite. In 'The Social Setting' we shall briefly survey the social context in which our elite performed their upper-class role.

After a general description of the elite and their position in Reeftown society, Part Two gives the career histories of the elite, and we follow their social mobility upwards in the actual educational and occupational mobility of the individuals themselves.

Part Three is devoted to a survey of the persons and personal influences which were important in shaping the careers of the elite.

Life and career histories have been used before in the study of social mobility and of elites.[34] It would appear, however, that the present study differs from those known to me in that the data have been presented in such a way that, in spite of their tabulation, their source in the individual life history remains constantly apparent. In most other career studies, not only the chronological narrative but also the direct personal touch – which is the quality *par excellence* of the life history – were forfeited in the logical and quantitative presentation of the material.

The life, career and family history is a personal document in which the subject is talking freely and 'off the record' and its value lies precisely in the fact that certain social processes 'can be seen with more intimacy and naturalness than if formal questions had been used'.[35]

Much has been written about the social sciences becoming ever more abstract and theoretical[36] in analyses in which the individual 'remains as a marionette dancing on the strings of (reified) culture forms',[37] and by techniques unsuited for the study of changing societies.[38] In this methodological impasse the life history can be useful. For surely the most practical and direct way of discovering how a culture is actually acquired is to go to the culture-bearing individuals themselves, and allow them to tell it in their own words, and as they want to.[39] While listening to the story, the reader not only 'learns something about the role of the individual in culture change',[40] but may be given 'an intuitive grasp of the full complexity of social life',[41] for when a culture is seen 'through the feelings of an individual it looks entirely different'.[42] But for this to be achieved the career history must be more than just a name for a group of specific questions relating to a career, and the life-history approach must be used not only to collect but also to present the material.

Though not based on actual life or career histories, the study on the French worker today by Andrieux and Lignon[43] does exactly this.

Like the present one, this French enquiry was based on material gathered largely without respondents being aware that they were interviewed. The authors, one of whom was a factory worker himself, initiated the conversations at the work bench and the conveyor belt, in washrooms and pubs, during lunch breaks and in many an odd hour, as well as during leisure times at the homes of the respondents. Like the present one it had no control group and was also, inevitably, based on a very small sample of only fifty-eight individuals. But the material was written up in such a way that intimacy was preserved; verbatim replies were quoted throughout and the workers were allowed to speak for themselves. Thus it has become a description of the French factory worker 'as he himself sees himself – of his hopes, his aspirations or the lack of them, as seen from within'.[44] The result (which is probably rare in sociology) is that the reader is given an understanding of 'what it feels like' to be a factory worker in mid-twentieth-century western Europe. And, inevitably, the findings come as a surprise.

It was, then, this beautiful French study which we held in mind when writing up our material; and it is hoped that the picture it conjures up is as vivid and convincing, and that it shows 'what it feels like' to enter, somewhat belatedly and precipitously, the modern world.

The great advantage of the life history is that it does not force an artificial framework on the subjects' replies, though this is precisely what poses formidable problems of analysis and patterning. However, besides the assistance of an African co-worker with unusual qualities, I had the tremendous advantage of many years of previous personal experience with Africans and an intimate knowledge of their locations and townships. I had the time and opportunity so seldom enjoyed by receivers of research grants and subsidies, to acquire personal knowledge of Reeftown and the Reeftowners – to get 'the feel' of the society from first-hand observations.[45] Consequently, the reader will find constant references to observed behaviour and to actual happenings in the township. Frequently, puzzling statements could be explained and supported by drawing on my knowledge of the total social context. In this way verbalizations could often receive meaning, and superficial findings depth. Here this study should make a real contribution.

I have striven throughout to reproduce the stories as near as possible as they were told, so that the reader can learn directly what the people were saying and how they were saying it.[46] I believe that the actual words carry a conviction and a meaning which is lost by paraphrase; they give an insight which is otherwise rarely obtainable. It may sometimes seem that the many literal quotations prolong the book unnecessarily, yet they lend intimacy and authenticity to the reports, and they provide the reader with the means of assessing for himself the validity of the interpretations offered. For that reason also certain histories relevant to particular points described previously, and reproduced exactly as they were told, are appended to some chapters.

It must be stressed that in these stories I have tried to follow faithfully the spokesmen's own logic and manner of expression, even in the passages which are not quotations. They reveal attitudes and sentiments which, though not purposely studied, nevertheless provide some of the most unexpected glimpses 'behind the scenes'. Hence the point of view adopted here is very much 'from within', and, therefore, the angle of vision is more closely focused on the intraracial than on the interracial situation. Since Europeans frequently assume that the side turned towards the European is 'all there is' in the African, and since Kuper[47] has specially highlighted the interracial situation, this book can act as a necessary corrective.

The necessity to conceal the respondents' identity has been a matter of constant concern. The main method has been fragmentation Each one of the sixty individuals is designated by a pair of initials, and for the sake of reference most of the quoted fragments relating to an individual bear these initials. It is possible that a reader could piece the fragments together; but wherever it really mattered, the initials have been changed. With regard to some longer reports, permission to quote was obtained. In this respect, the fact that some years have passed between the fieldwork and the appearance of this book is an advantage. On their never-ending search for promotion and advance, a majority of the elite will have left the township by 1970. While this does not invalidate the findings, it does impede easy identification.

In this type of study, in which the same group of individuals is looked at each time from a different angle, some repetition and overlapping is inevitable. Often a finding emerges from one context which later becomes confirmed by a similar finding from another. Many cross-references are required and these may sometimes be irritating. For this I crave the reader's indulgence.

For those readers who do not have much time – and there must be many such – every chapter concludes with a brief 'Summing Up' of the main points dealt with. For quick reference all headings are descriptive, and the main findings are reviewed in a final conclusion.

This study is the result of patient listening, verbatim recording, precise categorization and careful interpretation. No hypotheses were set up beforehand; the investigation did not set out to prove anything. The findings, and these were often unexpected and surprising for both investigators, have been allowed to emerge from the analysis of the data themselves.

There is no control group, but the siblings naturally offered themselves for comparison, and will be so used in a later book.

In many cases the validity of the statements could not be checked; reports about childhood, deceased parents, absent relatives and even about most of the siblings, had to be taken at their face value. The sample is small – too small for temporary variations in mood to be randomized. By and large, however, a plurality of periods of contact, interviews and contact situations, and the fact that the subjects formed an interacting group who knew one another well, contributed to eliminate inaccuracies which inevitably resulted from the spontaneous response of individuals in changing moods.

It must be stressed further that not only is the sample not necessarily representative for an elite taken over a wider area, but it is also hardly likely to be representative over a longer period of time. In such a rapidly changing society as that in which our elite were living, scarcely any predictions can be made from a study of people who were leading at one particular time. This is the reason why, after consultation with Professor J. E. Kerrich, Head of the Department of Statistics at the University of the Witwatersrand, I made no attempt at conclusive statistical evidence. Even though some of the figures are statistically significant – and in view of the smallness of the sample this would have been a desirable end – mention of this is generally omitted. For their validity, significance tests assume conditions which remain fairly stable, while I have stressed all along the general fluidity of the circumstances and the rapidly changing elite.

The material is presented in straightforward narrative. The tables have descriptive value only. Although sometimes words and expressions had to be used which in quantitative research have assumed a special technical meaning, they are not intended to have any other but their normal sense, as in general usage. For example, such words as, 'attitude' or 'motive', when discussing the reasons why certain decisions were made or the manner in which certain institutions were viewed. This is not an 'attitudinal' or 'motivational' research, but an attempt to encompass the total situational context. Lack of knowledge of such situational factors has, we believe, sometimes led quantitative researchers to misinterpretations or to the quantification of irrelevant concepts.

Our aim has been to describe the facts about a small group of people. It is not implied that they are necessarily similar to or different from other people of similar age, social position and educational level, whether in this or any other country, whether black, brown or white. Few comparisons with similar groups in this or in other countries have been made, for the simple reason that comparable researches about comparable groups hardly exist.

This book then presents a descriptive analysis of the lives and careers of one particular, well-defined elite of one particular well-defined Bantu township on the Witwatersrand of the Transvaal – the story of the lives and careers of sixty African men, as told by themselves. (The words 'African' and 'Bantu' will be used in the same meaning.) Everything said applies to these individuals only. No generalizations over a wider group of people have been made, nor are intended.

However, although a single case study as here presented cannot offer answers to the more general questions which arise in the context, it can stimulate the formulation of new hypotheses. And in this respect, the very limitations of this study may be its strength. The concentration on only a few individuals and the use of the life-history technique have made possible a penetration in depth as yet rarely attained in urban African research; areas have been reached as yet seldom touched by sociological investigation. These open up new fields of study and indicate a number of new questions which can meaningfully be asked. This will probably prove the main value of this research.

part one

The elite and their society

1 The setting

The historical setting

The people with whom this study is concerned lived in what was officially termed a Bantu township. Europeans in South Africa, always reluctant to change old conceptions, still called all places where black people lived 'native locations', while the people themselves talked about 'our village'. In reality, however, Reeftown was a subsidized housing estate, in many respects similar to those that, during the last twenty years, have arisen round London and other metropolitan areas in England and America, to house the overflow from congested conurbations and to clear slum areas from the city centres. As in England, these new housing estates were built well away from the city areas, and, as in England, the expectation was that more industries would settle in the neighbouring industrial areas to draw on the township's labour and provide jobs near home for the township's population. But also, as happened in England, this process has been slow and the synchronization of this double movement of decentralization of populations and industries has been defective. Consequently, many people still commuted daily over distances varying between eight and twelve miles.

Together with a dozen or so other black townships (which we shall call Reef towns), our Reeftown formed an almost continuous black belt south of the Witwatersrand. After a three months' general survey of these African Reef towns, it was selected without as yet any knowledge of its elite, for the following reasons: it had a capable and sympathetic white administration; it was near enough to my home for me to make frequent visits and keep regular contacts; it was safe enough to be visited by a woman alone, even after dark; it was old enough for its community life to have had a chance to

3

develop and to show something of the shape of things to come; and it seemed to possess the usual characteristics of social-status differentiation. Finally, it seemed to be a good average between Johannesburg and the other towns along the Reef.

Because of its core of long-urbanized people, Reeftown had a sophistication not far behind that of Johannesburg. Yet Reeftowners were said to be 'more helpful and co-operative'. But in comparison with the other towns on the Reef, Reeftowners were called 'less simple', 'less rural' and 'less friendly'. It had certain advantages over Johannesburg. Johannesburg's older districts represented earlier and probably disappearing patterns of community life, whereas its new and sprawling south-western areas, later called Soweto, were too vast and formless for a community study. By contrast, Reeftown seemed of the right size to be comprehended by a one-person research and not so unsafe after dark that it could not be visited by a woman.

People were happy to be in Reeftown and not in Johannesburg, which was 'too fast, too competitive and too dangerous'. 'In Johannesburg', they said, 'you can be killed any moment of the day, and any day, but in Reeftown there are whole blocks of streets where you can walk safely at night.'

As in any African area there was much violence and there were the usual murders, assaults and stabbings, particularly over the weekends. Generally, the motives were personal revenge or jealousy, and not greed. There were no large-scale gangs and no organized crime, though there were the usual Tsotsis or town toughs, as Monica Wilson calls them (Wilson, 1963, 7). 'The Tsotsis are violent and boisterous, given to smoking dagga and fighting with knives. They are a byword among the migrants and "decent people" in town for their "wildness" and the migrants will have nothing to do with them' (*op. cit.*, 23). In spite of this, the Tsotsis were small-fry in comparison with such Johannesburg personages as the bank-roll robbers, the big gang leaders, the hired murderers and the successful illicit dagga, gold and diamond dealers who frequented the shebeens of the City of Gold, and who were rarer in the Reeftown shebeens.

Reeftowners often said jokingly about themselves: 'Of course we're always "agin", we're old urban people', or, 'Naturally we're hard on the white administration. Honestly, it's a shame!' They agreed that their own white administration was 'not bad as they go'.

Among administrators, Reeftown was considered a 'difficult' township, almost as bad as Johannesburg. The people themselves blamed the bad inheritance from the old location for what they described as the general money consciousness, the heavy drinking and the low educational standards of the schools. The nearness of a hospital and of a chemical factory were given as reasons why people found it easy to obtain illegal spirits. 'There's always trouble in Reeftown,' people said. 'People are used to town life, used to having things and they always want more.'

Johannesburg, however, was said to be 'more progressive', while Reeftowners were 'not interested politically'. People were too dependent on a benevolent administration for loans and licences, jobs and recommendations. Politicians in Reeftown complained that if the people were not going 'to sacrifice', they themselves were not going 'to do all the sacrificing alone'. During 'The Emergency', Reeftown kept so quiet that it incurred a severe reprimand from Johannesburg political headquarters, and a black policeman, disliked by everybody, was quickly murdered to show local political zeal.

One resident summed up the exact place of Reeftown in between Johannesburg and the other townships on the Witwatersrand: 'In Reeftown you're already somebody with R100 per month, whereas with R100 in Johannesburg you're still nowhere. On the other hand, in Reeftown you need more money again than in the other towns.'

Thus the important fact was revealed that Reeftown represented a fair average between Johannesburg, which was entirely exceptional in South Africa, and the rest of the country.

The dual orientation

The removal of the African populations from the earlier, congested locations to the new spacious townships, which came to be known as 'The Removal', precipitated certain changes in the social structure of these urban communities – changes which were in some respects surprisingly similar to those reported in a number of community studies of New Towns and Housing Estates.[1] (Frequent references will be made to these studies in the text.) On the other hand there were also some very great differences.

First, there was a difference in scale. The new community of Reeftown was only one little spot in the Republic's huge housing drive, launched on a nationwide scale after World War II to make up in one tremendous financial and organizational effort, for an accumulated African housing shortage estimated in 1952 at 167,000 houses. An additional shortage for the next ten years was calculated to be 185,000 houses,[2] a housing project of truly mammoth dimensions upon which, up to the end of 1960, the Government had spent a sum of over R200,000,000 (inclusive of services and transport) and which by 1962 was expected to have reached its target,[3] when it was hoped there would be no more slums in the urban areas.

The new Bantu townships which, as a result, had arisen everywhere alongside the white towns, already at this stage, contained much larger populations than any one of the English communities studied and previously referred to. Reeftown, for instance, had between 40,000 and 60,000 inhabitants and was expected ultimately to accommodate 100,000. Each of the new townships established alongside the main capital cities of the country may, in 1961, have already had up to half a million or more inhabitants.

There was, however, a much more important difference. The people we are dealing with here formed a sector of the South African population which, in terms of twentieth-century developments, as expressed in the notions of urbanization and industrialization, were in an earlier socio-economic phase. In addition, they formed a sector which occupied the position of a culturally distinct and racially differentiated group which, as political principle and economic aim, had to be developed as a separate unit; while, at the same time, it was expected to participate wherever needed in the wider commercial and industrial (European) development of the country as a whole.

For instance, the project to house – and house well – all South African urban Bantu next to the towns in which they had found or could find employment was the most positive expression to date of the further integration of increasing numbers into the urban (European) economy. But, on the other hand, it was also the final confirmation of the basic national (European) belief in residential as well as social separation between the two main population groups. These new housing estates owed their very existence – after due mention has been made of all financial and technical operations and research by the Government as well as by the Municipalities – to the Native Building Workers' Act of 1951 which, for the first time in the history of South Africa, made possible the use of African labour on African houses at rates of pay less than those stipulated for builders of other races. Subsequently, each city council set up its own housing department and implemented a crash programme to train African building workers; and this, in its turn – particularly as the building trade in new countries was one of the pivotal economic activities – brought new occupations, new skills, new opportunities and new wealth to the African people. Thus, the introduction of a differential wage scale in the building industry – a race-discriminatory measure – became a basis for economic growth and development on a scale hitherto unknown.

Inevitably, therefore, this dual orientation imprinted its stamp on the social changes which were triggered off by what came to be called 'the Removal', and resulted in two seemingly conflicting developments: on the one hand these changes reflected those which were also occurring in the western world generally; and on the other, they revealed the effects of the separate development of the African sector

6

in the national (European) context, towards which these new urban Bantu housing estates provided such a strong stimulus.

In so far as these recent social changes stimulated in these African communities the growth of new social differentiations and the rise of a new elite, or elites, they are of concern to us here. For the new 'social' elite which emerged in Reeftown also carried the mark of this dual orientation: of participation in the changes currently taking place in a wider world, and of separate development as a more recently urbanized and industrialized sector of the South African population.

To sum up briefly those all-pervading changes in the western world as far as relevant to our subject, we should mention two inter-related developments. First, the growing centralization in government, in commerce and industry[4] and in communications.[5] In fact, the increasing power of the state at the expense of local authority,[6] and the gradual disappearance of local self-government[7] have been observed and described in a great many books and articles. But not only were the activities of the state becoming more centralized, they were also becoming immensely extended in ever-expanding, more costly and complicated social and public services.

In industry, and in the economic sector generally, a similar development could be observed; centralization and the extension of competencies and responsibilities gave rise to the national combine and the international corporation.

Secondly, the positions of influence both in industry and government were increasingly being occupied by persons with professional qualifications and specialized training. Thus, in Government service, we find the local notable and amateur being replaced by the expert, the trained civil servant, the professional politician and the trade union official,[8] while in industry we see how the individual entrepreneur, the industrialist, the privately-owned factory, the family bank were gradually disappearing to make way for the specialist, the manager, the technician. In short, and as Birch writes: 'The new men of power derive their income from salaries, not from profits.'[9]

Increasing bureaucratization in Government services was the inevitable consequence of mass democracy, while 'The Organization Man'[10] was the product of mass-production. These changes which, although in differing degrees and with differing speeds, were occurring everywhere in the modern world, were giving rise to what in Anglo-Saxon countries were called 'the new middle classes'[11] and 'the new elite'.[12]

These changes were also beginning to be reflected in certain happenings in South Africa. For corroboration one need go no further than the South African Hansard and the local press in which

7

THE ELITE AND THEIR SOCIETY

numerous reports appeared concerning the battle of the small, individually-owned chemist's, butcher's and grocer's shops against the increasing competition by the chain stores.[13]

In so far as the new African communities rising up around the big industrial centres of South Africa were able to participate fully in these general socio-economic developments, one would have expected to see in the public sector the rise of a new Bantu elite of professional politicians and higher public servants, and in the private sector one would anticipate the emergence of a Bantu managerial class.

However, for reasons already explained, developments were less homogeneous. We were able to observe the rise of the salaried professional and the public servant, and here the new Bantu townships only hastened a development which would have taken place in any case because of the expansion and the bureaucratization of the African sector. But with regard to the rise of a Bantu managerial class, this was probably delayed, possibly even diverted, by the establishment of these townships. Instead, the townships have promoted the growth of the independent entrepreneur.

Some more specific, although interrelated, aspects of these changes will now be briefly discussed: the change from the local notable to the national professional politician; the replacing of the European by the African official; the rise of the public servant and the emergence of the individual entrepreneur.

The change from the notable to the professional politician

The rise of the professional politician went together with the shift of emphasis from local to national politics. We were fortunate enough to observe this at close quarters in the change in membership and role in the Advisory Board of Reeftown after it had been moved from the old location to the new township.

In the old location, the Advisory Board had been composed entirely of notables.[14] These were mainly the 'stand-owners',[15] consisting of businessmen of repute, members of the tribal aristocracy and an occasional professional. These persons have been commemorated in the names of the sections of Reeftown.

When the Administration explained 'The Removal', these experienced leaders recognized the inevitability, as well as the advantages, of the move and had promised to co-operate in principle, on certain conditions. Subsequently, however, they found it impossible to communicate their unpopular decision to their constituents, who, in the meantime, had been organized for resistance on a national scale. For, like the slum-dwellers elsewhere,[16] the location-dwellers did not want to move, but, unlike elsewhere, the local removal had become 'The Removal' and resistance to it 'The Resistance Move-

8

ment' – a matter of race relations and national politics. The older local leaders found themselves powerless in the face of their own electorate; they also found that, while they had lost the lead to the national politicians, they were, nevertheless, expected to act as living symbols of the struggle by remaining in occupation of their houses and refusing to move. Consequently, most of them remained in the location whereas, ironically, more and more of the active resistance fighters themselves moved to the new township. When, eventually, the first hesitant location leaders began to move and to occupy the houses built for them or built by them, they found that new men had already entered upon the scene.

In 1950, the first elections for a provisional, small three-member Advisory Board were held in Reeftown, bringing three persons to the fore. Next to a traditional leader, bearer of the most illustrious Bantu name, and a second person who was a schooled businessman, there was a Mr S., a new man with no occupational or educational distinctions. He was a member of the African National Congress and had been selected for the job and introduced to the people by one of the present Reeftown elite. This happened at the time when this person was still politically active.

For some years the representative of 'Royal Blood' maintained his elected position while the new man fortified his, and succeeded in having his own protégés elected. Educated Reeftowners still speak of this time when the two leaders – symbolic of traditional and modern power – worked together and 'everything was good'. The traditional leader was a successful butcher and a highly-paid industrial worker; but he was not 'educated', his English was poor, he never gave a public speech and never organized his elections. In 1956 he failed to win the popular vote, and the new man gained a significant majority. After that, the tribal aristocrat joined the ranks of Council nominees, together with some educated traders.[17]

This was the position when, in the winter of 1959, the Administration finally prevailed upon a batch of the 'strongest' board members of the old location to move to Reeftown. The township manager, whom we shall call Mr Jones, as well as many residents, keenly anticipated the impact of these mature and seasoned leaders on the next election in the new township but, a week later, the oldest and most respected of them suddenly died. He had been an elected parent member of the School Board and had held a number of high-status positions. Moreover, he had been known as a personal friend of the Manager of Non-European Affairs, whom we shall call Mr Uiterwyck, and his new township house had been specially built for him in the most exclusive area.

His sudden death shook the township. The 'Removal' resisters considered it 'God's punishment for abandoning the battle', and the politically active masses of Reeftown saw in it unmistakable proof of the strength of the new leadership. But, as always in the face of death and in spite of the warring factions, the township got together, and a committee was formed to plan the funeral, which had to be 'a statesman's funeral with a guard of honour', and 'like that of Mr Strydom' who had also been 'the lion of the North'. (Shortly before, Mr Strydom, the Prime Minister of South Africa, had died and, on the initiative of its leading ministers of religion, the township had held a Memorial Service which had been attended by Europeans and Africans.) In this both friend and foe agreed, and all gave donations.

The funeral service was held in the Dutch Reformed Church to which the deceased had belonged. All the notables of Reeftown, Europeans and non-Europeans, attended. There were the Mayor of the white town, in gown and chain, the Chairman of the Non-European Affairs Committee and the Manager, the township manager, officials from the Department of Bantu Education and a number of other European personages with their gloved and hatted wives.[18] There were representatives of the School Board, the School Committees, the teaching staff and the schoolchildren; ministers from all the status Churches; representatives of the Crèche Committee, the Independent Order of the True Templars and all the other organizations to which the deceased had belonged.

Many of Reeftown's leading professional men and businessmen were present, as were many ex-members of the previous Advisory Board. Conspicuous by their absence were the Chairman and members of the new Board, who boycotted the funeral. They did not even attend the funeral banquet to partake of the ox which Mr Uiterwyck had donated in honour of his 'lifelong friend and opponent'. It was the last occasion at which the older leaders, henceforth to disappear from the political scene, acted as a group. With this historic funeral an old era passed and a new epoch in the history of Reeftown began.

Since then the undisputed leader, elected yearly by a large majority, has been the aforementioned Mr S., the township demagogue. All the elected Board members were his creatures. At first he had been somewhat inexperienced, but latterly he had received adequate training and expert advice. It was rumoured that he was only 'small-fry' in the hierarchy of the African National Congress, but this was of little import, since his power in the township depended upon his personality.[19]

Voting participation, which had been decreasing steadily during the last few years, was further diminished by the total abstention of the elite and most of the educated people. For neither the aristocrats of education, nor those of wealth, nor, for that matter, the older aristocracy, were willing or able to participate in the elections as these were currently conducted by the township 'bosses'; in which candidates were manoeuvred out of the way by threats of blackmail and violence, money was obtained partly from outside sources and partly through rowdy drinking parties, and votes were secured by money payments together with various forms of illegal pressure and extortion. In fact, the last elections which we witnessed made a farce of democracy. Consequently, township politics had changed from co-operation to resistance.[20]

Tactics were aimed at destroying the habit of acceptance, by criticizing constantly in simple concepts and by attacks upon and ridicule of individual officials. Deliberations were governed by the need to show results in some matter of detail such as by succeeding in delaying or entirely putting off some small unpopular administrative measure. In fact, all administrative matters came to be used for political purposes. The aim was to find unity through hatred and negation, rather than through any constructive policy; and, at the same time, to avoid confrontation with the reality of their own lack of experience in financial and administrative matters by projecting the blame on the white Administration.

The township elite, who understood a little more about administration, were sincerely contemptuous of a leadership that 'played to the gallery', and directed itself exclusively to 'the *hoi polloi*'. On the other hand, they watched the new politicians with a certain benevolence because, at least at first, they believed that they 'did the dirty work' for them.

Thus, the Advisory Board of Reeftown changed from a civic institution of township notables to a political pressure group of township 'bosses'; and, instead of a channel of communication, it became a barrier between administration and administered. Although the increasing bureaucratization which 'inevitably accompanies modern mass democracy in contrast to the democratic self-government of small homogeneous units'[21] would, in any case, have led to the rise of the paid professional 'in place of the historically inherited avocational administration by notables'[22] this change might not have occurred so quickly had not 'The Removal' and the subsequent settlement in a new habitat precipitated events.

As it was, the emergence of the professional politician led to the withdrawal of the best-educated and most knowledgeable elements from creative participation in township affairs.

The receding European

Together with this change from the co-operative to the protest leader, and from the earlier more mellow black–white relationships to the new corrosiveness of a political battle, there was the change from the earlier personal relationships between administrator and administered to the new impersonal attitude of a large organization and the inevitable decentralization of a modern bureaucratic society.

In the old location, Mr Jones was accessible to everyone without discrimination. Assisted by only one European, he was available to settle disputes, reconcile opposing groups, impose fines for trespasses and solve the hundred-and-one problems of urban living. Even in the early days of the township, Mr Jones, dressed in shorts and open-necked sports shirt, rode on horseback over the *veld*, chatting with every family, scolding and praising, encouraging people to general tidiness. Older residents remembered how he had welcomed every new arrival personally, had shown them how the new stove worked, had explained what the new garbage can was for, and told them how to apply the whitewash on the stones which were destined to form a provisional fencing of each individual plot. Reeftowners themselves told us how Mr Jones himself brought the first seeds and saplings which were to become the vegetable and fruit gardens; how none of the first hardships on the dusty open *veld* were so bad because Mr Jones and his family lived in the original farmhouse in the same area where they themselves had 'no sewerage, no water, no electricity, and no nothing'. Assisted by one clerk and a freely-elected body of vigilantes, he kept order and often himself brought the groceries from town. He also fulfilled the task of a midwife, until a qualified nurse-cum-midwife was installed in the temporary office, together with the first greengrocer. Nevertheless, many a time he would get up in the middle of the night to fetch the doctor for urgent cases.

Since then Mr Jones had retreated behind an army of European and African officials. He now arrived by car, dressed in a lounge suit, to spend the day in a solemn office in the main Administrative building, which looked as forbidding as the town hall of any country town. His fate was similar to that of the District Officer in Tanganyika, described by Liebenow.[23] For, like his rural equivalent, the modern urban administrator was increasingly cut off from the intimate contact and the sources of information which were the by-product of the foot-safari, and which were so particularly valuable because they 'humanized' the European administrator in the eyes of the administered.

The new elite of public servants

A veritable hierarchy of African officials now separated Mr Jones from 'his' people – a development much regretted yet persistently encouraged by this experienced administrator. But the people themselves regretted it even more. 'Nowadays we can't get through any more', was the eternal complaint of the humbler residents, who saw themselves increasingly removed from the all-powerful source of all benefits. They now had to tell their troubles and their secrets to other Africans, in whom they had no confidence. Consequently, they doubted whether their interests would be well served.

However, the retreat of the European was general in all departments and on all fronts of interracial contact. The European welfare worker and health inspector, the European minister and teacher, the European sports and music organizer, became rarities in township life where before they had entered personally into the lives and homes of the people. The policy of Separate Development required that all institutions, such as homes, community centres, crèches and day nurseries, as well as all welfare organizations and recreational facilities be handed over to African control. Consequently, the Europeans now worked from head offices in town, which they seldom left and from which they directed and co-ordinated the activities of an ever-increasing Bantu staff, who had taken their places in all fields of activities.

But, even if Government policy had not forced the pace, and often prematurely insisted on the Europeans vacating certain senior positions, the 'Africanization' of the services would, nevertheless, have had to come. More and more matriculated and professionally-trained individuals were clamouring for jobs. The European private sector did not need nor desire any further Africans other than manual, even though skilled, workers. White-collar jobs for Africans in the European sector were few and minor, offering limited chances of promotion. Consequently, for almost all senior executive posts, for any positions of status and authority, Africans had to turn to the public services. As these services, whether controlled directly by the Government or indirectly through the provinces and the municipalities, constantly expanded and required a larger and increasingly expert staff and personnel, the 'Africanization' of this growing bureaucracy was not only the fruit of the official *apartheid* policy but in line with the requirements of an ever more articulated and socially differentiated society. Here again the new townships, such as Reeftown, provided many new openings. More schools, better services, more clinics, larger recreational facilities – all these demanded a continually growing nucleus of professionals, experts and administrators.

In this emergent Bantu society in South Africa, the conditions were not so very different from those prevailing in countries like Ghana or Nigeria, where, as 'in all underdeveloped countries the state plays an especially important role in all spheres of life';[24] the state becomes, of necessity, not only the largest single employer, but the largest single employer of educated Africans.

13

The beginning of a managerial elite

At the same time, certain economic changes were taking place. Wider urban experience, improving skills and better education were bringing steadily rising incomes and greatly increased needs. Gradually, and at first almost imperceptibly, these brought a change in the position of the African sector in the national (European) economy from 'labour' to 'market'. With this, the function of those who had hitherto only been workers became enlarged into that of 'buyers', and the largest internal market of buyers in Southern Africa began to open up.

This development was considerably stimulated by the rapid expansion of the new housing estates. Houses needed curtains and carpets, dining-room suites and kitchen schemes; new tea-sets required doilies, and display cabinets required *objets d'art*; house-proud hostesses needed tea and polishes; generous hosts cigarettes; and children's parties sweets and cold drinks.

Consequently, an increasing number of European manufacturers and importers began to open up African branches to deal more particularly with the specific requirements of this growing African market. And it was these African branches which provided a new field of employment for educated Africans. For the first time the European sector now had a use for them, not *in spite of*, but *because of*, their being Africans. They were needed as experts and consultants on sales techniques and on specific methods of approach, on special publicity angles, on African tastes and preferences, on African languages. As a result, educated Africans were appointed as management, sales and market experts. In executive positions they entered the private sector of the European economy, where Africans served other Africans. They became managers of African personnel departments and heads of African research departments. They obtained well-salaried posts as sales promoters for cigarettes and cold drinks and as demonstrators of soaps, margarines and oils, radios, sewing-machines and kitchen stoves. The wife of one of the leading Reef socialites was head of the African sales department in a large European furniture firm, and an ex-nursing sister was in charge of the African branch of a well-known European soft-goods dealer.

It became essential to reach this growing Bantu society of the educated and wealthy by means of modern media, and so the Bantu press and the Bantu radio received a tremendous boost. They enlarged their scope and reach to such an extent that the earlier handful of African editors and journalists, radio announcers and photographers grew rapidly into a first recognizable elite of communicators. Ultimately, radio transmissions were to be in seven Bantu languages. Programmes would require announcers and producers, record com-

14

pilers, sports commentators, journalists, artists, script-writers and authors, typists and clerks. Bursaries would become available for a three-year B.A. course for these communicators; and, as and when they attained executive positions, they would begin to swell the exclusive ranks of a growing managerial elite.

It must be emphasized, however, that this potential or actual managerial elite owed their existence to their competence as Africans, and their services were used entirely for the development and the service of the African market, considered to have different requirements from the white market. Nowhere, to my knowledge, has an African on the Reef attained a managerial position purely on the strength of his abilities and in the service of European customers. (The few exceptions may be in those places in which these Africans can be screened off from European customers.)

The rise of an entrepreneurial elite

Whereas, for a number of reasons, this budding African managerial elite working for the African market in the European sector could never enjoy the general prestige in the social life of African society which their European equivalents can count upon in European society, the most undivided public esteem was directed towards the emergent entrepreneurial elite. Occupationally, all other things being equal, an African housing contractor and an African estate agent could enjoy in Reeftown greater prestige than an African manager of the African sales department of a cold drinks corporation.

This, possibly surprising, emphasis on the independent entrepreneur was evidenced by the fact that he was seen by some leading black[25] and some white[26] observers as the only sign and token by which the so-called African middle class could become a 'true'[27] middle class. This was the result of the current fashion among some Europeans considering African social differentiations entirely in terms not only of European class patterns, but even worse, of pre-twentieth-century European class patterns.

Whereas the earliest members of an incipient managerial elite among the Bantu have remained unsung, the emergent entrepreneurial elite (as was also the case with the first pioneers of an educated and professional elite before them) have been applauded and welcomed, investigated and recorded.[28] The entrepreneur rather than the manager has found his patrons and promoters among the Government and the Official Opposition alike. Even as the Government was making serious efforts to create a land-owning farmer-class in the rural areas set aside for Bantu occupation, so they were giving a similar encouragement in the urban areas set aside for African residence, to

15

the formation of an entrepreneurial class which, as soon as it became successful, was expected to transfer its capital and experience to the Bantu homelands, there to become pioneers of African development in providing employment and creating wealth for the rural Africans. The Official Opposition, however, hoped that by encouraging the growth of a Bantu business elite, they would help to create, on the one hand, a firm nucleus for a stable urban population, and, on the other, an independent political pressure group which would naturally be opposed to the policy of separate development (cf. p. 43) and would demand political power in an integrated society.

On moving to Reeftown, the shop-owners and merchants of the old location, as well as those who had been members of the location Advisory Board, all of whom automatically had the right to business premises, were given the pick of the trading sites. Thereafter, any-one who could show that he had the necessary capital and resources could apply for a licence and obtain a business site. On the principle of one man one shop, Mr Jones hoped to give all capable and enter-prising residents a chance.

In the geographical isolation of Reeftown, many a small Bantu investor or saver had an opportunity to try his luck and his business acumen in a small shop or in a business of his own. Many a first, tentative trading venture would never have had a chance of success had it not been assisted by official, local *apartheid* regulations, which prohibited investment by European capital and enterprise, and re-stricted the activities of non-African sales representatives – regu-lations increasingly enforced as a result of the repeated demands of the Reeftowners themselves. Official policy here ran parallel to the general preference of the present-day Africans for any form of independent business enterprise among their own people, rather than for Euro-pean employment, even though the latter might afford higher pay-ment and greater security. Despite this, it sometimes took a long time before a would-be African businessman appreciated the tremendous openings in this growing market, which European business interests had not been slow to discover and exploit, and which were now offered to him by what was called 'positive' *apartheid*. Even so, many an attempt failed and, in spite of repeated efforts by a benevolent local authority to obtain last-minute financial and technical assistance, and in spite of appeals to the white wholesalers and other creditors to grant a last delay so as to stave off final disaster, there were about three to four bankruptcies annually in Reeftown alone.

When investigators for Government commissions and private institutions came to the conclusion that the growth of African trade and commerce was handicapped by African limitations as much as, if not more than, by European restrictions, European volunteers came forward from all over the Reef from such organizations as the South African Institute of Race Relations, the Rotary, the Round Table, the Junior Chamber of Commerce, to organize lectures and courses for aspirant traders on such subjects as business methods, sales techniques and window display, on costing, stocktaking, profit-making and book-keeping.

I myself persuaded many a prominent European businessman to lecture in the classrooms of Reeftown's secondary school and to answer questions on how to open a shop, run a bank, start a news-paper, found a company, and on every aspect of business life, as the questioners conceived it.

Of even greater consequence, however, though less generally em-phasized, has been the rapid development of the self-employed trades-men and artisans in these new townships. Originally produced under the aegis of the building activities within the townships, and the training in the municipal housing departments (at the end of 1958 the Non-European Affairs Department of the white parent town employed about 1,450 Africans for work in its various sections and of these 650 were building workers), many carpenters and brick-layers, plasterers, plumbers and electricians came up and, wherever they could, set up independently as small entrepreneurs. When the news spread that in the townships there was money to be made in self-employment, several others left their jobs and apprenticeships as 'boys' to European artisans in the European economy and started an independent enterprise among their own people in any one of the new townships. Thus, Reeftown could count an increasing number of tailors and dressmakers, radio repairers, car mechanics, cobblers and watch repairers, and produced an entire economy of its own with its own price, cost and wage levels, similar to any one of the villages in pre-twentieth-century Europe.

At the same time, big European corporations with large sales in the townships speeded up the training of African salesmen and, one by one, we were able to see the European wholesalers' representatives and sales promoters disappearing from the township scene, and their jobs being taken over by Africans who had been eagerly awaiting just such a chance. However, it did not go fast enough and one day, when I was by chance in Mr Jones's office, I heard him tell some top European executives of a large American corporation that such and such a date was the deadline, after which no European sales worker would again be admitted to Reeftown.

The strictest control was exercised on Indian dealers who were not allowed to take orders or to sell their goods in the township but who could not be prohibited from delivering orders placed by Reeftowners in the Indian shops in town, or on the periphery of the township.

Fostered and pampered, the class of small African entrepreneurs

17

thus grew and the African salesman came to the fore. During the years of the field research, a favourite topic of conversation, even among the highest educated, professional Reeftowners was how to become a salesman, and many paid large fees to subscribe to courses in salesmanship held by both responsible and less responsible agencies.

Ever since, this occupation has been growing in prestige through the recruitment into its ranks of increasing numbers of matriculated, professional and even graduate Africans, as well as many underpaid and dissatisfied public servants.

A temporary phase of semi self-employment came to be seen as the best apprenticeship for the independence and the greater earnings of a dreamt-of business enterprise.

In conclusion, it would appear that, whereas the western world everywhere has experienced 'the death of the salesman',[29] he is only now being born in the closed world of Bantu development under *apartheid*.

The decline of the first urban aristocracy

'Even in the old location,' informants assured us, 'people had already classified themselves.' The earliest urban elite in the old location had consisted of the old 'stand-owners' (actually stand-holders and home-owners). These were not necessarily the wealthiest, the best educated or those holding jobs of highest status and authority. There may have been a minister or a school principal among them, but what counted was that they owned a house or several houses, or even business premises. They were the longest-established businessmen, a first, independent, moneyed class, comparable to the propertied classes or landed gentry in Europe. Many of them no longer did any work. They were landlords and lived off 'rooms to let', the scarcity of accommodation having raised the rents considerably.

Their status was unassailable and independent of the general appearance of their houses. Little money was needed for maintenance. Many houses were dilapidated, and made unsightly by the addition of corrugated-iron sheds or lean-to's. For status depended on the number of rooms to let. In this lay the wealth of the landlords. They were slum landlords for, as few Reeftowners failed to mention, the old location had been a slum.

Apart from home-ownership, this first urban elite had little in common with, nor was their way of life any different from that of, the sub-tenants and other slum-dwellers around them. (In their habits and tastes the earliest landed aristocracy in Europe, and particularly in eastern Europe, were not so different from the serfs and menials, and the social distance between master and servant could be exceedingly small.) In the happy gregariousness of congested location life, social prestige did not bring forth social exclusiveness. Moreover, all were equal under the European.

Nevertheless, even among the businessmen and landlords, there were a select few. These were 'the names'. They were the very cream of this elite. As in the case of any old aristocracy, these few did not 'need to show their status, for people knew the names'. In most cases it had been the father who 'had caused the status', and when he died 'the name' and its prestige had descended to his widow and children.

But, when these members of the earliest elite had to move to Reeftown, the situation changed. It is true to say that they began with considerable advantages. They had asked for and obtained a separate residential area and the township administration had built a series of five- to six-roomed houses to serve as models from which to choose. Mr Jones had suggested that these should be built under the expert supervision of his staff. With few exceptions, however, these houses remained unoccupied and uncopied.

The location stand-owners had been given the most generous compensation moneys[30] for their often slum-like properties; and in a desperate attempt to secure for themselves the greatest comfort and to remain in the lead, and in spite of all entreaties by Mr Jones and his assistants to 'put the money in the bank' and to use some of it to build up their new township businesses, they started building themselves the most ostentatious mansions. Thus there was much truth in the general saying that in Reeftown the new houses did not show class but only compensation moneys. Inexperienced as the ex-stand-owners were in modern building techniques, they were often grossly overcharged on materials and labour, and they generally built beyond their resources. Finally, little or nothing was left to tide them over until their new shop had acquired a new clientele.

In addition, circumstances had changed in the new township. Stand-owners could no longer rely on the loyalty of old customers, nor on a steady income from lodgers and tenants. A new wave of traders and merchants who knew something about display and salesmanship was emerging, bringing progressive ideas and much competition. Many a widow who in the old location had never really had to make an effort did not know what to do. Moreover, the next generation failed in every sphere. The children, brought up as wealthy heirs, had never learned to work; and now, in the new township they could not change their ways. Helplessly the old couples and widows and their good-for-nothing sons had to watch how 'those upstarts', 'those who had only been small-fry before', now had flourishing businesses and drove around in big American cars. These were only 'newcomers', whereas they themselves, were they not 'the veterans', the carriers of the 'big names'? They were an urban aristocracy,

19

experienced in urban ways, and here were the 'new rich', often un-
couth, whose fathers had been simple country folk. They still held
on to many tribal customs and their wives did not participate in social
affairs. These were the new business elite, not particularly educated
or refined, but they were ambitious, hard-working and pushing.

During the years of our field research, we were able to observe how,
one by one, the bearers of the big names were dropping out of business
life. They went bankrupt; they had to 'sell' their dying shops; they
just could not adjust to the change. Most of them continued living
in their large but unfinished houses, which were not easy to sell. The
'new rich' desired to build their own houses, and tastes were changing
rapidly.

Their sons and daughters, who had never gone far in education –
the standard of education in the old location had in any case been
low – were unqualified for the new positions which were opening up
in the ever-expanding new township. Even if the old location had
thrown up its normal quota of professionals, they would still have
been too few for the far larger and far better equipped Reeftown.

And so the veterans had to watch another wave of 'newcomers'
settle down upon Reeftown. These were the doctors and lawyers,
the public servants, the graduates and the trained. They and the
'educated' among the wealthy traders and merchants now occupied
the conspicuous positions in all township affairs. They introduced
entirely new social customs and manners, and they now set the tone
of the social life of the community.

Residential differentiation

The new townships also precipitated the development of social differentiation. Whereas in the old location, any existing status differences
had remained almost unnoticed to a visitor, in Reeftown the differences in the houses and the various districts leapt to the eye. From
the beginning, the Administration had prided itself on the fact that
it could offer its residents a wide choice in size and type of house, as
well as in size of stand (and in this respect, the Administration can be
justly proud). People had obviously eagerly seized the opportunity
and seemed to vie with each other in showing how different were their
tastes and interests, their patterns of behaviour and their styles of
living. Each neighbourhood had its own distinct atmosphere.
Whereas in the old location educated and illiterate, poor and rich,
long-urbanized and newly-arrived residents had all lived together
in the closest proximity, in the new township people of similar ways
of life and leisure tended to seek accommodation among like-minded
friends, and the increasing social differentiation was expressed and
emphasized in residential differentiation.

20

In this, Reeftown, with its core of experienced town-dwellers, reached a degree of sophistication unequalled elsewhere. To understand this important feature of our township, a brief historical review of the building operations and housing schemes in relation to origin and social class of occupants will be given in its main outlines and as far as is relevant.

The population was to consist of three different kinds of people:

1 the old and longer urbanized population of the old location, comprising (*a*) the so-called 'stand-owners' (as explained, these were in reality, either tenants in municipal-built houses, or home-owners living on rented municipal plots); (*b*) their tenants (these were actually sub-tenants, i.e. tenants of persons mentioned under (*a*));
2 the people from the surrounding farms and those who had, up to now, lived in European backyards, a heterogeneous lot from a wider area and with little urban experience;
3 anyone who had found work in the surrounding industries, and those who were engaged for the performance of certain essential township services wherever the 'locals' could not fill the vacancies.

Different housing schemes provided for the different needs of this population. For those mentioned under 1 (*b*), sub-economic, prefabricated houses with two to five rooms were provided for the poorer tenants, whereas for the more well-to-do and more ambitious home seekers the Administration developed a home-ownership scheme. For those mentioned under (2) there was a 'Site-and-Service' scheme to hasten their removal and resettlement. Each family was allotted a plot, laid out with a lavatory and a water tap, and permitted to build its own temporary shack on the understanding that, once the Council had completed the permanent home on the plot, the shack had to be demolished without compensation being given.

The first 200 of the poorest residents moved into the first sub-economic houses at approximately the end of 1949 and, in this way, the oldest section nearest the old railway station came into being. These first residents 'entered their houses with tears in their eyes', so Mr Jones told us. 'They knelt on the rough cement floor to thank the Lord in prayer', for the long-awaited chance to begin a civilized way of life had finally come true. Even now, at the annual Christmas party for the aged of the township (one of the many parties which we regularly attended), these old people sang the praises of Mr Jones, their 'father', and expressed their strongest disapproval of those residents who came after them and who 'are bad and get lawyers to fight Mr Jones – such a good man!'

After these grateful old tenants, came the less grateful and more demanding, and also much more numerous younger ones, those who had for political reasons originally resisted 'The Removal'. They also

21

received sub-economic houses; and, although they settled in quickly, they kept up their resistance.

At about the same time, around 1952, the Management inaugurated its first assisted home-ownership scheme, a truly pioneering venture in those days, for which they had finally succeeded in obtaining a special grant from the white City Council, and they proudly considered themselves to have been the first to start such an assisted home-ownership scheme. This enabled financially-sound applicants to build their own houses with the help of a municipal loan. The building was done by native contractors in the Council's employ and according to buyers' specifications. If so desired, the buyers could choose from a variety of plans designed by the Housing Department, in which the greatest elegance was combined with the lowest cost. In this way, the second section nearest the new railway station came into being.

The most well-to-do and enthusiastic home builders were allotted sites alongside the main avenue leading from the national road to the town hall. This avenue became the first status area.

The difference in house tenure marked forever these two oldest sections of Reeftown. The home-owners considered the tenants to be 'always causing trouble and being uppish though they haven't a house to call their own'. The home-owners constituted the earliest bourgeoisie. What was commonly expected that only freehold could achieve, was equally achieved by home-ownership: it became a stabilizing force, welding a highly mobile and restless population into a responsible, stable community. The tenants in their sub-economic houses considered the home-owners 'illiterate and politically backward'.

The sub-economic section, on the contrary, remained for a long time the seat of the revolutionaries, the resisters and the agitators, who considered themselves the intelligentsia of Reeftown and the leaders in the political struggle.

The 'Site-and-Service' scheme, which was developed for those mentioned under (2) was started at the other, southern, end of the township, at a considerable distance from the first areas. These ever-growing 'Site-and-Service' areas, spreading away from the actual social centre as far as the eye could see, have always (even a long time after they had become built up, and after even more and newer schemes had been started) remained beyond the pale for the residents of the older areas, who were united in their common pride in being 'the veterans', and who dissociated themselves from the 'Site-and-Service riff-raff'. These areas were considered to house mainly 'the rowdy element', 'people who do not know how to live in a house', 'people who do not know how to behave socially' or, briefly, 'the sub-tenants and even lesser fry'.

Nothing – barring exceptional circumstances – would induce a status-conscious Reeftowner of the older areas to go and live in the 'Site-and-Service' district. Since the inhabitants were considered to be the best customers for the doctors and shop-owners, some doctors had additional consulting rooms there; and a number of later arrivals among the businessmen were only too glad to be allotted business premises in these areas. Moreover, their shebeens were the most popular, and were regularly frequented by the better-class population – and wherever shebeens flourished there were customers for a great many other types of business.

In the meantime, the first stand-owners of the old location had begun to move in and, as has already been explained, they started to build themselves ostentatious residences on a scale hitherto unknown. In this way they began a status scramble among all who came after them. The subsequent housing history in Reeftown can be seen as the persistent attempt by newer residents to equal and surpass the older capitalists, if not always in cost and size of house, then by the introduction of novel features, original decorations and unusual styles and materials. Here again the Administration came to the rescue of the less well-to-do, yet more educated, status seekers by building, especially for them, a better-class house at a reasonable price right alongside the stand-owner's houses.

This came about as follows:

When the Government froze the number of sub-economic houses, all other houses in the sub-economic district had to be converted to economic rents. In order to ensure that the limited number of sub-economic houses were really occupied by sub-economic families, he council surveyed the population of the district. Among the sub-economic tenants were many middle-class families, and even some of the earliest and youngest members of the new elite. Some couples were found to have a joint monthly income of R120 to R180. When the local authorities decided to raise the rents to the economic level, some of these were in the forefront of the movement of protest against such a measure. As with the rent rebels of St Pancras, London, they rose in revolt under the leadership of Mr S., who had just become Chairman of the new Township Advisory Board and who himself lived in a subsidized house and was in need of some spectacular success to establish his position. He succeeded in delaying the proposed rise in rents. Public opinion had been roused to the issue. The newspapers had severely criticized the Government's attempt to restrict sub-economic housing to the very, very poor only, and the Management of Reeftown had to tread warily.

We mention all this for a reason which will now become clear. At the very time that the Government restricted the number of sub-economic houses in all the new townships throughout the country, the Bantu Housing Council laid down a cost limit of R400 for all assisted housing. The Management then devised a clever scheme by which houses could be built within the cost limit and according to all the building specifications laid down by the Health Board in such a way that poorer applicants could buy a house which had originally only two rooms. After these had been paid off, or as and when the family finances increased, one, two or even three further rooms could be built on. Buyers of these homes were assisted as before, with loans ranging between R300 and R400 at an interest of 3¾ per cent, repayable over ten years in monthly instalments of not less than R2. This scheme was developed particularly for the lower-income groups. Many Africans who lived on the Reef and who in the new townships of Johannesburg had been forced to occupy four-roomed houses which they did not need, at rents they could not afford (in its building programme Johannesburg had preferred speed to all other considerations), tried to move to jobs in the neighbourhood of Reeftown in order to become eligible as buyers under such conditions.

Then, when the Management was obliged to raise the rents of tenants in the rebellious district, they were able to offer to the poorer, but not sub-economic families, these houses built for growth.

The more affluent in the district then found the better-class houses previously mentioned to be much to their liking. These were four- and five-roomed houses, larger and of a more elegant external finish, though incomplete internally. As already explained, these houses were situated in the districts which were developing around the original stand-owners' residences. Moreover, in these same districts the Administration planned to encourage the new 'Upper Ten' of self-employed and professionals to seek residential exclusiveness. This movement had already begun, and the doctors and wealthy businessmen had already started building in these areas, and their houses truly, and for the first time, surpassed those of the ex-stand-owners in size and style, general elegance and appointments.

The four- and five-roomed special council houses, basking in reflected status glory, could be purchased for as little as R1,060 for a five-roomed house, at a deposit of not less than R200, the remainder payable within ten years in monthly instalments of not less than R10 per month. It was, then, with these houses that Mr Jones finally succeeded in enticing away, and out of the sub-economic district, the more educated and prosperous of Reeftown's residents. Where before people had complained that they could not afford a rent of R10 per month, they now gladly paid R15 and R20 a month in loan redemption for a house which would ultimately be theirs, and which brought them right into the most fashionable area of Reeftown.

24

Throughout the period of our field research, we witnessed a slow but steady trek to these houses from the original areas of Reeftown. To these houses also moved those of the 'newcomers' who had no accumulated wealth, but yet had achieved high status – the school principals and supervisors, the health inspectors and the top-grade municipal staff. All those, in fact, whose educational and occupational status required some residential exclusiveness, although it was high enough not to need the extravagant residential splendour of the uneducated but wealthy businessmen – a splendour which they, in any case, could not have afforded. The businessmen, moreover, increasingly preferred to have their shops right in among their customers in the spreading southern areas. They were given conspicuous corner stands, so that they could act 'as the proverbial Joneses'. Consequently, this internal residential mobility became the most objective indication of the general social mobility.

Thus Reeftown became characterized by an unusually well-developed differentiation in houses and residential areas. This had come about because, unlike most other and younger Reef towns, it had a core of long urbanized, experienced residents with some accumulated wealth; and because it had administrators of the calibre of Mr Uiterwyck and Mr Jones who, by encouraging home-ownership and residential differentiation, gave 'everyone a chance to express his advance in his house', as Reeftowners often told us. Thus, in 1959, more than half the township's houses were owned by their occupants.

Summing up

We would suggest that 'The Removal' from the small congested location to the large and spacious new township of Reeftown precipitated certain changes. Among these we mentioned the decline of the first stand-owning urban aristocracy and the emergence of new social differentiations and of new separate elites. In Reeftown the general social mobility came to be particularly emphasized and expressed in residential mobility and residential differentiations through historical circumstances and deliberate encouragement.

We further described how, in these new urban housing estates such as Reeftown, a certain inherent duality which had always characterized the emergence of a modernizing, urbanizing African group as, on the one hand, a separately developing and, on the other hand, a participating society was not only confirmed but accentuated. Thus, the new elite which was being produced and supported by the changing social structure in these new urban communities reflected this dual orientation. Consequently, while the modern world generally was being caught up in the change from a nineteenth-century

25

entrepreneurial to a twentieth-century managerial society, and the old elite of owner-industrialists and local notables was everywhere being replaced by a new elite of managers, national professional politicians and public servants, African society in South Africa showed simultaneously the emergence of both these types of elite: an elite of public servants and professional politicians on the one hand, and an elite of self-employed and semi-self-employed on the other.

Thus, in its elite, this emergent African society showed how it lived simultaneously in two different contexts: the one in which it participated in the more general changes occurring in a wider world, and the other in which it obeyed its own unique historical imperatives and followed its own cultural development.

The social setting

The rectangular shape of Reeftown, running from north to south, was surrounded by open *veld*. The railway ran lengthwise through the township, dividing it into Nguni-speaking and Sotho-speaking areas. Only part of the oldest northern section, which had been settled before the introduction of ethnic grouping, remained ethnically mixed.

Beginning with an original purchase of a piece of farm land of just under 1,000 morgen (one morgen is $2\frac{1}{9}$ acres), in 1948, the township had expanded to some 3,000 morgen, i.e. roughly $7\frac{1}{2}$ square miles. Subsequent purchases brought the total land area to 3,500 morgen, and the township was planned to have, ultimately, a population of some 100,000 people. The old location had occupied barely 70 morgen and had a population of 27,000.

In February 1958, i.e. nine years after the first families had moved in, the total population was estimated at 40,000 people living on 8,000 developed stands. The size of the average family was thought to be a little over five persons. But all population figures were only estimates; an illegal population of at least 5,000 residents had also to be reckoned with.[31] The ratio of male/female was 100/109, with a not inconsiderable surplus of adult females,[32] one of the typical products of long urbanization, and a constant source of worry to the Administration.[33]

The continuously changing social scene

Like all these new Bantu townships, Reeftown was planned as a model town with all social services and amenities – wide, tree-lined and tarred main roads; electric street lighting and optional electric light inside the homes; running water and water-borne sewerage with flush lavatories for every house; regular garbage removal, etc. The map showed sports grounds, children's playgrounds, open spaces and parks, swimming baths, tennis courts and golf courses. Each section of about 550 households was to have its own primary school. Sites were reserved for a trade school, a post-primary school, various clinics, crèches and community centres, as well as a bachelors' hostel, a nurses' home, an old-age home, etc. Beer halls and beer gardens were spread all over the township; also garages and petrol stations were planned, as well as a medical centre, a civic centre and various shopping centres. The main square at the end of the central avenue through which one entered the township was the centre of all communal activity. Here was the Head Office of the township Administration, with the Public Library and the Hall, arranged like a miniature Parliament, in which the Advisory Board members, dressed in academic gowns, would hold their monthly meetings. Here also the plan showed the sites for a cinema and a large communal hall.

During 1960–61 many of the amenities were still accommodated in temporary premises. There were, for instance, three temporary clinics which operated from strategic points easily accessible to most of the residents; and the branches of three European banks, which were accommodated in small corrugated-iron sheds. One large and one small hall provisionally filled the vacuum created by the lack of a communal hall, but many public meetings and larger gatherings, except jazz and dance sessions, took place in churches and school buildings and in one large room in the Welfare part of the Administrative offices.

Many improvements were still to come. Yet the progress was truly remarkable, comparing favourably with the rate of development in housing estates overseas.[34] In the three years of our field research we witnessed the completion of the new Central Station and the gradual opening up of three township stations; the building of the secondary school; the festive inauguration of the Stadium; the construction of a large hospital with eleven operating theatres and initial provision for 350 beds, which, when completed, would comprise eleven different buildings standing on seventeen acres of ground; the erection of the police station, the new jail, and a number of new sectional superintendents' offices.

Mr Jones had had great hopes that the new Magistrate's Court would be situated in Reeftown, and space had been reserved on the map, but it now seemed that the Court would be established elsewhere.

In the meantime the population continued growing. Early in 1958, when our field research began, there were about 40,000 residents. At the end of 1960, these had increased to 60,000. Thus in three years the population had grown by half.

In such a rapidly growing community, conditions naturally changed from year to year and nothing was ever stable. After the war all the

E

27

city councils on the Reef had made the necessary surveys to establish the housing needs of their non-European populations. The African survey of Reeftown was no longer available; but even if it were it would have been out of date by the time we started our research. As a result, few figures about the population of Reeftown were available to offset certain data about the elite. Similarly, there was no occupational survey. The Administration considered that a survey was useless so long as people were changing occupation all the time.

Extreme occupational mobility was, no doubt, the dominant note of the township's economic life. Not only did people frequently change their employers and kinds of occupation, but they scuttled to and fro between employment and self-employment; between self-employment and semi self-employment; between private and public employment and between different public employments. Many individuals combined working for a profit with working for wages. In addition, new occupations were arising all the time.

Each new development or amenity brought not only new occupations but also new opportunities for jobs in the township itself. The opening up of each successive school required new assistant teachers, and promoted a teacher to the office of principal; each new sectional administrative office brought new clerical jobs and promotions; each new church added another minister and a council of church elders. Each new development, therefore, brought additional positions of status. As a result, each successive improvement created new competition for jobs and promotions and sharpened organizational rivalries.

As in Greenbelt,[35] the settlement of Reeftown had been accompanied by a new social dynamism and organizational activity. When people moved from the old location, many were already members of existing societies and clubs. After an initial muddle, because half the membership was in the old location, the other half in the new township and many members got 'lost', members and organizations found each other again, new committees were formed and new programmes drawn up. In 1953, when we made our first friends in Reeftown, these confirmed that, 'all organizations and clubs do better in Reeftown than in the old location. I don't know why. I think it is the new houses.'

The early residents of Watling[36] formed a Residents' Association to promote their communal interests and all the more specific cultural and social services were provided for by sub-committees emanating from and co-ordinated with this overall Association. But the residents of Reeftown left the provision of their social and communal services to the professional social workers and to the Advisory Board's continuous pressure on the white Administration. They themselves formed those clubs and associations which fulfilled

28

certain needs considered to be purely Bantu cultural. Thus they continued and enlarged their Funeral and Burial Societies; they canvassed new members for their savings clubs, pooling and party clubs and Stockfels[37] among their new neighbours; and many a woman saw her chance to branch out on her own and to found a new Friendly Society.

Thus, not unlike Little-Town-in-Overspill,[38] a great many unco-operative and unco-ordinated groupings were formed. Sometimes with no clearly defined aims, often at cross purposes, and generally competitive with each other, these catered for the many different tastes and interests of a society heterogeneous in origin, unevenly involved in the process of culture change, and as yet uncertainly wavering between old and new patterns of association.

In this 'general rash of social and organizational activity',[39] people who, in the settled relationships of the old location, had given up the status struggle, now found new outlets for their ambitions. 'In the old location I was a nonentity', said one of our acquaintances, 'whereas here I have been mushrooming into prominence.' Each new improvement and enlargement in Reeftown meant for some people a new chance to rise to positions of leadership, and became a new vehicle for social mobility.

For instance, when the Stadium was inaugurated, disputes started at once as to 'who would control it', which meant who would collect the gate takings and administer the funds. Rival sports organizations began to canvas supporters, meetings were called, the books were brought up to date, so as to be ready for the battle to come. The Soccer Association considered itself the obvious leader and future 'owner' of the Stadium, and at once it held new elections so as to be able to present 'a strong front' when the time came.

When two new tennis courts were ready, the older tennis clubs split and a rival club was formed with a new chairman and committee. The explanations of these new committee members reveal the rationalizations used. 'Breaking up is progress,' they said. 'You get a reorganization. Old faults are corrected. Leadership is revitalized. Improvements are made and new people come to the top.' And who would dare to say that these are not the perennial fruits of all revolutions? Everyone starts anew, full of hope and good intentions.

With each new development there was again a reshuffling of social relationships and a realignment of rival groups, as the leading antagonists collected their 'followers' with promises and threats, and new status rivalries flared up. Thus cliques formed, broke up and re-formed; reputations were made and destroyed; new leaders came into the limelight and others sank into social oblivion.

As in all new and emergent societies, the prestige attached to 'having been the first' was immense. To have started something, an

29

organization, a new profession or occupation, or even to have established a new routine in an existing institution, lent lasting distinction. People who had been the first in any one of the fields of activity in the new township were known to the residents, and the fact was always mentioned in introductions.

'He was our first African doctor already in the old location' or 'She was the first nurse in the first clinic' or 'He was the first librarian we ever had' or 'He was the first Principal in our first school.'

'To have been the first' was a local prestige characteristic of no mean significance. Such pioneers in a new field inspired the same respect among black South Africans as the Barney Barnatos, the Oppenheimers and the Schlesingers in South African (European) history. Here black South African history was being made. Many of the township's pioneers in one field or another figured among the elite.

The opportunity 'to open up new avenues', 'to start the ball rolling', never given to the individual in traditional Bantu tribal life and denied the African in his dependent situation under the leading white group, mainly because 'everything is already there', drove the people inevitably – and in spite of all apparent integration – in the direction of self-sufficiency and of the separate development of the African sector, in which only they could function as innovators. After all, many persons in need of self-esteem would rather be big fish in small ponds than small fish in big ponds.

Occupational differentiation

The first impression visitors received when entering the township in 1958 was one of much empty space and open *veld*, with building operations everywhere in progress. The older northern parts had been nearly built up, but as one penetrated deeper southward, the feeling of isolation grew. Often houses stood alone and forlorn on the *veld*. As the residents said, there was 'lots of nothing'. The general sense of emptiness and the physical distance between the houses emphasized the social distance which had grown between the residents in the change from the old to the new place. 'In the old location everything was just around the corner and everybody knew everybody else, while in Reeftown everything is far . . .', was a usual complaint.

The two developments which contributed more than anything else to create this feeling of social distance between the people were: firstly, the growing articulation of the social structure of Reeftown in a number of institutional groups and occupational hierarchies; and secondly, the differentiation in housing standards, styles of living and ways of entertaining.

Dealing with point one first, we shall in this section give a review of the main institutions operating in the township with particular

reference to the emergence of new elites and the increasing articulation in the older elites, as well as to the differential measure of
local prestige these elites enjoyed.

The township's administration was the task of the non-European
Affairs Committee of the City Council of the white parent town. This
Committee employed a manager of non-European affairs, whom we
have called Mr Uiterwyck and who, together with a large European
and African staff, operated from offices in the white town, whereas
the township manager, whom we have called Mr Jones, with his staff,
worked in offices in the township itself. During the years of our field
research, the latter's staff consisted of six Europeans – two Senior
and four Junior Superintendents – some thirty African clerks and
a varying number of social workers. They were known collectively
as 'The Office', while the officials in the white town were referred to
as the 'The Council'.

Besides the Council, there were two other authorities and employing bodies. These were called 'The Province' and 'The Department'.
Between them these three agencies ran the township and provided
the necessary services in separate, though not always clearly defined,
areas of activities which sometimes overlapped and often were at
cross purposes. Electricity, water, sewerage and disposal services
were controlled by the local Administration. Transport and some
aspects of housing were government controlled and outside the com-
petency of the Management, who were, nevertheless, blamed for
deficiencies. Education was under the Department of Education, but
the Council was responsible for the building of lower primary schools.
With regard to higher primary schools and secondary schools, the
responsibilities were not clear.

Teachers' salaries were paid by the Department, but the School
Board had the right to appoint and dismiss assistant teachers. Cura-
tive and preventive medicine, the medical and the social side of welfare, were divided between two different bodies. Invalidity grants
and old-age pensions were paid by the Department of Bantu Administration and Development; tuberculosis maintenance and assistance grants came from the semi-official national organization called
SANTA (South African National Tuberculosis Association); tuberculosis feeding was financed by the Local Authority.

Moreover, regulations were changing or were expected to change
frequently in the gradual transition from local and independent to
state-controlled township administration. For the officials this
resulted in their often having to apply laws and regulations they did
not necessarily approve of, or knew to be impossible to enforce.
In many aspects of township life the Local Authority had, therefore, responsibilities without having control. For the large masses of
Reeftowners, 'This complicated division of functions . . . makes it

difficult for the residents to develop a straightforward interest in local Government.'[40]

As in Watling, so in Reeftown, most residents could not distinguish between the various powers who could be blamed for injustices or appealed to with grievances. For simplicity's sake, therefore, the wrongdoer was 'The Government', which was seen, like the former tribal Chief, as one man, and his representative was Mr Jones or any of the white Superintendents the residents had to deal with at 'The Office'. Here their mental vision ceased. Mr Jones, therefore, fulfilled the unenviable function of the universal scapegoat.

In 1958, we found the township divided into twenty-one sections comprising about 500 households each and named after township notables. For administrative purposes, the sections were grouped together into six Superintendencies, each responsible for some 2,000 households (about 10,000 people). The cost of running Reeftown was between about R42,000 to R46,000 per Superintendency per year. Each (European) Superintendent was assisted by an (African) Administrative Assistant. These six African clerks, being trained and in many respects already treated as Assistant Superintendents, occupied the highest administrative posts thus far available for Africans in Reeftown.

A brief description of the daily administrative routine will make it clear why they enjoyed such high prestige.

The Administration dealt with three main groups of problems. (During December 1959 we sat one morning with each of the two Senior Superintendents (white), and during March 1961 with each of the three Senior Administrative Assistants (black), noting down all the cases dealt with from 9 a.m. to 1 p.m. The ready co-operation of these officials must be here once more acknowledged.) First of all there were residence permits and work passes. Most numerous were the requests for accommodation, for transfers, removals and re-settlements. Of the sixteen accommodation cases dealt with by one European superintendent during one morning, only five were straight-forward and simple. Then came applications for temporary passes and visiting permits, as well as for passes for foreign Africans and for replacement of lost passes. The Administration also collected the rents and was responsible for maintenance and housing repairs. Complications frequently arose. Most troublesome were the numerous cases of rent arrears and absconders. Tenants sometimes disappeared overnight, removing all their furniture. Many also were the cases in which it was not clear which department was responsible; and, as in all bureaucracies, the 'buck was passed' among the officials of various Government Departments. Innumerable application forms had to be filled in and permits obtained. There were also the registrations of births and deaths, applications for cemetery space, for party permits (holding a party involved permission for the purchase of extra Council beer and for the ritual slaughter of a goat or an ox on the premises), etc.

Secondly, the Administration, and particularly the African clerks, had to deal with all manner of quarrels and conflicts. They had to play the roles of judges and councillors in all the residential and domestic disputes. The two main causes of domestic disputes were: non-support by the husbands, and husbands driving their wives out of the house. Simple disputes were generally dealt with by the Ward Committees; complicated ones going to the Administration. One administrative assistant calculated that he personally handled about three domestic disputes per week; another had solved, in January 1961, six domestic and three residential disputes, and in December 1960 only one residential but as many as nine domestic disputes. The main aim was always to endeavour to stop the disputants from 'going to court'. Disputes were frequent on all housing estates, but African disputants would incur high and unnecessary legal expenses rather than accept defeat. Clerks also had to settle many organizational conflicts: a treasurer ran away with the cash, or an outvoted secretary refused to hand over the books to an incoming secretary. Then there were the innumerable difficulties between European employers and African employees; between African employers and African employees; and particularly between European dealers and their lawyers on the one hand and the African buyers and hire-purchasers on the other. Finally, the Administration frequently had to arbitrate between European wholesalers and African traders. By and large, Mr Jones frequently stood as the last, and often the only, person protecting 'his' people against illegal and extortionist practices by European and Indian businessmen.

The Administration's third main task was to act as a general source of advice and information. Cases had to be referred to the relevant departments – cases of sickness to the clinics; T.B. cases to SANTA; applications for pensions, maintenance and invalidity grants to the social workers; anything to do with sports and recreations, parks and playgrounds to the sports organizer; job seekers to the labour bureau; parents desperate for a school vacancy for their children or a crèche opening for their infants, to Bantu Education or the Crèche Committees; cases of seduction or insolvency to the Law courts, etc.

People often came with letters of recommendation from European or African lawyers, but more often they were personally introduced by members of their Ward Committees or by other public personages. Usage had laid down fixed 'under-the-counter' fees for such services. R1 for one's case to be personally attended to by one of the white superintendents, but R2 for a promise to be seen by Mr Jones. For access to Mr Uiterwyck an intermediary charged R4.

What the unscrupulous European or African lawyers charged for their useless recommendations was not known for certain, but could be as much as R10 for a letter. The white staff always told those thus recommended that the recommendation was useless, hoping to stamp out the abuse, but people continued turning up with such letters.

It is far from easy to administer people who do not understand the simplest economic or administrative matters. This becomes even more difficult when the people are black and naturally suspicious of the whites and their ways and are made more suspicious by politicians and by all those who derive benefit from acting as intercessors between them and white authority.

In our experience, the white administrators of Reeftown performed a difficult task with patience and benevolence, applying the many restrictive and obscure laws and regulations with considerable personal discretion, often shutting their eyes and always giving the benefit of the doubt.

The greatest difficulty was that the administrators had a different, often opposite, point of view from their residents. While the latter always wanted to bypass the African clerks and go directly to a white official, believing that only he would know best, be more just, more discreet and more impartial, the white administrators believed that the African clerks had to be given more responsibility and greater authority so that they might gain the experience required against the day – not so far ahead – when they would take over the entire administration of the township.

As far as the graded township staff was concerned, Reeftown had been continually understaffed. Dismissals had been only too frequent. It was estimated that since the foundation of the township, 10 to 15 % had had to be dismissed annually. This continued during our field research, and we observed that the main reasons were bribery and corruption, excessive drinking and violence. Only the most senior clerks seemed to be exceptions to what had become the general rule. Before our entry into Reeftown, the Administration had given its clerical staff greater executive power; this had failed. It was common knowledge that the best 'status sites' had been 'sold' to the highest bidder. Up to quite recently 'Site-and-Service' sites could not be obtained without a 'fiver', and it was rumoured that obtaining one of the special better-class municipal houses cost much more. As a result, the European superintendents had again taken upon themselves some of the main clerical responsibilities, particularly applications for accommodation and for sites.

In spite of their bad reputation, the township's clerks held, in the eyes of the residents, high prestige. It rested on their social visibility as well as on their authoritative position, which gave them real power; on their leadership on committees and their conspicuous functioning in public matters. Essentially their prestige was based on their association with and access to European authority. The educated and self-employed middle classes resented their authority, while the professional elite refused to consider African clerks as equals because they were not 'professional'.

To circumvent the (black) clerical assistant and gain direct access to the (white) superintendents was almost a measure of social prestige.

The professionals among the municipal staff were the social workers and the librarian. The Public Library was housed in the Administrative building. In 1958 there were 3,763 books. Their number was steadily increasing. In 1960 there were 4,137 books. The Annual Circulation Statistics showed a total of 7,287 books lent out for the year July 1957 to June 1958, and a total of 6,740 for the corresponding period 1958–9. The reading of books was almost entirely connected with school education. During holidays circulation dropped markedly. The categories 'English', 'fiction' and 'Sotho' showed the greatest popularity.[41] Every morning Mr Jones added his own morning and evening papers to those in the Library. With its social workers the Administration had been particularly unfortunate. When we began our work in the township, we found, besides one female, three male social workers and, to give these greater freedom in their work, there was no European welfare officer. Of the three males, one soon left for further study in America, largely under false pretences; one was smitten with 'the native sickness', and desired transfer; and the third, who had to be instantly dismissed, disappeared from the township, leaving his wife and children to the good offices of the community and the Social Welfare Department.

Of the next social workers appointed, some had to be dismissed because of excessive drinking or financial irregularities. Some disappeared without notice. As a result of a total reorganization, a new set of social workers – three male and four female – was subsequently engaged and a European Chief Welfare Officer was again put in charge. One male and one female social worker left soon after their probation period. The only stable element in this continuous turnover of social workers was the original senior female, a coloured woman. Later, this woman, divorced from her African husband and without his protection, had to leave the African community. She now works among her own coloured people.

However, the prestige of the social workers and of the township clerks remained largely unaffected by their behaviour and by the personal performance of any individual.

The Social Welfare Department investigated mainly cases eligible for old-age pensions, blind pensions, disability grants, tuberculosis, leper and cripple assistance, and for other grants and allowances, as

35

well as cases deserving of rent remittal. It was estimated that more than half of the tenants were always one or two months in arrears with their rents. All cases were investigated and rent remittals were frequent. During 1958–9, 116 cases of rent arrears involving some R3,000 were written off. However, through the years other rent arrears continued to accumulate until in May 1959 they totalled some R70,000, but nothing could be done about it. 'You can't throw the people into the street,' said the township manager. In Europe such an action would be called harsh and inhuman, in South Africa it would be decried as race discrimination.

The Annual Report of the (European) Welfare Officer for the financial year 1957–8 mentioned, in addition, a soup kitchen distributing a daily average of 500 mugs of soup to pre-school age children during the winter months; about fifteen food parcels per week distributed as poor relief; and a total of nearly 700 blankets given to the aged and indigent. A special tuberculosis feeding scheme assisted 2,594 patients. This did not include welfare work done by private organizations, and assistance from outside the township.

During the year 1959–60 as many as fifty films were shown. The cinema show held almost every Saturday night was the most important of the entertainments organized by the Administration. Children paid 5 cents; average attendance was 300. Adults paid 10 cents; average attendance 60. But almost every month the Administration organized at least one other function such as a concert-and-dance, a dinner-and-dance, a variety show of local talent, or even a concert by local white or even overseas artists. These were also the responsibility of the Welfare Department.

Milk came from the original farm on the site and was sold in milk depots at the subsidized price of 4c. per pint. There was a plan to develop the farm later so as to provide the residents with fresh produce, to be sold in a projected fresh-produce market.

Recently, a labour bureau for adolescent males had been started. In the first two months it had already placed over 100 of the nearly 300 applicants for jobs. A labour bureau for women was operated in the white town.

Two different kinds of police operated in Reeftown. Each Superintendent, like his rural equivalent the District Commissioner in British colonies, was also an Officer of the Peace and, therefore, the Local Authority employed its own police corps. Thus law and order in Reeftown was maintained by the Municipal Police, called 'blackjacks' because of their dark uniforms, and the South African police who wore khaki.

In 1958 the S.A. Police, in Reeftown, consisted of 3 Europeans and some 55 to 60 Africans, among whom there were one first-class sergeant, 8 second-class sergeants, one Native Detective Sergeant and 3 Native Detective Constables. In the same year the Municipality employed about 75 African policemen, among whom there were 3 sergeants and 4 corporals. But Mr Jones had found the Municipal Police generally unreliable in emergencies.

As a body, the South African Police, with its higher wages and its pension scheme, enjoyed higher prestige than the Municipal Police, but there were individual exceptions. Mainly because of the prestige of the uniform and the not inconsiderable power they could exercise, the policemen were considered, quite generally, as belonging to the middle classes[42] and, therefore, as socially equal to the assistant teachers and the factory workers, though less educated than the former and earning less than the latter. Associatively only the constables, the sergeants and the detectives could be reckoned with the assistant teachers. Like these teachers some policemen could, as in Reeftown, reach the lower echelons of the upper stratum, or the upper echelons of the lower class. This depended on personal appearance and behaviour, on residential standards, and on the level of domestic arrangements, including the wives.

There were about thirty declared burglaries a month in Reeftown. On an average five cars were reported stolen per week, but many more car thefts occurred and were not reported as owners often preferred to trace the thieves (and punish them!) themselves. It was said that the township had had only two 'tribal' faction fights since its foundation.

In the domain of law and order two further personages were of great importance – the Messenger of the Court and the Court Interpreter. Upon the latter something of the immense prestige of the lawyer had descended. In fact, court interpreters generally considered themselves, and acted as, legal advisers.

As in the case of the policemen and the public clerks, a stigma was attached to the occupation of interpreter; yet in spite of this the prestige of the profession remained high. It was largely based on the personal power which resulted from their institutional authority.

An important township institution was the *Advisory Board*. For political purposes the township was divided into six Constituencies or Wards, each electing annually its own Advisory Board Member, who had to be resident in the area. In addition to these six elected, there were three nominated members. Each one of the six elected members chose, in his turn, ten persons from among his own followers to form a so-called Ward Committee, working under his Chairmanship. These Ward Committees dealt with all minor offences and petty complaints, as well as those marital and neighbourly disputes they could successfully handle. They were not required to keep detailed records nor to justify their decisions; only a general monthly report for statistical purposes was demanded from them.

According to Mr Jones, the system worked well. It filled a gap in those many cases involving personal and domestic relations which, as in the Urban Courts in the Copperbelt, are better handled 'in terms of norms to which the majority of urban Africans continue to subscribe'.[43] Although the elite assured us that they did not avail themselves of the services of these 'illiterate' Ward Committees, we personally followed two cases in the year 1960 in which members of the elite, in disputes between themselves, had appealed for settlement to their Ward Committees.

Thus in these Ward Committees the Advisory Board functioned as a responsible civic body. In them also we discovered one field in which ethnic grouping made sense, in so far as the Ward Committee members, belonging as they did to the same ethnic group as the residents, had the required authoritative knowledge of the particular 'tribal' norms and customs of their disputants. Following Mitchell's very useful distinction (Mitchell, *Kalela*, 1956, 30) we shall use the word 'tribal' for a specific ethnic and linguistic group within a wider system of social organization, and the word tribal, without inverted commas, to describe a system of social and political organization generally.

As a high-status body and a vehicle for social mobility, the Advisory Board no longer had any significance. When the educated talked about 'The Board', they meant the School Board. The first African body ever to have been given actual institutional authority over people and funds, the School Board had become the real instrument of supreme power and prestige for the educated, so much so that during our field research it was rumoured that the township demagogue was seeking election to the School Board. Its membership numbered ten: four members were elected by the parents and generally drawn from the parent members of the school committees; six were nominated upon the recommendations of various officials who tended to recommend persons whose names had appeared already on the school committees.

Like many other institutions in this 'difficult' township, the School Board of Reeftown was said by Africans and Europeans alike, 'to cause more trouble than any other School Board on the Reef'. It had become a hotbed of intrigue. In all the scheming and manoeuvring to get oneself or one's followers on the Board and one's enemies off it, many a promising career was destroyed. During our years of observation, the names of the elite still figured largely among its members. (The later trend was towards a different membership.) The happenings in the School Board were widely discussed among the elite, and had wide repercussions in the township. What happened in the Advisory Board sank, by comparison, into insignificance.

In the gradual establishment of the township, the schools had provided the first rallying points for the community. In the stage of transition, scholars and teachers suffered much hardship. The first school, with four classrooms, opened in temporary premises. The other schools followed in quick succession but never quickly enough. Although with the beginning of each new section, priority was given to its school there was, inevitably, a time-lag. The dislocation in education was considerable. Sometimes half the children of one school were still in the old location while the other half were already in Reeftown, being taught by some of their own teachers and temporarily housed in an already completed school. Until the secondary school was completed, the scholars living in Reeftown went every day by bus to the old location.

By 1959 ten primary schools with 300 to 700 children each had been built. Three of these schools had female principals, the others had male principals. The total number of children at school in December 1958, was about 6,000, while during the first quarter of 1959, more than 1,500 children were turned away for lack of accommodation. These children were later absorbed by the existing schools and taught by additional teachers employed as extras by the schools themselves. The number of officially employed primary school teachers in Reeftown during that time was about seventy-five. The status of these assistant teachers, male and female, varied – mainly according to appearance and behaviour. Moreover a teacher's prestige was greatly increased by his participation and leadership in extra-mural activities. Most of the teachers were ordinary middle class; many were young and unmarried. Some were considered to be 'not better than labourers', and a few were counted among the upper-middle class.

Whereas the social status of the assistant primary school teachers wavered thus uncertainly (shown in ranking tests by considerable scatter), that of a principal teacher was firm and fixed. However bad his moral reputation or his professional results, he was and remained upper class.

Together with the first schools, and only slightly later, had come the churches. At first they had functioned more or less in a vacuum, until Sunday services could be held in school classrooms all through the day, at staggered hours. Then in rapid succession, and often in visible competition, Reeftown's justly famous churches began to appear on sites allotted them by the Administration but built at their own expense. And near each church was room for a minister's residence.

To a very large extent Reeftown's social life developed around its schools and churches and, up to this day, no large township function has had a chance of success unless the co-operation of the teachers and ministers has been assured. Since these professionals could always rely on a group of faithful and often dependent followers, the prestige

39

of both professions was high. On the other hand, in both these professional groups, developments had taken place which had made them occupational hierarchies. No longer were all teachers and all ministers in Reeftown socially equal.

More than in the case of any other professionals, the status of the assistant teacher had become depressed through two approximately simultaneous developments. The one was the opening up of higher positions to fellow Africans in the profession itself, including not only the positions of principals and secondary school teachers, but also those of supervisors and sub-inspectors. The other was the creation of the School Boards and School Committees by which non-professional, yet educated, fellow-Africans had acquired considerable control over African teachers.

In the religious field, developments were partly similar in so far as, through the opening up of higher positions to trained African ministers, a veritable hierarchy had arisen instead of the previous professional equality; while through church councils, elders and synods, more control and influence had been put into the hands of laymen and secular persons. In addition, very pronounced prestige differences had arisen between the various Christian denominations. Contrary to European opinion, as often written or expressed, these prestige differences did not necessarily coincide with the division between the European mission churches and the independent African churches. It had simply developed that some churches in Reeftown enjoyed considerable local esteem and some did not. In this there were often local differences.

In Reeftown the prestige differences between the churches were, as one would expect, influenced by the general appearance of the church buildings, but even more strikingly by their siting. All the main status churches were established in the prestige districts of the older northern parts of the township. Here the African Methodist Episcopal Church, the Nederduits Gereformeerde Kerk, the Church of the Province, and the Methodist Church of South Africa had erected imposing structures and large ministerial mansions. Only the Roman Catholic Church was still functioning in a rather shabby provisional building, and the Roman Catholic priest lived in the greatest simplicity and monastic austerity. Whether the western virtues of poverty and celibacy coincided with African values was doubtful.

But the church and minister's residence of the A.M.E. remained the most luxurious of all, and with the highest tower it proudly proclaimed superiority over all the others in Reeftown.

Six different kinds of medical practitioners provided for the health needs of the residents. There were the European doctors of the clinics, and later, of the hospital; there were the Jewish and Indian doctors who had established their private practices on the outskirts of the township, and who were reputed to charge lower fees than the Bantu doctors; there were the African doctors qualified at European universities in the European system of medicine; and the African diviners and herbalists, who practised according to the traditional Bantu system of medicine. In addition, there were Africans who practised a combination of both systems within a religious frame, as faith healers; and finally, there were those who, calling themselves clairvoyants and magnetizers, practised on their own. All these did well.

Each clinic had between ten and fifteen trained African nurses and midwives. As mentioned above, these nurses were paid by the Council, while those of the new hospital were to be paid by the Province. The Province also employed and controlled the health inspectors under an African Senior, and a European Chief Health Inspector. In their care was the general hygiene of the township. They were supposed to check up on conditions, and organize and teach general cleanliness. All traders and sellers of foodstuffs had to submit to regular inspections by them. This group of persons was among the highest qualified of the public servants, and their educational level gave them high prestige, while their profession gave them authority even over long-established, older and wealthy shop owners.

No fully qualified lawyers lived officially and permanently in the township, but a large number of self-appointed 'legal advisers' fulfilled a greatly needed function and were consulted in divorce and defamation cases, and in a great many other disputes.

In all these fields to which education had given the people an entry, education itself was no longer a uniting influence. On the contrary, the greatest importance was attached to small educational differences until these became barriers to professional co-operation and social intercourse. Relations, for instance, between nurses trained after having matriculated and those trained after having passed Junior Certificate, between social workers by diploma and those who had a university degree, were strained. There was no bridge between European-trained and African-initiated medical experts; and among European-trained doctors as well as among teachers of Reeftown, competition was stronger than common interest. There was as little social contact between the clerical and professional groups as between the elite of education and that of wealth. A tenuous bridge between the last two was formed by some of the professionals whose wives managed a business, as well as by the four educated traders who were included in our sample.

The Reeftown traders were considered mostly as 'uneducated' and even as 'primitive', and they did not participate in the social life of the township. About seventy trading sites were spread all over the township. Originally the business premises were erected by the Council and let at monthly rentals varying between R40 and R60. Later applicants had to build their own shops. Butchers' shops were said to be the most profitable. Next came general dealers and restaurants, grocers and greengrocers. Although some general dealers sold soft goods (and frequently stolen goods hidden under legitimate permits), there were no shops specializing in articles of clothing, or in haberdashery. There were, as yet, no shops selling radios or electrical appliances, and no furniture shops. Only recently a photographer and a hairdresser established themselves.

Many of the more lucrative trades such as furniture shops were still in the hands of some Europeans on the periphery. With regard to kinds of shops, the Reeftown traders were said to be 'conservative'. 'They only go in for well-tried lines,' we were told. There was a printing press which was, however, far from flourishing, and there was talk of starting a dry-cleaning factory, as well as a petrol station.

In spite of Mr Jones's attempts to give a chance to as many aspirant businessmen as possible, he could not prevent the gradual concentration of businesses into the hands of a few more efficient and capable individuals or kin groups. Shops changed hands continually, and there was much underhand 'buying' and 'selling' of trading sites. Licences were often obtained in the name of someone else. Many shops were run by so-called 'owners' who in reality were managers for another trader or for a public servant. The official rate of yearly bankruptcies did not include the many cases of failure when a shop was taken over by a new owner and continued under the previous owner's name and licence, or when managers and partners came into conflict with owners. The difference between these legal personages was seldom understood and there was rarely a written contract or a precise agreement.

Thus there was also in this field considerable mobility, caused by the never-ending search of economically inexperienced people for self-improvement, for independence of the European and for a job near home. This mobility would probably only slacken off when most shops had become concentrated in the hands of a few successful entrepreneurs.

Although, as explained above, European capital was not allowed to be invested in the townships, the restrictions being very similar to those imposed in the Bantustans, it had entered and still did so under various guises, as it would no doubt succeed in doing in the Bantu homelands, if it became really profitable to do so. However, no written guarantees or sureties were possible, and capital could only be invested on trust, a fact which limited its operation.

Much individual enterprise was carried on surreptitiously, mainly because of ignorance as to what was legal or illegal and because of the confusion between the two. Licences for self-employment were hardly ever obtained; most of such undertakings were often pre-

carious and temporary, and tentatively begun. But all this was part
of the process of growth of a population as yet inexperienced in trade
and commerce. Only one craftsman, a tailor, had ever applied for
and obtained a licence. This visible token of legitimacy and per-
manence carried its own prestige. To much of this irregularity Mr
Jones closed his eyes, knowing that in this new society conditions
could not be the same as among the long-urbanized and long-
established merchants of the other ethnic groups, and that here
extra protection and encouragement were required.

Nevertheless, butchers found reason to complain bitterly of the
'unfair' competition of illegal (Indian and Jewish) sellers of beef
and 'mutton', frequently in the form of live oxen and goats. Dry-
cleaning depots suffered from competition, mainly from Indians, but
such competition from more experienced traders was only half of the
African merchants' troubles. Their greatest handicap was that the
better-class and richer citizens (those with cars), preferred to buy
their monthly groceries in the white towns, and often in bulk instead
of, as the traders complained, 'helping their own people'. All self-
employed, whether doctors, traders or salesmen, were unanimous in
their opinion that 'money should circulate within the colour line'.
They were never tired of demanding that the Local Authority apply
stronger *Apartheid* measures and of urging African buyers to buy
only from African businesses. All this is remindful of the theory of
the 'double duty' dollar, propagated by Abram L. Harris,[44] which
was connected with the idea of a separate Negro economy. According
to this theory 'the Negro worker would not only purchase with his
dollar the necessities of life, but he would provide with the dollar
he spent the wages for Negro workers'.[45]

By and large, economic life was, as yet, poorly developed. Investments were on a modest scale. There were few productive premises
of any value; there was little technical equipment; capitalization in
merchandise was restricted; shops carried small stocks. Car mechanics as well as bicycle repair shops kept few spare parts. When
needed by the customer, these were ordered from the white town
or obtained by pilferage. Moreover, probably the majority of car
owners had their cars repaired in the white town. Most mechanics
worked in the backyards of their homes. But as long as the higher-
income groups preferred to give their custom to European shops,
believing these to be cheaper, better and more glamorous, African
trade would remain limited.

All this contributed to the one important economic conclusion that
the Bantu employer of labour was slow to emerge, and the wages
paid by African employers to shop assistants and workmen were low.
Female shop assistants and waitresses received about R16 per month;
working hours were long and indefinite, and included most week-

ends. Domestic servants who did not live in received only some R5 or R7 per month. While Europeans were constantly reprimanded for not raising African wages quickly enough, and while African buyers never queried prices in European shops, the Africans themselves were unwilling to pay their own employees the same wages, nor would they consider paying the same prices to their own traders and merchants, craftsmen and artisans.

Although the African urban worker had reason to complain of competition from new arrivals from the country, African employers gave preference to rural employees, who were said to be 'less cheeky' and 'cheaper'. Many African craftsmen and artisans had their own underpaid 'boys'. (See pp. 184ff.)

Residents complained about transport, but considering the distance it was quite adequate and compared favourably with similar housing estates in England for instance. Situated at the crossing between two national highways, Reeftown had a direct connection with its parent town as well as with Johannesburg and other Reef towns. Internal transport was provided by a bus service, as well as by the railway, which already had three local stations. Many Reeftowners had their own cars and others habitually used taxis. These operated on what in Turkey was called the 'Dolmush' system. The taxis functioned as buses, following fixed routes at regular intervals, filling up with passengers at fixed rates per trip. The usual charge was 25 cents per person for a trip to the white town or to Johannesburg in the daytime. At night there was a double charge. Taxi stands were located at various points throughout the township. On the central square one never needed to wait long, and generally one or two taxis stood ready, waiting for customers. Many taxis also delivered parcels. To own a taxi was lucrative; taxi owners and drivers were considered among the wealthiest residents. Many businessmen as well as teachers ran taxis as a side-line, either driving their own cars or employing a driver. Licensed taxi drivers complained incessantly about 'pirate' taxis, and sometimes violent battles, in which blood flowed freely, occurred between them.

Together with skilled factory workers and lorry drivers, taxi drivers were said to be the organizers of the 'strongest' (i.e. most wealthy and popular) Stockfels – the surest sign of affluence. Yet their own status was not above middle class. However, in the shebeens, persons of these weekly-paid occupations figured as money-lenders to the poorer, monthly-paid assistant teachers and clerks. Moreover, there was considerable occupational mobility between these occupational groups. It was therefore expected that their status would rise and that of their educated shebeen mates would sink. All the more so as the status of education was visibly descending in general esteem and that of wealth rising.

Reeftown had its own Post Office; there was one postal delivery a day. Many residents preferred, however, to collect their mail at the Post Office. The etiquette of postal secrecy was still largely unknown and, if known, often unheeded. Daily papers were distributed by some adults and schoolchildren. Subscriptions were, however, not encouraged. Experience had shown that too many copies remained undelivered and were resold elsewhere. Our elite preferred to fetch their papers at the agencies in the township. There were some public telephones in call-boxes; the residents who had private telephones occupied one page in the telephone directory.

Summarizing, it would appear that in the change-over from the small-scale society of the old location to the large-scale type of society of the township, the structure of the community was becoming more complex; its field of social activity more articulated as well as expanded; and consequently new occupational groups threw up new elites and older occupational groups became occupational hierarchies. A plurality of separate if not always entirely disjunctive elites were arising, and the educated had become divided among themselves.

Although large segments were still totally unconcerned with social class, they did not remain entirely unaffected by what was happening among the so-called 'social classes'. The principal change which affected everyone, rich or poor, educated or not educated, was this: wherever the African turned, he now encountered other Africans in positions of superiority and authority over him. The earlier greater dependence on successful interracial contacts was changing to a greater dependence on intraracial relationships. Whereas previously all one had to do was to try and please the European in charge, now increasing numbers of people found themselves in the predicament most intensely felt and most frequently expressed by the assistant teachers since the Bantu Education Act had given members of their own race considerable power over them: 'Nowadays, we no longer know whom to please.'

Formal organizations

The increasing occupational and educational differentiation in Reeftown inevitably affected organizational life in the township. The changing tastes and needs demanded different organizational patterns; and whereas organizational leadership itself carried immense personal prestige almost independent of the kind of organization, some organizations, on the other hand, had already acquired high prestige, whereas others were thought of as being decidedly lower class.

But whatever the social or economic stratum, Reeftowners by and

45

large were great joiners, and formal organizations were well-developed in the township. Membership in an organization, club or society was a matter of pride and always mentioned. Organizational leadership was a vehicle for social mobility upwards, particularly if other status attributes such as education or occupation were socially insufficient. Serving on a committee or board, being an office bearer in an organization, however small and unimportant, was in itself a recognized status symbol. One was then said by others to be 'prominent in social activities'. (See also p. 96.) but best of all was to be a founder.[46] To have founded an organization was a distinction which remained attached to one's name for ever after. In fact it was clear proof that one had not lived without leaving an imprint. It was a guarantee of immortality, for by it one was sure to be remembered.[47]

Inevitably, therefore, organizations continued to appear all the time. But most did not last long, and it was sometimes difficult to know whether an organization existed, was fading out, or had temporarily ceased its activities. The general, and typically noncommittal, expression used was that such and such a society was 'pending', or its members were 'resting'.

In the context of this study only a brief picture of the township's organizational life, in broadest outline, will be given. It covers the situation during the years 1958–60, while the figures given can be only approximations.

Football (soccer) was by far the most popular sport. There were some sixty teams in about thirty clubs represented on the Reeftown Soccer Association, the leading sports body. There were also about four active baseball and netball clubs, four not so active boxing clubs, and one rugby club. In addition, athletics, judo and bodybuilding had a limited appeal. Most of these sports were assisted and the funds at least somewhat supervised by the Administration, the Senior Welfare Officer and/or the African Sports Organizer.

In many sports organizations, the supreme leadership was in the hands of members of the upper-middle and lower-upper classes.

Four different uniformed youth movements functioned satisfactorily under European control. They were branches of two different Boy Scout and Girl Guide organizations. There were also the clubs of the Southern African Association of Youth Clubs with a mixed membership of boys and girls. The organizers and leaders were mainly assistant teachers and ex-teachers. However, the higher-status committees were again predominantly manned by the upper-middle and lower-upper classes.

Of the church organizations, perhaps the church choirs should be mentioned first because the choir-masters were persons of no mean status in Reeftown. These were mainly teachers and clerks. The choirs were of varying strength, and members came and went. Choral singing was the most important artistic expression of the Reeftowners and therefore the most popular, but also the most disputed item on all the programmes of official and semi-official township functions. Besides the church choirs there were teachers' choirs, nurses' choirs, school choirs and interdenominational choirs. These regularly gave performances of religious or contemporary music, and frequently competed for trophies in intertownship competitions. Of all the non-denominational choirs only one had emerged as the recognized leader in 'classical' music: its choirmaster was a clerk and a member of our elite.

It was then the sports clubs and the choirs which commanded the widest and most lasting interest among the largest number of people. Nearly every week-end some sports or music competitions were organized by schools and churches, and prizes were presented by notables, higher teachers and other members of the elite.

By far the most popular general organizational type prevalent among the upper-lower and the middle-class groups, was the 'Stockfel' in its many variations, from the simple pooling of fixed weekly amounts among a small number of associates – preferably not more than four – to the large societies in which a number of smaller pooling and saving clubs joined together in a weekly party at the home of one member who was 'the host or hostess of the week', and who thus was enabled to make a handsome profit from the sale of food and drink to members and their guests. The basic 'Stockfel' pattern also operated in the numerous friendly societies in which participants came together to render assistance in times of death, illness and other emergencies.[48]

These various forms of the 'Stockfel' were the only kinds of organization which, combining as they did 'business with pleasure', worked without European assistance to the entire satisfaction of large numbers of participants and continued to exist and to cater for the most general economic and social needs of the majority of the residents, in spite of persistent European condemnation.

In addition there were, for men and women separately, the various church prayer groups and fund-raising groups; of these the women's groups were more numerous and influential. In these so-called 'Manyanos',[49] women in conspicuous and distinctive uniforms came together every Thursday to pray and dance and to organize their various activities.

Through a system of mutual visiting between their branches and a strictly upheld code of reciprocity, the members of these two types of organization, the 'Stockfel' and the 'Manyano', travelled up and down the Reef and even further afield to join in and contribute to each other's activities. Thus a widespread network of social relationships was established and maintained, bringing much gossip and news,

47

so that people were generally well informed about what went on elsewhere.

There were a great number of 'tribal' societies in which 'tribes' and sub-'tribes', or even large clans, came together and recalled the great moments in their past history. Some of these societies functioned at the same time as mutual aid societies, providing funeral aid and other forms of assistance. To this same category of 'tribal' association belonged many of the smaller indigenous churches, often consisting of not more than the members of one clan or kin group.

The educated considered the 'Stockfel' 'primitive', the 'tribal' societies 'backward', and the church organizations 'conservative'. They had, however, no organization of comparable membership, cohesion and appeal, except perhaps the IOTT (the Independent Order of the True Templars), an organization just as 'African', but modern African.[50] Of all organizations the IOTT was probably the most cohesive and most strictly organized. It was a semi-religious, non-denominational, highly formalized organization with the professed aim of total abstinence. Directed by a European woman in the Cape, it was otherwise entirely African. The twenty-one temples in Reeftown had an estimated membership of 1,300 to 1,500. They met once a week. The bulk of the members consisted of factory workers. drivers, policemen and self-employed persons. About one-third of our elite were IOTT members, generally holding leading executive positions.

As our review proceeds from the organizations popular among the masses to those supported by the more educated, we see that membership becomes more sectional and aims more specific.

Tennis, golf and table-tennis were organized independently by the participants themselves; mainly teachers, clerks and factory workers. Some three different tennis clubs, each with six to eight members, played on the three courts, while an eighteen-hole golf course, badly in need of repair, was used by three or four small, independent golf clubs which formed and reformed round different committees. Golf was not considered an upper-class sport since it began among ex-caddies. Some doctors played, but not in Reeftown. The Administration had plans for renewing the old and possibly laying out a new eighteen-hole golf course. This would, however, require better organization and at least some co-operation on the part of the golfers.

Table-tennis was played daily after office hours by a club of some ten to fifteen members. Players were chiefly municipal clerks and assistant teachers. At the office was also a piano at the disposal of those who wanted to practise.

Each profession had its own professional organization. Some, like the Ministers' Fraternal, the Principals' Council and the Traders' Association, were purely local groups. Others, like the Health

Inspectors' Association, the Social Workers' Association, the TIAMA (Transvaal Interdenominational African Ministers' Association) and the TUATA (Transvaal United African Teachers' Association) had a regional or national scope. Most of these organizations were, however, split into two or three opposing camps in Reeftown, and their membership was generally quantitatively not representative.

As elsewhere only the clerks had no professional association. And for similar reasons. Clerks and social workers had, and possibly still have plans to form a graded-staff association. As the social workers considered themselves the natural leaders of this venture and the higher-graded, much older, municipal clerks resented this, there was a deadlock. As an informant mentioned, these two groups were 'strange bedfellows'.

As everywhere else[51] the women were 'the mainstay of local corporate life'.[52] Unlike the men, they formed organizations catering for more general communal needs. In this they showed a greater sense of civic responsibility than the men. Two large women's organizations had branches in Reeftown, each with some twenty to twenty-five members. Both were rather upper and upper-middle class, though not intentionally. They played a prominent part in the social life of the community by catering at functions, organizing charity shows, collecting funds and contributions in kind for various deserving causes, and generally participating in all township functions.

When their Annual Conference took place in Reeftown, their evening entertainment was a big 'social' affair, attended by a large number of leading citizens. No large function, whether official or private, could be organized without the assistance of one or the other of these organizations. Their mutual relationships oscillated between fierce rivalries and temporary appeasements. Very few women, except some wealthy Xhosa widows, succeeded in being members of both clubs, because in reality each consisted mainly of 'followers' of the founder. The two founders were among the most powerful personalities of the township. One group was predominantly Sotho-speaking, and the other predominantly Nguni-speaking.

As will be noticed, the organizational groupings often followed broadly 'tribal' lines. This was a natural result of the origin of most organizations in small friendship cliques, rather than of conscious planning or ethnic grouping.

The 'cultural clubs'

Having proceeded from the more general to the more particular, and having given only the briefest mention to each organization, we

49

must say a little more about one special type of organization, the so-called 'cultural club', which functioned chiefly among the educated, and those with whom this study is concerned.

These clubs were indicative of the perennial need and the equally perennial failure of small groups of people, who wanted to spend some leisure time together, with a view to the 'typical middle-class aim of self-improvement'[53] – at least so it would appear – and who were incapable of doing so unless within an organized formal frame.

The idea of these clubs had originated in the desire to continue 'something which we had at college'. They were modelled upon the well-known debating and lecturing clubs founded by Dr and Mrs Ray Philips at the Jan Hofmeyer School of Social Work, Johannesburg, and subsequently extended all over the Reef. After the Philipses left South Africa, and their continual guidance and selfless advice came to an end, these clubs generally died a slow death.

Such a cultural club had existed also in the old location, but it had deteriorated into a group which organized beauty competitions and dance nights. It was rejuvenated in the general enthusiasm of the new habitat into a cultural club which provided occasional lectures and regular ballroom dancing. As such it existed for two or three whole years, and was an active social and cultural force when we started working in the township. Gradually, however, it lost its earlier upper-class leadership, and it also failed in its subsequent attempt to obtain at least upper-class patronage. It had a paid-up membership of nearly forty young men and women, predominantly factory workers, with a sprinkling of assistant teachers, nurses, typists and clerks. In the years under study it again became limited to ballroom dancing; this resulted from the fact that members of the Communist Party had infiltrated into its committee in order to use it for their own purposes, which entailed pleasing the membership first.

Another similar group, a discussion group, called 'The Council of the Blood', which consisted mainly of Basuto, was founded 'in competition' against the allegedly Nguni-dominated Cultural Club. It made a brief appearance, set up two Committees, planned to perform Shakespeare's *Julius Caesar* because 'costuming would be cheap, as all the actors could wrap themselves in bedsheets', and then proved itself to be only a 'flash in the pan'.

Yet another group whose destiny we could follow, was opened with a lecture from a European staff member. It subsequently fizzled out. Generally, this was what happened. After European members of the Administration and some well-known African speakers from outside had given lectures, the list of suggested subjects and speakers was exhausted and interest waned.

The insoluble problem of all these 'cultural' clubs was that most members did not quite know what was meant by the 'culture' they wanted to promote and, at the same time, they were not particularly interested in finding out, although they felt that they ought to be. Moreover, as the African research assistant explained: 'They want to attend a cultural club for, if a Press photographer should come and take a picture, they want to be in it.' (In this they were not so different from many a white committee on the Reef of Gold.)

Only two subjects could draw full attendance in Reeftown – etiquette and politics, in that order. Not even a better type of film could bring the educated to the cinema, unless it had been let out beforehand that this was going to be a film which only the educated residents could understand. No doubt the greatest incentive towards cultural activities and cultural borrowing was snobbery.

Williams reports a statement by one of his informants: 'I can't recall any movement in the village that ever had any success unless someone of the so-called higher classes took an interest.'[54] This we found fully applicable to the Reeftown situation. In earlier times this traditional upper-class role had been filled by the European. He was willing to make the unpopular decisions, to act as arbiter, judge and scapegoat, as secretary, treasurer, man-of-all-work and, generally, doer of the only solid work done. But nowadays, not only was the European forced to recede, but the increasing trend among the Africans was 'to run things among ourselves and without European interference'. However, the African upper classes were disinclined to play the, previously European, role of scapegoat.[55]

The people now turned to the social workers, who were expected 'to harmonize people', 'to organize social gatherings and activities', 'to stimulate social life generally', and, most important of all, 'not to get involved in quarrels'. The social workers, however, seldom fulfilled these high expectations.

In 1958 we met a highly capable cultural organizer who worked hard 'to bring people together'. Inevitably, he became involved in some of Reeftown's permanent social divisions and became a highly controversial figure, splitting the entire upper class into violent pro- and contra- camps. Since he left, the Administration has been unable to find a suitable candidate for this most exacting position of cultural organizer.

Recently, the elite themselves founded their own cultural club, called Reeftown Study Group. It was started, upon the initiative of a small group of the elite, by one of the leading socialites, whose wife was the most admired upper-class hostess of Reeftown. The motives were mainly 'to win friends and influence people'. Membership was to be granted upon invitation only, and only to 'those in the top drawer'. However when it became clear that the recognized 'Upper Ten' were mainly uninterested, members of the next following social strata were invited to attend and join. The educated middle class watched with interest 'the antics' of their social superiors – 'those higher-ups' – and confidently predicted that 'those fancy ideas, it will not last!'

Yet there was a very great need for people to come together in clubs with a cultural and educational purpose, for lectures and debates. This was the only way in which the educated hoped to find a remedy for the dismal failure of informal, unorganized social life in Reeftown.

Informal association

The inability of the higher-income groups among the educated and business people of Reeftown to come together in informal association and friendly home entertainment was probably the most important social fact about the township.

'Socially,' said a member of one of the leading families on the Reef, 'Reeftown has disappointed me. People do not want to come together. They do not mix. They have no fun. Life's boring in Reeftown. Nobody entertains and there is nothing on.'

'In Reeftown people do not know how to be free.' That was what it amounted to.

Reeftown was considered to be 'dull' by the educated residents and their visitors alike. People in high positions, who went around the new housing estates on the Reef to choose where they would like to settle often preferred it for that reason, and in spite of Reeftown's excellent housing conditions, any one of the other townships where, it was said, people still lived mainly in municipal-built, rented houses; and, although there also they may have been no longer equal, they 'at least appeared equal'.

For, 'It is the houses,' people said.

'With all these fine houses, there is the evil of pride. There are petty jealousies and there is competitiveness in everything among the better classes.'

'All these people who have new, fine houses – the sense of ownership has overwhelmed them to the point of making them stiffish. They do not get together and everyone is isolated.'

'Everyone holds back. People dare not be free with each other.'

'This upper class coming into positions; it has made everyone artificial.'

Status anxiety has always been the hallmark of suburbia everywhere, and insecurity the characteristic of all social upstarts. The house has a special importance also for the white parvenus who make up the bulk of the European population of the Reef of Gold, and who had, frequently only one generation earlier, come out of the slums and the ghettoes of Europe. However, many more factors contributed to the failure of spontaneous social intercourse in Reeftown

We spoke of the invigorating effect of the new habitat. During many years Reeftown had been building and furnishing, moving and improving. People had been planning and organizing full of enthusiasm and good intentions, for now things would be different. But it did not last.

In Greenbelt[56] it took four years for the general jockeying for positions to come to and end and for the people to sort themselves out into new social-status and interest groupings. In Reeftown it may have lasted longer. Yet, when we arrived in 1958, i.e. nine years after its foundation, the township had already acquired a recognizable system of prestige differentiation. Some people's houses were already better and nearer completion than others, and the same names had begun to appear on the principal township committees. It had already become less easy to climb the social ladder by means of entertaining and organizational leadership. There were already a number of recognized 'hostesses' and 'leaders' in all the social strata of the population. To start new clubs and associations was considered detrimental to vested interests. Trends to monopolize the recruitment channels of leadership were already noticeable. A network of alignments and cliques in ever-narrowing social circles had formed, and visiting someone belonging to another clique was often considered a betrayal of friendship.

Flush lavatories do not change people overnight, and better houses do not necessarily make better citizens. After the earlier enthusiasm and good intentions had spent themselves, conditions were very much the same as before. Only now everything happened behind drawn curtains and burglar-proof front doors.

It must be remembered that this was still a primitive community – and a segregated one. People eyed each other with suspicion, and there was the self-hatred, the guilt feeling and the intra-aggression of the ghetto.[57]

There was as yet little that could give these people the sense of belonging together. Not even a common hatred for the European could unite them. What they did have in common was their dependence on the European – a common need which ranged from the necessity for actual material assistance to the psychological urge for recognition. And so this shared need for the favour of the European was yet another reason for rivalry.

If anything did unite the residents, it was the overriding desire to prevent at all costs the European 'finding out how bad we are'. This was the strongest unwritten code in the township. People suffered widely from personal threats to life and property, from blackmail and assault, reinforced by the practice of witchcraft and by mutual fear. The severest sanctions followed any betrayal of a fellow resident to the whites. Consequently many evil practices, much corruption, bribery and blackmail, and all terrorization continued to exist with impunity.

Many people were, or at one time in the past had been, involved in unlawful actions; many a household had a skeleton in the cupboard; many families had black sheep. People knew such things about each other but said nothing. 'But when you want to destroy someone, such knowledge comes in handy.'

A great many people had learned that in Reeftown it is better not to become too intimate with anyone.

And so, inevitably, anticlimax had set in. New developments still brought each time some reshuffling of the cards before new hands were dealt, but the players were becoming fewer. There was a general social apathy, particularly among the educated – an apathy about which almost every one of my acquaintances complained, but about which nobody seemed able to do anything.

It was in vain that Mr Jones had chats with leading people, inviting their advice and co-operation in creating a community spirit. It was in vain that large township functions were encouraged and every pretext for community celebrations was eagerly grasped, fostered and subsidized, for 'some form of "ceremonial" in the sense of joint symbolic activities is necessary to maintain group loyalty in an acephalous community',[58] as Frankenberg found in his investigation of Pentre. On such occasions, executive committees with many members were formed by the known organizers of the township and anyone could join. If these committees managed to survive until the actual day, the function generally went without too many hitches. Two annual functions succeeded in running for two successive years. We were able to follow happenings from the first inaugural meetings to the last quarrel. As in Pentrediwaith studied by Frankenberg, 'loyalties and enmities forged outside these specific activities are carried over into them',[59] and in this way found a healthy airing. Subsequently, after some sort of compromise had been found at the last meeting, and the ultimate blame for all the conflicts had been satisfactorily put on one of the European staff members, a new harmony and unity were temporarily achieved.

However, when the third year began and the time came for the preparation of the first of these two functions, the antagonisms expressed and created by earlier functions had grown to such an extent that the celebrations had to be called off after the first few preparatory committee meetings. The best community functions were those organized spontaneously by the residents at short notice, mostly on the occasion of a disaster or death and through *ad hoc* committees, which, after the last quarrels about missing funds had died down, could be disbanded and forgotten.

The educated – the only group that could organize large township functions – were divided among themselves. 'We are too competitive,' they explained. 'There is no companionship among us.' 'We only watch each other jealously.' 'We use each opportunity to pull each other down.' They were astonishingly frank about themselves and their own failings.

No doubt Epstein was right when he wrote that inconsistency and disharmony should be recognized as integral parts of the nascent social system and as 'an important source of its dynamics',[60] and certainly Sprott was correct when he wrote ' . . . quarrels may be taken as evidence of vitality'.[61] However, anyone who, like the present investigators studied some of these trends, may have also come to agree with those worried residents who complained that 'in Reeftown it goes too far'. In the end too much was destroyed and too little achieved. Too great an emphasis placed on social mobility has its toll in insecurities, in social conflicts and in damage to personality development. As people become involved with trying to get ahead rather than with developing any lasting and sure sense of the community and its needs, the result is a 'diffusion of insecurity'.[62]

After all, unlike the village of Pentre, for instance, studied by Frankenberg, which was an organically grown community, Reeftown was a housing estate. And the hard truth is that no community centres nor community functions can create from above, so to speak, a community spirit which can only arise from the living source of informal contacts and neighbourly 'droppings-in'.

With nostalgia the people remembered life in the old location, where 'everybody was equal, and people were kind and hospitable'. This was expressed as

'In the old location there was that general feeling to please,
to give, to entertain.'

'It was a slum really. It was terribly congested and filthy,
with all the social evils of drink, violence, prostitution and
worse. But it was real life, people belonged together. Africans
knew that they were all Africans together. They were aware of
their common evils and sought redemption in friendliness and
generosity.'

In this fond remembering there was something of the romance of the *Staedtel*, so noticeable in Jewish literature during the early years of the Emancipation, and so well described by Simon Halkin.[63]

In the *Staedtel*, according to the memory of the emancipated Jew, 'the fanatical rabbi becomes the utterly selfless saint . . . and the helpless, dull and cruel teacher evolves into the ideal pedagogue, whose love for the children is unbounded'.[64] Similarly, in the memory of the lonely Reeftowners, the most rapacious slum landlord and the most ruthless shebeen queen of the old location became generous and hospitable benefactors. The misery, the filth and the congestion were forgotten, and what was remembered was the human intimacy, the warmth and the fun of a social life which still possessed the proletarian quality of casualness,[65] and which was uninhibited and spontaneously joyful.

The most satisfactory informal social contacts were provided by drinking parties among the males. These often began at home and sooner or later moved to the shebeens, or they began in the shebeens, where friends were made easily. The shebeen, where people felt relaxed and at ease, was the only leveller of social inequalities. In the shebeen nobody worried about what was the correct form of behaviour, or what one's house looked like.

Reserving the first anxiety for later, we shall first take up the second reason for embarrassment. For the awkward and mortifying truth was that of approximately 250 owner-built (and also of the special municipal-built houses mentioned on pp. 23-4) on which Reeftown prided itself at the beginning of 1958, only a very small number were internally complete. Only the doctors and the most successful traders had completed their houses, whereas in almost all other houses not only were there rooms which still had no furniture, but rooms which were not yet really rooms. In this the house owners followed a procedure similar to that of the Administration.

In order to make houses available for purchase at the lowest possible figure, the Council had to leave many structural features unfinished. Most houses were, therefore, sold without inner doors or ceilings, with only roughly plastered walls and at best, roughly cemented floors, without bathroom or kitchen equipment. When the municipal buyer moved in, his house was frequently no more than an empty shell. When he then had saved or earned some more money, he started upon a series of 'improvements'. These 'improvements' were often unproductive and solely inspired by considerations of status. Thus, among the first 'improvements' was often the building of a new front façade of face brick and the erection of that most coveted badge of prestige, the *stoep*. Yet, unlike many Europeans who almost live on their *stoeps*, Africans do not use their *stoeps*. This shows again that cultural borrowing is not governed primarily by practical considerations, by need or by use.

Those who built their own houses proceeded similarly. The houses were generally designed and planned almost without regard to the money in hand. Then, when finances threatened to run out, the interior had to remain unfinished and the last available money was spent on external features and embellishments. Fancy burglar proofing and venetian blinds, window-boxes, walls and gate-posts of yellow face brick, wrought-iron and Slasto, were some of the absolute 'musts' for the status-conscious Reeftowners. It was often quite disconcerting to pass through so much splendour into rooms without doors or floors, and with roughly-bagged dark cement walls.

The speed and cultural 'know-how' with which the subsequent improvements were made were important status characteristics. A not untypical example of the procedure followed and the amounts paid by a sensible young educated couple of my acquaintance can be given. They had bought one of the special, municipal-built houses – a four-roomed one in the high-status area costing R710 – and were paying it off at the rate of R11·25 per month. They had already put in the ceilings, which had cost them between R120 and R140. The walls had been plastered and painted at some R30, and they had had their own electricity installed at the cost of R224. All this was done in just over one year.

It was estimated that in this manner the township population had, by 1959, spent some two million rand on the building of houses and the addition of improvements, which means that this sum had been invested in property by the people themselves, over and above the loans granted by the Council. This shows clearly the power of the social pressure towards improving and beautifying the houses.

Inevitably, the strain of this tremendous effort affected the social life of the community. First, because people were saving their money for home improvements rather than spending it on hospitality. And indeed, we were often told: 'In the old location money was not spent on houses, but on entertaining royally', or 'Here everyone holds back, but in the old location people gave themselves completely.' Secondly, until her house was finished, a house-proud housewife was not going to have Mrs So-and-so in for tea, in case she scrutinized everything and ran to her best friend to tell her: 'And you wouldn't believe it, but she hasn't even pelmets yet!'

The unfinished state of their houses caused everywhere acute embarrassment. 'Not until my house is finished', was the ever-recurring reason given for social isolation. Even some interviews were said to be possible only 'when we have got nicely settled'.

In Reeftown the shame was not only social but also cultural. It was not only that 'They will say that we had nothing before, that we are upstarts and now want to play high', but also, and particularly, that 'People take it that you are still primitive and backward, and that you don't know that there should be a bookcase in that corner there.'

The houses were the main bone of contention between the educated and the businessmen. The wealthy said about the educated: 'With all that education, and look where it got them! I have lifted myself up without education and you should see my house and furniture!' The educated, however, explained: 'A house is not everything; you must know how to live in it!' They pointed to the traders' houses, where the lavishly furnished lounges and dining-rooms displayed the owners' wealth, but were untouched and unlived in, while the family congregated cosily in the warm kitchen. They pointed to the completely tiled and multicoloured bathrooms with their built-in baths, as shining and spotless as they had come out of the shop, and then to the worn and dented enamel wash-stand which stood in the corner – obviously the only thing in daily use. 'It just shows you . . .', the educated told each other cattily.

Whenever one of the rich businessmen gave a party celebrating some home improvement, the educated and the nurses, who would be invited to lend glamour to the occasion, remarked that, 'What he did was all wrong; you don't enter a bathroom from the kitchen!' To me they then described such 'primitive rich' in a genteel way as 'rather conservative, you know, Mrs Brandel'. Among themselves they could be overheard calling them 'real Kaffirs'.

How often had we not been told, 'Wait until my house is finished' and then we shall make a splash!' But even when the house was nearing completion, nothing changed. The point was, as the African research assistant said, 'They don't know how to make that splash.'

For social class is not only typified by the style of the house and its interior decoration, it is also expressed by the manner and forms of entertaining. Guests tend to 'place' their hosts socially by the kind of refreshments and by the way in which these are served.

The connection between social status and forms of hospitality was well demonstrated by an event which happened during our field research. Every year Mr Jones used to give a Christmas party for his entire staff, and after all the customary speeches were made and songs sung, the free distribution of beer, meat and bread was the main attraction. But not only this. The food was served in large, shining tins which were destined later to become freely distributed garbage tins. These had to be used as they were the largest available containers to hold the enormous quantities of foodstuffs needed. None of the beneficiaries had ever objected to these. When, in 1959, Christmas time approached again, the women social workers, considering themselves a superior group of public servants, and desiring to demonstrate this fact once and for all, used the occasion of the Christmas party to create a clear social distinction between themselves and all the others. They informed Mr Jones that 'We feel out of place in a form of entertainment suitable for the ordinary labourer.' To me they complained that moreover they could not partake of food served from such unsuitable vessels! (Having forsaken most of their own original ritual, they were obviously rapidly adopting new modern rituals!) They then organized a separate party for the professionals among the municipal personnel at which tea was served with iced cakes, scones, tarts and sandwiches presented in the correct manner on the proper china dishes complete with neatly displayed doilies and serviettes, and nibbled with the prescribed ritualized hand gestures and mouth movements. To this party they also invited the senior administrative assistants; and only after they saw that 'there was food enough', did they invite the junior clerks as well because they (so truly and endearingly African), 'felt sorry for them'. Mr Jones was invited as the guest of honour and made a speech and it became, as one of the hostesses told us, 'a really civilized party'.

All this does not apply only to Africans of course. Also a great many European houses have been built to dazzle visitors rather than to provide comfort for the occupants, and architectural gimmicks are introduced with the sole aim to impress guests. Also in white houses the proper appointment of reception rooms often takes precedence over the furnishing of bedrooms and living-rooms, which are often left unfinished. Also white hostesses from among the *nouveaux riches* on the Reef vie with each other in the quality and quantity of their dinners and their cocktail snacks, the eminence of their guests and the originality of their parties. Sociologists are not yet very clear about the similarities and differences between class acculturation and ethnic acculturation, and it may merely amount to a difference in degree and emphasis. From this point of view and taking for granted that entertaining and hospitality are important expressions of social status, and often most effective instruments of social mobility upwards in many different cultures, it is still true that in Bantu tradition party-giving has always been and still is specially emphasized and greatly practised. There were therefore in Reeftown probably many more parties than in any other housing estate of the same size in Europe or America. There were weddings, funerals and baptisms; baby-coming-out parties, coming-of-age parties and matriculation parties. Each new feature added to a house was celebrated with a party. Every time someone went overseas or received a scholarship, his family or friends gave a party. Every possible occasion was used to give a party. Although even at such parties sometimes conflicts arose between the new urban and the traditional rural patterns, between tribal and kinship obligations on the one hand and the new demands of friendship and prestige on the other, such parties generally went off to everyone's satisfaction. Each guest knew his own position in the social situation and his role derived clearly from this position. For all urban innovations were grafted as single traits on what were

G

broadly and basically traditional patterns, known by everyone. These patterns of entertaining derived mainly from the old and familiar 'Stockfel', where everyone knew his function and role, and the principal of reciprocity was strictly observed.

As an African social science graduate explained to us, 'All social life among my people emanates from the "Stockfel" and all parties are fundamentally based on the "Stockfel". The trouble begins when they do not want to do this "Stockfel" type of entertaining because then they have nothing with which to replace it.'

The educated and the social snobs wanted, and needed, what they called 'European parties' and European forms of entertainment. One of the important and very necessary items on the overfull programme of a women's organization such as the Zenzele YWCA Club was instruction and practice in the European ways of giving parties – parties in which food and drink were not paid for by the guests, and in which the hostess did not receive 'presents' or services in return.

But such ways of party-giving were still very unfamiliar. 'If there is free drink or food, and if you do not make them pay like the "Stockfels" do, they help themselves freely, and they turn the house upside down to find more drink. Moreover, they bring any number of uninvited guests and behave in the most shocking manner.' If there was not this general 'Stockfel' pattern, there was simply no pattern at all.

In numerous conversations in which we tried to understand the difficulties, we were always told the same. 'Those who try to entertain in the European way, do so because they want to show the others how advanced they are; and the others only come so as to learn how things should be done.' People would sit on their chairs along the walls – just sit – each trying to behave with decorum and dignity, each uncertain with regard to the correct behaviour expected by the others as befitting his or her new status and social position. For that was the way in which, traditionally, all behaviour was controlled, determined and regulated. Less socially and more individually determined behaviour was still almost unknown. The uncertainty of perhaps committing oneself by the 'wrong' behaviour, that is by either 'shining too much' or 'betraying one's ignorance', was agonizing. There was nothing to break the inhibitions and in the fear of behaving either 'too low or too high', nobody enjoyed themselves.

The problem was that those who wanted this 'social entertaining of the Europeans', that is 'without presents and with just conversation but on an elevated plane', had not yet succeeded in finding the appropriate patterns.

This inability of our elite to come together in friendly informality was the subject to which any general talk with this investigator always returned, for it was a matter of great concern to them. 'Please, Mrs

Brandel, we do not know what is this "social" of the Europeans. Please show us how to behave.' In fields such as this the lack of easy black–white social contact was most acutely felt.

And so, rather than incur censure and ridicule from their peers, the upper class of Reeftown kept themselves to themselves. They barricaded themselves behind their new residential splendour and were lonely in the midst of their new possessions. When I told them that they ought to do something about this, that they ought to meet people and make friends (I even taught them jokes to start breaking the ice) they invariably replied, 'You can't do anything about it. It's the new houses.'

Some community-conscious Reeftowners among the educated even went so far as to say, 'The Council has given the people a chance to live according to their status, and they meant well; but it should have been done more gradually.' And, indeed, like all revolutionary developments, it had happened too suddenly.

Summing up

As against the proletarian insouciance of the old location, Reeftown showed the status anxiety which is the hall-mark of suburbia. The new social inequalities which had appeared far too suddenly, and which were made more apparent by the increasing occupational differentiation and the differential housing standards, had created well-nigh insurmountable social barriers. The changing patterns of home-entertainment and party-giving, combined with the state of incompleteness of most houses, caused acute embarrassment and inhibited easy sociability. By contrast formal organizations and all manner of organized clubs and societies, run on the pattern of the familiar 'Stockfel', flourished. But for the educated and well-to-do who desired to distinguish themselves from the ordinary Reeftowners by more western patterns of social intercourse and hospitality it was difficult to find new bases for personal relationships and for the creation of an integrated and life enhancing social existence. While individually the people seemed to be emerging rapidly from previous habits, beliefs and values, socially the rise of new ways of social interaction and the formation of new group loyalties were painfully slow.

In the never-ending pursuit of individual self-improvement, people were highly mobile – occupationally, residentially and socially. Competition in the general status struggle was fierce and ruthless. Whereas before, everyone had been equal under the European in charge, now the residents encountered in all fields of their lives fellow Africans in positions of relative superiority and inferiority, so that intraracial relationships became of greater concern than interracial relationships. Reeftowners found themselves in situations either of power or of submission *vis-à-vis* other Africans, and the consequent uncertainty as to the appropriate status behaviour caused considerable unease and increased the feelings of guilt.

For, in spite of all comparisons with housing estates elsewhere – comparisons generally favourable to Reeftown – this township consisted of people who, hardly yet freed from the traditional bondage of a kinship-dominated, custom-bound society, had suddenly been thrown into the unmitigated status struggle and the relentless competitiveness of the modern world in the *milieu* of a ghetto. Consequently, behind the façade of suburban respectability smouldered the mutual suspicions and jealousies, the fears and personal revengefulness of a primitive society, as well as the self-hatred, the guilt-feelings and the aggressiveness of the ghetto.

New social divisions had been introduced in juxtaposition with the old ones; divisions common in the modern world had now been added to the traditional divisions of an ancient, tribal world and there was, as yet, little that could unite these people. The emancipation from tribal restraints had engendered an extreme individualism.

Only once a year were all quarrels and rivalries forgotten; people loosened the shackles of enforced gentility and the social pressure towards conformity with certain, supposedly superior, ways of living. This was around Christmas time, mainly from 15 December onwards. Then, individuals who had not spoken to each other for months were suddenly seen walking arm-in-arm through Reeftown and everyone visited everyone else freely.

Then there were parties every day – parties full of good cheer and of the old good fellowship. The Council gave its many Christmas parties for the children, for the old-age pensioners, for the police and for the township staff. All the churches had Christmas parties. All the schools, the crèches and the day nurseries, and even the clinics held their parties when sweets and toys were distributed. Friendly societies gave their annual parties when 'the pot was turned'; and the high-class women's organizations had their more sophisticated celebrations complete with Christmas tree.

In all the homes there were family and neighbourhood parties. In some families the traditional goat was slaughtered and the pieces ritually distributed among the kin and neighbours. In other families there was a Christmas turkey and a dinner party for 'social' friends. Some drank Kaffir beer, others vodka and whisky, but everyone drank. Alcohol flowed freely everywhere; the shebeens were full every night. And so were the casualty wards of hospitals and clinics where the staff worked overtime.

People felt generous and hospitable towards each other and nobody worried about whether 'the pelmets were already up'. Moreover, friendships healed or sealed in a blissful state of alcoholic euphoria did not commit one to a more sober future if the gesture turned out later to have been a mistake.

Christmas had become for these people the uncontrolled outlet which they had once had – institutionalized and regularly – in the tribe.

During these weeks, the European was forgotten; the present tense came alive again, and people felt 'clean'. They knew once more that in spite of all the new social divisions they were still 'all Africans among ourselves'. In this general catharsis something of the sheer goodness and togetherness of the *Staedtel* was felt again by everyone.

2 The elite

Main characteristics

Occupation, education, income

A general description of the social elite of Reeftown is best begun with their occupations, for occupation was after all the most important though not the only and not even an indispensable indication of upper-class belonging. Moreover, for Europeans, occupation seems to 'place' a person quickest. Table I 2:1 presents the elite by their occupations and shows at the same time the occupational categories adopted for analytical purposes in this study.

Occupationally, then, the elite consisted of teachers and clerks, employed and self-employed professionals, ministers of religion (for reasons of anonymity all priests, pastors and ministers will here be referred to as 'minister'), traders and salesmen. But not all persons of these occupations belonged to the elite. Of the teachers only the assistant teachers of the secondary school and all the principals; of the clerks only the higher-graded personnel; of the ministers only some of the many residing in Reeftown; of the traders and salesmen only those considered 'educated', 'enlightened' or 'social', those who 'associate with doctors', as appeared to be the most frequently used criterion.

The group contained some border cases. These were individuals who occupationally and educationally belonged to the local upper class yet were socially inconspicuous; their social activities were not such as befitted people of their education.[1] Or inversely, they were socially so outstanding and so generally active that it made up for educational deficiencies or a lack of authoritative position.

Certain occupational characteristics of this elite are worth recording. First, almost three-fifths were professionals. The distinction

64

Table I 2:1 Numerical distribution of the elite by their occupations and by the occupational categories used

Occupation	Number	Occupational category	Number
Sub-inspector of Schools	1	Higher Teachers	9
Supervisor of Schools	3		
Principal and Teacher of Secondary School	5		
Principal of Primary School	7	Principals	10
Assistant Teacher of Primary School	1		
Secretary of the School Board	1		
Clerk in Department of Bantu Education	1		
Government Clerk	1	Clerks	17
Court Interpreter	3		
Messenger of the Court	1		
Municipal Clerk	7		
Township Librarian	1		
Sergeant of the Municipal Police Force	1		
Privately employed Clerk	3		
Health Inspector	4	Younger Professionals	6
Social Worker	2		
General Practitioner	3	Doctors	3
Minister of Religion	6	Ministers	6
Trader	4	Businessmen	9
Sales Promoter ⎱ Insurance Agent ⎰	5		
Total	60	*Total*	60

For analytical purposes the elite were assembled under seven broad occupational categories, because certain individuals tended to have a common educational and/or occupational background. That is the reason why, for instance, the Police Sergeant and the Court Messenger have been grouped under the public clerks employed by the Municipality of Reeftown. Sometimes, all educationalists will be referred to as 'The Teachers', or, when the ministers are included, as 'The Older Professions', to distinguish them from 'The Newer Professions' or 'The Younger Professions', as which we designate the Health Inspectors, the Social Workers and sometimes, but not without specific mention, the Librarian.

between them and the non-professionals was of the utmost importance and ran through the entire careers. Secondly, three-quarters were public servants, employed by either of the three powers: the Government, the Provincial Administration or the Local Authority. There were sometimes interesting differences between the Government, municipal and private[2] clerks, to which attention will be drawn.

Obviously, to be a professional, to be employed in the public service and to be self-employed were the three occupational characteristics most highly esteemed by everyone.

Educationally the elite varied considerably. A distinction must be made between professional and purely academic qualifications. Academically speaking, as many as one-third had only Junior Certificate and ten had not even that.[3] Fifteen held as their highest academic qualification a Matriculation Exemption, and eight had a degree, usually B.A., although one had a B.Sc.

With professional degrees and diplomas, however, they were well supplied. Three-quarters had one or more of these, while 65 per cent held one or more teachers' certificates. It was mainly owing to this large number of teachers that there was an accumulation of professional diplomas so that every three professionals held among them four professional certificates. In addition many had special diplomas for languages, commercial subjects, journalism, physical training, etc. Eight clerks, two ministers, three of the younger professionals and three businessmen were ex-teachers. Of the clerks, the Government clerks were highest, and the private clerks lowest, qualified. The Department of Bantu Education employed the largest number of graduates.

While, therefore, in some cases upper-class position could apparently be achieved with little education, a university degree always and without exception conferred elite status upon its holder. The twelve graduates of Reeftown were, therefore, all members of the elite. The point was to be able to carry a 'name' (an *Umsila*) which 'displayed' your education. While 'failed' graduates were also highly esteemed in the community, the habit had developed of calling these by the number of years successfully passed. (Possibly by analogy of such teachers' qualifications as NPL_3 and the older T_4.) One was, then, not a 'failed' B.A. or B.Sc., but a successful 'B.A.$_2$' or 'B.Sc.$_1$'. Consequently, in the eyes of Reeftowners, almost 40 per cent of the elite had some university status.

Two further expressions showed the enormous need to have some 'nameable' education. 'Drifts', my assistant explained, were those who had not failed an examination but started their studies and then drifted.[4] Other interests had intervened. Studying no longer seemed so necessary, or it had turned out more difficult than expected. But the possibility of still taking the examination remained open. This was closely connected with the idea of 'planning' or 'doing'. After passing J.C. one was 'planning Matric', and after Matric one was 'planning B.A.'. It sounded better.

Of the three western dimensions of social status, income was probably at this stage still the least important. Education was still a more important status characteristic, and it was generally agreed that 'wealth with education' was better than 'wealth without education'. Only 'very great wealth' could stand on its own, but representatives of 'wealth only' were rather to be found in Johannesburg than in Reeftown.

Table I 2:2 Showing the average incomes of all salaried individuals by present occupation

Occupation	Average monthly income in Rands
Higher Teachers	119·66
Principals	95·16
Government Clerks	109·00
Municipal Clerks	69·00
Private Clerks	71·34
Younger Professionals	86·34
Total average	92·54

The average monthly income of the salaried individuals among the elite was R92·54. (See Table I 2:2.) Of all the salaried groups, the higher teachers and the Government clerks received the highest financial remuneration, while the municipal clerks and the private clerks had the lowest salaries. The average salary of the latter in our elite was unusually high because of their rather exceptional employment. Two of them were in charge of two of the local branches of European banks, and the third was employed in Johannesburg by a semi-public institution. Usually, however, private clerks were considered to be lowest-paid and lowest-status of the three clerical groups.

With regard to the teachers, their salary depended on professional and academic qualifications, and on seniority. The figures for the Reeftown educationalists were slightly lower than they should have been because some teachers had incurred loss of seniority as a result of disciplinary measures. Principals had an additional special principal's allowance according to the number of children in their schools, and a primary-school principal could, therefore, earn more than a secondary-school teacher.

No doubt the average monthly salary of not quite R100 for the top public servants of an urban Bantu township seems low. (These

figures refer to 1960–1. In the meantime, there have been considerable rises in salaries of the teachers and the other public servants in
other departments.[5] A general increase in salaries also occurred in
private employment.) Understandably, a large number had, therefore,
additional sources of income. Before dealing with these, the incomes
of those whose earnings can only be estimated must be considered.

In terms of mere salary, ministers of religion were probably the
lowest salaried group. Their stipends ranged from R14 (the R.C.
priest) to R80 (the Anglican priest, who was the best remunerated
of his colleagues of the European mission churches), up to probably
R120 or more for ministers of the independent African churches. But
all ministers had, in addition, free accommodation in well-built and
well-equipped houses next to their churches; and the Roman Catholic priest had all his living expenses paid. Moreover, ministers enjoyed
free transport, good quality cars, pensions and provision for the
education of their children. Some ministers contributed to pension
funds. But all ministers received additional incomes from baptisms,
funerals and weddings, as well as from special fund-raising functions.
However, more and more power and control over the ministers and
the church funds was being exercised by African church councils and
synods, so that most ministers were gradually learning that 'L'état
c'est moi' no longer applied to them. Nevertheless, offerings of
various kinds proffered by faithful parishioners (and more especially
by less faithful parishioners who wanted a church wedding or a
proper baptism) continued to be the custom in Reeftown. In comparison with the generally higher educated public servants, the
ministers of religion were far from badly off. They were certainly
relatively better paid than their white colleagues.

The salesmen averaged between R100 and R120 per month,
although their actual earnings varied from month to month, ranging
from a minimum of R70–80 to a maximum of R300.

No estimate of the traders' profit was possible. Two of the four
who merited elite status were highly successful and engaged in
extensive business activities in the township itself, as well as in their
homelands. The financial position of the other two was tenuous; in
the one case this was due to marital difficulties, and in the other case
to irresponsible actions and overspending on status symbols. Both
had temporarily taken on what can be called 'agencies' to carry them
over their difficulties. A normally successful trader in Reeftown
should show at least a net profit of R200 per month, but could earn
much more. No doubt there were many traders in the township who
earned more than the two above-mentioned. They were, however,
generally considered 'uneducated' and not counted among the 'social'
elite, although they had ostentatious, fully completed and fully
furnished houses, and drove around in large, shining American cars.

The income of the doctors was disproportionately high in relation to the general salary and profit level of the other Reeftowners. Their high average earnings were due to a number of factors. Fees charged varied according to the purchasing power of the area. Generally, the nearer to Johannesburg, the higher were the fees; but, on the whole, fees were high everywhere. Consultations (including examinations and prescriptions) at the surgery cost for adults between R2 and R2·50; for home visits doctors charged between R2·50 and R3. (Since then fees have gone up, together with the rise in European medical fees.) Children paid about 50 cents less. In addition, African doctors were their own dispensers. While normal prescriptions were included in the fees, any unusual medicines as well as injections were charged as extras.

Frequently physicians' wives acted as secretarial and nursing assistants; African doctors had few, if any, administrative or office expenses. Patients paid cash and sometimes, as with African lawyers were asked to pay in advance. There were few bad debts. African patients willingly paid their doctors the high fees charged. European and Indian doctors, practising in Reeftown from rooms on the periphery were said to charge less. This was felt by the African doctors to be unfair competition, and they never ceased demanding the total removal of these doctors.

Information from authoritative sources enables us to state, with certainty, that a monthly income of about R400 was considered an unsuccessful medical practice, while the average practice brought in between R600 and R800 per month. If a general practitioner did not reach this last figure after six months in one place, he moved elsewhere. The only profession said to be more profitable was that of a lawyer.

However, these incomes from their occupations did not give a true picture of the actual monthly earnings of the elite. Besides the contributions from working and earning wives, which will be discussed later, additional amounts of money were derived by just over half of the elite from a variety of income-producing activities and investments. They were owners of, or partners in, various kinds of business undertakings from taxis to shops; they ran agencies for insurance companies and burial societies; they had urban and/or rural property in those areas in town or country where Africans still had, or again had, freehold rights. Many others were owners or occupiers of land which, whether held in leasehold or freehold, was 'looked after' by tenants against some compensation whether in cash, produce or stock. Some owned houses or business premises which were let to tenants.

Although it was, of course, impossible to obtain complete and precise information on such matters, our case records would suggest that at least one-third of the elite owned (or had owned and since sold) urban or rural property, sometimes only land, but generally houses or shops, mostly freehold but sometimes leasehold. The rise of a new occupation, that of estate agent and property dealer showed that the Bantu were becoming aware of the possibilities in these fields. Although the new housing schemes, in the urban areas, depressed the rents, it was still considered that one urban property could carry up to fifteen tenants who paid about R5 per room per month. This was the main reason why urban Africans wanted freehold rights. In addition about six of the elite had inherited or bought their own farms in freehold areas, which they operated from town, while some elite had shares in rural property, and others again were expecting to obtain this after some relative had died or some dispute had been settled.

Quite a few of our elite had obviously learned how to speculate in land, and had profited or hoped to profit from the rising land values.

Our enquiries about savings, capital investments and insurances, though again far from complete or detailed enough, led to further findings. Thirty-nine of the elite of Reeftown were definitely known to have contracted for insurance, and about thirty-three made an average monthly payment of R10·64. Five individuals paid R20 or more per month in premiums, and eleven paid R10 or more. The remainder paid less than R10 per month. Generally speaking, we concluded that the insurance contracted for seemed excessive, the premiums very high and without functional relationship to the incomes professed.

Savings were noted many times. The elite seemed to prefer building societies' subscription shares to savings bank accounts. No one had Post Office savings. These were considered only for domestic servants and other poorly-paid low-class workers. Whenever someone had inherited Post Office savings from an older member of his family, he at once converted them into other capital investments.

Though it was impossible to give any overall figures, we can say with certainty that the elite were great savers. A saving of R20 per month on an income of R100 to R110 was nothing unusual. One school principal earned R88 per month, his wife an additional R40 per month. He paid off R20 per month on his house, R5·75 in insurance, R15 on his furniture, and still saved R10 per month. A secondary-school teacher told us that during one year's teaching in 1944 on a salary of R24 per month during the first six months, and of R30 per month during the second six months, he saved R110 in one year!

One of the administrative assistants who earned R72·50 and his wife, a staff nurse, R62 per month, spent per month: R15 on house instalment and rates, R5 on furniture instalment, R13·10 on insurance and R12 as an instalment on his car. They had three children. In addition, the couple managed to save another R40 per month towards the purchase of a property in their own homeland.

All this seemed to point to either considerable additional earnings or far smaller living needs than is generally supposed, but most likely to both: extra earnings and fewer needs. Certainly, in most cases our calculations led to the conclusion that amazingly little money was left for what the cost-of-living surveys call the basic necessities of life, such as clothing and food, fuel, cleaning materials and transport.

It will be noticed that some occupational groups were not represented in our sample. First, no lawyers figured among the Reeftown elite, and we have explained the reason. Second, no Advisory Board members or any of the political leaders, whether traditional or modern, were included in the established upper class.

Some members of the tribal aristocracy as well as the one bearer of an illustrious Bantu name mentioned in Chapter 1, had come to settle in the township, but their status was generally restricted to their own co-'tribalists' and, although among these it was very high, it was not of the nature of a social status as defined by us. (Since the establishment of the first Bantustan and the independence of the former British Protectorates in which chiefs and royalty played a large part, the prestige of the 'tribal' aristocracy was rising again.) And even if, as sometimes happened, their status was recognized by others who did not belong to the same 'tribe', it was based on different criteria and was expressed and maintained by different means. Unlike some tribal aristocrats and chiefs in other parts of the country, the traditional nobles living in Reeftown had never attempted to convert their tribal status into modern social status. After our departure from Reeftown a member of the royal family of one of the (ex) Protectorates settled there as a medical practitioner.

With regard to the modern political leaders, some aspects of this leadership have already been described in Chapter 1, and will be further discussed in a later book. In contrast to national political leadership, which may have been in the hands of persons of high educational or professional qualifications, or of persons of wealth, royal blood, or of those descended from chiefs, local political leadership had passed to persons who were semi-educated, working in manual or semi-manual occupations, and belonging to the low- or medium-income groups. It was these individuals who had been chosen or who had offered themselves for training, and who now formed a small group of professional, paid politicians, whether operating through the Advisory Board, the Trade Unions, the underground continuation of the banned African National Congress or the Pan-Africanist Congress, or through other types of organization.

Whatever feelings of gratitude and admiration the educated elite of Reeftown may have entertained for these representatives of modern resistance politics, they did not admit them to their social circles; and the ladies of the upper-class women's organizations, as well as the members of the middle-class 'Manyanos' and other church organizations, never invited the politicians' wives to their social gatherings and fund-raising functions. Consequently not one of these politicians belonged to the social elite of the township. They had become political leaders without reference to their social status, and whatever prestige they had gained was due entirely to their political power.

Their leader was Mr S., described already in Chapter 1, p. 10. He was a van driver and changed jobs frequently. He lived in a small rented council house and his domestic life was far from irreproachable. In straightforward-ranking tests he was seldom mentioned, and if his name came up there was generally some hesitation, for 'he could not possibly be put in the same class as Dr So-and-so'. Like that of the 'tribal' leaders, his power position could not possibly meet the criteria of social status. He was a perfect example of highest sectional, yet small generalized or social, prestige.[6]

Age and religion, 'tribal' and provincial origin

The average age of the elite of Reeftown was 44·3 and the median age 44. The youngest member was 24 and the oldest 75. But most of them were between 36 and 50. The ministers of religion formed the oldest occupational group and the health inspectors and social workers the youngest. In the clerical group and in that of the younger professionals there were considerable age differences. The Government clerks were, as one would expect, the oldest clerical group and the privately-employed clerks the youngest.

Almost two-thirds of the elite belonged to the two largest school missions in the Transvaal. (See Table III 5:5.) The largest group, as much as 40 per cent of the total, belonged to the Church of the Province. The next largest group consisted of the Methodists, who formed a quarter of the total. Whereas the indigenous churches constituted the largest religious group among Africans in South Africa as a whole, only 13 per cent of the elite belonged to an independent African church.

It may be noted that, if one considers that most of the elite came from Methodist parents, and that among the fathers the proportion of Anglicans to Methodists was almost the exact converse of that among the sons, considerable religious changes must have taken place during the childhood and adolescence of the elite.[7]

The 'tribal' composition of the Reeftown elite was entirely unrepresentative of that of the township itself (see Table I 2:3) and,

Table I 2:3 Numerical and percentage distribution of the elite and percentage distribution of the population of Reeftown by 'tribal' affiliation

Tribal Affiliation	Elite No.	Elite Percentage	Reeftown* Percentage
Nguni-speaking			
Swazi	3	5·00	10·6
Zulu	8	13·33	26·4
Xhosa-speaking		30·00	11·3
Xhosa	8		
Hlubi	5		
Fingo	5		
Sotho-speaking			
Northern Sotho		31·67	13·6
Pedi	7		
Tswana	7		
Khatla	2		
Ndebele	3		
Southern Sotho (unspecified)	12	20·00	31·7
Other			6·4
Total	60	100·00	100·00

* Provided by the Non-European Affairs Department of the township.

for that matter, of the 'tribal' composition of the entire African population on the Reef, during that same period. (The test used was the normal approximation to the binomial.)

In comparison with the township population, its elite showed two striking points of difference: in the Sotho-speaking groups a significant predominance of the Northern over the Southern Sotho; and in the Nguni-speaking group, an even more significant predominance of Xhosa-speaking individuals. However, since the elite were considered 'newcomers' in Reeftown,[8] and in fact had been recruited mainly at a later stage and not from the 'veterans', there was no reason why they should show the 'tribal' composition of the township. The 'tribal' composition of Reeftown was not very different from that of other Reef towns. For instance, Johannesburg had in 1960 31·3 per cent Zulu, 4·35 per cent Swazi and 12·22 per cent Xhosa, i.e. also about three times as many Zulu and Swazi as Xhosa.

Were they then representative of the Transvaal? Possibly, in so far as the Sotho-speaking group was concerned. For in the population of the Transvaal, the Northern Sotho were the indigenous people and consequently they were in the majority over the later immigrants, to the extent of constituting still the largest group (about 40 per cent) of the Transvalers, who, in any recruitment, may have had preference.

However, the predominance of the Xhosa among the Reeftown elite had no such explanation. Nor can it be said that they or their parents had come to Reeftown via a longer or shorter sojourn in the Orange Free State or the Transvaal, as was the case with some Zulu and all Swazi. A scrutiny of the elite's provincial origin revealed that those born in the Cape, and more particularly in the Eastern Province, formed the largest single group.

The predominance of the Xhosa in our elite cannot come as a surprise to anyone with practical experience of African organizations; for it was a fact of common observation, often discussed among welfare workers, that on the boards and in the committees of important European-type organizations, the Xhosa seemed to be conspicuous everywhere on the Reef. In fact, there appeared to be a disproportionate number of Xhosa among the office bearers.

Until further investigation, we may suggest two points in explanation. First, distance from the original habitat has sometimes been put forward as greatly contributing towards quick assimilation in a new environment.[9] However, cultural mobility does not necessarily imply social mobility, and speedy urbanization does not necessarily lead to positions at the top of urban society.

It has often been said that the Xhosa have been longest exposed to western missionary education.[10] They were the first Bantu with whom the white Cape Colonists came into contact. In this connection, it may be noted that, in our sample the Xhosa-speaking individuals were not significantly more often third-generation 'in civilization'.

To our mind, other factors should not be left unconsidered in their effect on successful acculturation; and among these factors we found, in the case of our sample, the phenomenon we called inter-'tribal' mobility, which will be described in a later book. This inter-'tribal' mobility occurred as a historically well-established fact in the case of the Hlubi and Fingo,[11] who constituted the majority of the Xhosa-speaking individuals among the elite, and without whom the Xhosa-speaking group would not have been significantly large.

However, in many situations in their lives, the elite attached more importance to provincial than to 'tribal' origin, and in moments of conflict, provincial origin could become a new focus of identification. There was, for instance, acute rivalry between 'the people of the Transvaal', who considered that the Reef belonged to them and that its top positions should rightfully go to 'true' Transvalers, and 'the people of the Cape' who were 'intruders'. In this rivalry, the Zulu and Swazi often sided with the Sotho in their common resentment of 'those conceited Xhosa'.

And again, the Zulu from Natal felt little in common with the Zulu of the Transvaal, to whom they ascribed the characteristics which the white Natalians ascribed to the white Transvalers. The Transvaal Zulu were 'upstarts', 'noisy' and 'ill-mannered'. They were said 'to come with their big American cars and flashy clothes and shout all over the place'. But the Transvaal Zulu retaliated by considering their Natal co-tribalists 'sleepy' and 'backward'.[12] This was only one example of the many cases in which the Bantu, without losing their own social divisions, were taking over the social divisions of the European South Africans, as well as the corresponding stereotypes. A very interesting example was the fact that, although the Bantu in the towns had their own 'out-group' in the so-called 'foreign native' and clearly talked about and treated him in much the same way as the gentiles talk about and treat a Jew, they had taken over, in addition, much of the diffuse anti-Semitism of their white compatriots.

Provincial origin was not always co-extensive with 'tribal' affiliation. Among our elite was a Swazi-ized Tshangaan. None of the Swazi actually came from Swaziland, and only half of the Zulu hailed from Natal, or even from Zululand. Ten individuals came from the Orange Free State but in six cases their ancestors had originally come from Basutoland, Zululand, Bechuanaland and Swaziland.

Nevertheless, the two main provinces of origin of the Reeftown elite were the Cape (twenty) and the Transvaal (nineteen). After these the Orange Free State (ten) contributed the most. Natal (four), Basutoland and the Reef itself (seven) contributed the smallest numbers.

Social origin

The parental background of the elite

The elite of Reeftown came from educated Christian homes. With only one exception their parents had been born or had become Christian. Only ten fathers had been entirely illiterate. Almost three-quarters had belonged to the three largest school missions in the Transvaal, the Methodists, the Anglicans and the Lutherans, in that order. As many as thirteen fathers had had teacher's diplomas; three had been ordained ministers of European mission churches, and five had been evangelists.

The strongest impression which remains from our elite's stories about their early childhood and their lives with their parents was that of extreme mobility: residential, occupational and even religious mobility. This mobility makes precise categorization according to occupation almost impossible, while taking only their last occupation gives an erroneous impression. Broadly, however, four main groups

H

can be distinguished: the so-called 'farmers';[13] those who combined this farming with one or more other occupations; the white-collar and professional workers; and, finally, the smallest group, the labourers.

All but one of the fathers had been born and brought up in the country, and almost all had begun their lives as farmers. Although quite a number had combined this farming with other remunerative activities, farming had remained the main occupation of half of them. But even those whose main occupational emphasis had shifted to any one of the new clerical or professional occupations did not for this reason relinquish their farms entirely. Town was a temporary stage; their investments were land; their values were counted in heads of cattle. Most of them, even those who came to settle in town, continued to look to the country as their only security, their main purpose and their ultimate destination; as the proper place for their children to be reared and for themselves to die.

More than three-quarters of the fathers had, in the terminology of their sons, 'trekked', and the majority of these had trekked more than once. Most of these had been rural migrants. They had lived and worked for longer or shorter sojourns on one or more white-owned farms or rural mission stations. They would return for a spell to some 'tribal' territory or native reserve and move away again.

A smaller number had been urban–rural migrants. They went to work for shorter or longer periods in the mines and the newly arising mining towns, in Kimberley or on the Witwatersrand. Only one or two remained thereafter in town, but most returned to the country, using their wages to buy more cattle and generally to supplement and improve their rural way of life. For, whether by means of rural or of urban–rural migrancy, the aim of most fathers was to try and maintain the ancestral way of life while they were being irrevocably and almost against their deepest wishes drawn into a new and different world. This new world came to them while still in the country, and without even going to the towns, in the form of white farmers and missionaries, white traders and government officials, white supervisors and foremen; from these the fathers of the elite picked up new ideas and new customs.

Quite a few had tried their hand already at some forms of self-employment. Some had been transport riders and some had combined this with a simple form of hawking; others had been artisans and craftsmen. They had learned the trades of cobbler or tinker, tailor or blacksmith, carpenter, builder or wagon repairer either in the service of the white man or in the vocational training classes of the rural missionary institutions.

More than half of them were reported by their sons as owning or having owned some landed property, whether urban or rural or both.

Their urban property consisted of houses on municipal stands or of freehold stands on which a previous owner or they themselves had built a house or business premises. Such houses or shops were then let at relatively high rentals. As to their rural property, it was not always easy to discover its exact nature, but a careful estimate seemed to show that thirteen of these were definitely 'farms' in the normal sense of the word, some inherited and some bought, and these provided the family with a permanent place of residence as well as a means of livelihood. The remainder of the rural properties were probably no more than 'plots', bought with the idea of developing them later, or of selling them at a profit, as the need might be, and in fact some of our respondents still remembered the purchase and sales prices. In addition, six fathers had taken part in communal land and farm buying and developing – a form of co-operative which at that time was very popular among Africans. However, all but one of these six had failed to make a success of this venture.

Thus the fathers moved between urban and rural occupations, between traditional and modern means of livelihood; between employment and self-employment; between farming and trading. They bought and sold urban and rural properties, and from being farm owners some became urban landlords, always in search of better conditions of life and opportunities for advancement.

Even the educated professionals among them were characterized by occupational mobility. Of the seventeen fathers who had professional qualifications, only thirteen worked at their professions. Of the thirteen teachers only three continued to teach; all the others left their professions for more lucrative occupations.

Ultimately, twenty-two fathers settled in urban or semi-urban areas where only seven of them became 'labourers', a word used by our informants for urban workers but never for rural or farm workers. Considering that such labourers must have constituted the majority of urban or semi-urban Africans, this number of seven is remarkably small. It shows that the elite's fathers were in the majority either well-educated for those times, or if not, then successful farmers or resourceful and enterprising jacks-of-all-trades. They had already made an early and not unsuccessful entry into the modern world, even though many of them had never left the rural areas.

The same can be said of the elite's mothers. Although more of them had had no education at all, they were not far behind the fathers. Two-thirds of them had had at least some education or could read and write; nine held teacher's diplomas, while some had taught without proper qualifications. Furthermore, many mothers came from families of some educational, tribal or farming status and a handful belonged to aristocratic clans or royal houses. But even those mothers who had received little or no education showed themselves as progressive and capable, with the highest ambitions for their sons' education. This was all the more important as many of our elite had lost their fathers during their formative years and the widowed mothers, thirteen of them, became important figures in their backgrounds.

As our elite remembered them, most parental marriages had been monogamous but, according to Bantu custom, all widowed fathers remarried, with the result that eleven of our elite had had or still had step-mothers. These usually caused considerable sibling conflicts and inheritance disputes.

Almost 20 per cent of the parental marriages were inter-'tribal', but most of these concerned two different Xhosa-speaking 'tribes'. Nevertheless, it is noteworthy that 6 per cent of the marriages were unions between Nguni- and Sotho-speaking persons. This also shows that de-'tribalization' had already started in the parental generation. As an interesting aside: almost all parental marriages had been solemnized in a Christian church and in five of these the spouses or their parents had relinquished the *lobolo* custom. (*Lobolo* is the payment to the bride's parents to assure that the children of a marriage belong to the man's family.) Against this, the marriages of the elite themselves had all been celebrated by a church wedding and not one had not adhered to the *lobolo* custom!

The rural background of the elite

Just as in some contexts provincial origin seemed to be becoming increasingly more important than 'tribal' origin, so there were a growing number of situations in which the urban–rural dichotomy seemed to be increasing in importance. In fact, it was clearly developing into the main social division in Reeftown.

Already as early as 1953–4 an Inspector of Bantu Education[14] had discussed the effect of this growing urban–rural differentiation with his colleagues, as it directly affected the problem of the adaptation of the syllabuses in the different schools. The Inspectorate had come to the conclusion that, with regard to the general school situation, the difference between the rural-born and the urban-born Bantu was greater than that between urban-born whites and urban-born blacks. The needs of urban children had diverged so much from those of rural children that the same syllabus could hardly be applied to both. What seemed, however, a simple matter of differentiated education required in a culturally so multiform society as that of South Africa, became in this case complicated by the fact that urban children were by no means all urban born. In the towns on the Reef, not only in the secondary schools but also in the primary, and particularly in the higher-primary schools, there were many children who had spent

Table I 2:4 Numerical and percentage distribution of the elite by the place where they were born and brought up according to whether this was urban, semi-urban or rural

Area	Born		Brought up	
	No.	Percentage	No.	Percentage
Urban		6·67		31·67
Reef	3		15	
Large Town	1		4	
Semi-urban		15		18·33
Village or Country Town	9		11	
Rural		78·33		50·00
Native Reserve	29		21	
European Farm	12		3	
Rural Mission				
Station	6		6	
Total	60	100·00	60	100·00

As six individuals were brought up in several places, the last place they called 'home' before reaching 16 years of age was given.

the first ten years of their lives in the country, and who, from the point of view of educational needs, should be treated as rural children.

In terms of actual urban residence, our elite were not very urban at all. On the contrary with only four of them born in a large town or city (see Table I 2:4), they were according to the conventional way of reckoning very rural indeed. This rural predominance of the leading citizens of an increasingly urbanizing population[15] added a further dimension to the already considerable social distance between the elite and the majority of the residents of Reeftown. As a social division this urban–rural cleavage was becoming more profound, though less obvious for an outsider, than the growing social class distinctions; and it was more destructive to the traditional kinship relations than the new prestige differences with which it frequently coincided.

In a way this rural–urban division among the South African Bantu was similar to that between the South African whites. Among the many points which separate the English-speaking from the Afrikaans-speaking Europeans there is also a rural–urban component, in so far as the Afrikaners were historically the more recently urbanized group and some of the differences, such as in educational eagerness, or in the prestige rating of certain occupations and professions, could be ascribed to differences in length of urbanization.[16] (During the years 1964–6 the superiority in the examination results of Afrikaans-

79

speaking over English-speaking schoolchildren was a frequent topic of discussion in the press.)

Reeftown residents had become very conscious of this rural–urban difference. They had very definite ideas of what they considered to be the effects of urbanization on themselves, and these were similar to the usual sentiments on this topic expressed by the white South Africans.

The two main points concerned manners and social behaviour on the one hand and the attitude to money on the other. Rural people were said to be more reserved, more polite, more dignified. Urban people were socially more relaxed and adaptable; but they also were more cheeky, rude and noisy, more disrespectful. In dress, rural people were said to be more meticulous and rigid, urbanites more nonchalant. Rural people spoke a purer and more beautiful Bantu, the language of urban people was corrupted with Afrikaans, English and Fanakalo. Rural people were slow and ponderous, urban people more alert and quicker on the uptake. They laughed at different kinds of jokes.

Urban people were greedy, too money-conscious. 'They won't do anything for nothing.' A trader had his shop painted, and in the course of a chat he said: 'Now take this boy of mine[17] [the painter]. He works for R3 per week and is quite happy with it. He's rural of course, and he doesn't know any better. A Reeftown child, if he'd work for another native at all, wouldn't do it for less than R6 per week. But he wouldn't be so concerned about the wages as whether he could make something on the side. Now a rural native is much more honest . . .'

Reeftown housewives preferred for domestic help to have 'older ladies from the country', although after a while in town 'they also get spoiled and become even worse than the urban servants'. Country people thought townsmen wanted 'a lot of rubbish', 'aping the Europeans' and doing it 'all wrong anyway'. 'They just make themselves ridiculous.' 'In the rural areas you wouldn't get away with that nonsense. In the country you have to be true.' (Typical African expression meaning that your behaviour is in accordance with your status.) While it was taken as self-evident that all teachers drank, it was generally agreed that urban ones drank more, and their behaviour was worse.

In line with these behavioural differences, were the differences in attitude towards the Europeans. Briefly, a rural African did not consider a European as a human being. In town every African wanted to be like a European.

But more important then the difference in social behaviour, even more important than the difference in attitude to money, though not unconnected with this, was the different attitude to education, and this is the reason why the subject is discussed here at all.

It was widely believed that, 'Urban people don't have the urge to be educated. There are so many ways of making money in town without education. But in the country education is the only salvation.' Also, 'A rural child knows that if it wants money it must be educated first.' The same applied to the parents. In town, parents were said to be 'more interested in boosting their income'. 'They force the children to go to school for a few years, for a little bit of education makes a big difference in earning power,[18] and then they force their children to leave school and go to work and bring money into the house.'

'Africans in town are becoming like the coloureds,' we were told. 'At the age of 16 they take a job in the factory, and the more the trade unions will raise the wages, the more it will be so.'

School supervisors made similar observations. They told us that 'Teachers in town never bother with private studies, whereas in the country the teachers try to improve their qualifications by correspondence courses. And this is true in spite of the fact that in the country there is no one with whom they can discuss their study problems and here in town many educated people could help them.'

Some European observers seemed to expect otherwise,[19] but, Reef-towners were convinced that the most highly educated Africans in town were predominantly rural. 'Prominent positions in town', we were frequently assured, 'are all occupied by people from the rural areas.' Examples quoted were doctors and lawyers, school sub-inspectors and supervisors, graduate teachers, high-graded public clerks and holders of university degrees. A rough census undertaken by the African research assistant among some of the leading Africans on the Reef, did not bring any significant support for this assertion. But at that time I did not realize yet that informants used the term 'urban' and 'rural' in a cultural and not in a geographical sense. Many had, in fact, come from rural areas but had called themselves 'urban'.

Most of the German and American urbanization studies, so it would appear, showed this same trend. Social-mobility-through-education as a characteristic of the first generation in town, as against social-mobility-through-achievements in the arts and business (i.e. achievements not requiring much education), as a characteristic of the second generation in town, was noted as a fact by Sorokin among the rural migrants in America.[20] The authors pointed out that the farmer-peasant's son who reached the urban upper classes, had most often done so via the ministry, pedagogy or the public service – 'the underpaid professions',[21] i.e. such occupations which required, in the higher echelons, higher academic and professional qualifications. On the other hand, such fields as the arts and business, both of which could be explored with little education, were found to be more often the media for social advancement for the urban born. 'Education and religion,' the authors explained, 'are connected with the schools; entrance into them requires no capital, and they appeal to the idealistic and religious nature of farmer-peasants' children. These three factors seem to explain why pedagogy and the other professions and politics are the occupations that most often enable farmer-peasants to rise in the urban world.'[22]

Thus, the observations made by urban Africans seemed to resemble facts already noted and explained in other societies and may, therefore, presage similar developments for the future of the Bantu in town. This would mean that a not so educated elite of independent businessmen (and also of politicians) would increasingly rise from among the urban born, whereas a more highly educated elite, needed to take up positions which require higher professional and academic training, would have increasingly to be recruited from the country.

As a group, our elite with an average age of 44·3 years, cannot lend support to Sorokin's research findings, for their rural background may simply be a matter of age. (The four urban-born individuals were among the youngest.)[23] However, within the group were some interesting differences bearing on the rural–urban component in their background. First, the highest educated of the elite were almost all among the 50 per cent who were brought up in rural areas, or among those who were semi-urban born and/or brought up. In this respect there was a striking difference between the higher teachers and the primary school principals. These last were mostly urban by upbringing. As a matter of fact, the small country town emerged as the distinguishing characteristic in the background of the doctors and the higher supervisory and teaching personnel.

Furthermore, with regard to the age and the manner of coming to town, there were interesting differences between the professionals and the non-professionals. First, the professionals came, by and large, later to town than the non-professionals and only after a longer or shorter stay in one or more country towns, whereas almost all the non-professionals came to town straight from a Bantu reserve or 'tribal' territory.[24] In other words, the non-professionals had a more 'tribal' background upon their arrival than the teachers.

Summarizing our findings with regard to the urbanization of the elite, it would appear that the distinguishing characteristic of the professionals and the most highly educated of these upper-class Reef-towners was not so much that they were so little urbanized that only 6·67 per cent of them had been born in a large city, but that their urbanization had occurred slowly and gradually, and that it had proceeded via areas which in geographical terms cannot validly be called 'rural' nor in socio-cultural terms 'tribal'. As a more than average educated group, most of our elite came late (i.e. after 20 years of age) to town, as one would expect.

When we later find a number of unmistakable signs that our elite had reached an advanced stage of de-'tribalization', this should be recalled.

The domestic scene

The wives of the elite

Three members of the elite were not married: the Roman Catholic priest, one of the privately employed clerks, and one of the younger professionals. However, this professional lived with a woman as though they were married; and he was, therefore, included with the fifty-eight married persons. Four individuals had been officially married to and divorced from one or more wives before their present marriages. In two other cases the first wife had died. In addition, one member of the elite lived unofficially separated from his third wife, but in open concubinage with another woman who was wealthy but of bad repute. The most successful, most educated of the businessmen had, after his wife died childless, married her younger sister.

Settlement in the new suburban environment had at first brought a spate of divorces. Of these we have of course no first-hand knowledge; but during the years of the field research, we experienced, besides a number of minor marital conflicts, four major marital disputes among the members of our elite. All of these ended in divorce or judicial separation. A further major dispute was just beginning after the schedules were completed and has since ended in divorce. In four cases the cause was the husband's misbehaviour: in two cases this consisted in habitual adultery, in one case of irresponsibility and neglect, and in the fourth case of mental and physical cruelty. In the fifth dispute there was considerable misbehaviour by both husband and wife. The number of divorces in such a short time was excessive, but in the general upheaval of removal and resettlement, these divorces may have been part of the readjustment demanded by the new and improved living conditions and the desire for a new respectability.

A wife could be a very important status symbol and co-earner. The wife of an upper-class Reeftowner, therefore, must ideally be not only educated but professional, not a teacher but a nurse and preferably a staff nurse. In fact 70 per cent of our elite had professional wives. (See Table I 2:5.) Most of them were teachers – chiefly primary-school teachers. Some were domestic science teachers. Many of the nurses had originally been teachers. Of the nurses about half were not

Table I 2:5 Numerical distribution of the wives of the elite by profession and education

N = 58

Professional wives	No.		Non-professional wives	No.
Teachers	26			
Primary School	16		B.Sc.$_1$	1
Domestic Science	7		Matric	1
Kindergarten	1		J.C.	4
Unqualified	2		Above Std. VI	3
Nurses*	14		Std. VI and below	8
Qualified	7			
Unqualified	6			
Unregistered	1			
Social Workers	1			
Total	41	41	Total	17

* Nine of these had originally been teachers.

qualified; this meant that they either had failed their examinations or had become pregnant before completion of their training. Two were still in training.

But a wife was not only an important expression of a man's status, she could also be an important status raiser. It was generally agreed in Reeftown that 'a wife can pull her husband up'. This applied particularly to those cases in which the man's education or occupation was not quite sufficient to give him upper-class status. Hence the large number of businessmen who married nurses. Our policeman was another case in point. He just managed to be counted among the elite of the township because his wife was a highly respected and prominent woman, an ex-teacher, now staff nurse and midwife. On the other hand, if a higher professional, say a doctor or lawyer, had a wife who was merely a lower-qualified teacher or even one who had only J.C., he would not lose his status as a member of the Upper Ten.

Husbands were eager that their wives should improve their qualifications and their earning power, and many wives became nurses or more highly qualified teachers, only after their marriages. One husband sent his matriculated wife to the office of an African lawyer to become articled, but he soon called her home again because her office life exposed her to too many temptations.

In 25 of the 58 households the wife and mother was not working at the time; but in the majority of the marriages the wife worked either in a regular and salaried job, or as assistant or manager in her husband's business. In some cases she was or had been active in a business enterprise of her own. The average earnings of the twenty-two salaried wives (the two student nurses not included) amounted to not

Table I 2:6 Showing average joint monthly incomes
of the salaried husbands and wives of the elite
by husband's occupation

Occupation of the husband	Average joint monthly income (in Rands)
Higher Teachers	150·34
Principals	114·90
Government Clerks	150·50
Municipal Clerks	95·00
Private Clerks	148·00
Younger Professionals	146·00
Total average	126·50

quite R40 per month. The nurses earned, of course, twice as much as
the teachers, and one cannot help wondering whether it was at all
worthwhile for married women to teach. The average joint monthly
income of all salaried husbands and wives among our elite was
R126·50, and so a wife's salary did not add more than one-third, and
generally less, to her husband's earnings. (See Table I 2:6.)

In view of the rural background of the elite, it was of particular
interest to discover that as many as almost 60 per cent of the
marriages were inter-'tribal'. Ten were between different Nguni-
speaking 'tribes' and eight between different Sotho-speaking 'tribes',
but in as many as fourteen marriages a Nguni-speaking and a Sotho-
speaking 'tribe' were united. In two cases even the wife was coloured
(i.e. of mixed black–white descent).

In this high incidence of inter-'tribal' marriages we have one of
the recognized signs of a high degree of de-'tribalization' if not of
de-tribalization. A further examination of the elite's marriages
brought to light an even more interesting sign of the changing
patterns, in so far as almost 60 per cent (58·63 per cent) of the
marriages were between partners who had the same origin with
regard to the urban–rural component; both had been either urban
or rural born. In comparison with this large number of same-origin
marriages, the number of same-'tribe' marriages was small, only
39·65 per cent. Here we see clearly in our elite's generation the shift
of emphasis from 'tribal' to urban–rural differences.

The houses of the elite

Even more than by a wife, social status could be expressed and enhanced by a house. In itself, to live in a house and not in a hut, was

85

of the greatest social and cultural significance. It not only showed that one had 'arrived' socially and culturally, but it demonstrated for everyone to see that one had arrived among human beings.

Also, a house had wider visibility than a wife, and it spoke in a language which even the most primitive and backward Reeftowner understood. To own a house and, even more so, to have had it built according to one's own specifications, and in a manner indistinguishable from the best European house in the European areas, was the ultimate victory over the darkest forces.

'The people always look at the houses,' we were told. 'When we were in the old location, they never thought much about us. Then when we built this, they got their surprise.' In ranking tests, an informant would say, 'I don't know him very well. I must first see his house.'

However, this applied mainly when the husband's education/occupation were 'merely ordinary'. Introductions at women's tea parties showed this clearly. A new arrival would be introduced: 'This is Mrs So-and-so. Her husband is Principal So-and-so. You must have met him already.' And the next guest would be mentioned as, 'This is Mrs So-and-so. She lives in that beautiful pink house on the left when you enter the village.' (The husband drove a bread delivery van.)

'A house,' it was explained to us, 'makes no difference in the case of a school principal, nor with a top-class clerk. But in the labouring class it makes a big difference. Now Mr X, for instance, his wife is just an ordinary housewife, and he works in a factory. They're nothing, but he has a very nice house and people wonder how he got the brain to have such a nice house, and then you start respecting him.'

Thus, a house, like a wife, had varying status significance. An uneducated businessman or a well-to-do but otherwise 'ordinary' man needed a house in the same way as he needed a wife, to 'pull himself up', whereas as we explained earlier, the occupational prestige of a health inspector or school supervisor was such that it had less need of special residential support.[25]

It was almost the general rule that the higher one's occupational/educational status in the township, the less did one's social status depend on the house. It was in the new middle classes, among the skilled factory workers, the lorry- and taxi-drivers, and the semi-educated businessmen that the house assumed the all-important status significance which had to compensate for deficiencies in education.

As we have explained already,[26] the earliest owner-built houses expressed compensation money rather than status; and even in Reeftown's later development, the most expensive houses, and those

86

most elaborately and completely furnished, belonged, in the majority,
to the not so well-educated businessmen – the shop owners, the coal-
and-wood merchants, and the building contractors, whose residential
know-how and aspirations often emanated from their professional
wives.

Nearly 70 per cent of the elite were home-owners. (See Table I
2:7.) Of these, just over half had built their own houses which were

Table I 2:7 Numerical and percentage distribution
of the elite according to house tenure

House tenure	Numbers	Percentage
Home-owners		
Self-built House	20	
Council-built House	19	
House in other Reef town	2	
Total home-owners	41	68·33
Tenants		
of Council-built House	10	
with Widowed Relative in		
Self-built House	2	
with Family in Council-		
built House	1	
Total tenants	13	21·67
Free Living in Church-built House	6	10
Grand total	60	100

of ostentatious design and materials and markedly different from the
houses built by the Council, in which no money was wasted on
luxuries and useless adornments. The division between the owners of
Council-built and self-built homes did not coincide with the social
division within the elite into upper-upper, middle-upper and lower-
upper status groups. Of the twenty owners of self-built houses, half
belonged to the middle-upper and lower-upper strata, and among the
owners of Council-built houses as many as half belonged to the
upper-upper and middle-upper strata.

What all the elite had in common, however, was that (with the
exception of some traders) they all either already lived in areas of
highest status, or intended to move there shortly. This move to high-
status areas figured largely in marital disputes. The wife would press
for a better-class neighbourhood, where she would be among congenial women and all the other housewives would be her friends. But

the husbands were frequently against living among their social equals. Two reasons were given. First, they would think with apprehension of the social pressures which would be exerted on his accustomed way of life. 'I tell you how it will be, Mrs Brandel. We won't be able to live as we like. We shall have to eat vegetables and rice every day, not just meat and pap. That won't be good enough when we live among those people.'

The second reason which women gave for their husbands' resistance was that the men preferred to live among their social inferiors for 'they then would feel themselves more important'. Moreover, a weekly-paid factory worker or van driver next door was useful to give a monthly-paid husband credit for the shebeen.

However true all this may be, it was a fact that the wives were mainly instrumental in these residential status moves.

The average cost of the 200 to 250 owner-built houses which we found when we started our field-work was estimated at some R1,700. There were, however, considerable variations, from about R800 to as much as R5,600 or R6,000. Of course, thanks to the double economy, building costs were below those in any equivalent middle-class European area. (In those days a skilled African brick-layer's wages were R14 per week; those of a skilled European brick-layer were R34 per week. Building materials could be obtained from the stocks of the Council at cost price plus 6 per cent handling charges.) According to a European estate agent who, at my request, examined these houses, a house which cost in Reeftown, for instance, R5,000, would cost R8,000 in an upper-middle class suburb of the white parent town, and about R10,000 in the upper-class parts of the northern suburbs of Johannesburg. (Here the differential land values play a part in the purchase price of the houses.) But that same house would probably not be good enough for these areas. An African graduate school principal's house in Reeftown, built by a municipal contractor, had cost him 95 cents per square feet. In a better-class white area the same house would have cost him R2 per square foot.

In these owner-built houses one could distinguish three different grades, according to the size of the house, the number and disposition of the rooms, and the kind and finish of additional appointments and outbuildings. (See Table I 2:8.) About eight elite lived in first-grade houses, which had cost them an average of R4,000. These were large, seven- or eight-roomed houses, with wide and low windows, elaborate *stoeps*, heavy decorated imbuia front doors with 'ding-dong' bells. They had double garages built on to the house, with detached servants' quarters, as was compulsory in the European areas, where the minimum distance between the servants' rooms and the master's house was laid down in a by-law. However, whereas the servants of the wealthy Europeans had their own bathrooms, or at least wash-

Table I 2:8 Numerical distribution and approximate cost of the three classes of self-built houses of the elite

Class of house	Number	Cost range in Rands	Average cost in Rands
I	8	3,600–5,600	4,000
II	5	1,400–1,900	1,600
III	7	800–1,200	1,120
Total	20	800–5,600	2,580

Note that these figures cannot but be approximations, and are based on information by the owners themselves.

rooms with hot and cold water, the wealthy of Reeftown provided at best a cold-water tap for their servants.

The internal arrangements of the best houses showed an L-shaped lounge and adjoining dining-room, a so-called 'master-bedroom' leading into the bathroom with a built-in bath, fully tiled in at least two contrasting colours – favourites being green and pink. For the children there was a separate washroom or shower cubicle and a separate W.C. There was always a fully tiled and appointed so-called 'American kitchen' with stainless-steel sink, built-in cupboards, a refrigerator and an electric stove. Such houses generally had a separate entrance hall which the medium-type houses did not possess. (A more precise compilation of inventories of a sample of housing exteriors and interiors failed. After only a few attempts our African research assistant was forced to discontinue, owing to growing resistance and animosity. This shows the extent of the housing sensitivity of Reeftowners. We had, therefore, to content ourselves here with generalizations.)

Medium-type houses cost an average of R1,600 and they had coloured and polished cement floors instead of the parquet of the best houses. They had linoleum on the kitchen and bathroom floors, whereas the better houses had plastic tiles. Although they did have a *stoep*, it was of simpler construction. Whereas the best houses invariably had large and elaborate Slasto-decorated fire-places in the lounge, with built-in jetmasters, the medium-type houses had simpler heating arrangements. Also, their kitchens were simpler, but there was always a panelyte-topped chromium-legged kitchen table and matching chairs, and a kitchen cupboard resembling a juke box.

An interesting status struggle was going on as to the relative merits of the large wardrobes, which went with the bedroom suites, and which, until recently, had always been the most desirable and first-to-be-acquired status symbols, and the built-in cupboards, which were increasingly regarded as more 'upper class' (and which had, in fact, been preferred by a doctor's wife), and which were putting the heavy, ornate wardrobes into disuse.

The most expensive houses had 'studies' or 'dens' which were, during our time, the last word, but there was not yet one appropriately furnished or in use.

The medium-type houses still had their *stoeps*, not necessarily jutting out and elegantly appointed, but often contrived from a corner of the house. They also had separate, single garages. The simplest, self-built houses had no *stoeps*; they were often just square blocks, frequently plastered and painted in gay colours. There was a lean-to or a pillared pergola for the family car. Their average cost was R1,120.

All the houses were single-storeyed. Only in Johannesburg was the first two-storeyed residence appearing, and in this could be seen a measure of its greater socio-cultural sophistication. When we made our first survey, the houses in Reeftown had corrugated-iron roofs. Only four had roofs of red tiles, which were considered the height of luxury. Their proud owners were two court interpreters, one doctor and one independent businessman. Since then, however, further improvements and refinements have been introduced and developments will, of course, continue.

The ministers' residences were in no way inferior to the best owner-built houses, though there were differences in size and appearance. The monastic austerity of the Roman Catholic house has already been mentioned; but as the Roman Catholic priest had, at the same time, the highest educational distinctions, his personal prestige was not unduly affected by his poverty.

It may be of particular interest to mention in this context that among the home owners who had built their own houses, thirteen were salaried employees. It was calculated that their houses costing an average of R2,136·16 per house, were built on an average monthly salary of R98·62. On these houses no municipal loans were received.

Private behaviour and personal tastes

While, in their public role, the elite presented an image of decorum and restraint, their private behaviour was characterized by inconsistencies. Underneath the surface of suburban respectability, violence flared up easily and at the least provocation. In this proneness to violence our elite resembled a western lower class.[27] Next to the ideal of self-improvement which they shared with a western-type middle class,[28] and in the service of which some leisure time activity was devoted, stood the time spent in the shebeens, with their casual contacts and general promiscuity.

The most common forms of disrespectability prevalent among our elite were said to be drunkenness, womanizing and financial irregularities. Among the sixty individuals comprising our sample, there were five who must be called 'drunkards' because they drank excessively, regularly and openly, during working times and on days off. In four cases only the man drank, and in one case both husband and wife were regularly drunk. In one further case only the wife drank. In addition, some twenty-odd persons were repeatedly seen by the European investigator in an advanced state of intoxication at official functions and at their work. Some interviews had to be abandoned because, upon our arrival, the interviewee was found to be drunk.

A great number, probably the majority, were known by their wives to be 'unfaithful', at more or less regular intervals in extra-marital relationships which varied in duration and intensity. Extra-marital children were sometimes known to exist in the township and elsewhere. However, as long as such escapades were kept within certain limits, and certain proprieties were preserved, the wives preferred to close their eyes.

Drinking and womanizing were reported often to go together. More than half of the husbands were known to visit shebeens regularly. Some of them maintained a certain gentility; but with most of them the shebeens meant periodical carousing with gangsters, getting involved in street brawls and car accidents, and mixing with females below their status. In some cases the husbands were also heavy gamblers. All doctors and most teachers were said to be heavy drinkers and often drunkards. This fact was widely known, and acknowledged everywhere as a general rule.

A third form of disrespectability quite openly mentioned by informants as of frequent occurrence among the elite, was bribery or corruption, as well as illegal appropriation of funds. The frequency of what is termed 'the illegal appropriation of funds' in the Bantu Education Department, has made a special departmental ruling necessary. During the period of our field research ten upper-class persons were dismissed or transferred mainly because of such financial irregularities, but also because of excessive womanizing or drinking. (For similar reasons promotions were often missed and seniority lost. The surprisingly low salaries were sometimes due to this.) Five of those dismissed were members already included in the sample, while the other five would have been included had it not been for their untimely removal from the scene and their replacement by others. Among them were three ministers of large European mission churches, one supervisor and two school principals; the others were municipal employees.

The general lack of cultural interests among the elite was often commented upon by the few who thought of themselves as exceptions. While about half of our sample were regular newspaper readers, only about five were interested in reading books and these only occasionally. At one time, it had been our intention to investigate in a more precise way the role of books and reading generally in the elite's formation and, particularly, what they actually got out of their reading; but, in an already overfilled programme, this had to be abandoned. However, we found in the course of our other investigations that two of the sixty elite had been directly influenced in their career by certain books. The one individual was influenced to choose his present career by an American book on salesmanship. The other had been influenced by a book written and published in the previous century. Both persons appeared to have learned mainly how to be successful and to earn more money.

One member of the elite was interested in western sculpture and painting, and had tried his hand at it, not unsuccessfully. He was also the only one who had preferred modern, contemporary furniture to the linenfold, ball-and-claw foot imbuia style which was then the height of fashion.

About three or four individuals were interested in listening to records of European chamber music, or of symphony concerts. Of European music it was generally only songs which pleased the elite, and quite a number of them could accompany soloists on the piano. Choral singing, however, attracted a much wider group of the educated and the professionals; but our elite, rather than participate in the choirs, preferred to function as conductors and choir-masters, or as appreciative audiences in the reserved seats, as they saw the Europeans do.

The elite's tastes in art and literature inclined towards Victorian standards. Furniture had to be heavy and ornate. Stories should have a moral; evil should receive punishment, and virtue should be rewarded. Dickens was a favourite. They also liked to read biographies of famous people – Napoleon, Catherine the Great, Hitler, Marx, Churchill and other figures in history. The interest here was in discovering why such individuals had achieved fame. What was their personal magic?

Here indeed is a wide and fascinating field for research which is as yet almost untouched. We hope that our few observations may awaken someone's interest.

Another point worth considering would be the fact that, unlike the present tendency in the West where people, as Riesman showed so clearly, were becoming, more and more, observers rather than participators, the people of Reeftown seemed, also in this respect, to resemble the Europeans of an earlier age. They did not want to read books but to write themselves; they did not like listening to a play, but longed to act; they wanted to join in rather than to watch. To quote only one example: one day we had the opportunity of bringing a well-known European *Lieder* singer to Reeftown. Knowing how the people enjoy singing, we discussed the plan with some of the younger socialites, explaining that this singer could give them an idea of the tremendous wealth of beautiful songs to choose from and thus to enlarge their repertoire beyond the 'Last Rose of Summer' kind of song, so dear to the social set. The result was a quarrel about which Reeftown quartet, quintet, soloist or choir should appear on the programme and on the stage together with the European singer. The dispute became so heated that, on the advice of the senior social worker, the concert was cancelled. In Reeftown people do not want to look on, they want to participate.

However, except for a few individuals, the elite of Reeftown was uninterested in cultural matters.[29] They were, however, profoundly preoccupied with the attempt to acquire the correct attitudes towards such cultural matters. They considered a show of interest in western art, music, literature and drama to be the correct status symbol. Therefore, every now and again they made an effort. Someone bought a book with an impressive-sounding title; another went to a concert given by a world-famous European pianist or violinist; others again visited an exhibition of modern paintings, especially if the artist was an African. But, with few exceptions, interest could not be sustained, and what was experienced appeared incommunicable.

So-called 'cultural clubs' were started with enthusiasm, but their continued functioning could be achieved only by practical, financial advantages and by social snobbery.

Snobbery was a cultural weapon quite often consciously used by responsible educationalists, like my friend P.Q. He had tried to organize an evening of serious drama, which had been a flop. Then, the next time, when *A Tale of Two Cities* ('that's high-brow stuff!') was to be shown, he had spread it around that 'only educated people' need come because 'only educated people' could understand this film. Then they came – the teachers, the clerks, the salesmen, the university graduates, because they all wanted to show how educated they were.

Thus, on the Reef one can learn to recognize the tremendous social value of snobbery as incentive towards acculturation; and one learns not to laugh at its manifestations among the white and the black parvenus on the Rand of Gold.

While in this way interest in western art forms and styles was gradually being acquired through the stimulus of snobbery, there was no interest at all in expressions of African culture. On the contrary, all true African art, such as tribal dancing and Bantu music, was held in profound contempt. Similarly, all modern jiving and twisting was abhorred. 'Ballroom dancing' was the only form of dancing admitted. And so, at weddings and other festive occasions, a spectator could watch the elite dancing, unsmilingly, the tangoes, the fox-trots the quick Viennese waltzes and the slow English waltzes – those hardy perennials of the European dance floor, which whites can only dance as an occasional change from the samba, cha-cha, bossa nova or whatever the contemporary dances are called.

Consequently, with only a normative interest in western culture, and with a total rejection of African culture, the elite of Reeftown lived in a cultural no-man's land. Similarly, having in principle forsworn all African forms of fun and fellowship with which the unenlightened created among themselves the easy insouciance of an urban proletariat, and unable as yet to imitate fully the typical social ease and unconcern of a European-type upper class, those among our elite who did not find compensation in the shebeens led lonely, drab and dull lives.

The position of the elite in their community

Newcomers and insiders

The elite formed only one-half of 1 per cent of the total population of Reeftown. That is the elite as defined in terms of an 'educated' 'social' elite. If the other elites were included, i.e. the 'uneducated' but wealthy business elite, and the political elite (which would have to include the traditional and the modern), then the total elite of Reeftown would represent about three-quarters of 1 per cent of the population and might increase to almost 1 per cent. The importance of this small group of people in their community was of course entirely unrelated to their small numbers.

In Reeftown, the elite were considered 'newcomers'. This was not quite applicable since 60 per cent of them had already been known to the people from their work and residence in the old location, from which they had moved to the new township, together with the rest of the location population, or as the various institutional activities in which they were employed became transferred. But only three had been born and only five had been brought up in the old location. Therefore, only these few were what was termed 'children of Reeftown'.

But it was precisely the most highly educated group of upper-class residents who were indeed newcomers. When our field research started we were often told: 'Not one child of Reeftown has ever passed Matric', and 'All our university graduates are imported!' We have already explained the low educational standards of the old location. (Since then, the first 'child of Reeftown' has graduated, and the residents gave him a large public reception, with many speeches and much singing and dancing.)

When they arrived, the university graduates, school supervisors, doctors and health inspectors had been received into the community by official celebrations of welcome in which they had been introduced to the residents, their function explained and their status as VIPs confirmed. For Reeftowners were slow to admit the newcomer, particularly those who called themselves proudly the 'veterans', and who sensed that here was serious competition. They complained that they were 'always passed by when new jobs came up', while the new-comers said that they were 'not allowed to speak up in social gather-ings', because they were considered new and inexperienced.

In the normal run of township affairs, this antagonism did not matter much, but in moments of crisis and social conflict, the gap between 'newcomers' and 'locals' aggravated any other divisions.[30]

The elite were also described as 'insiders'. This name referred to a shared characteristic which has not yet been explored, and which was of no mean importance in their prestige. It has already been mentioned that, in the main, they were professionals and that almost all of them were either public servants or self-employed, thus em-bodying certain highly-esteemed qualities, all of which were related to the fact that their jobs concerned the residents of Reeftown itself. They were 'insiders' because their job was 'inside' the community, and consequently, the Reeftowners themselves benefited directly from their occupational and educational eminence. (This is connected with the popular notion of 'Service' which will be dealt with in a later book.) The teachers concerned themselves with the education of Reef-towners; the doctors and health inspectors promoted their health and hygiene; the ministers of religion looked after their religious needs; the traders and salesmen provided essential goods and services; the municipal clerks assisted and advised the people of Reeftown in a great many of their daily problems; the messenger of the Court could daily be seen on his rounds; and the privately-employed clerks were constantly observed working in the banks. Even the third private clerk and the Government clerks, who worked outside the township, conducted or had conducted up to recently certain public activities which had great status significance because these touched a large number of people in what were considered certain valuable aspects of their lives. It was, therefore, through various forms of social participation or, as it was termed, 'social activities' that they shared with the true 'insiders' something at least of the functional sig-nificance which appeared as the *fons et origo* of upper-class status in Reeftown.

As in Glossop, there was also in our township no necessary con-nection between a man's success in his profession and his prestige in the community in which he happened to live.[31] However high his occupational status in the European sector might be, whether he was a highly skilled and highly paid worker in a European factory, or a head clerk in charge of several minor clerical workers, or a boss boy in a responsible position over a large number of workers, and, as a result, had the high occupational-elite status, which we distinguished from social-elite status, this counted little in Reeftown. Like the proverbial justice which must be seen to be done, so also social status must be seen by the people. It must be 'shown' or 'displayed', as it was said.

As with the chiefs and headmen of old: 'The headman has to put up a show. He has to make a display of social activities, that is he must give beer parties and extend hospitality. He must kill more cattle than others for his guests. He must receive more people and go and visit more people. If he does not show his headmanship in such ways, his people do not consider him a real Induna.' So with the teachers. As the teachers were the first group to represent prestige in the new order, and certain problems of this new kind of status had to be first faced with reference to them, they were always quoted as examples. It was said, for instance, 'A teacher must behave like a teacher, otherwise we do not recognize him as a teacher', or 'Teaching ability in itself means nothing. You must give the display due to your status as a teacher, then Africans will respect you; only then will they think you are somebody.'

For what counted in the original communal society was not status as such but status communally expressed, status socially operative, status actualized in society. Only when status was displayed in overt conduct, in concrete and visible signs, did it 'serve' the community. Only when thus displayed did status evoke its proper response: respect. Respect (*hlonipha*, Zulu, and *thlompho*, Sotho) again must be shown in appearance and behaviour.

There was a vital interdependence between 'showing the status' and 'showing the respect', and in this was reflected the vital interdependence between man and his group in a communal society. Referring to Hilda Kuper, who wrote: 'The *incwala* is first and foremost a ceremony which, as the Swazi say, aims at "strengthening kingship", at "showing kingship", "to make the nation stand" . . .',[32] we suggest that in showing his status, a member of a communal society 'strengthened' his community and by showing respect, the community in its turn 'strengthened' the man of status. For by displaying his status in the correct and accepted manner the person of status made his status fruitful and beneficial to his community, and it was by showing the respect that the community confirmed the person of status in his status. Thus status display stood for the expression of a person's self-evident awareness of his group-belonging, and its confirmation by the community. It stood for a person's vital place and function in the communal whole. It stood for his true communal self.

In the tribe, status was shown in general appearance and bearing, in language and ways of speech, in manners and forms of address, in property and possessions, in a large kin group and a big following, in hospitality and generosity. So similarly in Reeftown, status had to be made manifest to the residents either by the visible and tangible evidence of wealth in the elegance and size of the house, car and furniture, by the unmistakable proof of educational eminence in a university degree, or even a failed degree, but especially and mainly by visible social activities, by certain expected forms of behaviour, by the assumption of a public role, and by the practice of a profession or occupation in the community, for all to see.

Public figures and social leaders

The elite were conspicuous by virtue of the functional significance of their jobs and spare-time activities. They were, in a sense, public figures whose public image, with all its idiosyncrasies, was widely known and talked about by the other residents. They acted as speakers at township functions as well as at yearly conferences and annual general meetings of one or another of the many clubs and associations of the more European type. Frequently, upper-class persons were defined as 'those who know that a speech must be prepared'. They opened exhibitions; they adjudicated at public debates; they presented the prizes and trophies at sports and music competitions; they officiated as judges in the selection of beauty queens and in demonstrations of ballroom dancing. They featured prominently 'on the platform' and occupied, as a matter of course, the front seats during township celebrations, concerts and variety shows.

In fact, they were increasingly performing the functions which had hitherto been the duty and privilege of the Europeans. During the years of our field research we were able to observe how, as the European receded as an active worker from the immediate affairs of township life, the upper-class African was expected to step into his shoes. Where before the European would be invited as guest of honour to the opening of a new crèche or to the launching of a fund-raising function, now leading Africans from Reeftown or from neighbouring townships would be invited to perform this role. Also, as Europeans would be invited to attend upper-class weddings 'to lend glamour', or 'to raise the tone' of the occasion, now the elite were invited by the status-aspiring members of the middle class to attend their celebrations, particularly those which followed a European pattern. At such family occasions the elite were allotted a place of honour with the nearest kin and oldest relatives at 'the great table'; they were naturally seated with any Europeans who might be attending the function; they were served first and had the right to use whatever china and cutlery was available. That, however, in their upperclass role, the elite felt the European guests as direct competitors was, I believe, rarely realized by those whites who were so eager to promote better race relations.[33]

From among them were elected, and among them rotated, the Chairmanships and higher offices in the township Boards and Committees, such as the School Board, the Crèche Committee, the Adult Advisory Committee of the Youth Clubs, the governing bodies of the sports associations, etc. In fact there was not one important board or committee in Reeftown on which members of our elite did not figure.

Like their Negro cousins in America, the elite of Reeftown were those whose position in the township caused them to play the roles conventionally the prerogative of an upper class.[34]

To a certain extent also they were beginning to form a privileged class. They had no difficulty in placing their infants in the overfilled subsidized crèches and day nurseries; they could choose their children's schools according to their requirements; they had the right connections to obtain scholarships and bursaries. They travelled first class on the trains, or, if travelling free, their season tickets were, as a matter of course, first-class tickets. Having their own cars or using the joint taxi system, they never needed to use the overcrowded buses or trains if they did not want to. They could often choose their town of residence as most township administrators were keen to accommodate individuals of high standing and good repute; there was even some competition between township managers for the favour of such law-abiding citizens. Consequently, they enjoyed a certain measure of freedom of movement unknown to the other, less privileged town dwellers.

Inside Reeftown itself, they enjoyed a certain immunity from police interference; their houses were not raided and no local policeman would dare to ask them to show a pass. In fact, they did not accept the authority of the black policeman. Outside Reeftown and wherever they were unknown, they often complained about 'the lack of discrimination' by the police, for they expected the preferential treatment due to their rank. The discrimination they did not want was racial discrimination only.

As was to be expected, these leading residents had free access to the highest white authorities. In fact, the latter would often seek them out, try to win their confidence and obtain their advice and cooperation, but generally they failed in this, owing to widespread jealousy and suspicion.

Besides *de jure* and/or *de facto* exemption from Influx Control

Regulations, from the curfew regulations and from service contracts, there were many smaller and larger areas in which the elite enjoyed a privileged position. It was only when one studied those few exceptional cases like our elite, that one realized how much the other Reeftowners were controlled, and often handicapped, hindered and obstructed by legal and conventional restrictions.

As high officials in church organizations or sports bodies, in Education and Health Departments, they had gone and were going abroad, to attend international conferences, on study trips or on overseas scholarships. They never had difficulty in obtaining the necessary passports.

Their names and pictures appeared frequently in the Bantu press and occasionally in the European press. Some of them attended multiracial lectures and conferences, or were invited as guests to the multiracial consular parties. Some went occasionally to multiracial functions like concerts or shows at the University of the Witwatersrand in Johannesburg. Their family events, their parties and meetings featured in the social columns of the press. They figured as 'The Man of Taste' or 'The Fashionable Person' in advertisements for cosmetics and clothes. This was interesting, as it showed how they differed from the white social elite in so far as they had not (yet) differentiated their functions from those of the elites of the show and sporting worlds, who, in white society, were the only ones to lend themselves to commercial publicity purposes.

In sum, 'They stand in the limelight', or 'They catch the public eye', as it was said. They were 'spottable', as the expression was. They were known, if not in person, then at least by name and hearsay. In ranking tests, therefore, their names came readily to mind, and they stood out by frequency of mention. They also stood for certain qualities. They often figured as the prototypal person exemplifying a particular social stratum. 'Now Mr and Mrs So-and-so', a ranker would say, 'persons like these would have to be placed together with Supervisor X.'

In fact, for a European participant observer and a regular visitor to the township, it was almost impossible *not* to notice the elite.

In setting the taste patterns and consumption styles, the elite were the recognized status leaders of Reeftown. In terms of etiquette, they were said to know 'how Europeans are doing things'. As social leaders, they acted as the channels through which the hundred-and-one small idiosyncrasies which together were supposed to make up the European way of life, flowed to the others.

One morning we were suddenly interrogated by our various hostesses in the township about the etiquette of serving at table among Europeans. Upon enquiry, it was revealed that one of the doctors had learned from a dinner with some white friends that plates were

99

handed on the left side and removed from the right of each diner. It seemed unbelievable, but very important to know. But it was feared that the doctor's wife, anxious to remain exclusive, was purposely misleading her imitators from among her status-climbing friends. Even male acquaintances accosted me in the streets for reliable information on this important aspect of western etiquette. Among those interested was also a taxi driver, son of one of the township's 'veteran' widows, who was known as a 'strong' 'Stockfel' member, and who saw in this novelty a refinement which could bring profitable results at his expensive 'Stockfel' dinners.

Similarly, we followed the introduction into Reeftown of that delicacy, mayonnaise – token of more refined tastes and less utilitarian trends in food. Its many uses had been demonstrated to the ladies of the Reeftown branch of the more fashionable of the two women's organizations at their mother club in Johannesburg, by a woman member who had for many years been 'cook in a wealthy Jewish household, and the Jews know how to cook'. This woman, although an ex-domestic servant, was a valued member of the club because she 'knew how Europeans are doing things', and no one was particularly perturbed about the apparent incompatibility of her two statuses: on the one hand her high social prestige as a culture carrier to a club of well-to-do housewives and professional women, and on the other hand her low status as a domestic servant.

The mayonnaise thus introduced to these ladies subsequently figured at a fund-raising tea, together with such cultural titbits as celery curls, radish roses and prunes stuffed with cream cheese, and it was daintily tasted by the guests. Thereafter, it began to make its appearance on tables at weddings and other family occasions. Many a time it remained untouched, since many guests preferred the familiar meat stews and mealie rice, potatoes and pumpkin to the fashionable cold salads and snacks. Even so, it stayed – a symbol of the new way of life and a reminder of the ultimate goal.

As in the domestic science classes, held in the Reeftown high school, where the teachers preferred to demonstrate the more expensive extras rather than the wholesome and inexpensive but dull dishes, so in the general life of the community, the social classes were more attracted by the accidentals of western civilization than by what Europeans themselves, and particularly the European teachers and welfare workers, think of as the substance.

On the subject of who actually were the fashion leaders in clothes, many discussions showed that here the elite had strong competition from the workers in the garment factories who were said by some to be the true leaders of fashion. They had the first opportunities of seeing and wearing the styles which would, in the next season, become 'high fashion'.

But the field in which the elite's social leadership was undisputed was of course that of houses and furniture and of all residential appointments generally. It was, for instance, one of the doctors who introduced to Reeftowners the double garage not as a separate out-building but as part of the architectural design of the house.

It was another member of our elite, one who was unique in having a natural artistic sense and a playful temperament, who started the craze for rockeries which for a short while dominated fashionable Reeftown. Rockeries are a typical feature of South African gardens and much ingenuity is displayed by white garden lovers on the Reef in building and planting their rockeries. Reeftowners had no difficulties in building their rockeries but trouble began when the pockets had to be filled with plants. I was asked frequently for rock plants. I explained that the real fun of a rockery was in collecting your own rock plants from the *veld*, and suggested they go out on a Sunday with the family, have a picnic and search for the plants themselves. But upper-class Africans do not go on picnics and do not sit around the *veld*. Only Bantu herbalists searched for plants, and no self-respecting Reeftowner would want to be seen doing this. No wonder that the interest in rockeries soon waned and attention was directed to making neat borders, flower beds and lawns, regularly watered by sprinklers or servants.

Interesting observations could be made with regard to the introduction and spread of new residential fashions in Reeftown, as well as with regard to the changes in preferred styles and tastes in the designs and materials of the houses. We were fortunate enough to watch the process at first hand, and a brief description might inspire someone towards a more thorough investigation from which, without doubt, much can be learned about cultural borrowing and social imitation. In the following I have had the expert guidance of Dr Doreen Greig, ARIBA, a former President of the Transvaal Provincial Institute of Architects in Johannesburg, who was kind enough to accompany me to Reeftown, and give me her opinion on the housing styles there.

The first Reeftown houses, built by their proud owners around the years 1949–50, looked like modest versions of the style which had been originally introduced by Herbert Baker, the English architect who practised in the Transvaal between 1902 and 1912. After World War I this style spread all over Johannesburg and the Reef towns; it was the most favoured style not only for the expensive houses in the (originally English-speaking) better-class white suburbs such as Houghton and Saxonwold in Johannesburg, but also for the new houses being built in established (predominantly Afrikaans-speaking) lower-class and lower-middle class suburbs such as Melville, Cottlesloe, Turffontein, Norwood and Mayfair. Characteristic of the style

101

were the precast loggias and pergolas and *stoeps* of the houses, whether they were designed for mining artisans or mining magnates. Then, about 1950, when the middle-class Johannesburger would no longer think of building such a house, it appeared again, now in Reeftown. Cheap little houses of drab-coloured brick, their *stoeps* supported by debased 'classical', or precast concrete columns. These houses built by the home-owners during the earliest years of the township were then the pride and glory of Reeftown.

Eight years later, when we began our field research, the favourite style of Reeftown had changed. Now the most desirable houses had become more solid and larger, and also more expensive, showing the rising living standards of the more successful residents. They were built of yellow face-brick with hipped roofs of red tiles or red-painted corrugated iron. The windows were large and horizontal. One of the popular gimmicks was the corner window or the wide window with one rounded end. Instead of classical columns, now face-brick, often of a darker golden or purple colour, or 'moderne' triple pipe supports, were used to support the *stoep*, which was generally placed asymmetrically on the façade of the houses, whereas the Herbert Baker *stoeps* had always been arranged in neat symmetry. Again, as in the Baker houses, the *stoeps* were of highly polished red cement.

Such yellow face-brick houses had become fashionable in Johannesburg in the mid-thirties and were built in lower-middle and middle-middle class suburbs, like the (predominantly Jewish) Cyrildene and Highlands North. When this distinctive style had run its course in the white suburbs, it was taken up in Reeftown, where the two first yellow face-brick houses were built by the wealthiest of the earlier 'uneducated' traders and made generally desirable in a more advanced form by one of the doctors. Yellow face-brick, sometimes laid in intricate patterns, was also lavishly used for building the garden walls, while the wrought-iron gates swung between yellow face-brick garden posts.

Thus, a style current in the white areas around the thirties, represented the ideal house type of our township some twenty years later, and yellow face-brick remained for quite a while Reeftown's preferred building material.

In the meantime, however, the inhabitants begun to experiment with a variety of styles, materials and decorations. The 'status' houses were alive with the gimmicks which sold surburban speculative houses in the white districts inhabited by emergent Afrikaner society: the display of as many different building materials as possible, the mixing in one house of different coloured and textured plasters, different colours and textures of brickwork, combinations of plaster with slasto, timber, ornamental grilles, chimneys, boxed windows and all kinds of embellishments.

102

Dr Greig remarked that 'there was a disappointing lack of indigenous decoration on the external walls of these houses – of the multicoloured abstract patterns of the Sotho, the Ndebele and the Zulu. The process of urbanization of the African seems to deprive him of such valuable aesthetic exercises and expressions.'

During the period following our field research, in the years between the beginning of 1962 and 1966, new styles emerged. Among these two deserve mention. There was, first, the use of the monopitch roof at all angles. This was a post-war affectation and its Johannesburg prototype was, according to Dr Greig, built around 1950, in a then lower-class, cheap (my own) white suburb. However, the monopitch, developed into a clerestory-windowed house, soon became popular in other white suburbs, and has become greatly favoured in expensive suburbs all over South Africa today. In Reeftown, the first monopitch roof appeared around 1962 on a house built by another doctor. The style has since been chosen by some wealthy traders.

In these later years the first white, gabled-roof houses have also appeared in our township. Their European prototypes emerged during the last ten years in speculative building for lower-middle and middle-middle class white suburbs, and later the style was being developed in many small variations by package-deal firms of good calibre.

These plain, whitewashed or white-plastered, rectangular houses with their recessed *stoeps*, are characterized by their gable-ended roofs covered with black slate or dark cement tiles, their economy of line and harmonious finishes. They represented, according to Dr Greig, a great improvement in standards of building and taste. This style has now become dominant in the newer and less expensive parts of the extended 'Northern Suburbs' of Johannesburg, as for instance, Parkmoor and Blairgowrie. To these parts were moving waves of new, white immigrants from overseas and from the country areas of the Republic, as well as many of the newly prospering status aspirers from the Southern Suburbs. The inhabitants of the Northern Suburbs of Johannesburg have always regarded the Southern Suburbs as almost proverbial lower-status areas in a manner similar to that with which the older Reeftowners looked down upon their own 'site-and-service' areas. These people – and this might be stressed – were caught up in a process of socio-cultural mobility similar to that which was taking place among Reeftowners.

However, these white-gabled houses did not gain ready acceptance in Reeftown. To abandon the much-admired face-brick for the simpler whitewash and plaster was not so easy. Here the natural preference was for what was furthest removed from the often whitewashed, daub-and-wattle hut of the past. For the same reason, the two 'rondafels' added to my own house and lending it great charm

103

in the eyes of my European friends, are invariably viewed with disapproval by my African visitors.

Another point worth mentioning was that, as far as we could notice, not one householder had so far discovered the advantages in the Transvaal of a northern orientation. It had also taken white people in South Africa some time before they ceased building their houses to face the street.

Summarizing, we could observe how each time the population of Reeftown, in their rapid socio-cultural advance, tended to find their own level from among the culture traits offered to view by the Europeans living next-door; how after a delay in time, each time becoming shorter, they adopted a particular style but passed through it at a quicker tempo; and, finally, how direct imitation was modified by some selectivity.

Above all, it seemed to us of particular importance to see how the Reeftown home builders, in their social imitation, passed, in only a few years, through changes in styles and tastes which it had taken the Europeans several generations creatively to evolve – an illustration in a small field of what, in our view, was happening everywhere in Africa over a larger domain of human activity.

With regard to the elite's social leadership, evidence suggested that it was the elite – the doctors and the wealthy traders – who first introduced novelties in Reeftown and these were then gradually accepted by others. In all the cultural borrowings and adaptations, the elite often figured as the experimental guinea-pigs who had to swallow an apparently delectable western morsel first while the community watched and waited – could it be digested by a black stomach, what were its after-effects, did it work?

With regard to the acceptance of western values – which the Europeans distinguished from fashions and etiquette, but most Africans did not – the process was not much different. It was the elite who were supposed to show whether a new feature 'worked', which meant whether it could help in the struggle of life and could benefit the people in the pursuit of their goals and aspirations.

Theirs was a great responsibility indeed.

Power and social immunity

The elite were also in a favourable position *vis-à-vis* the Europeans. They were in regular and personal contact with them, not only in their work and because they occupied the higher positions often directly under the European in charge, but also in their spare-time activities. Therefore the authority and influence of the Europeans devolved upon them. The value placed on organizational activities and leadership was in no small measure due to the opportunities which this brought of meeting and making friends with Europeans.

'Europeans only take notice of office-bearers', was a remark frequently heard. The great advantage of multiracial social gatherings was precisely in the fact that one was 'spotted by Europeans'. For in such gatherings Europeans would seek them out and start friendly conversations with them, and this could lead to a profitable relationship. Therefore, the elite were frequently described as 'those who, at social functions, can be seen to talk with Europeans'.

It was in such European contacts that the elite found confirmation and justification of their social prestige. But in addition, from such contacts, they derived much of the power and influence they could command. For, after all – although probably in a slightly lesser degree than before separate development – the Europeans were still the source of all privilege, and whoever had the ear of Europeans was assured of certain benefits. Other less-privileged and less well-connected Africans had to appeal to him to intercede for anything they needed and for any project in which a European could be of assistance. And that was practically everything.

In this intermediary position between black and white the elite could, therefore, command and manipulate a source of actual or potential power. Consequently, the competition among the educated for the favour of the Europeans, whether white civil servants, welfare workers, church, social or political contacts, as well as European employers, was probably as acute and ruthless as the competition for jobs and offices. There was a pronounced tendency to monopolize the channels of black–white communication and, once 'a European had been acquired', to prevent others from joining in the spoils.

The power and authority which the elite thus enjoyed in Reeftown as a result of their intermediary position made it essential for others to remain in their good books and to do nothing which would antagonize them. In our opinion, this was the main reason underlying the fact that, although the Reeftown elite said of themselves that they were 'like all high trees', catching 'the wind' of public criticism, this was not allowed to come into the open. Many of them were surrounded by 'followers' who, in the hope of recommendations and assistance, performed certain services such as spreading bits of information, originating malicious gossip, canvassing support for the election to a honorary office, communicating promises or threats, compelling witnesses to silence, striking up friendships with possible prospects, and performing a host of other such activities which together form the mechanism of power manipulation.

In this respect, the elite were beginning to share an important characteristic with the western upper classes in that they enjoyed a certain immunity from whatever social sanctions could otherwise be brought to bear on disrespectable behaviour and infringements of the proprieties of Reeftown society.

For, as Lipton saw clearly, the upper class, the aristocracy, whether by descent or by wealth, has probably always been characterized more by its vices than by its virtues. Respectability, defined as behaviour in accordance with certain general norms of a society, was a middle-class, not an upper-class, characteristic, he wrote. 'To be as good as the upper classes,' Lipton explained, 'you have to be as bad as the upper classes – and get away with it, as they do.'[35]

Lipton brought this subject up to use the disappearance of this earlier upper-class 'privilege of amorality' as evidence for his thesis of the general levelling-out of class distinctions in present-day America, manifest 'in the trickle-down process' of upper-class characteristics through 'the middle class taking over the mores of the American upper class'. Reeftown was, obviously, at the opposite end of the development; it was at the stage of the first rise of an upper class and of the earliest appearance of the upper-class privileges so that Lipton's 'principle of amorality' was again applicable to it, and to its new elite.

The phenomenon had been brought to our notice as early as 1958, as a result of the following incident. A member of the Upper Ten of the township gave a house-warming party, and among the guests was the chief of one of the Northern Sotho tribes, who brought with him his 'town girl', 'a very smart nurse', by whom he had some children. Township gossip had widely praised the qualities of the chief and the elegance of his girl-friend. At the same time, however, one of the local educated businessmen, himself a member of the elite and otherwise highly esteemed, was not invited because at just about that time his wife was divorcing him, and he had not yet married the mother of another lot of his children. Therefore, in this case, what was tolerated in a chief was not tolerated in a member of the local elite.

Since then, however, developments have continued, and we were able to watch how this new tolerance began to spread to the new chiefs of the towns. Soon afterwards, an adopted daughter (the wife's sister's child) of one of the elite became engaged to a very wealthy matriculated businessman from another township. The latter had not only just divorced his wife, but had divorced her by a rather shameful, treacherous procedure frequently used by African husbands to rid themselves of a less well-educated wife, married in an earlier stage of their careers, and now felt as a hindrance in their social ascent – an occurrence apparently typical for highly mobile societies. It consisted in obtaining the wife's consent to a divorce on the pretence that the marriage in community of property was disadvantageous for business and had to be changed into a new marriage by ante-nuptial contract. (Reef wives were, however, now becoming alerted to the trick.) Consequently, there was talk among the social classes of Reef-town of boycotting the wedding. However, when it became known that the wedding would be a 'very grand' affair, that all the elite from the Reef had been invited, and that doctors and lawyers, court interpreters, school inspectors and health inspectors would be there, no Reeftowner had the courage to refuse the invitation.

The upper classes on the Reef had already too much to offer and too much to withhold for others to dare be too critical when they offended certain proprieties.

A good example of the differential value judgements according to the prestige of the referrants was the following: Some assistant primary-school teachers came to be placed in the upper–lower ranks because they were heavy drinkers, even drunkards, and 'had let them-selves go'. They were, moreover, not members of the Teachers' Association or of any clubs or societies. They consorted with low-class people, were rowdy and generally untidily dressed and sloppy. But not so with regard to one of the doctors. During the earlier years of our field research he was a habitual drunkard and a regular shebeen customer. Every week-end he could be seen drunk, fighting and shouting, together with his friends, who were described as 'the lowest of the low'. During a series of successive week-ends he smashed a number of cars. He came drunk to his surgery, or failed to turn up at all; he refused to participate in social functions, and never attended the exclusive parties to which he was invited because of his high-status profession. His clothes were untidy; his home dirty. It was a small rented Council house 'like that of a labourer', and 'there was nothing in it'.

The same things were, therefore, said of him as of the primary-school teachers, and possibly even more. Yet he was, with only a few exceptions, ranked in the upper class, even in the upper-upper stratum. This was then explained as: 'Well, in his case, he must be classified in the European way, and then it is status that counts – that is profession/education.' Some informants then added: 'But he is degenerating', as though in this way paying lip-service to 'the African way'.

The few who decided that he could not possibly be placed together with the other members of Top Society, explained their decision by pointing out that: 'He has not been able to accumulate wealth. Have you seen his house? And in spite of all that education!' Thus, neither in his promotion to top rank nor in his demotion from top rank did the criterion of 'respectability' count at all. Yet his drunkenness was known all over the township and commented upon and disapproved of by everybody, and in no way different from that of the assistant primary-school teachers.

While it cannot be repeated too often that a great deal more re-search on this subject would be required, we might recall, for the time being, Frazier's findings about 'the changes in the canons of respectability' among the new and wealthy generations of Negroes in America.[36] Maybe we were observing here in Reeftown the earliest signs of a similar development.

It was not only in this regard, however, that the Upper Ten of the township were ceasing to play the social-status game according to the rules generally accepted by the middle classes.

Social participation and social exclusiveness

We have seen that among the expectations about the role of an elite was the general requirement of organizational leadership and social participation. This requirement had no doubt originally been ful-filled by the earlier pioneers of education,[37] but during the time of our field research, the elite's patterns of social participation had begun to change. As a result we were fortunate enough to be able to observe at close quarters the birth of another new development, namely, the rise of a socially-aloof upper stream.

Considering that in Reeftown organizational participation was the vehicle of social mobility upwards, particularly if other attributes such as education and occupation were not quite sufficient, it was not surprising that the most enthusiastic and tireless participants of Reef-town were to be found among the upper-middle and lower-upper strata, that is among those whose social position hovered tenuously on the borderline between middle- and upper-class status. Under-standably, therefore, the Upper Ten, secure in their status, had never been particularly noted for their organizational activities, although they had functioned as guests of honour or as patrons, and they had shown interest in what 'the lower orders' had been doing for the general well-being and cultural progress of the community by some-times honouring their activities with a brief appearance.

In this kind of social participation, which was not really participa-tion but simply patronage, the educated elite had always differed markedly from the business elite. The educated complained bitterly that the wealthy traders and entrepreneurs did not take part in town-ship functions nor desire to be office-bearers, not even presidents or patrons of voluntary associations, nor were they willing to put their roomy reception rooms at the disposal of committees to be used for meetings and other gatherings. Kuper quoted an informant who gave two reasons for this detachment from involvement in community affairs.[38] First, the trader felt that if he became 'mixed up' with the people, predominantly so poor, he would 'be tempted to help them'. Second, the trader feared that the people might do him harm because he appeared to be well-off. In traditional society exceptional achievement had always incurred the risk of an accusation of witchcraft on the part of the less successful.

Certainly these two reasons also applied to the businessmen of Reeftown, but, at least in our township, there was more to it.

To understand this it must be remembered that Reeftown was split by social divisions and all manner of other, more permanent differences – those which derived from more traditional antagonisms and those which had arisen in the urban circumstances. These divisions were particularly noticeable among the social classes who, as a socially interacting group, met each other frequently in a variety of social situations outside kin and work relationships, situations for which no traditionally laid down patterns provided a basis of interaction and in which, invariably, the absence of shared rules of intercourse increased the mutual antagonisms and rivalries which seemed to gain the upper hand over common interests and similar goals.

Not only were the elite forever competing against each other for the few status positions on leading committees and important boards, as well as for the few promotions and new jobs that became available as the township expanded, but they were more or less permanently divided into two major and some minor 'camps' (as the cliques were called), each centred around one person, each implacably antagonistic to the other. Each of these personalities had collected a small nucleus of permanent 'followers' from among fellow members of the elite, while the others were aligned and realigned with each successive conflict.

In view of such continuous rivalries every social participation meant entering the arena and taking sides. For social participators could not avoid being drawn into the conflicts; everyone's support was, at times, mobilized. To play a leading role in a township function, to accept office on a committee, necessarily meant becoming involved in the inevitable disputes.

One of the doctors explained why he could not take a more active share in community life: 'Now, for instance,' he said, 'there is that new cultural club again, and then immediately there is a counter club. So you can't join because then you are supposed to take sides. A doctor can't do that.' Whereupon his wife added: 'We must be friends with everybody.'

Surely the main reason why all over the world such housing estates seemed to harbour and originate so much quarrelling and backbiting, so much antagonism and conflict, was the fact that they were mere dormitories. Most residents were commuters and their incomes were derived from sources outside the estate. Even if they worked in the housing estate, their wages or salaries were paid by absentee employers and they were, therefore, not dependent for their livelihood on the goodwill of the residents, and on their general standing in the community.

It was the need to keep on friendly terms with everybody which drove those whose income was dependent on the residents' goodwill to withdraw from social involvement.

This applied first of all to the shop-keepers, merchants and the other self-employed, the builders and the increasing numbers of independent artisans and craftsmen – all these could simply not afford to turn potential customers into enemies. During our field research we were able to observe how the doctors learned their lesson in this respect. Soon others followed their example and also began to cultivate a safe and neutral attitude of non-committal.

In the growing shift of emphasis from interracial to intraracial dependence it became even more necessary than before to keep out of all entanglements. We were able to see how some of the higher public servants began to follow the example of the doctors and traders. The municipal clerks had probably already been advised earlier by their supervisors not to become involved. Rather than, as one of the traders told us, 'put my head in a hornets' nest', these persons preferred to withdraw, the one from the presidency of a cultural club, the other from the chairmanship of a youth organization, yet another from the board of a sports organization. For the same reason, it became increasingly impossible to induce any of the more highly educated, non-teaching yet professional individuals to accept office on the School Board.

This movement of withdrawal from social responsibilities was aggravated by political developments. For as politics entered the scene and political disagreements began to penetrate an increasing number of township activities, so that political factors became more and more intermingled with social, economic, ethnic and other differences, more and more of the higher professionals and clerical workers found it expedient to withdraw from active leadership in the social life of the community, and to narrow down the circle of their friends.

For when politics were involved, what was before merely 'bad for business' became a threat to life . . .

The educated middle classes complained bitterly of the unwillingness of the 'top people' to take up the leadership expected of them, and to which their position would entitle them. 'Our top people are not true,' they said in typical African fashion. They accused this non-participating top stratum of 'uppishness'; they called them 'selfish' and 'the stiffs'.

The fact that the most highly educated and the wealthiest residents – the people of highest social prestige – were withdrawing more and more from their social responsibilities ran so contrary to the people's deepest convictions that it was almost unacceptable, and many a middle-class, community-conscious individual confidently predicted the downfall which was expected to follow such isolation.

And to make matters worse, they had to stand by while another development took place before their eyes. Not only were the elite beginning to replace the Europeans and taking over some of their most disliked attitudes towards their less privileged fellows, but they were beginning to function as substitutes in town for the tribal chiefs, the former aristocrats and nobles of 'the Royal Blood'. As, on the one hand, they sought to meet the European as their social equal so, on the other hand, they tried to re-establish contact as between equals with the tribal Chiefs, thus preparing themselves for all possible future developments by securing a foothold in each camp. For the large interior market and an expansion of their clientele could, so they reckoned, only come with the support of the great and powerful rural leaders, such as the chiefs, the religious founders and the witch-doctors.

Social antagonism faced our elite from two different strata of the population. The more traditionally-minded were horrified by their frequent neglect of ceremonial duties and kinship obligations, by their brushing aside of family ties in favour of the new ties of friend-ship. The sensibilities of the respectable middle classes, however, were offended by their lack of church attendance, their marital in-fidelities, their internal squabbles and intrigues, their public drunken-ness, their preoccupation with trivialities. How often were we not told of the social and political leaders' lack of respect for an old mother, of their neglect of a father's grave, of the betrayal of their first less educated wife, or of their desertion of their children.

But the most frequent accusation against the top people, and at the same time that on which all the different social and cultural groups agreed was: 'They are doing nothing for their own people'. It was then explained how 'In the country a rich man gave to the poor. But now? Nothing. On the contrary, the richer the meaner, the greedier, the harder grabbing.' Among welfare workers it was common know-ledge that the wealthier business people were the least likely to give financial support to the African welfare organizations. Frequent complaints were to the effect that: 'Our leaders are letting us down', or 'They are only interested in earning money for themselves', etc. The community expected their leaders to lead and advise, to instruct and to help. In the general estimation they should have been leaders in church, education and politics. They were supposed 'to stand up for us against the Europeans', 'to speak for us', 'to defend our rights', 'to get us privileges'. It was felt that the leaders were letting their people down badly. They did not play the role assigned to them by the community and few of the high expectations of the people were fulfilled. Typically and inevitably, as prestige was gained so the people's respect was lost.

Thus, apart from the fact that it would be almost impossible for any elite to satisfy the divergent role expectations of a society in all stages of development, the elite did not even fulfil the most universal and insistent demands of the common people, for leadership and particularly political leadership.

Summing up

The elite of Reeftown consisted mainly of public servants and self-employed. Among the public servants we found teachers and clerks, health inspectors and social workers. While of the two older occupations, those of teachers and clerks, only the 'tops' had elite status, of the newer professions, those of the health inspectors and social workers, all belonged to the elite. The self-employed consisted of the independent entrepreneurs and the doctors. Some sales representatives and insurance agents also were reckoned among the elite. Of the numerous ministers of religion only those belonging to the main prestige churches, whether European or African, had elite status.

Three-quarters of the elite held one or more professional diplomas. Sixty-five per cent had teachers' certificates. This resulted in an accumulation of professional certificates shown in the fact that forty-five individuals held between them fifty-nine professional diplomas. Twelve members of the elite were university graduates and another ten or twelve were failed graduates, thus more than one-third had some academic experience. As many as half of the sample held only Junior Certificates, or not even these, as their highest academic qualification.

Their incomes varied greatly with a lowest salary of about R54 and a highest income estimated at not much below R800 per month. In addition, over half of the elite had incomes from additional enterprises, investments or property either in town or in the country. The average salary of the public servants was not quite R100 per month.

The elite appeared to be a relatively mature group with an average age of 44·3 years; the ministers of religion were the oldest, and the health inspectors and social workers were the youngest professional group. Of the clerks, those employed by Government were most mature in age. They were also the best qualified and the best paid of all the clerical workers.

The religious affiliations of the elite reflected the general distribution of religious adherence among Africans on the Reef; three-quarters belonged to the three missions which ran, at the time, well-known secondary schools or teacher training colleges in the Transvaal. The largest number of the elite were Anglicans, and the

112

third largest group after the Anglicans and the Methodists was made up of the independent African churches.

An analysis of the 'tribal' affiliations of the elite showed a significantly high percentage of Xhosa-speaking individuals, and among these Fingo and Hlubi specifically identified themselves. These Xhosa were evenly distributed among the various occupations and income groups. As to the proportion of Northern to Southern Sotho, the elite reflected significantly the tribal distribution of the Transvaal rather than that of the Reef. Thus, as to their 'tribal' affiliations, the elite were entirely unrepresentative of Reeftown itself and of the Reef.

Of all the provinces, the Eastern Cape contributed the largest quota to the elite of Reeftown, closely followed by the Transvaal. Only four individuals came from Natal.

Only four of the sixty were born in a big town or city, and almost half were born in a Native Reserve or Tribal Territory. But the point which, in our opinion, was of importance was not so much that our elite were not very urbanized (only 6·67 per cent of them were urban born and not quite one-third had been urban brought up), but that for most of them their urbanization had come gradually and after they had reached the age of 20, when they came to town to look for work or to take up waiting posts.

Investigating the urban–rural component in their early residential mobility, it was found that only seventeen individuals had spent their earliest formative years uninterruptedly in a Bantu or 'tribal' area. All the others had come to town after a longer or shorter stay in areas that cannot be called 'tribal' – areas such as a European farm or a mission station – or in areas that cannot be called 'rural' – areas such as one or other of the small provincial towns.

We believe that it is this gradual urbanization, strongly typical of the professionals and the most highly educated among them, which was characteristic of our elite; and it was in this that an explanation must be found for the fact that they, though not very urbanized in terms of length of residence, proved to be, in some important aspects, highly de-'tribalized'. The first of these aspects encountered in this chapter, was the large number of inter-'tribal' marriages contracted by them. Almost 60 per cent had married wives of a different 'tribe' and among these were two who had married coloured women.

About 70 per cent had wives with professional qualifications; nearly twice as many of them were teachers as were nurses, but only just over half of the wives were working at the time. The average earnings of the salaried wives were not quite R40 per month, and it was noted that the educated upper-class households of this new Bantu township, in which both parents were salaried employees, had a joint average income of not quite R130 per month.

Nearly 70 per cent of the elite were home-owners. Of these just over half lived in self-built houses varying in size and elegance, and having cost their owners on an average at least R2,500. The salaried individuals who built their own houses spent an average of R2,136·16 per house (information from the house builders themselves) on an average monthly salary of R98·62. The Council-built houses in which the other half of the home owners lived cost an average of R850. The majority of the loans were still being paid off. In their preferences in styles of houses and furnishings, the elite had followed closely European housing developments and changes, but with a decreasing time-lag and at a quickening tempo.

Subsequently a few words were said about the private behaviour as well as the cultural and artistic tastes and interests of the elite – these people in between two cultures and at home in none.

In their community the elite were considered 'newcomers' and from another point of view they were 'insiders', because their jobs concerned the well-being of the people themselves and did not serve 'to enrich the Europeans' as those who were working on the other side of the colour line were said to do.

They were the social leaders who introduced fashions and styles, manners and morals. They set the standards and showed the people what heights Africans had already reached. They were the goal – the beacons pointing the direction of all endeavour. As public figures they had wide visibility. They were gossiped about and widely criticized, and sometimes even ridiculed because of their 'antics'. However, such criticism seldom came out in the open; the elite had, already at this stage of their development, too much to give and too much to withhold. For by means of their authoritative positions and their European contacts they controlled the sources of all privilege and enjoyed considerable power and influence.

We finally described how, in spite of the stress on social participation, we could witness the beginning of a new development, namely the rise of a socially exclusive group; and we explained this in terms of the necessity for those whose livelihood depended on the goodwill of the community, to remain uncommitted, particularly in view of the intense and continuous disputes which accompanied all social activities whether formal or informal. This avoidance of social involvement, this shirking of social responsibility by their top people, was against the most dearly held values and deepest convictions of the Reeftown community; it was contrary to all social role expectations. But even worse, and this referred not only to a top stratum but to the whole elite, was their total refusal to take up the political leadership to which their high status entitled them, and which was expected of them.

'Our top people are not true', seemed to sum up the position of the elite in their community.

part two

Mobility

3 Educational mobility

Primary education

Introduction

In this chapter we shall deal with the process of socio-cultural change as manifested in the educational advance of our elite.[1]

A first point to make is that all of the elite had completed their primary education (the last completed Std. VI in 1951) before the Bantu Education Act, No. 47 of 1953 had been implemented in April 1955. The median year of the elite's completion of Std. VI was 1932, and the densest cluster was between the years 1927 and 1939; in these years 32 of the 60 individuals finished their primary education. The general conditions of primary schooling in those days can be learned from two investigations. The one deals with schools on the Reef in 1937[2] and the other describes the situation in the Transkei in the forties and as recently as the early fifties.[3] These two theses can be used here in corroboration of the statements by our elite themselves.

By and large our respondents spoke unfavourably about their primary education, giving many telling examples from their experiences. Parents were generally lax about sending their children to school when they reached school age. This was so, even on the Reef.[4] Naturally, without compulsory education, everything depended on the parents. In addition, the teachers were said to have been 'incapable', 'badly qualified' or 'lazy';[5] they were subjected to little or no supervision by their superiors. While in those days NPL_3, i.e. Std. VI plus three years' Teacher Training, was practically the only, and generally the highest, qualification for teachers, a great many teachers had no qualifications other than Std. IV and some years' Teacher Training, while 'you could already teach after having passed

Std. IV twice'. Many a mission school was founded and headed by a barely literate and sometimes even illiterate evangelist. The method of teaching, as well as the range of subjects, left much to be desired. 'It was mainly dull and memory work', 'The Ten Commandments were more important than the multiplication tables', 'It was nothing but drill and you were not allowed to ask questions', are some of the statements by members of the elite. Only three books were required up to Std. VI.

One respondent summed up as follows:

'All that was necessary was that you went to church and you learned to speak beautiful English. Our heroes were those who could use the most complicated sentences, flowery images and lots of difficult words. I realized only later that whether they spoke sense or facts was unimportant. While nowadays . . . well, of course, nowadays, the most popular boys at Fort Hare are the ones who can speak Tsotsi language and do some jiving. . . .'

Attendance was irregular and equipment poor; classes were over-crowded and school buildings often entirely inadequate, even on the Reef.[6] 'In our school there were no lavatories', was often stated. Schools were few and far between. Some schools only went to Std. II, others to Std. IV, and many had no Std. VI. One respondent said that he and his brother walked twenty miles to and from school every day, only later could they go on horseback. Another attended a school of 1,000 children with no more than eight teachers. Not only were different standards taught together in one session by one teacher,[7] but also children of the most widely divergent ages sat in the same class. Schoolchildren were frequently obliged to do the schoolmaster's home chores. They were, in fact, every teacher's free domestic labour.[8]

In a sample of twelve schools on the Reef, the average age of boys in Sub A for the term ending 25 March 1937 was 9·5 years.[9] Very few children ever completed Std. VI, and the average age of school-leaving was 11 years 8 months.[10]

Statistics of the Department of Bantu Education show that even as recently as 1956–7 the problem of early school-leaving was considerable. By the time the second Sub-Standard was reached, one in five children had already left school. And by the time Std. VI was reached three-quarters of the children had dropped out. In 1960–61, the time of this study, the situation had not improved, for Professor J. L. Sadie,[11] estimating the school grade survival ratio, wrote that 'out of every 100 who enter the first school grade, fewer than 10 complete the last primary grade to enter the ranks of the secondary school children, who during 1960–61 constituted 3·2% of the 15 to 19 age group.'

The main defects of Native Primary Education in the Transkei up to 1951 were listed as follows:[12] frequent admission during the year; overcrowding; unequal division of work between the teachers; the 'Small A' class; the wrong medium of instruction ('the official language of instruction was introduced too early, contrary to Departmental regulations'); irregular and inadequate requisitioning; and irregular attendance.

The 'twin evils' of native primary education were said to be 'excessive retardation in the Sub-Standards and a heavy rate of retardation after the Sub-Standards'.[13]

In some schools in the country (and the Reef towns were no better in those days) conditions must have been truly Dickensian!

Finally, and to cap this far from amusing tale, we may quote that in the Transkei, the most closely missionized and earliest organized school-area of South Africa, it was found that, 'Until 1947, the curriculum of the Native Primary Schools in the Transkei had been the same and had remained unchanged since 1933.'[14]

It is in this general situation of African Education before the Bantu Education Act – a situation at present too quickly forgotten – that we must place the early educational history of the elite in order to be able to judge their achievement.

The general attitude towards education

In those days, not more than a generation ago, the value of education was beginning to be realized in even wider rural circles. Education stood for many things. Probably originally, and still for those parents who consider Std. III enough, it stood for that new magic, the letter – the letter which made it possible to maintain contact with a son who had gone to the mines or a daughter who was in domestic service in a near-by town. Those with higher aims, however, thought first of the prestige that would accrue to the family through having a son, to 'carry' or 'preserve' your name, as was said.

There was much rivalry between the families, the clans, the villages. The people saw teachers and ministers, the two earliest prototypes of the educated person, and they saw that 'they were valuable in the community'. Respectfully people pointed them out to one another, saying: 'This clan has produced so many teachers or ministers.' Even today people on the Reef will say: 'Our township has so many B.A.s but Y township has not yet produced one.' At weddings the educated persons of the two families were enumerated, and their praises sung as the deeds of the warriors and hunters were in earlier days. Those who could be said to be 'serving their own people' were accorded fame and prestige.

The new literate groups fulfilled many community functions. They were the advisers to the chief; they functioned as interpreters between the authorities and the people; they were the scribes of the villages. The African teacher in those days performed the same function as the early teachers of the American frontier and enjoyed the same prestige.

All this, however, did not necessarily apply to the daughters. 'They married anyway and all that education was wasted.' It was only after it became more widely known that a daughter's educational qualifications raised the *lobolo* (the child or bride price) because her education increased her earning power, and that therefore 'education paid' – even and especially for girls, that the African women of South Africa became as well-educated as they are today.

Much of the slowly, all too slowly, awakening interest in education was due to the untiring efforts of the missionaries and teachers, who, as many respondents told us, went from hut to hut and from kraal to kraal visiting the people, explaining about education and its advantages, trying to persuade these conservative farmer parents to send at least one of their sons to school, or to give at least one of the younger sons to be trained as evangelist or minister.

The missionaries were, no doubt, helped in their endeavours by the dwindling rural economy, the increasing impoverishment of the countryside, and the decreasing grazing lands. Many parents wished to have at least one educated son as a 'stand-by' for an uncertain future. Respondents told us: 'Educated people do not depend on the weather.' A Xhosa proverb quoted to us was: 'Education is that wherefrom, come rain or snow, one will always eat.' Respondents reported increasing drought, diseases and soil erosion, and consequently a greater number of inheritance disputes and family quarrels with the inevitable accompaniment of black magic and jealousies.

The following quotations underline this:

'He has gone to make a name for us by education. It is good, he is no longer in this terrible place; he is away from jealous relatives and neighbours. Higher learning brings both prestige and more money.'

'Education is better than merely cattle in the new age which is awaiting us. It is also better than land from which you have to move so often to make way for the whites.'

It was not poverty which delayed or prevented education. Poverty entered as an important factor in secondary education but at this stage it was never mentioned. Yet only eleven of the elite as children received their primary education free while a further nine had had their school fees reduced. The small fee of 15 cents per quarter was in twenty-six cases paid by father, either with or without the help of another relative. In fourteen cases it was the mother alone who had paid for the entire primary schooling of her son.

Thus people began increasingly to choose 'education instead of cattle'. And this obtained particularly among those who stood to inherit little, or whose inheritance was disputed by other relatives, for they then said to themselves: 'Never mind, I don't need cattle, I have education.'

But in spite of this, children did not start school as early as the urban Bantu now consider the normal age to be. When our elite were young, nine years was the usual age of starting school.[15] Respondents were generally conscious of the fact that this would, nowadays, be considered late, and they explained: 'there was that feeling among Africans that a child should not go to school too early', or 'there was a general belief that if you started school early you would go mad'. This belief was widespread, and even up to this day many of our elite have country cousins who are watching their 'mad' kin, and whenever a mishap occurs they blame it on 'too much education' and 'too early mental strain'.

Conditions differed throughout the country. There were so-called 'progressive' and 'backward' areas. But our elite must have been, on the whole, socially privileged as almost half went to school earlier than the normal age of nine.[16] The unsystematic nature of Bantu education in those days however does not always make it easy to determine when schooling had actually started. Some little boys just sat around with their older brothers or sisters because these were supposed to 'look after them'. Others, who had to do herding in the day-time, were taught in the evenings by an elder sibling. All children brought up in an urban area went early, mainly because 'school was safe', 'it kept us out of mischief'. But again some rural children went early because 'there was nothing else to do'. Sometimes a late school start was explained by saying that 'school was too far', but by and large the impression was gained that, if the parents were really keen on getting their children off to an early start, ways and means were found. Very often one can read through the carefully-phrased replies in which respondents tried 'to show the respect' to their parents, that the real reason for a late start had been parental neglect or the desire to have the child at home for company or work.

The fathers' attitude to education

How much the desire for education arose from social and economic insecurity can be seen from the fact that precisely the wealthiest farmer-fathers, and those of high and secure tribal status, were against education.[17] 'Prosperous parents were not eager to send their children to school', many respondents explained in impersonal terms, so as not to condemn their own fathers in the eyes of the European. 'We cattle-possessing people,' the sons explained, 'we were never thinking of coming to Johannesburg to eke out a miserable existence.' 'We were cattle-people and proud of our ways. But later we also got mixed up with these whites and this western so-called civilization.' Such statements revealed the seignorial tradition of all pastoral peoples.

Not only in the Eastern Cape, but also in the Northern Transvaal there were proud farmer-fathers. A Pedi among our elite explained:

'My mother's family were very well-to-do, more so than my father's people. They all had their own farms. In those days I lived with my mother's people. We had a very big house and there was nothing we lacked. All my mother's many brothers still have each his own farm; and they're rich. One of them just bought a tractor for R2,000 and paid it off in one year. People could get wealthy around Pietersburg.'

If father preferred farming to education, then it did not matter whether the cattle were held on a European farm, or in a Bantu reserve, or whether the land was held by customary allotment from a chief, in freehold or on sufferance on a white man's farm.

'. . . Our house was lucrative on that Dutch farm. If father had been educated or had wanted education for his children my family would have been big. But father said education was to be given to lazy people. He did not want to send us to town for proper schooling but employed a teacher on the farm to teach us something. Then when I was about 13 or 14 I had an injury to my arm, inflicted by an ox. My father felt that I wouldn't be strong enough to carry a bag of mealies and so I had better get educated . . .'

Many prosperous farmer-fathers wanted both cattle and education, or 'property and knowledge' as one respondent called it. Combining the two could be a severe strain:

'We were well off in that reserve. Because I was the oldest my parents wanted me to go to school and to do the herding and general looking after the cattle. The trouble is you can't have cattle and education, but my parents wanted both and I was always torn between the two.'

Others found a solution. Like any other white farmers, they took on paid farm labour:

'A young man was employed as general labourer for herding,

122

milking, ploughing at R3 per month, so that I could go to boarding school. It's not a good solution because native labour is bad . . .'

While most of those who were against education were wealthy, and particularly cattle-wealthy, those fathers who were for education were some of the educated, professional or white-collar workers, or also the poorest fathers. In fact, the higher father was educated, the more he encouraged and enforced his son's education. All the doctors, who all three had professional fathers, started school early, very early. All the ministers who came from wealthy farming families in which the head of the family had little or no education himself, started school late; and were not encouraged to go to school and sometimes even prevented.

The category 'indifferent' contained no clearly identifiable sociological group. Here we found rich and poor fathers, illiterate and educated fathers, professional fathers too busy with their own careers, and the father who was a national political leader and always away. These were the happy-go-lucky fathers, as their sons called them; those who 'couldn't care less', who 'did not have the push'. Here it was a matter of the individual personality and differential reactions to similar circumstances.

Quite clearly, in a society in which education was not compulsory few of these children would have been educated had the choice been left to their fathers.

The children's attitude to school

The children themselves were not too eager; only 30 per cent of them had a positive attitude towards school.[18] For most of these, however, school meant school sports and organized games, singing, music and all those other things which, in a rural African childhood, only school could provide. Only very few enjoyed the actual learning, or 'being taught' as the general expression was. Whether the teacher was harsh or kind, the school far or near; whether they were hungry or well-fed, cold or hot; whether they had difficulty in understanding or whether things came easily, these felt they were undergoing the glorious process of 'being educated'. They stared in fascination at the teacher, 'How is it that he knows all that, and he is black like me . . . !' They wanted to become like the teacher.[19]

Another 30 per cent felt completely negative towards school and education. They tried passive resistance and sometimes succeeded in delaying an early start, particularly if they were the first-born in the family. Some had to be forced by father, 'who used the rod unsparingly'. One youngster 'always had to repeat things and then felt

L

123

so sleepy. So my parents finally tied me on to my cousin . . .' Then there were the active resisters who played truant and ran away to work on various farms and earn money, or made for Durban to cut cane, or went to visit relatives. One of these runaways reported how: 'At first I never wrote home for fear I would be dragged back, but later I was only too willing to get back home and to school; the farmers in Durban sjambokked us.'

By and large we found confirmed what knowledgeable informants had told us. For instance, the following:

> 'In the past the parents were keen, not the children. But all the same rural children were more eager for education than urban ones. In the country education was your only salvation. But even if you did not like school, the parents in those days had more authority over the children and the children were easier to control.
>
> 'Moreover, with rural children, once you get them started on education, you can be sure that they will complete.'

Herding was the greatest single factor which interrupted the rural boys' schooling. More than half of our elite had been herd boys at some stage in their childhood and nearly all loved it. They certainly preferred it to school. Even today they commended it to us. 'Herding cultivates a sense of responsibility and ownership,' they said. Most boys alternated between school and herding, or school was interrupted for one or two years to do the traditionally required herding. Not even settlement in an urban area could absolve a youngster. 'I had to go back to my paternal grandfather who had remained on the European farm to herd for him, though my father was keen I should start school early.'

School mobility

As it had been with the fathers, so it was with the sons: mobility appears again as the keynote of the elite's childhood and adolescence. First of all, there were the changes in environment caused by the moves between urban, semi-urban and rural areas, the changes to and from tribal territories, white farms, mission stations or small and even larger towns. In Table II 3:1 we have tried to show these sometimes radical changes in social environment and from the table it can be seen that over half of our elite had already known different kinds of urban or rural ways of life before reaching the age of 16. Second, a not inconsiderable number of them had as infants or youngsters known already different kinds of homes and rearers. According to established Bantu custom, and often as a result of the insecurity and fluidity of their parents' lives, they had been given for a while to

124

relatives to look after, and quite a few boys had been shunted around the kinship system during most of their early years, almost always irrespective of their own wishes and needs. Finally, when studying the primary schools attended by our elite, we found a great many school changes. In fact, no more than just over one-third of the children had started and completed their primary education up to and including Std. VI in one and the same school.

Table II 3:1   Numerical distribution of the elite by the kind of area in which they were born and brought up, and trekked away from or to, before reaching the age of 16

Area	Born in/on	Trekked: away from	to				Brought up in/on
Bantu Reserve	29	12					17
European Farm	12	10				1	3
Mission Station in a Rural Area	6	2			1	1	6
Village or Small Town	9	2			2	2	11
Large Town or City	—	—			1	1	2
Reef, including Johannesburg	4	—		1	5	5	15
'Several Places'	—	—	2	1	1	2	6
Total	60	26	2	2	10	12	60

This table should be read as follows. For instance, with regard to the rural mission station, of the six individuals *born* in such an area, two *trekked away*, one *to* the Reef and one *to* 'several places'. Two *trekked to* such a mission station, one *from* a Bantu area and one *from* a European farm. As a result, of the six who were brought up on a mission station, only four had been born there.

(Of the six who trekked to 'several places' before reaching the age of 16, four settled afterwards again in a Bantu area, and two in a large town.)

Taking these three types of mobility together, mobility between rearers; mobility between areas; and mobility between primary schools, it was calculated that just under 20 per cent of the children had never experienced any changes at all. These do not, however, form a definable group. Lack of mobility was found at both ends in Bantu reserves and in location streets.

A total of 123 schools were attended by 59 boys (see Table II 3:2). This means a general school mobility of 2·08 schools per child. But not only that, it was also found that of the almost two-thirds of the mobile children, 22 had attended two schools, 12 had attended three schools and four had attended four or more schools. An analysis of these school moves revealed some of the factors which contributed to the fluid and mobile backgrounds of these African children and which must have had an influence on their subsequent careers.

Table II 3:2 Numerical and percentage distribution of the elite by the reasons for the primary school changes

N = 59*

Reasons for school changes		Number	Percentage
School-organizational		29	35·36
School had no Std. V	9		
School had no Std. VI	12		
School had no Std. III	1		
No school at birthplace	3		
Other	4		
Parental mobility		29	35·36
'Father always trekked'	15		
Parents moved	11		
Widowed mother trekked to town	3		
Relatives		21	25·61
Sent to relatives for proper schooling	10		
To help relatives	8		
Because father died	3		
Other		3	3·67
Total		82†	100

* One individual's educational history was not obtained.

† Of the total of 123 schools attended, 41 were in the child's birthplace, and therefore only 82 moves need to be explained.

There was, first of all, the fragmentary and unplanned state of African education in those days which in itself demanded a considerable mobility of the children and necessitated sometimes frequent school changes. This may need some explanation. Only 8 per cent of the schools attended by the elite had been governmental, while a small percentage had been tribal or community, farm or mine schools. The great majority, as much as 80 per cent, had been founded and run by missionaries.

These untiring and devoted missionaries often acted, not only without co-operation, but also with a good deal of competition between themselves. The schools were erected at places dictated by missionary requirements and resources, as well as by the funds and the teachers available in the individual missions rather than by the actual needs of the communities. In some areas schools were clustered together, and in other areas there were none at all. Many schools did not have the required number of Standards; while some went up to

126

and including Std. II only, others went up to Std. IV or Std. V. Moreover, schools were sometimes started as a temporary measure and discontinued when the required number of pupils did not enrol; when the only teacher became indisposed or left; or when the school could not obtain registration. In such cases another school had to be found and this frequently involved a move to another town or district.

With regard to the methods of teaching, the subjects taught, admissions, promotions and examinations – in fact, all important educational matters – there was lack of uniformity and an almost entire lack of co-ordination in the curricula and the rules of the various schools of the individual missions.

As a result of the competition among the different missions for the soul of the African child, it could happen, for instance, that parents whose child had failed, say Std. III, in one school, took him to another school belonging to another and rival denomination, where a sympathetic Principal would allow him to join Std. IV. Urban parents still nowadays reportedly try this method of promotion. Every now and again a failed child disappears from one school in Reeftown and is later discovered in another school in the next standard. Conversely it happened that missions gave preference to the scholars of their own denomination. One is struck by the sometimes arbitrary manner in which scholastic and administrative matters were decided. Our most level-headed and knowledgeable informant could relate such happenings as the following: in a college, one of the famous ones in the country, where he did his Std. VI, the entire Std. VI class, including himself, was declared failed by a superintendent because 'he was anti-German and, moreover, resented Africans being taught by Europeans'. That was in 1928.

The missionary authorities usually ruled supreme. The importance of personal relationships and connections, personal favouritism and influence was apparent from a great many of the stories told to us. On the other hand, it may well be that it was precisely thanks to the supreme powers of the missionaries that many of our elite were saved from years of superfluous drill and drudgery, and were often moved about and up by personal intervention.

A number of school changes became necessary because the boy did not do as well as he was supposed to:[20] he was spoiled by his rearers, particularly if these were his mother's people; or he got out of hand, played truant or preferred herding to schooling. Sometimes mother considered that father was not strict enough, and so she prevailed upon him to send the unmanageable child to another relative, who promised to exercise better control. These moves for disciplinary reasons or for reasons of better or continued education and in which relatives offered to take the child for a while, cannot always be distinguished from other moves in which the relatives also played a part, but in which they wanted the child for their own sake, to work for them or to keep them company.

The following was an interesting example. The boy was staying with his parents in a Bantu reserve and it had been planned that he should attend school daily in the near-by town. A friend of the family, a minister, 'who knew my parents, suggested I come to him in Pimville, Johannesburg, because schools were near'. When the lad arrived in town he found that he had to look after the minister's cows! (In those days there was a piece of land in Pimville which served as a sewerage disposal area for Johannesburg. The land was fertile and many urban African residents used to plough parts of it or have their cattle grazing there.) The little boy had to milk the minister's cows and sell the milk before going to school. In addition, the minister ran a horse-and-cab, providing transport as a means of livelihood, and the boy had to act as groom. Only after his father died could a resolute mother call her son back home so that proper schooling could begin.

In about one-quarter of the school moves the relatives entered actively upon the scene, sometimes retarding the child's progress, but, particularly in times of crisis, coming to the rescue and saving an otherwise hopeless situation.[21] We have several cases on record in which father's death caused a complete change of plans. In three cases, the widowed mother could not cope and found a good temporary home for her children. We have three further cases in which a school move became necessary because a widowed mother took control and trekked to town, where she herself could find work and the children further education.

Another one-third of the school moves came about as a result of the parents' lack of residential stability.[22] Consider these cases. Father was a school principal who was sent round the country by the missionary superintendent to open new schools. Moreover, during these years mother died and father remarried. The children were sent first to mother's parents, then to stepmother's father; and for short spells in between these moves, when father had suitable accommodation, they stayed with him. As a result, the son attended seven primary schools in the eight years it took him to complete his primary education. In another case, father was a well-known Anglican priest who was 'always transferred to start new mission stations, as he was very senior'. His son told us: 'I always arrived at the next school just in time for the next examinations which I then passed because I was brilliant, and so I was promoted to the next standard, after which I had to leave again.'

To discover whether such frequent school changes caused much retardation, we compared the one-third not-school-mobile children in our sample with the two-thirds school-mobile ones. It was then found that the not-school-mobile group had started at the average age of 9·30 years and completed primary school in 8·75 years, whereas the school-mobile children had started at 8·66 years of age and completed primary school in 7·85 years. Hence, on both these counts, the school-mobile children did better; they started earlier and advanced faster.

We can suggest two explanations, the one referring to the reasons for, and the other to the effects of, the parental residential mobility. We would recall that much of this was in the search of better living conditions, occupational and economic advance, and educational opportunities. In many cases, therefore, the degree of parental geographical mobility was a measure of progressive attitudes. As it also appeared from our study that the parents' and rearers' active concern shown in the child's education was the crucial factor in his educational progress,[23] it was exactly these mobile, progressive parents who encouraged and supported most actively the continued primary schooling of their children.

The second point concerned the effects of this school mobility on the young boys. Not one of our respondents ever expressed regrets or even irritation, or feelings of insecurity or homesickness at having moved away from their parents, or from one home to another and from one school to the next. The parents were, after all, only one element in a more inclusive set of kin and the children showed throughout an unruffled placidity and easy adaptability in all environments.

On the contrary, there was sometimes mention of the stimulating effect of this mobile childhood. Spokesmen talked of 'an adventurous spirit I acquired through having professional parents who were always transferred', 'I learned a lot by moving about', and of 'the desire for freedom and exploration those frequent changes created'.

However, these are only some suggestions in explanation of a possible positive relationship between the children's extreme geographical mobility and their educational progress.

The elite's educational aptitudes

Besides a fortunate social origin, a greater capacity for school learning than usual was probably the only concrete factor which can be adduced to throw some light upon the later success of our elite. In view of the general retardation in the primary schools of that time,[24] which resulted in our informants stating that: 'Ten years till Std. VI was a good score in those days', and 'To be in Std. II at the age of fourteen was quite normal', our elite had done rather well. They took an average of 8·25 years to complete Std. VI at an average age of

16·42, and this in spite of a wide scatter. There were those who did not start school till they were twelve years old, and a few took as long as twelve years over their primary education particularly if they had attended a 'tribal' school. But these were the exceptions; and not even these exceptions reflect unfavourably on the ability for learning of our sample, as the general environmental conditions and the educational quality of the schools must be taken into account. As a matter of fact, the elite often failed to secure promotion, and on the other hand they frequently jumped classes. 'I did Std. III and Std. IV and then again Std. V and Std. VI in one year,' said one respondent proudly. Again another said: 'I was always promoted. I was among the best scholars in Basutoland. If it had been now, I would have had scholarships.' The relative independence of the mission schools and the tremendous power of the superintendents obviously favoured the brighter boys.

When, therefore, our elite said of themselves: 'I was extremely bright', 'I always topped the class', 'My brilliance was obvious to anyone', this was not vain boasting, but a statement of fact by persons who had not yet been conditioned to western hypocrisy. One had to be decidedly outstanding to overcome so many obstacles and to do so much on the basis of so little.

The later educational careers of the elite did not afford any further opportunities for precise evaluation of their mental gifts, although it was exactly in their post-primary education that certain gifts of personality and character appeared, such as persistence and ambition.

Some educational histories

An early 'adventurer'

When the 60 adolescents completed Std. VI the urge to continue education was not equally strong with all of them. Fifty-two proceeded immediately to the next stage in their education, while seven had a break from school.

The story of one of these (the Rev. N. T.) is worth relating here because it throws an interesting light on the various factors involved in obtaining an education. The person in question is now an ordained minister in one of the European Mission churches.

His well-to-do farmer father, a Sotho, felt no particular urge to have his son educated and so the boy started schooling late. When he had completed Std. II he had to leave school to herd the cattle on his father's farm. He told us: 'As a small boy you were just tossed about, it seems to me. I was just told to herd. Only after grandfather died, could I do as I wanted, which really was to earn money.' So he went to work in a cheese factory in the neighbourhood. Soon he found that 'there was too little money for too much work'.

He then went to Durban where he was recruited as a railway labourer. But this was even worse and he did not like it at all. 'I had lice between my toes,' he said. Moreover, 'to go on looking for another job each time was too difficult'. So he decided, 'I must go back to school and get educated in order to have easier jobs.' In these noble intentions he received considerable encouragement, after a rebuff by 'a beautiful girl, who wanted nothing to do with me because she did not like uneducated people'. He was then nearly 18 years old.

He obviously had quite a struggle to make the grade, and when he finished primary schooling, he was 22 years old. His younger brother passed Std. VI in the same year, and, 'as I had wasted my time, I said to my father that if he couldn't or wouldn't pay for both of us, he should at least send my brother to college. For I would go to Johannesburg and earn money first'. Father, who had three other sons and two daughters to educate, gave in to this argument and consented to pay R44 per year for the younger brother's training in Lovedale.

So the present minister was recruited to the Mines and left for Johannesburg as an underground miner on a three months' contract. He renewed the contract twice, and then decided: 'This is too much. I've had enough. The work is too tough. There's nothing left for me but to go back to school.'

So finally, at the age of 24, he selected the cheapest training college he could find, and went there as a boarder to be trained as a teacher. He did his J.C. in record time, which showed that he was a bright young man.

Although the fact that he broke off schooling twice may be somewhat exceptional among our sample, the attitudes and sentiments expressed by him are typical.

Battling against circumstances

'I had to struggle for my education,' was how Mr R. Z. began his story. He had 'an average home', as he put it. There was nothing much to say about it, except that 'it had the Christian way of living'. Father, who had been the only son of a fourth wife, had worked for a while as a migrant labourer on the Reef. R.Z. was born on a Bantu Reserve in Zululand, the first of seven children. Soon after his marriage father began trekking from one European farm to another, hoping to improve himself. He then became a Christian and joined one

131

of the independent Bantu offshoots of the Methodist Church. When R.Z. was ten years old his father settled down on a mission station near the Swaziland border and became an evangelist. He 'knew nothing about civilization except Christianity.' His mother felt that the children should be educated, but the father said he couldn't afford it. R.Z., as the first-born, had to do herding. He was one of the few in our sample who did not like herding. He had other plans for his future.

However, as luck would have it, a relative of father, also an evangelist, lived next door. He had no children and decided 'that I was bright and he took me up to school'. It was a tribal school and in five years, R.Z. completed Std. VI, although, to placate father, he had to alternate school with herding.

Mother then decided something had to be done. She thought it would be best if her bright son was taken up by the American Board Mission, where her uncle was. With this goal in mind she persuaded father to send her first-born to a school in Nongoma, the one nearest her uncle's American Board Mission. In this Methodist mission school he had to complete Stds. V and VI again, and he failed the first year. He explained: 'I wasted my time. I had nothing to do. I did not go regularly to school, and all the subjects were new.' Later, and in another context, he said that at that stage he no longer wanted education. The tribal school had apparently cured him of his earlier enthusiasm. However, the American Board Mission relative did not take him on after he had completed Std. VI because another relative – his grandfather's brother – insisted that he stay with his son. The grandfather's brother had gone to Swaziland in his early manhood and had become the Prime Minister to King Sobhuza. Now, his grandfather's son's son went to the Royal School in Bremersdorp, and as 'the Chief knew we were closely related to to the Swazi Prime Minister', R.Z. could also attend and board there. He did his J.C. in the normal three-year period. He never applied for a bursary, since he didn't know they existed.

He then returned home and wanted to go to Adam's College, but his father wanted him to work and help with the other children. This he did for six months, when he summoned his second brother, and commanded him to do the work and look after his cattle while he went to town to try and get on in his own way. This he did successfully.

A stroke of luck

K.E.'s father was an Anglican but he came home only occasionally from work in Johannesburg and he had never shown any interest in his son's education. Mother, struggling alone at home, in the semi-urban location where the children had been born, had allowed this important Anglican contact to lapse, although she remained an Anglican, and the son had been brought up in that faith. Because she did not like him to loiter, his mother sent him to the near-by government-aided school, which had only 2 Subs and 4 Standards. K. E. does not remember much of those early days. His recollection starts when father died in a train accident and 'I began to see things.' Mother then went to Johannesburg to work and the children were given to mother's mother, who came to live with them in the same semi-urban location. The boy, however, had to go to another school to complete Stds. V and VI, and it was then that Mr M. (an African) suggested that the boy should come and stay with him to complete primary school.

Mr M. was a trustee of a number of African-owned farms. In those days people were buying freehold property all round the little town. This was both before and after Union. Many places were sold and many were very large, consisting of 1,000 acres or more. It was difficult to buy such a large area by oneself, so several people would band together and buy the land communally, forming syndicates, with each one owning some 100 acres. They had to choose a trustee to look after them all, and Mr M. was such a trustee. He needed boys to work the plots, because his son had become a teacher and 'no longer worked'.

At 3 a.m. the lads had to get up and work the farm, ploughing, weeding and looking after the cattle. They then went to school, but as soon as school was over they had to work again. They received no pay, merely board and lodging, and the food was meagre. It was very hard work; 'You were really used as a sort of slave, and you were never one of the family.' He nevertheless completed the two last standards in two years.

Then a wonderful thing happened. Mother received R200 from the Government as compensation for father's death. 'Really, father's death was a stroke of luck.' With the money he could do his J.C. in one of the large rural boarding schools. He had wanted to continue to Matric level, but there was no more money; and he could not get a scholarship from the Anglicans because he had never been to an Anglican school, and no other Mission Church would help him as he was, at that time, still a practising Anglican.

The bright boy who got all the scholarships

'Exemplary, wonderful!' is how J. O. described his home life. 'My parents owned a large property, about 300 Morgen, and I had a popular father who had a stock of pedigree cattle which is still, up to this day, the pride of the home.

'Father was of the opinion that successful farming did not need education. He himself had only Std. III.' He had been a a first-born and had acquired his grandfather's property by a simple business deal. Grandfather had willed his property to be shared by all his children, by division, and father had subsequently bought up all their shares, for which he paid cash. To do this he bonded his property and the lawyers advanced him the cash, nearly R2,000. But there was still R400 plus interest outstanding, and when J.O. grew up and, as eldest son, was going to inherit everything, his father required him to pay this bond which he did during the first five years of his working and earning life.

An Anglican Mission school was near, so he went there when he was seven. 'I had to do herding and I went to school only once a week', J.O. explained. Nevertheless, after only eight years and at the age of 14 he completed Std. VI. J.O. himself was not too keen on education but 'the European teachers always preached the need for education and gave me private tuition'. All the time his father had been against his first-born's education, but 'father was surrounded by the Anglican missionary teachers, who always visited our home', and finally had to give in. He did not have to spend much on his son, because J.O. won all the scholarships. But not at first. At 14 he was under age (the usual age was 18) for teacher training, 'so we cheated my age and the African Principal of the primary school forged father's signature, for his permission. When father saw the application form with his signature he was tongue tied, for he respected the teacher. So father had to agree, although he had wanted me to work on the farm.' He passed his first year N.P.L. 1st class at St Matthew's (Anglican) and obtained a scholarship for the remaining two years. When J.O. returned home after that first year, father started boasting all round the community that he had a brilliant son who had won a scholarship and would be an asset to his people. Then he bought his first-born a new set of clothes, and became interested in his education.

'At that time,' Mr J.O. explained, 'there was a general inspiration for advancement in our area. After the frustrations of the war, there was a general upsurge and consciousness about education. People heard lectures from missionaries, teachers and ministers, and learned that their sons must be educated in order to fit into the new social pattern.' Each time he obtained yet another scholarship the Anglican fathers told him that they helped him so that he could, in his turn, help his own people.

'Moreover, I was the eldest. I had to pave the way for the others. The way I went determined the fate of all my brothers and sisters. Had I not done well, the others would have been doomed.'

He did well. Having completed his N.P.L., he followed this with J.C., also at St Matthew's on a scholarship, in one year. A European teacher gave him private tuition. He then won another scholarship for N.P.H. at St. Matthew's. 'I always passed first-class,' Mr J.O. added, and he ended this part of his life story with, 'I certainly was their bright boy!'

Three lucky boys
  Mr G. G.

Mr G.G. was an only child, until his mother died and his father married again. His father, who belonged to the Amazizi clan of the Fingo, qualified as a teacher and became, in addition, a preacher in the Methodist Church. He was once a delegate to the Synod 'which shows his position'. Also, through the premature death of his elder brother, the father had inherited the family farm, which was on a 20-acre plot, and with it came many cattle, sheep, goats and horses.

Mother was also a teacher, and all her people had been teachers and were interested in education. She had higher aims than just teaching; she wanted him to obtain a university degree at Fort Hare. As both parents were always moving about, he was brought up with his mother's people, who were even more important than his father's people. First his maternal grandmother had looked after him, and, when she died, his mother's sister brought him up. They had a big farm and he had a very comfortable life. He had everything he wanted and was thoroughly spoiled. He never did any work on the farm. He started school at the age of 7 and by the time he was 14 had completed Std. VI. As he was then still too young to go to college, he spent a year with his mother's sister, who had in the interim moved to an urban location. Her husband was a minister.

He should really have gone on to high school, but in those days only Lovedale (Presbyterian) gave secondary education, and his parents were staunch Methodists and did not like it. However, all his mother's sisters had been trained at St Matthew's (Anglican) and had a soft spot for it. So when he was old enough he entered St Matthew's to begin training for N.P.L. He passed his first year with a first-class pass and as St Matthew's had no higher course in those days, he moved to

135

Lovedale for N.P.H. Father had in the meantime retired, and mother paid for this phase of his education. He then obtained a Principalship and registered as a Matric student with the University of South Africa, because most other principals had Matric and he said to himself: 'I'll show them!' He 'just got the syllabus and the books', after which he continued to be promoted, but then he had 'bad luck' and was demoted to a simple assistant-teacher's post at a secondary school in the Transvaal. There he found that 'all my colleagues were graduates and I was always snubbed by them, although I was told that I was a better teacher'. He had to do something about this so he registered with the University of South Africa for a Bachelor's degree, which he obtained five years later, majoring in Native Administration and Xhosa.

Mr L.L.

Mr L.L.'s father had always been very progressive, although he was a first-born. This was why he had left his father's father's place (obviously father's father did not share these progressive ideas), and gone to father's father's second brother 'who lived nearer to education', and whom he persuaded to allow him to go to school. His father then passed his J.C. at Lovedale and even obtained a Higher Teachers' Certificate. He never taught, but instead became a clerk in the Native Recruiting Corporation of his area, for he had his own farm and was a successful agriculturist.

In spite of his education, father had inherited a large part of his own father's cattle and money, although most of his father's possessions had been divided up among the three brothers. This inheritance enabled him to buy himself a good farm.

So much for father.

Mother too was a 'higher-qualified' teacher. She was the daughter of the founder of one of the largest high-status independent African Churches, to which father also belonged. This was how they had met and married.

Father's farm was 'prolific', and he made good profits. 'We had lots of eggs, milk and meat. All types of vegetables were in our garden, and the fields produced plenty.'

Mr L.L. went to school at seven. This was early, and was due to the fact that his older brother was being held back to wait for him, as they had to go to school together. School was far away and 'we had to walk quite a bit every day, but that made us healthy.' Later, however, they went on horseback.

He completed Std. VI at the age of 14, and at 15 had entered Lovedale as a boarder to train for N.P.L. 'as a stepping stone to whatever would happen later'. He and his older brother went together to Lovedale, after which he studied for his Matric, also at Lovedale. 'When you do Matric after Teacher Training', he explained, 'you get a concession, so that you can do it in a shorter time.' But he failed his first year. (He told us that he was doing commercial Matric, and the teachers for that course were scarce.) He was then advised to complete J.C. first, which he did after which he passed his Matric.

Because of this delay, his three younger brothers as well as his younger sister 'were coming up' close behind him, and they were now ready for higher training. Father could not afford to send all of them to Fort Hare, and as the two eldest brothers already had a profession, they had to 'go out and start work'. Two of the younger brothers then went to Fort Hare, the sister started training as a nurse and the younger brother was sent to an agricultural college, because he was to continue to run the farm for all of them and look after the parents in their old age.

During all the time that the six children were being educated, two squatter families lived on the farm and kept it going.

'No, of course, the squatters' children could not go to school. School was not for squatters' children. My father wouldn't have allowed them to stay on our land if their children did not work for father.'

At present the youngest brother is looking after the farm. Mother, who is now a widow, lives with him, and our 'lucky boy' goes there regularly on holidays because, like all the other siblings, he considers it 'home'.

Mr N.G.

His father's father had been 'a sort of Headman with three wives', and father had been the third son of a Junior House; and those sons 'take more readily to education as they have no cattle inheritance'. Whereas his father's father had been somewhat suspicious about education, a European minister had put pressure on him, until his father received permission to stay with the minister at Lovedale.

In the afternoons his father had worked in the house and garden, and in the mornings he received training as a teacher. After completing his training, however, he had found employment at a Fraser shop. He told his son afterwards that teachers were very poorly-paid, and this job gave better remuneration. After a while he left the shop for a near-by country town, where he started his own business.

137

Father was very keen on the education of his children. N.G., a first-born and only son, however, 'hated school'. In the location of the little country town where he was born he went to school at 10. But that was when he had started schooling in earnest. Before that he had run away several times to work on various farms in the neighbourhood, and he had been brought back each time by his father.

'My father did everything for me. He brought me up, he paid for all my education.' However, after six years' schooling in his home town, and when he was 16 years old, he had become so naughty that it was felt that another relative would be better able to control him and so father sent him to mother's brother's place.

He then ran away again, refusing all further education. He spent two years in various jobs as 'general labourer', until the hard work finally taught him to have high aims. The work was really too strenuous and it was an insecure existence, going from one job to another. When father finally called him back he was ready to go to school again.

He completed J.C. in two years, which was a mistake because he had no Latin or Maths and therefore could not do Matric. Instead he had to be content with S.C. Father then sent him straight on to Fort Hare where he obtained his College Education Diploma and a B.A. in three years. He was then 25 years old.

Immediately thereafter he married a girl who was also a teacher, and he got himself a job in a large and important high school, in which job he stayed seventeen years, the longest job duration in our whole sample. His salary in those years became finally four times as much as it was when he started.'

Secondary and higher education

Introduction

A thumb-nail sketch of the history of post-primary education in South Africa and some of its developments with particular reference to the academic and professional education of our sample,[25] may show something of the educational desert through which the elite had somehow to find their way to the small oases spread few and far between.

In 1841, Lovedale was opened by the missionaries of the Glasgow Missionary Society, and its name commemorates the Rev. John Love, the Society's first secretary. It started as an institution for the training of catechists and teachers, the two most urgently needed professions.

It was a mixed white–black institution; classes and literary societies were mixed, but dormitories and dining-hall tables, as well as all games were racially separated. In addition, land was acquired for agricultural purposes, because 'it was intended that students should labour on the land, partly for their sustenance, partly for their health while otherwise engaged in sedentary pursuits, and more than either that they might be able to instruct their countrymen afterwards, in the art of cultivating their own soil as well as in the things of religion'.[26]

Ever since those early days the controversy on certain issues, such as the medium of instruction, the inclusion in the curriculum of manual or practical work, and differentiated (i.e. adapted) education for Africans, has raged in South Africa.[27]

In 1916 the South African Native College of Fort Hare was opened by General Botha, and in 1924 the first graduation ceremony took place.[28] Fort Hare began by preparing Europeans and non-Europeans for the Cape University Matriculation Examination, and later restricted itself to post-matriculation work. In 1923 it became a University College, and the training of African Bachelors of Art began. In 1934 a Medical Aid Course was added and a B.Sc. Course became possible. In addition it provided Diplomas in Education, Theology and Agriculture.[29]

The first African university graduates from Fort Hare caused 'a real B.A. fever' to spread among the people, as we shall later hear one of the elite explain. Respondents told how everybody worth his salt wanted to do a B.A. Those who could not go to Fort Hare tried the coveted Bachelor's Degree through correspondence college courses. Here the sometimes unscrupulous college salesmen's talk and the often unethical promises and activities (which up to this day are still uncontrolled) contributed their share of casualties.

The Bachelor of Arts or Science Degrees remained the highest academic aspiration until, in 1940, the Johannesburg Hospital Board agreed to admit non-European students to the non-European wards for clinical instruction; and, in the next year, the first African students were invited to apply for the Medical Scholarships offered by the Bantu Welfare Trust. Therefore it was not before 1941 that the Witwatersrand University admitted Africans to its medical school. (The Natal Medical School, intended primarily for Africans, did not begin teaching until 1951.) Since then a thin but steady stream of African general practitioners has come from the so-called 'open' universities of the country. 'So-called' because only some University Departments were open for a limited number of Bantu, who were allowed to follow classes with the white students, but were debarred from the social and sports life of these 'open' universities. Fully multiracial universities with admission for all qualified students of all

M

races to all departments and to all their facilities and activities have never existed in South Africa.

By 1955, as many as fifty-five Bantu holders of state scholarships had gained the degree of M.B., B.Ch. until the Extension of University Education Act (No. 45 of 1959) refused registration at European universities to any further non-white students except by special permission of the Minister concerned. This permission has sometimes been granted.

In the years 1959–61, the period of the field research, two new University Colleges were opened exclusively for Africans: the University College of the North at Turfloop near Pietersburg, mainly for Sotho students; and the University College of Zululand at Ngoya for the Zulu and Swazi groups. New African students admitted to Fort Hare were henceforth to be selected mainly from the Xhosa-speaking tribes, while the University College of the Western Cape was opened near Cape Town, for coloured students. In 1961, the University College for Indians was opened in temporary premises near Durban. In 1961, there were 515 African students registered at the three Bantu colleges.[30] But over 1,000 Africans are registered annually for the correspondence classes of the multiracial University of South Africa.

Henceforth, all non-European medical students in South Africa received their pre-clinical training at Wentworth, near Durban. By June 1961, there were 112 Africans studying medicine in South Africa.[31] 105 of these students could have been receiving Government bursaries in any one year, but because of failures only 68 were doing so at the beginning of 1961. In 1959 there were 67 African medical practitioners and 18 interns registered with the Medical and Dental Council,[32] while the number of African lawyers was even smaller.

It was not until 1945 that the first two Africans were registered at the University of the Witwatersrand for the degree of LL.B. Neither of these two pioneers, however, completed his degree. Both left, probably after the second year, one to go into business and the other to continue, but working for the attorney's admission examination instead, as this can be prepared for by private study while the student is articled.

This line of study, for a law diploma rather than for a law degree, has since been followed by the majority. The study of law seems to be even more difficult for the South African Bantu than that of medicine, and the wastage in the University Departments of Law has always been high. We were told that of 30 entrants, an average of only one or two finally gain their LL.B. In June 1961, 29 Africans were taking law degrees and 50 were doing law diplomas in South Africa.[33] The number of African lawyers in the whole country varied. Unlike Bantu doctors, Bantu lawyers tended to enter the field of active politics; and, in recent years, a number have had to leave the country or cease practising.

In spite of these two important points of breakthrough, in medicine and in law, in 1961 Bantu still could not train as dentists and chemists, architects, chartered accountants or quantity surveyors – all those professions which coloureds or Indians had already entered. In June 1961 the first three Bantu were studying for a degree in engineering.

The rise of these higher professions eclipsed the light of the B.A., which thereafter lost some of its former glamour. After all, it was of pure academic value only. Unless one had in addition some form of specialized training, it had no practical value. In 1961 67 Africans received Bachelor's Degrees (against 37 coloureds and 79 Asians); only three obtained an Honours degree (against 5 coloureds and 9 Asians); only one a Master's degree, and only one a Doctorate.[34]

When, however, the universities offered Africans a degree in law, this did not necessarily mean that it was now also natural and easy for them to become articled, nor was the opening up of a science degree accompanied by the provision of suitable occupational opportunities for African science graduates. A flagrant example of the unplanned and uncoordinated development of African higher education and occupational opportunities was the institution of the B.Sc. Hygiene.[35] It had developed at Fort Hare, out of a course originally set up with the aims of supplementing the traditional skills of African 'witchdoctors', with some scientific training, thus equipping them as 'medical aides'. It had been generously subsidized by the Chamber of Mines, so that the B.Sc. Hygiene course was taught in the most lavish buildings of all at Fort Hare. However, there was not a great demand for training as medical aides; instead other degree-eager Africans avidly grasped this opportunity to obtain a university degree, whatever it was, together with the bursaries attached to it. After some years, however, it appeared that there were no jobs requiring this degree for Africans, nor jobs which offered a salary equitable for university graduates. The first twelve B.Sc. Hygiene graduates produced were all found to be employed in professions having nothing whatever to do with health or hygiene. One was found to have become a photographer – probably the nearest to the chemistry learned! Later, about 1953, the grant was transferred to the Department of Physiology at Natal, and the B.Sc. Hygiene as a degree disappeared.

We shall find among our sample a few persons who did or hoped to do this degree because 'there was a bursary attached to it', and 'as a stepping stone to Medicine'. Another person found, on arrival at Fort Hare, that the B.Sc. Hygiene he had wanted to do and for which he had obtained a bursary had, in the meantime, been withdrawn. He entered for B.Sc. instead, because for this he could obtain another bursary from the Government. In this endeavour he subsequently failed, and his bursary was withdrawn. Fortunately, he could then enter a newly-instituted Health Inspector's course, and he chose this because 'it was the nearest I could get to an independent profession'.

Some responsible and knowledgeable Europeans realized this lack of synchronization, but were powerless to do anything about it because the fields of African education, African occupational opportunities and African administration were controlled by a number of different institutional and official agencies, and influenced by opposing socio-economic forces and policies. The missionaries, who controlled education in the days when the elite grew up, saw only two needs: the need for teachers and for ministers for their ever-increasing African schools and congregations. At the same time the need for more and more African administrators and public servants, to man the ever-expanding public and social services in an emergent society, arose in a world beyond their vision and naturally fell outside their competence.

When the universities opened some of their departments to Africans, Matriculation received its first boost. At the start it had been mainly a prestige qualification, probably because of its general uselessness. Those professions and white-collar jobs which needed matriculants were generally still closed to Africans. Neither had the European private sector any need yet for African matriculants.

Up to 1932–3 students prepared for Matric at only one institution in the country – Fort Hare; and even the Junior Certificate could be obtained in only two schools in Natal and two in the Cape. In the Transvaal it was not until 1934–5 that three colleges started, more or less simultaneously, to train students for J.C. These were Kilnerton (Methodist), St Peter's (Anglican) and Lemana (Swiss Mission). By 1940 the first two colleges could offer matriculation. In 1942 Orlando High and Madebane High, both in Johannesburg, added two more high schools to this small number, but this time for day scholars only.

This means that up to the late thirties, in the Transvaal and the Free State, all post-primary education and in the other two provinces most of the post-primary education was limited to teacher training. It also means that when World War II was over, there were too few mature matriculants with which to begin the building of a trained Bantu civil service and to proceed with the rapid Africanization of Bantu Administration. Yet only such a Bantu public service could provide suitable high-status jobs for well-educated Africans who had not been trained as teachers, for the process of increasing African employment in responsible jobs in the private sector of the country was proceeding at a snail's pace.

For the nascent African public service this meant that the earliest recruits had to be drawn from people who had been trained for a

142

different purpose and had insufficient academic background. For African education it meant that for many years to come the educational system was burdened with a great many teachers inadequately and too hurriedly trained – persons who should never have been teachers, never wanted to be teachers, inevitably proved bad teachers, and who, ever since, have been moving out of the profession. A spate of them left after, rarely because of the promulgation of the Bantu Education Act, profiting from the mood of sympathy which the Act engendered among wide circles of Europeans both in and outside South Africa.

The result of this can be seen in the careers of the elite. Almost two-thirds of them had been trained as teachers, and as many as twenty-six had originally only the Native Primary Lower Certificate. From this point of view their subsequent educational and occupational history can be seen as one long and painful struggle to compensate for earlier educational inadequacies, or wrong vocational choices.

The colleges

After Std. VI had been successfully passed, almost all scholars could at once proceed to the next educational step. Five refused at first. (There was a six-months' period between the end of primary school and the beginning of term in the colleges. These six months, when the young men 'loitered around' or 'went for confirmation or initiation', were a great temptation.) Later those five were, however, only too glad to return to school. Only two were prevented by unfavourable family circumstances from continuing their education, and had to start working. This shows that we were dealing with an exceptionally privileged group, whose general circumstances were favourable to the new orientation. Either they themselves were eager to enter the modern world more fully, or they had parents or rearers who were education-oriented and well-connected, and who were, if necessary, able to control those adolescents who needed it.

Post-primary education, particularly for the older members of the elite, meant almost automatically teacher training. 'It was the thing to do; there was nothing better if you wanted to become an educated man,' they explained. 'Teaching was popular; everyone wanted to become a teacher'; 'It was the only type of education considered as "educated" ', or 'It just came like that. I didn't think any further'. It was 'the only attractive profession'; everybody wanted their children to be teachers. Such had been the most frequent reasons for entering a teacher-training college.[36] Obviously, the parents and missionaries sometimes exerted considerable pressure, and quite a number of our respondents confessed that they had simply been 'told' to go to college by father or mother or by father's brother or by an elder brother; or perhaps by the bishop, the missionary or the school superintendent. In fact, someone else had made the decision for them, and they had simply done as they had been told.

Parents were often anxious for their sons, particularly the eldest, to complete their teacher training quickly, so that they could start earning as soon as possible and help with the education of the other siblings, while the missionaries were anxious to fill the many teaching posts vacant everywhere. This was the reason why even those who had sincerely wanted to teach after completing J.C. or Matric, had to content themselves with a lower teacher's certificate. However, some of the elite, and especially the younger ones and the ones from the Eastern Cape,[37] had been more privileged than the others, and were able to obtain a higher teacher's diploma.

About 17 per cent of the teacher-trained chose the profession as a *faute de mieux*; they had failed in a more ambitious project and this had left teaching as the only profession still open to them with their current qualifications. It was also thought that a teacher's certificate could still be 'a stepping stone' for something better later – and indeed it often was. Moreover, this thought provided a consolation for the fact that one had had to settle for something which was at present considered rather lowly.

All these neutral and even negative reasons for entering upon teacher training really amounted to the fact that teaching was the shortest cut to a profession. Mphahlele wrote: 'While guest speakers continue each year on school speech days to tell you that the African must make the best use of his opportunities so as to "uplift" his fellow men, you know nothing could be farther from your intentions. You want to get a better job and earn a living and support your parents and their other children. You are dogged by a ghastly sense of insecurity. You must seek a short cut to a profession. Teaching is the nearest.'[38] It did not matter what this profession entailed. Moreover, in most colleges teacher training seems to have been slightly cheaper than Junior Certificate. On the other hand, it could not be done by correspondence course, but only in relatively expensive missionary teacher-training colleges. When Africans talk about 'my college', they do not mean a university, as Americans would, but a post-primary institution, possibly because it almost always meant a teacher-training college, or possibly because of the custom of 'Up-naming' (see pp. 186ff.).

Again, like the primary schools, almost 80 per cent of these colleges, i.e. most secondary schools and all teacher-training colleges attended by our elite, had been founded and were run by missionaries, with or without Government subsidies. But unlike the primary schools, these missionary colleges and the education received in them were almost always praised by our respondents for the excellence of their teachers ('Mine were mainly imported from Europe and these are far better than our own. And they did not mind whether they were teaching natives or Europeans.') and the quality of their teaching ('Now we have South Africans, whites but particularly blacks, and they're all bad, and the results are weaker'). There were as many strikes as today, 'but in those days the strikes were about food; nowadays they're about politics'.

A number of individuals mentioned that they had had great difficulties in adapting themselves, and here the difference between urban and rural boys showed. (Cf. Chapter 2, pp. 79ff.)

Some of the defects of the decentralized system of education which we noted in primary-school education, were also evidenced in secondary schools. Missionary rivalries often prevented inter-college sports competitions, although in all fairness it must be added that this was before 1938. In the tremendous upsurge in African education which followed Dr W. W. M. Eiselen's appointment as Chief Inspector of Native Education, many new and younger white teachers, English and Afrikaans, brought new and different attitudes into the mission schools. Soon Kilnerton and Bochabelo got together to arrange the first inter-sports competitions.[39] Some of our elite were, at first, handicapped in their careers because, as we shall see on p. 178, they had been brought up in the 'wrong' religion, or had studied the wrong subjects. In some colleges Afrikaans was not taught and the teaching and speaking of Afrikaans was even forbidden. In other colleges English was badly taught. Later such omissions were serious handicaps. Bantu languages gave similar trouble.

But most criticism dealt with the limited number of subjects taught. Not that the elite wanted more academic subjects. Interest in purely academic topics appeared almost nil. But they would have wanted 'more technical subjects', or 'more arts and crafts'. They did not mean fine, or even applied, art but useful subjects such as electricity, radio assembly, motor mechanics and particularly commercial subjects; in fact, any subject which would help them to earn money in self-employment.

One is filled with admiration for those European college teachers who needed all the devotion, the patience and the capacity for hard work they could muster in order to cope with students from an entirely different world, with the most varied educational backgrounds, of widely divergent educational levels and ages, who were, in addition, not always quite sure that they wanted to become teachers at all. Yet there was seldom a failed N.P.H., and very few failed N.P.L.s among the elite. (See the explanation of these terms on p. 301.)

Some of our more mature respondents realized the tremendous efforts of these early missionaries to enlarge the syllabus and to transform the prescribed subjects into more general civilizing media, but most respondents complained of a supposed discrimination.

In spite of all these minor criticisms, however, almost all the elite had the happiest memories of their colleges, and they wanted their children to go to these same rural colleges, although they suspected that great changes had taken place. They blamed these changes on the disappearance of those gratefully remembered missionary teachers to whom all that was good was due, and on their replacement by Africans.[40]

Bursaries and scholarships

Second only to the generally restricted and restrictive conditions of education, poverty was probably the most important obstacle to be conquered in the educational progress of the elite. Post-primary education was expensive. In those days, liberal opinion was paternalistic and assimilationist, and it was still widely believed that Africans could benefit from western education only if they were removed as far as possible from their home atmosphere. Consequently, all post-primary mission schools were boarding schools. In the Transvaal the first two high schools for day scholars were started by the Government. Cf. p. 142.) This increased educational expenses considerably. Parents now had to provide annually anything from R20 to R50 for fees and some R10 to R14 for books, as well as the train fare to and from college, and the not inexpensive uniform and other special items of clothing.

Although most parents were said to have been quite satisfactorily situated, their wealth was still mainly counted in cattle and land use. R50 annually for a son's schooling seemed a heavy burden indeed on the basis of salaries which rarely exceeded R10 or R15 per month. A son at college meant, therefore, the sale of cattle, and many a father needed considerable reassurances about later repayments to consent to this what he called, 'sacrifice'. It is telling that *Ego* himself never paid for his own teacher training. (See Table II 3:3.) He had either a bursary or, far more frequently, his parents and other kin paid for his teacher training, and this explains why the careers of the teachers were more than usually influenced by family considerations. (See p. 178.) Thus, in the case of our elite, actual cash poverty could hardly be distinguished from the oppressive family commitments which came to burden any educated member of the kinship system.

Added to this, many parents had the wrong idea about the possible cost of their sons' education, owing to the exaggerated reports which circulated among the families. 'Out of pride and jealousy', as we

146

were told, neighbours exaggerated the amounts of money which their children's further education was costing them. It was a matter of no little prestige to have 'a son at college', and prestige thrives on rarity. Having already made the sacrifice of selling some heads of cattle and doing without his son's labour, a father wanted his son at least to be the only or the first one with a college education in the community. In this, as in so many other fields, Africans did not contribute much to the spread of new ideas among themselves. On the other hand, it was precisely this competitive spirit which encouraged further education and helped the missionaries in their recruiting drives.

Table II 3:3 Numerical distribution of all respondents by the main examinations, certificates and degrees attempted,* according to how the fees were met

Educational level	Bur-saries/ scholar-ships†	Ego	Parents and relatives	Parents and Rela-tives and bursaries/ scholar-ships	Ego and bursaries /scholar-ships	Total
Junior Certificate	6	15	30	—	—	51
Senior Certificate and Matricula-tion	5	28	13	—	—	46
Teacher's Certificate	8	—	26	7	—	41
Other Types of Professional Training	16	8	1	2	1	28
Bachelor's Degree (B.A., B.Sc., B.Com.)	6	10	3	—	1	20
Total	41	61	73	9	2	186

* Failures and drifts are included.

† In our respondents' reports, scholarships, bursaries and loan bursaries could not always be reliably distinguished. Although some respondents knew that scholarships were 'for merit' and bursaries 'for poverty', the distinction was not as clear cut. Among some respondents there was, moreover, a tendency to mention financial assistance as scholarships rather than as bursaries. For this reason we did not insist on a distinction.

The tremendous financial effort which the further education of the elite represented, can be appreciated only if it is realized that many of them were not scholarship boys. Certainly, a total of 52 bursaries/ scholarships were counted among the 60 persons, but these bursaries concerned only 30 individuals, and covered only one-quarter of all the main post-Std. VI courses of study attempted. (See Table II 3:3.) Half of these 30 individuals had only the one bursary. Of the other half, most had two different bursaries and some had received three or even four bursaries for different courses of study. While some of the bursaries, therefore, definitely seemed to have had reference to the particular gifts of a particular individual selected for advancement by the bursary givers (e.g. The 'bright boy', p. 133), it would appear that most bursaries aimed at selecting individuals for specific posts or professions. All seven ministers and all three doctors, but only one-third of the teachers, received all or part of their professional training through bursaries. (See Table II 3:3.) Of the more recently opened-up professions, the majority were filled by bursaries.

The lowest number of scholarships were for academic training. In those days it was still considered to be without much practical value. And indeed, most of the scholarships for J.C., Matriculation and B.A. were given to those who already had teachers' certificates in order to assist them in improving the qualifications for their current profession or for a different occupation altogether. This system of attaching bursaries to certain professions rather than to certain deserving individuals, not only contributed to the lack of opportunity for acquiring a general, rounded-off system of knowledge, but it also encouraged the already prevalent non-directed attitudes towards education.

The elite never tired of assuring us that, in their youth, scholarships were rare. In view of this, we were rather surprised to find that no more than half had ever tried to earn some money towards their educational expenses during out-of-school hours or during college holidays.

The kind of holiday jobs done were as follows: (Unpaid) Pastoral/Agricultural Work only, 16; (Unpaid) Pastoral/Agricultural Work and Paid Jobs, 18; Paid Jobs only, 13; No (unpaid) Pastoral/Agricultural Work and no Paid Jobs, 13.

This cannot be explained by the fact that more than half of them had to spend their out-of-school hours herding the family cattle, for by the time the lad went to college, he had given up this duty and it had devolved upon another member of the family. Herding was not considered a job of work, but rather part of the rural way of life (similarly the domestic chores some young urban men had to do were considered part of urban life), for which no payment was expected. But other forms of farm labour, and particularly 'ploughing', were always mentioned separately, usually as onerous impositions on individuals who considered themselves to be budding white-collar workers. Nevertheless, most of the paid jobs which the young men could obtain were manual or semi-manual, as this seems the usual characteristic of all stop-gap and temporary jobs, as, for instance, in the U.S.A. (see Chapter 4, pp. 215ff.)

Also the kinds of jobs they had taken on seemed the usual ones. They had worked in shops as delivery boys and cleaners; packed or unpacked groceries; acted as hawkers of sweets and oranges; cleaned cars and bicycles; been dish-washers, waiters, etc. Newspaper sellers were in the majority. 'Daka boys' and golf caddies came next. The following attitudes appear typical.

'During holidays I worked for a private building contractor as Daka boy, mixing and bringing the cement, and the year after that again. That was when they were building the Pretoria Hospital. I earned R1·50 per week. That was big pay. After a while the foreman discovered that I was educated and talked English, and he took me round on his inspections and I interpreted for him. Later when they found out that I could read and write English, they asked me to write their letters for them in English. Most of the white building workers were illiterate. This I did during Saturdays and Sundays and I got 10 cents per letter. This money allowed me to have a tailor-made suit made by an Indian tailor for R8. A little later I could afford to have the waistcoat made for R1. Also I was buying books.'

'While working as a caddy, I was always thinking about the future. Naturally, you want to imitate your man. He was very rich, a Jew, but very kind. I thought that when I was educated sufficiently I would also play golf. But he couldn't write a letter without mistakes. Still, he was always willing to help me . . .'

The money earned was generally spent on clothes, seldom on books and only once on university fees. It was quite amazing how well remembered were those first ties and shirts and waistcoats!

Certainly these people had been used to rely heavily on the missionaries and on the benevolent attention and assistance from their European contacts. Most of our respondents were very concerned about the changes which had taken place since. 'True, in those days bursaries were scarce, but it was easy to get them. Nowadays there are more bursaries but it is more difficult to get them.' Frankly, they did not like the present situation in which the earlier missionary paternalism and the personal influence of the European were increasingly being replaced by the state and by the impersonality of a growing bureaucratization. 'In the olden days you needed only one person who liked you, and then all was easy. Now you must have so many recommendations and references.' Many such statements during our conversations on these topics showed the growing unease of people for whom all relationships were still conceived in terms of

149

personalities. 'In these days you can't get through any more,' they complained. 'The trouble is that nowadays we do not know any more whom to please.'

Certainly, not to know 'whom to please' was far worse than 'having to please someone', for people who had been accustomed from the start to depend on the more wealthy and dominant sector of the South African population and on overseas benefactors, all of whom were anxious to encourage the education of Africans. 'To please the missionaries was easy, you only had to go to church for it. But nowadays . . .' Moreover, when the elite were of school age, Africans knew many more Europeans, while now, despite increased social contact with private individuals, 'there are no more mixed committees where you get to know them'.

> 'Before, you only got scholarships when your father was well-known to the Europeans. You had to get on the right side of the missionaries because everything was in their hand. To a certain extent it is still like that, only now it is no longer the missionaries and you don't go to church for it.
>
> 'Now with all the Government people giving scholarships, all you have to do is to work hard, show good results, and forget politics. This, of course, creates the habit.
>
> 'But with the Anglicans and the Institute of Race Relations it's different.[41] They like you to be political and pro-English, because they themselves are against the Government and they do not like the Afrikaners.
>
> 'So you see, Mrs Brandel, you've got to know well beforehand where you want to apply for your son's bursary . . .'

As always, *Paris vaut bien une messe*; and this applies today even more than it did when our elite began their careers.

Study by correspondence course

In addition to the fact that further education, so persistently pursued, had for the most part to be undertaken without the aid of bursaries, most post-primary education, particularly the more purely academic examinations, had to be undertaken by private study while the students were employed in full-time jobs. In terms of examinations this meant that for about half of the academic examinations attempted by our elite at the secondary level, study was by correspondence course. (See Table II 3:4.) The higher the examination the less likely that it could be taken in an institution and after full-time study. One-third of the Junior Certificates, nearly all of the Senior Certificates, and the majority of the Matriculations had to be completed by correspondence courses. And on the university level only a minority of the various university degrees which the elite had hoped to obtain, were attempted at a university with the stimulating companionship of fellow-students.

However, it is even more important to look at the people concerned rather than at the examinations. Seen from the point of view of the individuals, the pathetic fact is revealed that only eighteen of them, i.e. not yet one-third of the total, never attempted to take any examinations by correspondence course. And, among these, four never went further than J.C. or not even up to J.C. The others comprised all three doctors, and more than half of the ministers and younger professionals – those who, in other respects, were shown to have been specially privileged. It would appear that the greatest belated educational efforts were made by the present school principals and the clerks, nearly all of whom tried to pass not only one

Table II 3:4 Numerical distribution of the elite by the results of all academic examinations attempts by correspondence course or at college

Educational level	By correspondence course		At college or university		Total	
Junior Certificate:		17		34		51
passed	14		32		46	
failed	1		2		3	
drifted	2		—		2	
Senior Certificate:		13		2		15
passed	6		2		8	
failed	3		—		3	
drifted	4		—		4	
Matriculation:		17		14		31
passed	11		11		22	
failed	4		3		7	
drifted	2		—		2	
Bachelor Degree:*		13		9		22
passed	4		6		10	
failed	1		4		1	
drifted†	8		3		11	
Totals	60		59		119	

* Those who tried to do an examination by correspondence course as well as at a college have been placed under the institution which they attempted last. If these double attempts had been added, the number of exams attempted and failed by correspondence course would have been higher.

† 'Drifted' here includes those who failed first or second year and discontinued, as well as those who let their study drift at the first- or second-year stage, without trying to pass the next examination.

but even two educational hurdles through private study. Four persons tried to pass through as many as three successive educational stages by private study.

Considering the piecemeal way in which further education was so often painstakingly and belatedly acquired, and the amount of study by correspondence course which this entailed, the failure rate cannot even be called high. Naturally, correspondence courses resulted in a greater number of failures and these increased on the higher levels. The lowest number of failures occurred for J.C. and the highest for S.C. This last examination was generally taken as an alternative to Matriculation if the latter proved too difficult, or after the student had already failed it. S.C. lent itself to study by correspondence, because it could be taken a few subjects at a time. The passing of the S.C. was often a person's last hope of reaching a higher salary scale in his job. Of all the occupational groups, the higher teachers, the doctors and the younger professionals showed the fewest Matric/S.C. failures. However, Table II 3 : 4 does not show how many examinations were passed after one or more failures. Neither does the table show the number of interruptions between the various educational stages.

Our case records revealed that scarcely one-quarter of the elite were able to go as far as they went without interruption. However, in most cases this was not very far; generally only to J.C., and in three cases to Matric or N.P.H. Twenty-two individuals had had one interruption in their educational progress, sixteen were interrupted twice, and as many as seven reached their present educational level after three or more interruptions.

However, 'interruption' is not really the correct term to use. It implies that the young man planned his scheme of education beforehand, and that in between the different stages he worked until he had saved enough money, persuaded parents or kin to give him the money, or succeeded in obtaining a bursary for the next stage. To some extent this applied to those who had been driven by circumstances into seeking an early professional qualification in N.P.L. until they had earned some money and/or fulfilled their family commitments, and could allow themselves the luxury of an 'egoistic' pursuit of the missed J.C. or the N.P.H. In this manner 17 of the 26 N.P.L.-qualified teachers completed their J.C.s at a later stage, and most of them had to continue teaching while doing so. But even among these lower-qualified teachers it was not always easy to know whether this later J.C. was part of a well-thought-out earlier plan, or simply an idea which arose later.

For this was what generally happened. Respondents began the work for which they were trained, and did not undertake further training until it became clear that any further promotion or increase in salary was impossible unless a further qualification was obtained, or new occupations and professions or higher executive posts in their own lines became available for Africans.

Consequently, our elite usually took more than the normal number of years over their exams and degrees, and they did not pass the various educational stages until at a very much older than the normal age. (See Table II 3:5.)

With regard to the first point, the average time which the elite needed to complete the two years from J.C. to Matric was 2·73 years, while S.C. took an average of 4·12 years. Similarly, it took our elite an average of more than four years to complete the three years' Bachelor's Degree course.

With regard to the second point, the average age at which Matriculation was obtained was 23·68, but S.C. was not acquired until the members of the elite were nearly thirty-five years old and again the Bachelor's gown could not be donned until an average age of nearly thirty-five years was reached.

Table II 3:5 Numerical distribution of the elite by the average age at which they completed and the average number of years they took to complete the main academic examinations

N = 59

Kind of examination	Number of individuals	Average age	Average number of years
Std . VI	59	16·42	8·25
Junior Certificate:			
at once	29	19·55	2·93
later	17	26·59	1·77
Senior Certificate:			
at once	2	21·50	2·50
later	6	39·34	4·67
Matriculation:			
at once	10	21·30	2·20
later	12	28·67	3·67
Bachelor's Degree:			
at once	2	23	3
later	6	35·67	4·50

However, these averages conceal the differences between the lucky ones who could pass the various educational stages in the proper order, without too many interruptions, and those who had to acquire their education in bits and pieces, often in a somewhat erratic manner. In Table II 3:5 the two groups have been distinguished. Take, for instance, the J.C.'s: the lucky group of twenty-nine individuals who could do their J.C. immediately after completing primary school, averaged 19·55 years of age, whereas the unlucky group of seventeen individuals was 26·59. The former group took 2·93 years to complete it, while the latter took much less time, namely 1·77 years as most of them had already N.P.L., after which J.C. could be done in one year. Comparing the lucky ten who were able to complete Matric at once after J.C., we found that it took them an average of 2·20 years, but those who had to pass Matric later in their working lives, needed 3·67 years. Furthermore, the lucky group had an average age of 21·30, about the same as those who passed S.C. immediately after J.C. But an unlucky majority could not pass their Matriculation until they averaged 28·67 years of age, and S.C. was not acquired until they were almost forty years of age.

The two who were able to study for their Bachelor's Degree immediately after Matric (and did not fail) averaged twenty-three years, whereas the six who had to complete later in life were as old as 35·67 when they finally obtained the degree.

Educational mobility

Excluding the doctors, we found only four persons among those twenty-two who ever tried to obtain a university degree who were able to go straight to a university after completing Matric. These four were, not surprisingly, the two youngest health inspectors, one secondary-school teacher and the R.C. priest – people who had, in one form or another, enjoyed exceptional support and assistance. One of the health inspectors became the recipient of one of those B.Sc. Hygiene bursaries mentioned on pp. 141–2; the other health inspector and the secondary-school teacher (Mr N. G. – see p. 137) had exceptional fathers; and the priest was an exceptional case altogether.

In contrast to the other ministers who had all received their ministerial training after they had already been working for some years in other capacities, the R.C. priest had been selected and trained for the ministry at an early age. Undoubtedly the most systematically and carefully educated person in Reeftown, he showed what could have been achieved with these culturally mobile, eager and pliant human beings if their education had been from the first better planned, adapted and guided. Unfortunately the benefits of his better-integrated knowledge never reached the community at large because of the lack of participation of the R.C. Church in township affairs.

It is only when contemplating such exceptions that the educational careers of our elite can be seen as the haphazard, happy-go-lucky things they had been. As many as three-quarters of them reached their present educational levels in several (ranging from two to five) disjointed, time-separated and badly integrated educational spurts.

That such a manner of improving the originally inadequate educational qualifications required a considerable mobility was self-evident. This general mobility (an educational mobility in a much wider sense than the usual) expressed itself in various kinds of changes and changeabilities. We noted continuous changes from one diploma to another, and from one college to another; from private study to institutional study, and back again to private study in the course of attempting only one educational stage; from employment to school and back again to employment; from self-payment to bursary, and after failure back again to self-payment. It was a mobility which also operated in a switch-over from the favours of one protective missionary or Government agency to another; an easy forsaking of one bursary giver for another; the abandonment of one denomination for a more powerful, richer or more generous church; the change in political adherence or organizational membership. And finally, this mobility also obtained in the capacity to turn an educational failure in one direction into a subsequent success in an entirely different direction.

In order to show something of the actual dynamism of the educational progress of the elite of Reeftown, the educational chart has been devised. It is far from perfect. The need for anonymity and the desire for clarity necessitated certain simplifications. Except the three types of teacher training and doctor training, other types of specialized training, by which persons could be identified, have been left unspecified. Minor professional courses, for instance, in a language, physical education, book-keeping, journalism, salesmanship have been omitted. The many interruptions, as discussed earlier, nor the number of years taken, have been indicated. As to Matric/S.C. it has not been shown whether Matric was tried and failed and subsequently S.C. was granted or obtained in a second attempt, or whether S.C. had been intended from the start. Similarly, various failures in attempting some examination until ultimate success was achieved have not been shown. Only the final result appears on the chart. Some of the Drifts (shown as D) may in reality have been Failures (shown as F). The expression frequently used was: 'I did not complete'. Thereupon it was often preferable not to pursue the painful matter. But we hope that the chart can, nevertheless, convey an overall impression of ceaseless endeavour against great obstacles.

The main stages in the educational progress of fifty-nine individuals have been set out, starting from the moment of completion of primary school, when the group split into two streams: the N.P.L. stream and the J.C. stream. The former contained those who were induced to seek the shortest, and often the only, route to a profession. The latter consisted of those who 'were lucky'. These

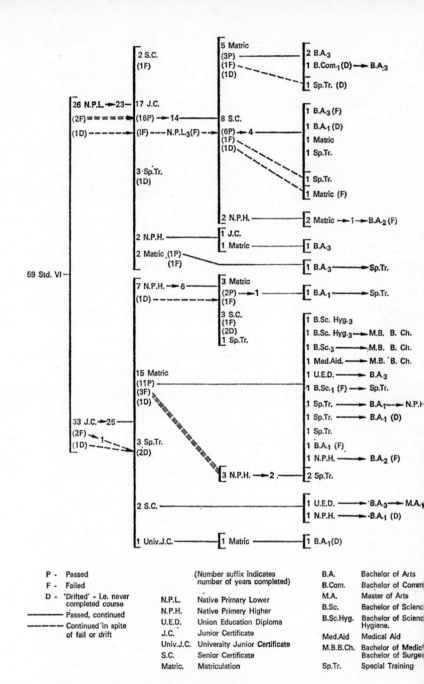

Figure 2 The progressive development of the elite towards their present educational level

156

two streams represented the first educational inequality in our elite.

The J.C. stream contained more people from the Eastern Cape. The manner in which education originally arose in the Eastern Cape and from there spread northwards gave tremendous initial advantages to the people of the Cape, who belonged mainly to the Xhosa-speaking tribes. But, even more important, the J.C. stream also consisted of individuals who were younger than those in the N.P.L. stream. The average age of those in the J.C. stream was 40·56 (median age 41) years, while the average age of those in the N.P.L. stream was 49·68 (median age 50) years, i.e. a difference of almost ten years. In a world of rapidly widening horizons, each new generation begins again with a somewhat better start and at a somewhat higher level than the previous one. Each new generation finds again the going slightly easier and, what is more important, expects to find more opportunities on its way. This was clearly evident, for instance, in the educational histories of the three doctors, see pp. 167ff. This is an important source of the frustrations inherent in a quickly changing society (and will be discussed in a further book); it undoubtedly tends to deprive the older generation of a sense of achievement, but on the other hand it spurs them on to renewed efforts to keep pace with developments.

The N.P.L. stream then split into two main branches: the one consisted of those who took the longer and, possibly, more cautious road of first doing J.C. and only afterwards attempting Matric/S.C., or the higher teacher's certificate of N.P.H.; the other branch contained those who went directly for these aims. Of these only one reached the B.A.₃ level. The immense effort this must have represented can be gauged by the fact that it took him about ten years to complete Matric and B.A. Hence, as to time needed, his *tour de force* did not save him much in comparison with those who first did J.C., then Matric and then B.A. The two who did N.P.H. after N.P.L. were bursary cases. One of them made use of the concession given to holders of an N.P.H. certificate to complete Matric in one year, after which he then reached a B.A.₃. The other N.P.H. undertook the seemingly retrogressive step of a J.C. He was one of those cases who 'just bought the books'. He said he wanted 'to further his knowledge'. But, having thus found himself in a somewhat blind alley, he subsequently gave up the struggle.

The fortunate younger men in the J.C. stream also went two different ways: the one aimed at Matric/S.C. directly; the other, while ultimately arriving at the same goal, did so via a higher teacher's certificate, and a job. With these latter, as informants explained: 'The parents discovered that it was more expensive than they thought to keep a boy at college. How many more years does it take until my son brings back my money with higher learning?'

Nevertheless, the majority in the J.C. stream followed the direct Matric/S.C. road.

As was to be expected, a greater number in the J.C. stream reached university level than those in the N.P.L. stream (42 per cent as against 24 per cent). But if the doctors are excluded, then the N.P.L. stream really did better.

We see also the general trend towards teaching; first as the one and only educated profession, then as 'the poor man's profession', and finally, as 'the last hope profession'. This was particularly so after a Matric failure. Whereas a 'B.A. failed' was still something in itself, a 'Matric failed' remained nothing. One had 'nothing to call oneself by'. Yet the student's aspirations had been raised and it was difficult to reconcile himself to 'some form of manual labour'. A 'failed Matric' was more likely to become frustrated than a 'B.A. failed' and there were more of them too. Luckily many of our elite succeeded in finding openings in some form of specialized training after their Matric failure. Some of these had however been allowed to drift again. These were courses which were entirely unsuitable, or undertaken without proper guidance; or it was later discovered that there were either no examinations for Africans at the end or no occupational openings for Africans so qualified. Here is a great need, and more specialized courses with clear 'names' attached would be one solution to the increasing problem of the failed or second-class Matriculants.

One sees clearly, however, that our elite appeared to have been fortunate in having chanced upon some of the few special training courses which, besides training for the ministry, could still lead to a position of professional prestige after academic failures.

It was at first surprising to note the number of failures and drifts even in a generally successful group of people; the number of times a failed examination was tried again, and, when failure in one direction had finally to be acknowledged, the undaunted manner in which something else, sometimes even more difficult, was attempted. No less than 14 of the 25 'faileds' or 'drifts' (follow the dotted lines on the chart) stumbled on another field in which they then often succeeded.

The most extraordinary case, one which appears to combine a number of typical features, was certainly the one N.P.L. who left college before completing the courses (possibly because he failed the second year – though this was not clear: he complained about 'those bad teachers'). He then went to another college to have another try at J.C. but failed again. Having worked for a year as a clerk, he returned to college intending to make another attempt at N.P.L. but failed once more. Subsequently, he abandoned all attempts at further education and passed through a series of jobs in which he gradually advanced to better positions. Fifteen years later he returned to his books, intending to sit the Matric examination through correspondence course. After eight years he finally completed all the subjects and was awarded a S.C. Immediately after this he registered with the University of South Africa for a B.A. course 'in preparation for law, because I wanted to become a lawyer, and so I took a professional B.A. with law subjects'. This was ten years ago. Recently, he decided that it might be a good thing for a man in his position to do Afrikaans 'on the Matriculation level'. He was expected to take this exam towards the end of 1960. In spite of all these failures, and possibly because of his tremendous determination, he occupied one of the highest-status positions in Reeftown, living in a face-brick house of six rooms with tiled bathroom and American kitchen – one of the four tiled-roofed houses of the township. He was also a leading member of the highest and most powerful body, the School Board.

In the educational stories evidence abounds of the widely prevailing ignorance, through the difficulty of obtaining correct information about kinds of training, types of courses, and the meaning and requirements for a particular certificate. In one case, for instance, the young man had passed J.C. and, for some reason, thought this was the 'wrong' kind of J.C. It was only later that he discovered that his original J.C. had been perfectly valid. Another bought the 'wrong' books. 'I only discovered afterwards that they were those of the previous year, and I had to start all over again.' Yet another person had passed an S.C. which had not been valid as a university entrance exam. Nevertheless, he registered at a correspondence college for a bachelor's degree, bought the books for the course and started study ing. After three years he took the first-year exam but failed in two subjects, and was then told that his S.C. 'was the wrong one'.

We know of many more students besides our elite, who later found that they had taken the wrong subjects, followed the wrong course, bought and studied the wrong books, or had applied for and been accepted for the wrong bursary, etc. Considered from this angle, the elite would probably appear as that group among the whole population who, in the vast opportunities for choosing wrongly, had made the fewest wrong choices. It was probably mainly a matter of luck if one ultimately arrived somewhere.

The enormous struggle, the waste of time, money and effort, the heart-sickening disappointments which this could mean, emerged clearly from the educational stories. Yet, the overall impression gained was one of surprise at how lightly it had been taken and how quickly it had been forgotten. It seemed to mean so much less than it appeared to the European observer. It seemed to matter so little in view of the all-conquering aim of socio-economic advance.

Moreover, the general educational mobility which we have

159

attempted to demonstrate by means of the educational chart, and which was rather encouraged by the fragmentary and uncoordinated manner in which educational opportunities were – always belatedly – made available to the South African Bantu, as well as by the lack of synchronization between educational opportunities and occupational openings, was also of another – an actually qualitatively different – kind. This other kind of mobility had its roots in the cultural immaturity and the lack of deep involvement of the individuals caught up in the process of cultural mobility.

Vocational attitudes

'Of course, in reality, with my people', said P. Q., 'they did not really know what they wanted nor what it all meant. All they knew was that they wanted to be pioneers of African development.'

The choice of a next step in the educational struggle towards the top seems to have been determined mainly by such factors as: what one could get a bursary for; where one knew a friendly missionary or had established contact with another helpful European; by the kind of books the aspirant already 'had from a brother who had tried it before'; by the type of course one could buy second-hand from a friend; where one could get free accommodation because a relative lived near by; whether it could possibly bring a free trip overseas; whether it paid its dividends in higher income and status; and also often whether it was something new and one could be 'the first in the latest', as the African researcher always called it.

This almost blind thrust towards higher education is well expressed by the following spokesman:

'With us Africans, after J.C., or in my case Matric, you just apply anywhere for any bursary you can get for any subject or study or profession. Never mind what. And then you do whatever comes along. Now with me, for instance, I got a Government bursary for B.Sc. Earlier, at school, I had no idea what I wanted to study, then after I had done J.C. I still had no idea. Then, when I got that bursary, I thought that's as good as anything else, and I thought I might do this B.Sc., possibly as a stepping stone for Medicine afterwards. I had no idea what B.Sc. meant.

'A few months after I started the course I regretted it. I did not like the subject. I then wished I had done Arts, it seems there's a greater variety of subjects there . . .

'You mean to do what? I don't really care, and I really only want something which can make me into something nobody has ever been before. Professor of Economics, or Head of the Observatory, or anything of that nature.'

160

In the narrow range of training choices open to Africans, the young men, avid for recognition, threw themselves at any new opportunity offered, without much knowledge as to where it could lead, what type of studies it involved, whether they had the capacity, whether the subjects were congenial, whether jobs would be available in which this particular qualification would be required and adequately remunerated, what sort of work the job would entail, or whether they would actually like that work.

In fact, the educational progress of our elite appeared to have been determined by any considerations other than educational. Moreover, their generally undirected search received little guidance from the haphazard and often impromptu and entirely uncoordinated though well-meant efforts by those responsible for African advance.

The usually neutral and sometimes even negative frame of mind in which the forty-one teacher-trained members of our elite had entered upon their professional training has already been discussed. (See 'The Colleges', pp. 143ff.) The vocational mood of the eight ministers (besides the six who were employed full-time, there was one who was fully ordained but worked only part-time and was unremunerated, and another who was a graduate, in 1960 being prepared for high office by his [European] church) had not been much different. In fact, these two oldest professions were generally considered as interchangeable. The ministry was not a financial improvement on teaching, but the training was always free. With three ministers the actual word 'pressure' escaped them, but this was at once rectified with a statement such as: 'But of course, it is a matter of vocation.' Another said: 'At that time I saw possibilities in it, although now I see that it does not pay, of course.' Two ministers had chosen their profession because they had 'always been interested in higher education'. One minister, originally trained as a teacher, had finally decided on his present profession because he did not have enough money to pay for medical studies, and his past record was such that he could receive neither promotion nor bursary from the Education Department. The case of this minister as well as the one of the graduate, in which badly-reputed teachers were accepted and even selected for minister training, were symptomatic for a most regrettable situation: the loss of contact of some European missionaries with their own African parishioners and with the African public generally (which cut them off the sources of much valuable information), as well as of the lack of co-operation between these missionaries and European officials – a state of affairs utterly detrimental to missionary work.

With regard to the more recently opened professions, Dr R. (see p. 167) wanted to become a doctor of medicine already at a very early age. The two other doctors studied medicine because that was what their fathers expected of them. However, from the moment they qualified, none of these ever looked back. The other seven entered upon their present professions because their original plans had not materialized. In the case of the oldest and the youngest this was a job which they failed to get or which did not come up to expectations. With the other five it was a failure in one of the preliminary educational stages towards a more lofty academic goal. These failures were of a different nature – failures in passing an exam, in securing the necessary bursaries, in following up an opportunity when it appeared within reach; failures also through poverty and family commitments, through lack of persistence of singleness of purpose. In most cases several considerations and circumstances had operated together, and had resulted in the ambitious, possibly over-ambitious, young men having to settle for something less.

The following two cases histories may show the interrelationship between these various types of failure.

Mr T. O. related:

'After I had failed my Matric in two subjects I could not do it again because the exams were only once a year and it would have meant waiting a whole year. . . . So I thought I had better do this training course. You could get bursaries for that. I would in any case never be able to go to Wits without Matriculation.

'But then my parents said, "No, look now, you are already old (he was then 23 years old). You must come home and marry so that your wife can look after us and nurse mother." Mother was ill. They advised me to do teacher training in a college near home, so that I could join them and help. I thought it was a pity because I knew that if only I had Matric I could manoeuvre myself into any post, though I could not be an interpreter because I was not proficient in Bantu languages. But with all the money already paid for me at high school, I felt I should consider my parents' advice. My brother was also training as a teacher, and I felt this was in any case secure.'

His mother died just before he completed his training. He stayed for a while at home with his father, after which he obtained a bursary for his specialized training for which he did not require Matric. His father then agreed, on condition that he continued helping his younger sister.

Mr M. F.'s failure is somewhat more complex:

'I had wanted to do Medicine, but I had received a bursary for a bachelor's degree . . . I thought I'd take that in any case as a stepping stone.'

He then completed the degree, after failing once and having to repeat one year. 'I then tried Wentworth. I wrote for forms, and got them but somehow never filled them in or sent them back.'

'Why?' you ask? 'I was discouraged by friends. They said Wentworth was offering something inferior to Wits . . . What? No, I never tried Wits. I thought I'd have a holiday first. Some time off from books, you know. Have a good rest and so on. After that I would start thinking seriously again about going back to school . . .

'Well, I drank a bit, and och, you know, nice times. . . . Then I thought I shall work first, and I got a good job. . . . Then my brothers were coming up fast behind me and I decided to lessen the burden of my father and help them first. I had after all a good job already. . . .'

If it is found by sociological and social-psychological researchers that the greatest frustration prevails among the younger professionals, our finding that, among our small sample, all of them failed to achieve a more desirable or higher aim, may point to an explanation.

Concluding, it would appear that of the fifty-nine times that any one of our elite had entered upon some kind of professional training, this had only in ten cases been done in a positive frame of mind (see Table II 3:6), and among these were none of the ministers and not one of the younger professionals. A quite sizeable majority had simply drifted into a profession, with as little concern and committal

Table II 3:6 Numerical distribution of all respondents who had entered upon some professional training by whether their attitudes towards this training had been positive, negative or neutral

Type of training	Positive attitude	Negative attitude	Neutral attitude	Total
Teachers' Training	9	7	25	41
Ministers' Training	—	1	7	8
Training in the more recent professions	—	5	2	7
Doctors' Training	1	—	2	3
Total	10	13	36	59*

* Several individuals had received training in more than one profession.

as they drifted out of it again and into another profession or occupation if the mood or the occasion arose. This can be demonstrated by studying the reasons why, for instance, 16 of the 41 trained teachers left the teaching profession after some time. Of these 41, four had never taught, three had not completed their training and one was the

163

R.C. priest who simply obeyed his bishop. Too little money, no prospects of promotion, and the gradually decreasing status, which was the lot of the simple assistant teacher, were the main reasons. A more lucrative employment or training offered itself, or the need for adventure and for escape from parental control could only be satisfied by leaving the teaching profession altogether. In fact, the reasons why these teachers left their profession were no different from those put forward as reasons for leaving most jobs. (See Table II 4:2.)

As is inevitable in South Africa, the question must arise of how far discriminatory legislation was responsible for teachers leaving the profession. In this case the relevant legislation is the Bantu Education Act. Three of our ex-teachers left in the years 1954, 1955 and 1957, that is, after the Act was promulgated. All three were failed Matrics, and had undertaken teacher training because they could not attend university, and teaching was 'at least some kind of profession'. They had never wanted to teach and had left teaching gladly when new avenues were opened to them. Two of these three frankly confessed to this reason, never mentioning the Act. The third one's explanation merits verbatim quotation, so that the reader can judge for himself why Mr T. S. left the profession.

> 'Yes, I resigned. I wanted to leave teaching, I did not like the education offered to the children now with Bantu Education and all that. The standard of education was inferior. Also the pay was no longer so attractive to me. (He earned just under R40 per month.) Also I was disappointed. The school I taught in was Higher Primary and Lower Primary combined. And when it was reorganized, I was attached to the Lower Primary part, although I had the Higher Teaching Certificate, and so I lost interest. . . . A European Church contact then gave me the idea of applying for a newly opened clerical post with prospects . . .'

To shield oneself from one's own shortcomings, family obligations (as in Mr T. O.'s and Mr M. F.'s case) can serve as well as colour discrimination or the Bantu Education Act (as in Mr T. S.'s case). The surprising discovery was how free from such rationalizations our elite usually were.

Social scientists, particularly those of a non-anthropological bent and, therefore, inclined to approach the African situation with categories derived from the study of western peoples, have sometimes been tempted to compare this lack of personal involvement and apparent lack of goal-directedness with similar phenomena in other highly mobile societies such as the USA. Such comparisons of certain isolated traits are misleading, and worse, can shortcircuit a better understanding. In our small sample many other considerations and circumstances must be taken into account. There was, certainly, much ignorance of what was involved in a particular job or profession, and this was part of a more general and more comprehensive lack of experience concerning the requirements of the modern world, resulting in an over-simplification of issues which is naïvety – not a personal but a cultural naïvety. There was much evidence to suggest that these people generally lacked the moral values and mental notions by which the various professional and educational concepts, as evolved in the western context, could be distinguished and judged and the distinctions considered of importance.

As it was at present, education was the handmaiden of occupation. A profession was almost always a means to an end. There may have been a lack of definition of the means, but the end was always very clear.

Educational inequalities

We have seen how certain social differences had already affected at an early stage the educational histories of the elite; even in this generally privileged group one could in fact observe certain social inequalities. But besides the accident of birth and social origin, we also noted how history and geography brought out early differences favouring the people from the Eastern Cape as well as the younger generation who had grown up in a world in which educational opportunities had already increased somewhat more. We also saw and will see again how certain circumstances appeared to conspire to encourage or impede educational progress. By and large, each occupational group showed a distinct pattern in its educational history.

Throughout, the **doctors** appeared to be the most privileged group. Not only did they pass the two main post-primary stages without interruptions, but they also started school earliest, completed Std. VI earliest and in almost the shortest time, and they were also the youngest group to complete J.C. and Matriculation. In fact, up to and including Matriculation their education proceeded without a hitch. All three had highly qualified, professional fathers who were personally and actively determined to see their sons not only educated, but highly educated; and all three sons responded well and were intelligent and studious. They all received bursaries for their medical training. (See the educational histories of the three doctors, pp. 167ff.) Nevertheless, the older members of this specially privileged group had encountered several obstacles.

The members of the more recent professions, such as **health inspectors and social workers,** appeared to be the most privileged after the doctors. They started their education at the more or less customary age; only the doctors started younger. They took longer than any other group to complete primary school, but they were all able to complete J.C. immediately after Std. VI; and only the doctors passed J. C. and Matric at an earlier age. Also, not one of them needed to be satisfied with S.C. instead; and all passed the various educational hurdles in the right order. Their educational patterns, however, varied considerably, and the average was somewhat inconclusive.

As a group, the **ministers** started school latest and, consequently, completed Std. VI at the latest age, although they passed the six standards and two sub-standards in the shortest time. They were 'second sons' of wealthy farming stock. Their educational histories show wide divergencies: the D.C.R. minister failed in more than one attempt to complete his J.C., and he was the only minister without one or another teacher's certificate, while the R.C. minister had not only an N.P.H. teacher's certificate but was also the only one of the six who had passed Matric and his first-year Bachelor of Arts examination.

The **clerks** had had, throughout, the most unfortunate educational history, as one would expect of the only non-professional, non-self-employed or semi self-employed group. They started school latest of all, with the exception of the ministers. Although they completed primary school in slightly under average time and completed J.C. in well over average time, they took longer than any one of the other groups over their S.C. and Matric, which they were able to tackle only in later life, generally by correspondence course while employed in a full-time job. They were, too, the oldest by a long stretch to complete J.C., S.C. and Matric in the later part of their lives. Not one of them went further than J.C. in his early youth. In addition, the clerks had the largest number of failures in Matric exams. They even had some failures and drifts in teacher-training colleges where failures were extremely rare. Not one succeeded in obtaining a Bachelor's degree although two (both Government clerks) had tried.

Comparing the educational histories of the **higher teachers** and the **principals**, it may be observed that the latter were, on the whole, less fortunate than the former. Indeed in some respects they resembled the clerks, for it was among these two groups that there were the greatest number of those who had to try J.C. and Matric in later life, as well as the greatest number of failures. Between the two teaching groups there was litle difference in school-starting age and in the number of years taken to reach Std. VI, but the principals took at least one entire year longer to do J.C. and S.C. than the higher teachers, and not one of them could do Matric after J.C. Their failure rate in S.C. was the highest of all. Further, the principals generally came from poorer backgrounds than the higher teachers.

The **businessmen and sales representatives** occupied, as far as their educational destinies were concerned, an intermediate position between the most fortunate groups (the doctors, health inspectors, social workers and higher teachers) and the least fortunate groups (all the clerks, principals and ministers).

The educational histories of the three doctors

The oldest of the three doctors whose school years were earliest will be described in greater detail. This may serve as an introduction to some general facts. Again it must be stressed that the stories here are reproduced as much as possible as they were originally told us by the persons themselves.

Dr R.

As a young lad there was never any doubt in his mind that ultimately he was going to be a doctor of medicine. There had been 'many famous witch-doctors in the family, on mother's as well as father's side', and from his earliest years he had been filled with the desire to continue a long and honoured family tradition. This desire had been greatly strengthened by the frequent visits to his parents' home of a European doctor who had been a friend of Dr R.'s father. 'He gave me his name when I was born, and all through my childhood I was known by this name. Everyone called me Dr Smit.'

Dr R.'s father had left the Dutch Reformed Church for the Anglican Church because he wanted to learn English. He then became a Minister and wanted his son to follow in his footsteps; but Dr R. 'was not keen'. The father then thought that the next best was to be a teacher, and after Matric, to do a B.A. plus a Higher Teacher's Diploma. But Dr R. was definitely not interested. 'Just then, luckily, they started this course of Medical Aid for Africans; I believe, in 1936. This course was Matric plus four years, and I chose that. And we got the money.'

'It went like this. After Matric there were difficulties because father did not have the money to send me to college, and suggested I take a job in the Native Commissioner's office in the place near where we lived to save money for further studies. But a Native Commissioner in those days could only employ Africans as Police Clerks and I detest uniforms'. His father, however, had the right missionary connections. The boy's J.C. and Matric studies had already been made possible through 'special concessions in school fees' at the Anglican colleges. Now it was also through Anglican missionary influence that he obtained a bursary for Fort Hare, but to take B.A. This was not what the boy wanted, but he decided 'it was the next best thing'.

Medicine studies for Africans did not yet exist in South Africa. Those who could afford it or had the bursaries had to go overseas. 'Only in 1941 did Wits offer Africans opportunities for medical study. Cape Town had been first, but they only allowed Africans for the two-year pre-medical course, and you had to go overseas for your clinical. Then just when I had managed to get that B.A. bursary, this Medical Aid for Africans was introduced and I gave up my B.A. bursary and applied for one for Medical Aid. I got that bursary. It gave me R60 per annum for four years. It included tuition and board and lodging, but I had to pay for train fares, books and clothes myself.

'All this had taken so long that I joined Fort Hare only in April 1937, two months late for the course which had started in February. My Matric at St Peter's had had no physical science, but geography and Latin instead, and so I had to do this from J.C. upwards. It was hard work. The first year particularly was heavy going. You needed 40 per cent in all subjects: Zoology, Botany, Chemistry and Physics, which were all new to me. There were ten or twelve non-Europeans in my group.'

In 1940 he then completed the four-year course and did his one-year probationary period in McCord's Zulu Hospital. 'It is like housemanship.' 'There were no African sisters then, only nurses and staff nurses. All the sisters were European; we were not supposed to give orders to the sisters, we worked under Dr Taylor. Black–white relationships were very good . . . the spirit generally was that of a happy family. In 1942 we took our posts in out-stations under the Union Health Department. I was sent to X in the Northern Transvaal because the people there belong to my language group and you needed to know their language and customs. It was a completely African area, consisting of Native Trust Farms, African-owned farms and the Reserves. The area had lots of huge farms bought up by Africans forming Companies, It was the so-called communal buying.'

Dr R. liked his work and the country. He was amazed to see how tremendously it had developed since his childhood. Although many of the leading missionaries 'who ran the place' were kind to him – he lived with a relative of one of the missionaries – he came up against opposition from one European missionary doctor and one African nurse: the European 'had a colour bar' and the African nurse 'was afraid that I would do her out of a job'.

So he decided to give up his earlier plan, which had been to work there for a few years and save up for further studies – moreover the salary was 'too low'. He resigned at the end of 1942 and applied for a bursary for Fort Hare itself.

'When I took up that post in the country, I had heard already that Wits [the University of the Witwatersrand, commonly called "Wits"] was opening up for African medical students, and I had started preparing by working at a private correspondence course in Botany, Sociology, Physics and Chemistry. I could not do any practical work, but I thought I'd start theory anyway.

'I got the bursary. Now in 1943 the situation was like this. A first-year B.Sc. at Fort Hare served as the one year pre-Medical course if you had 50 per cent in all subjects. Those who had less had to continue and do the full B.Sc. three-year course, for which you only needed 40 per cent. Then, after that you could still do medicine at Wits. I passed 50 per cent and was one of those selected for a scholarship from the Native Trust Medical Scholarship Funds, and in 1944 I entered Wits. There were two groups ahead of us. In our group there were five, I believe. None of these first African medical students had ever paid for their own studies, except one who had either been sent from Basutoland or had private funds. The Scholarship was R400 per year. Out of this we had R26 allowance for board and lodging and about R40 for books. These scholarships were repayable, but the two groups before us had refused to repay theirs, and so we also refused. We've never been asked since to repay the money.

'At first at Wits I felt quite out of place . . . although some European students did their best to make us feel at home. There were of course always those who . . . They tried to make things unpleasant. . . . But by and large they were helpful; some invited us to their homes. . . . With me, of course, provided all are absolutely equal and all can join in everything, I would prefer a mixed University. . . . I myself did not miss sport at Wits, and I did not care for European dances, but if you're a keen sportsman, then you suffer at Wits. . . . Nevertheless I think most would have been quite satisfied with the knowledge that they could join if they wanted to and would then still have preferred to go to their own functions among their own people. What irked them were the restrictions. . . . But mixed classes do stimulate us Africans. You feel that you must prove that you can do the same as the whites. We had lots of extra assistance from the senior students and from the professors.

'There were no residences for us. I first lived with my sister. She had a small three-roomed house and I had to sleep on a stretcher in the dining-room. I only stayed three months. Then we, another student and I, got a room in a cheaper European district. But we failed to get a permit to live in that area. Other students lived secretly in the backyard of a European in another area near the University. . . . We then found a place in

Sophiatown. That was grand. Two comfortable rooms in a huge seven-roomed house owned by an African lady who was only using the kitchen, one bedroom and one sitting-room. So the four of us took those rooms, two to each room. It was very comfortable. We paid each, I am not quite sure whether I remember correctly, but I believe it was R9·50 or R11·50 per month for the room, dinner, laundry, furniture, electric light, a piano and a radiogram. We had our breakfast in a tea-room in Sophiatown and lunch and tea at the University. We had a gay time.

'The scholarship money was not sufficient. I did not earn anything. During the holidays I went to work at Lovedale Hospital to gain experience and the pay there was R16 per month, of which R12 went back for board and lodging. Both my elder sisters who had always helped me were now dead. But one sister was already a staff nurse and she helped me as much as she could. Also they helped me now and then from home. My father's salary was pitiful, but my mother ran a laundry business...

'In 1949 I did my housemanship again at Lovedale Hospital. This was still only possible in Mission Hospitals. Baragwanath was not yet open to African housemen then. The other housemen at Lovedale were Indians. They formed two groups of two and were always at loggerheads with one another. Two were politically active and two not. I was with the ones who were not, because I had no political interests.'

About his education generally, Dr R. says: 'In high school I would have liked more study in two subjects: firstly more instruction in musical instruments, such as piano and violin. All the music we had was choir singing. Then more Afrikaans; we did not have to study that and now this is a disadvantage.'

With regard to his medical study, he feels that it would have been better if he had learned typing and book-keeping. He would also have preferred more normal psychology. 'We only had abnormal psychology.' He would also have liked to continue English on the B.A. level, and in particular, he thinks that History of Medicine should be taught. After the medical course there should be study of Bantu Medicine, which would by then have already been put into its true perspective through the study of History. 'There is,' he says, 'a difference between the Bantu curing and Witchcraft. This knowledge which the Bantu have of herbs and cures should not be lost.'

So far then, the educational history of a remarkable man. Dr R. never failed, he always obtained the highest marks and it took him as much as twelve years after Matric to become a doctor! The circumstances which were against him can be summed up as follows: the belated opportunities for medical training of Africans in South Africa; the unimaginative and sketchy planning of medical study for Africans, and the lack of funds. His advantages were: a sense of vocation, and great sincerity, adequate brains and hard work, singleness of purpose and the right missionary connections.

Dr. L.

Dr L. also did his Matric at St Peter's because his father was a School Principal at that time and he wanted to have Latin and Mathematics, and 'There were then not many high schools that did not specialize mainly in Teachers' Courses.' His father wanted his son to be a doctor. 'He himself was already a teacher and I had to be better than he.' His father had made this decision, although St Peter's was an Anglican school and father himself was a Methodist. Dr L.'s mother died when he was eight years old and father remarried soon afterwards. When he passed Matric in 1939, 'father couldn't afford Fort Hare. [The stepmother considered it a waste of money.] The two children following me, a brother and a sister, were also at college both doing J.C. So father got me a teacher's job at home.' But Dr L. did not like teaching; 'there was no money in it'. After six months there was a series of events, culminating in the father's sudden death, after which Dr L. decided to go to Johannesburg. [Only after his father's death (cf. Mr K. E., pp. 132–3) could Dr L. follow up his father's original wishes.] Through St Peter's (Dr L. had in the meantime become an Anglican) he obtained a job as laboratory assistant, but it was 'very badly paid'. He then found a better-paid job, and 'I got my younger brother in the same job after he had passed Matric in 1941'. They were then earning about R9 per month each and started saving. 'The first year was difficult because among other things my sister got married.' During the second year, however, they managed to save about R8 a month each and by the end of that year they had accumulated some R200. 'We then had a discussion and we decided that since I was the eldest and had already sacrificed to get my brother through college to Matric, I should now have the first chance to continue school.' He finally decided to go to Fort Hare. He could have gone to Wits, since it had been opened to African medical students, but 'it was not easy to decide on a five-year course with only R200 in your pocket'. It seemed less difficult to commit oneself to a Bachelor's degree, which took only three years. 'There were no medical scholarships yet except those given by the Native Trust,' he says. [He obviously failed to obtain such a scholarship.]

o

171

When he arrived at Fort Hare in 1944 he found that there was an extra bursary going for B.Sc. Hygiene and the registrar suggested that he apply, because he only had R200 and a younger brother to see him through his studies. He got the bursary and did his B.Sc. Hygiene in the shortest possible time. He then heard that the Native Trust was again offering medical scholarships (in 1947), and with his B.Sc. Hygiene he stood a good chance. The competition was keen, but he won his scholarship and so he completed his M.B., B.Ch. in 1951 at the University of the Witwatersrand in Johannesburg, commonly called 'Wits'.

He found Wits 'far more stimulating than Fort Hare', and 'those European boys work much harder than we Africans'.

Like Dr R. and for the same reasons, he did his housemanship in mission hospitals, but he does not regret it. He feels he received far more experience. In those smaller hospitals, 'you had to do far more yourself, your own X-rays, your own dispensing, etc.' In Baragwanath 'all that is done for you by specialized departments and you don't learn anything about it'.

Dr L. was fortunate in having been born later than Dr R. when Wits had been opened to African medical students. In spite of a professional father, keen on education, unfavourable family circumstances developed. Father's sudden death, though tragic, seems to have been liberating however. An iron determination, and an immense capacity for saving did the rest. Dr L. knew what he wanted, never failed, and yet his medical training after Matric took him nine years.

Apartheid suits him fine. He does not want to be with Europeans anyway, and he earns more money as things are.

Dr P.

As far as parental origin and background were concerned, Dr P. was born with a silver spoon in his mouth. His father, who had been a matriculated school principal, was descended from a wealthy farming family who had their own farms, lots of cattle and grew tobacco as a cash crop. 'He looked after us well and we were never in need.' The boy had completed his J.C. in Lovedale and his Matric in a well-known high school in Cape-town. Dr P. wanted to become a teacher, but 'father wanted me to be a doctor'. He wanted his son to be 'one better than he himself had been'. Father paid for most of his schooling. The family being well connected in the Transkei, his father got him a B.Sc. bursary from the Bunga for Fort Hare in 1949. B.Sc. Hygiene had at this stage been stopped. The bursary covered only part of the fees, but father provided the rest.

172

Having finished B.Sc. in three years he 'was accepted for a loan scholarship offered by the European students of Wits', and there he took seven years to finish his medical training. He liked Wits, and he did not dislike his education. 'I got on well with the European boys in the same business,' he says, and he still has many friends among European doctors. After completing the course, he did his one-year housemanship at Baragwanath Hospital. He complains that African housemen at Baragwanath were paid only 'the highest salary for a staff nurse', i.e. R90 per month.

In this, our youngest case, there were eleven years of training between Matric and the opening of a practice.

Ten years separate the time when Dr R. and Dr P. left Witwatersrand University to start out on their careers as general practitioners. The world had changed in the interim. Everything which before had been considered the due reward for hard work and continuous individual effort, was now taken for granted and accepted as by right.

Summing up

Briefly summarizing the main points about the elite's education in an earlier era, in which almost all education depended largely on the devoted but uncoordinated and somewhat arbitrary efforts of the mutually competitive Christian mission churches, we found that in spite of differences among individuals and occupational groups, the elite as a whole appeared to have been fortunate in their parents and rearers, in so far as the majority could start school early or at the customary age of the times, in spite of a general prejudice against early entry into school, particularly in the rural areas, and although only one-third of them really liked school and learning. And again in the post-primary stage they were lucky in so far as all but two could, and did, continue their education after Std. VI with a majority going on to J.C. and some even to Matric.

Moreover, in spite of individual differences, they also seemed as a group to have been more gifted than average for school learning. In a time of general and excessive retardation, it took them on an average only 8·25 years to complete primary school at the then relatively early age of 16·42.

This deserves all the more attention as we found among the children a high rate of geographical mobility of three kinds: moves between different rural/urban areas, among different rearers and different schools. Less than one-fifth of the children were brought up by and with both parents and attended only the one school in their birthplace. However, this almost excessive mobility did not seem to

173

have had a retarding effect. On the contrary, evidence suggested that this very mobility was positively related to educational progress.

A similar mobility was found to have been the keynote of the elite's post-primary education. The fact that African education was at first mainly geared to the rapid production of teachers; that educational opportunities became only very slowly available and these were generally uncoordinated with occupational opportunities (a coordination particularly necessary in an expanding society): briefly, the general fluidity of the African educational situation as well as the lack of central and thorough planning; poverty and heavy family commitments as well as the lack of educational fervour – all this resulted in a majority of the elite having had to start their working lives with insufficient academic and professional qualifications. Hence their further educational careers can be seen as one long drawn-out and much interrupted struggle to make up for earlier academic deficiencies and wrong vocational choices.

The tremendous effort represented by this educational struggle towards the top is only realized if it is known that our elite were not generally speaking scholarship boys. All the bursaries ever received between them covered only one-quarter of all the post-primary-school examinations attempted. Hence about half of all academic examinations on high-school level and two-thirds of those on university level were acquired in later life through correspondence courses while the students were employed in full-time jobs. The majority of those who reached a level beyond J.C. attempted to pass two or even three successive examinations by private study. Rather than earn the money for the next educational step by taking on temporary jobs, as the modern working student does, more than half of our elite never worked at all in any paid jobs to pay for their education (and those who did work, paid only for their clothes and rarely for books), the elite went the way of the student employee. Thus there emerged a picture of occasional spurts of earnest, though unsystematic, endeavour to acquire bits and pieces of usually poorly integrated knowledge in the form of certain subjects learned by heart at odd moments in between and after work.

Considering this the failure rate cannot, we believe, be called high. But inevitably, each stage took much longer than was normal, and most qualifications were acquired at a much later age. The second important characteristic of the post-primary education of our elite was, therefore, this belated piecemeal accumulation of various educational and professional qualifications, the change-over to another course of study if this one threatened to become a failure, and the change of professions.

Hence the third main characteristic of the elite's educational careers was the considerable mobility these careers required and, in

174

their turn, engendered. We use this term mobility in a much wider, and actually qualitatively different, sense than is generally understood by the term educational mobility. By this we mean not only the continuous change from one institution of learning to another, from one patron to another, from one course of study to another and from one educational goal to another, but also the easy adaptability with which a particular educational aim was replaced by another when the first had failed, and the manner in which external circumstances and accidental factors were allowed to determine the aims. A precise analysis of all the considerations and circumstances which had weighed upon the professionals in the choice or change of professions revealed the prevailing neutral and even negative attitudes towards their chosen professions, showing a high degree of personal non-involvement.

All this led to a further main finding, that the need for further education arose almost entirely out of occupational aspirations. Hence the general lack of interest in purely academic subjects. This entirely utilitarian way of viewing education was not discouraged by the fact that in those days, very few bursaries were granted for academic study and then mainly to those who had already a profession and needed further academic qualifications. This also influenced the careers of our elite along particular lines and often against their personal inclinations and individual talents. Mercifully they themselves showed few personal preferences.

We noticed too the huge optimism about their own capacities, and the happy expectancy about the outcome. The door was never shut for our elite. Both the optimism and the expectancy were probably not unconnected with a general ignorance of the ideals of those who brought education to the Africans, as well as with the lack of a realistic appraisal of a given situation and their own potentialities within it. On the other hand, all this may well account for the tremendous drive and persistence behind this educational struggle towards the top, this education by trial and error, this almost blind thrust forward, and for the enormous dynamism which emerged so vividly from a detailed study of these careers.

4   Occupational mobility

Introduction

While in the previous chapter we described the process of social mobility with special reference to the educational progress of our elite, we propose in this chapter to deal with what was essentially part of the same process, their occupational advance.[1] Instead of school and study changes we shall now investigate job changes.

'Job' has been taken to mean any full-time gainful occupation after Std. VI. Herding, holiday jobs and spare-time jobs were not included. 'Odd jobs' which sometimes represented the first occupation in a working life, had to be taken as one job only.

We call 'job change' all changes in the employing body or in the area or place of employment as well as changes in the type of employment under the same employer. Hence, what are often called intra-job and inter-job changes have not been distinguished; both are, in our definition, job changes. Transfers and promotions under the same employer are included in the term, but not mere salary increases. In the case of the self-employed, all changes in practice, removals of shops or the opening up of new lines of business have been taken as job changes. Job changes also include changes between employment and self-employment, except where self-employment was tried while other employment was still held.

The recent transfer from the old location to the new township had also to be taken as a job change. Such movements have happened before in the history of the Bantu people; they are part and parcel of the total mobility picture of the South African Bantu. (See, for instance, the successful career of Mr P. Q., p. 209.) Sometimes such removals precipitated promotion or even a change of employer or occupation.

In our treatment of the subject, the first job has been singled out

176

for separate discussion. After this the total job histories will be described, giving first the extent and then the nature of the job changes.

But a word of caution is perhaps necessary. While some check was possible as to the exams passed and the certificates acquired, there was little we could do with regard to verification of the data supplied about past jobs. Reliance had to be placed on what was verbally expressed and explicitly mentioned, while the correct interpretation could often be guided by other information supplied in other contexts. It may be assumed, however, that, particularly in the case of short-period employment, stop-gap jobs and low-status jobs in the earlier stages of the careers, some full-time employment might have been forgotten, although the dates and years which we always requested made some check possible.

Throughout the job histories ran the social differentiation between the professionals and the non-professionals, or more precisely between the professional and the non-professional jobs. To these differences due attention was given.

The first jobs

Professional and non-professional jobs

When the time came to take up the first full-time paid job, it became clear why so many of our elite had gone in for teaching, and why even today Africans want to become 'professional'. As a rule the inspector had already gone the rounds of students in their final year and offered them a choice of vacancies. (See Table II 4:1.) The students usually took one near home and frequently even in the same country schools in which they had once been a scholar. From then onwards the teacher, if he so wished, became incorporated in a countrywide and usually benevolent organization, and as long as his teaching came up to certain moderate expectations, he knew where he could turn for the satisfaction of his needs.

This is as one of them explained it:

'In those days we were very much under missionary influence. The missionaries were the superintendents of the schools. If you were a regular churchgoer and pleased them, you did not need to apply. You simply said that you wanted a job or a change, and they would appoint you to a vacancy. It was all very easy. The superintendent of your own mission generally had several schools under him. You went to tea and had a chat and all was settled. Whereas nowadays with the school boards . . .'

There was a rapidly expanding market for teachers; schools were opening everywhere in the country, and quite a few of the young, as yet inexperienced, adolescents with N.P.L. as their highest qualification (or even with no teacher's certificate at all) were offered principalships in newly opened schools. Although a better job, or a job a little further away from the family, might sometimes have been preferred (witness the few 'nothing betters') the first jobs can be assumed to have suited the teachers well enough, at least for a start.

As long as the applicant wanted to teach all was well. If he did not want to (two of them 'hated' teaching), or could not obtain a satisfactory post (three of these had the 'wrong' religion, which meant that, although they belonged to and wished to remain with one denomination, they had been trained by an institution belonging to another denomination), his first job chances were reduced to the level of that of the non-professionals.

And then 'nothing better' jobs prevailed. In the country, where most of them still lived at this stage in their careers, there were hardly any jobs suitable for young men with J.C. or even Matric. Clerical jobs were only to be had in a few places. Among these were the local Pass Office, the local Recruiting Office of the Mines and the Magistrate's Court. Consequently, most non-professionals began their working lives with just any jobs because: 'It was absolutely the only job I could get', 'They were the first to answer my application and I could not afford to wait', or 'It was the next best thing to pick-and-shovel work'.

Some did not even make the effort. When it became clear that any further education was out of the question, either because the family could or would not afford it, or because life at home had become unbearable, or simply because of the lure of the big city, they packed up their belongings and left to try their luck in town.

The family entered more frequently into the professionals' first-job choice than in that of the non-professionals. (See Table II 4:1.) After all, parents, rearers and other relatives had been the prime movers in sending the young man to teacher-training college; they had generally paid the fees. Now that the first fruits of their joint efforts were beginning to appear, they demanded their *quid pro quo*. No wonder then that throughout their careers the professionals remained more kin-tied than the others, with whom the desire for 'pastures new', as this was often called, and for escape from family obligations, were stronger. The desire for education could sometimes give an additional impetus towards a change of habitat. ('There was every chance of furthering my education in town, and it was town-life I wanted, because of the bioscope and all that.')

The age at which our elite started their working life in earnest was, on an average, about twenty-nine, but the ages varied widely from as young as thirteen to as old as thirty-four years. It was not an im-

178

portant figure in these histories as it depended, of course, largely on the level of education previously attained. Generally speaking, professional first jobs were, for this reason, obtained at a later average age than non-professional first jobs.

Table II 4:1   Numerical distribution of the respondents by all reasons for taking their first jobs according to whether these were professional or non-professional jobs

N = 56*

| Reasons | For taking first jobs | | For leaving first jobs | |
	Professional first jobs N = 28†	Non-Professional first jobs N = 28	Professional first jobs N = 28†	Non-Professional first jobs N = 28
Vacancy	14	—	—	—
Nothing Better	3	19	—	—
Money	2	2	3	9
Prospects	—	1	5	5
Status	—	—	2	2
Family	10	4	8	2
Adventure	4	6	4	3
Education	2	1	5	6
Promoted } Transferred }	—	—	4	4
Other	—	4	3	2
Total‡	35	37	34	33

* Excluded are the Roman Catholic priest and two doctors who never had any other but their professional jobs, as well as one trader about whom our data were incomplete.

† These were twenty-seven teaching posts and one job of another profession.

‡ Frequently more than one reason was given.

With regard to the average earnings, too many variables make such a figure meaningless. Earnings depended on such unrelated circumstances as the period in time (the years in which the first jobs were taken ranged from 1921 to 1955), the province (the provinces have always had different wage scales for teachers and public servants, as well as for domestic servants and labourers), as well as on the type of job and employer and on the educational qualifications of the applicant. For example, in 1909 in the Cape, an N.P.L.-qualified teacher received about £50 a quarter; in the Transvaal, two similarly qualified ones received (one in 1929 and the other in 1941) exactly the same salary of £11 per month. In 1947 on the Reef, a J.C.-educated sweeper in a clothing factory earned R16 per month. One teacher-trained person worked in 1949 as a cleaner in the Capetown

University for £3 per week; after eight years he discovered that 'there were no holidays unless one was tired'. He was, and went home to the country where he joined the South African Police. Some jobs included food rations and/or free accommodation. Even so, the average salary of the professionals was slightly higher than that of the non-professionals, approx. R17·50 against approx. R13·50.

During the first jobs, their incumbents had had time to look around, to form a clearer idea of what they wanted from their jobs, and learn where they could find the kind of jobs that could give them what they wanted. They also learned what kind of persons had to be contacted, and in what manner, in order to secure for themselves the better jobs. In other words, they were beginning to learn the ropes. Moreover, through the first jobs new needs had arisen, and aims became more diversified. Some of them were thinking of marriage and others had already got married. The main considerations which came into play in most of the subsequent job changes were becoming apparent (see Table II 4:1); first, the complex money–prospects–status; second, but achieving more importance as the occupational histories advanced, the first promotions and transfers. A very small number seemed to have found in their first jobs already a little niche promising future advancement, but most individuals discovered that the first job held few prospects, so they looked around for and found more promising openings. This was the beginning of the never-ending search for new opportunities, higher status and better pay. With the teachers, money was seldom explicitly mentioned, but with the non-professionals it soon became their avowed purpose, mentioned without embarrassment. Money was the only way in which the non-professionals could be compensated for the lack of professional status.

As a result of the first job, educational reasons greatly increased in importance, which was typical of the African situation. (See Table II 4 : 2.) These occurred among those persons who had discovered that there was no hope of advancement unless another diploma or degree was acquired. They had saved up some money for a correspondence course, or had obtained a bursary.

Again family considerations weighed heavily in the decision to leave the first job, and again more with the professionals, who now wanted to try their luck somewhat further away from the family and from parental control; some non-professionals had now definitely made up their minds that only town could satisfy their ambitions.

It was not surprising that the employees did not stay in their first jobs very long, and that those in professional jobs stayed somewhat longer than the others. The figures here were: the professional first jobs lasted an average of 2·76 years and the non-professional first jobs an average of only 1·60 years, which last figure compared favourably with the findings from researches on Bantu labour turn-over and jobs, with samples consisting almost entirely of industrial and unskilled workers.[2]

Table II 4:2 Numerical distribution of the elite by all reasons for taking or leaving all jobs (first and other jobs distinguished)

N = 55*

Reasons	For taking a job			For leaving a job		
	First jobs	Other jobs	Total	First jobs	Other jobs	Total
Promotions, Transfers	—	87	87	8	74	82
Money, Prospects, Status	5	98	103	26	65	91
Vacancy, Nothing Better	36	42	78	—	—	—
Family Considerations	13	22	35	9	14	23
Desire for Adventure, Change, Freedom	10	23	33	7	13	20
To Acquire Further Education	3	7	10	11	19	30
To Use New Qualifications	—	12	12	1	5	6
Denominational Reasons	3	3	6	1	2	3
To Gain More Knowledge or Experience	—	5	5	—	1	1
To Test Myself	—	2	2	—	1	1
Did not like the Job	—	—	—	—	7	7
Illness	—	—	—	—	5	5
To go into Business	—	—	—	—	5	5
Human Considerations	—	2	2	2	23	25
Technical, External Factors	—	2	2	1	12	13
Total†	70	305	375	66	244	312

* Excluded are, besides one trader, the Roman Catholic priest and the two doctors (who were excluded also in Table II 4:1) also the other doctor.

† Total number of reasons exceeds total number of jobs because sometimes more than one reason was given with reference to one job. The job changes here considered do not include those of the ministers and the traders after they had become ordained or self-employed.

First jobs in town

At a certain stage in their careers the workers wanted to come to town. This stage occurred in the job histories of the professionals as well as in that of the non-professionals, but in that of the former it came later and was a more gradual process, while in that of the latter it happened earlier and more abruptly. (Cf. Chapter 2, p. 82.)

181

Essentially, as Lawrence Lipton has brought out so well, town was a relative thing. He writes:

'The big city was the golden goal. It was a relative thing. In Chicago we yearned for New York; in Omaha, I found, they were yearning for Chicago. In Lincoln, Nebraska, they yearned for Omaha. Sometimes they took it that way, by stages, and when they had had their fill of New York, some who were harder to satisfy made the golden journey to Paris. But the picture they cherished was the same everywhere: the big city was the place where you could realize yourself and let yourself go, by which they invariably meant sexual fulfilment. Somehow the notion of financial fulfilment was tied in with it, so that it added up to the rags-to-riches Cinderella story of the American dream.'[3]

The African *trek* to town, as well as presumably the expectations accompanying it, has a parallel in America which may so far not have been sufficiently considered in labour researches. However, the desire to *trek*, to move to an urban or simply a more urban area, or just to somewhere new ('I wanted a change', 'I wanted to see new people and places') has throughout influenced the careers of our elite, although to a diminishing degree. Symbolized as 'Adventure' in the Tables II 4:1 and 2, it often combined with the reason symbolized as 'Family', either positively or negatively, i.e. the desire to move was frequently strengthened by the need to be either nearer to or further away from a particular member of the kinship system. But apart from this *trek* to town common to Americans and South Africans, the total situational context within which an African career took place was so different from that anywhere else as to preclude meaningful comparisons. For a move to town by a black person in South Africa as well as in some other countries on the African continent, involved its own special difficulties, and required its own peculiar preparations.

There was a common saying in Reeftown: 'The move into town was made via the Teacher Training College or the Mines.' The truth of this saying was fully confirmed by a study of our elite's first jobs in town.

For the teachers (as also for most other professionals) the move was relatively easy. Their position was that of public servants anywhere in the world, and the new breed of managers in the western world. Transfers, if carefully planned, could be effected within one large organization, and frequently these represented promotions. The job histories showed how the gradual *trek* to town was made via one or more, each time slightly bigger or more important, country towns and examples were not lacking among our elite's progress, of teachers whose gradual *trek* to the city was not only accompanied by educational advance and occupational promotion, but also fitted in with a variety of other aims and purposes. Mr Y.Z.'s geographical/ educational/occupational mobility was instructive. (The italics serve to highlight the relevant points.)

After having completed his N.P.L., Mr Y.Z. applied and was accepted for a job as *principal of the 'tribal' school of his home district*, where he himself had done Std. V and Std. VI. The next year he registered with a correspondence college in Johannesburg as a J.C. student. After two years he left because he 'wanted a bigger school, less to do and more time to read', and he apparently found all this in *an assistant teacher's job at a mission school in the near-by country town*, to which he had been recommended by the missionary supervisor. In addition, his previous salary was raised from R10 to R11. He then obtained a mission bursary for N.P.H.

'I was young (25 years) and I wanted to get further away from home' (and a strict father who had treated him harshly), 'and I also wanted to learn Afrikaans.' So he applied for and got a job as *assistant teacher in a mine school in a country town*. In the interim, a general increase in teachers' salaries had brought his monthly earnings to R16. He 'impregnated' one of his girl students and as he was 'madly in love' with her he married her.

Two years later he decided that he 'wanted to be nearer Johannesburg to further my education'. He had heard that there were classes at the Technical College. He succeeded in getting himself recommended as *an assistant teacher in another mission school*, but now *in one of the smaller Reef towns*.

His mother's brother lived there and he could stay with him, which was cheaper. At the same time he could in this way repay something of his debt to this maternal uncle, who had provided him with a home in his childhood when his parents were travelling round the country – both had been teachers.

In this Reef town he at once registered himself as a Matric student with a correspondence college, never taking advantage of the classes at the 'Tech'. His salary was then R24 per month.

Two years later he was promoted and invited to accept the position of *principal in a primary school in one of the larger Reef towns*, where his starting salary was R32. (This did not include his principal's allowance.) He got himself nominated on the Advisory Board and his special Afrikaans language qualification was useful. After a few years' faithful service he obtained the B.A. bursary which was yearly given by the (Afrikaans) Township Administration to the most promising resident, and he went to do his B.A. in Fort Hare. He passed his first-year examination but failed his second and his bursary was not renewed.

183

MOBILITY

(He told the African investigator that he had enjoyed himself immensely at Fort Hare. To the European investigator he explained that his wife became ill and that he had to return to look after his family.)

Anyway he subsequently became *principal of a large higher primary school in another, important Reef town.*

By contrast, for most non-professionals, the move to town meant starting again at the very bottom of the occupational ladder. A glance at the kinds of employer and employment which these non-professional Bantu found for their first jobs in town showed two important features of the South African occupational situation as this affected non-professional Bantu (even though schooled up to Junior Certificate or Matriculation, and teacher-trained but unwilling to teach) when not born and/or brought up in a town or city. These two features are such important factors in the South African Bantu's job history as to make most comparisons with conditions elsewhere invalid. They were the institutions of 'the Boy' and 'the Pass'.

The 'boy'

In the non-professional first jobs those of the so-called 'boys' predominated: delivery boys, messenger boys, tea boys, cook boys, office boys, etc. In those early days, private European employers had hardly any other use for Africans of some education – suit-wearing Africans. This occupation of 'boy' appears as a typical feature of the South African, as of all colonial, situations, where between conquerors and conquered the main contact was in the master–servant relationship. In fact, the notion 'boy' was expressive of a personal relationship rather than a category of work; a 'boy' was attached to someone whom he addressed as 'master' or 'baas'. In the job history of our elite, his post was an extension of the post of domestic servant into the occupational (industrial or commercial) domain, where a 'boy' was an individual personally attached to a European or group of Europeans in a particular occupation. Furthermore the function of a 'boy' became connected with the all-important feature of South African life: the division between manual and non-manual, between unskilled and skilled labour. In this context, the 'boy' represented the manual side of the 'master's' non-manual job, or the unskilled part of his skilled job. In South Africa, the distinction not only between manual and non-manual work, but also between skilled, semi-skilled and un-skilled jobs became very important.

Every white South African tradesman, for instance, had a 'boy who held the ladder, handed him his tools and cleaned up the mess afterwards. And, inevitably, the boy learned to do, and sometimes did, most of the job for him, while the white 'master' sat smoking his

184

pipe, and drew the recognized white-labour wages. Being a 'boy' to a white artisan has generally been the only (unofficial) apprenticeship for Africans (see the 'Daka Boy' mentioned in Chapter 3, p. 149). and many a now self-employed electrician, plumber and carpenter in the townships started out on his career as just such a personal 'boy'. In many such cases the role of the 'boy' in South Africa was probably nearest to that of the medieval 'factotum' who combined the functions of 'man of all work' and 'servant managing his master's affairs'. The 'Daka Boy' wrote his master's letters!

In the original scheme of things, the 'boy' was, without doubt, a valuable stage in the occupational development of the Bantu; and, in the dearth of vocational training schools, he is still an indispensable preparation for self-employment, particularly since Africans, according to the research assistant, prefer to receive their training while being paid a weekly wage as 'boys', to having to pay for their training in a vocational school. Moreover, and this should be stressed, in addition to the actual training such 'boys' received in particular skills and work methods, they benefited from the frequently close contact between 'boy' and 'master' which served as an important bridge for the mutual infusion of cultural traits.

Its functional importance can be judged from the fact that just as successful Bantu farmer owners now invited, in their turn, squatters from among their own people on to their land (see, for example, Chapter 3, Mr. L. L.'s father, p. 137), and just as prosperous African plantation owners were, in their turn, becoming employers of African migratory labour all over Southern Africa,[4] so the prospering independent Bantu artisans in Reeftown – the plumbers and electricians, the builders and bricklayers – now in their turn made use of the services of, and talked about, 'my boy'. Many such institutions, formerly seen as typical colonial abuses, can now be recognized as having a socio-economic basis. Consequently the 'boy' institution will, undoubtedly, remain useful as long as there are large numbers of occupationally inexperienced South Africans.

'Delivery boys' were the men employed by European shops such as grocer's, butcher's, baker's or dry-cleaning firms to deliver the goods and collect the orders. They corresponded roughly to errand boys, though they might be of any age. Frequently, they were the drivers of delivery vans, carried a measure of responsibility and were well paid. 'Shop boys' acted as personal attendants and assistants to white shop assistants, and served customers only if they were black. Office boys and messenger boys were in status probably nearer to minor clerks. In the case of our elite, such 'boys' served as general utility men. They cleaned and dusted and washed up; they served the tea and fetched the lunch sandwiches for the European staff; they collected the mail and did the personal shopping for the white clerks;

185

they 'delivered parcels for important customers', and were 'window dresser assistants', while some also performed minor clerical duties such as duplicating circulars, addressing envelopes and packing and stamping mail. It is not easy to classify the jobs of these 'boys' in the categories used for non-Africans in other countries. Implying both manual and non-manual duties, they make exact comparison with the job situation elsewhere difficult. There was moreover a tendency for our respondents to 'up-name' these jobs in terms of 'assistants'. 'Up-naming' we called the widespread custom of talking about persons and jobs in terms borrowed from white society but applicable to higher-status or higher-qualified jobs or persons. For instance, an electrician might be called an 'electrical engineer', a bricklayer 'a builder' and a builder 'an architect'; a packer and sorter was called 'a despatch clerk', a herbalist 'a chemist' and someone who, in his spare time did the books for a trader, 'an accountant'. Outside the hospital, male nurses sometimes called themselves 'doctors', nurse-maids 'nurses' and nurses 'sisters'. Similarly a son might call his father who had been a kitchen boy 'hotel cook' or even 'hotel chef', and his domestic servant mother 'a housekeeper'. The owner of two butcheries or of one butchery and one grocery store was referred to as 'a chain-store owner'. Someone who had a general store and a taxi was called 'a director of companies'. The same phenomenon could be observed when our spokesmen talked of any cattle, land, huts or other possessions in the country, in terms of 'the family farm'. The custom seemed to be the result partly of a misunderstanding or ignorance of the exact meaning of such European terms, but mainly of the tremendous thirst for status, and particularly, equal status with the whites, even if only in name. Its corollary 'down-naming' is described on p. 187. To find a way out of the difficulty all such jobs as 'boy' or 'assistant', except those of personal service 'boys', were classified as semi-manual.

Indicative of the master-servant relationship, the word 'boy' was in South Africa felt to be derogatory, particularly since it was extended as the usual form of address to all Bantu, including even the most venerable and those who did not work for any particular European, or were not employed by white concerns. Consequently, and to inaugurate the advent of a new era in black–white relationships, a determined movement had been started, to drop this word 'boy' altogether, not only as a form of address, but also in job designations. In 1963 Johannesburg City Council unanimously passed a recommendation to increase the wages of its Bantu workers and, at the same time, it decided to remove the word 'boy' from all job designations. For example, the word 'boss-boys' would be replaced by 'supervisors', and 'furnace boys' would in future be called 'furnace attendants'. In the meantime the new educated and professional classes of Africans in the newly independent states of Africa seem to continue to use the word quite freely to designate their own personal servants, who reply with 'master'. But when, for instance, educated Nigerians talk about 'my boy' (see, for instance, Chinua Achebe's novel *No longer at Ease*) nobody objects!

In the meantime however, the term as well as the accompanying so-called 'White' attitudes have been taken over by the South African Africans themselves to designate positions of inferiority and dependence in their own intraracial relationships. Its use was an example of the habit of 'down-naming'.

According to this habit, professionals talked of all non-professionals as 'just ordinary people', or 'merely an ordinary man'. All persons who did not actually and conspicuously sit behind a desk in an office were generally described as 'only labourers'. Similarly, a manager, as against an owner of a business enterprise, was often disparagingly said to be 'only a boy'. For instance, one of our Reef-town friends, talking about a trader who, as manager, ran a shop put up with European capital said: 'He parades in the village as the owner, but he is only the boy . . . '. (The two researchers in this study sometimes had a good giggle when thinking of Mr Harry Oppenheimer, Chairman of the Anglo-American Corporation, and the uncrowned king of South Africa, who according to this 'down-naming' custom of the elite would have to be designated as 'only the boy'.) In another case, one of our group of elite went into partnership with his brother-in-law, to manage a newly-opened branch of his relative's original shop. A few months later he explained to us: 'My brother-in-law was doing no work at all, he made me his boy and I had to do all the work. So I bought myself out . . .' Thus Africans were now using the word to designate all those who stood in a relationship of personal dependence towards a fellow African; they used it to describe in the same derogatory meaning the one who does all the work while the other gets the honour and the pay!

The 'pass'

The word 'pass' has never been precisely defined, but the so-called 'pass laws' aimed at, or were considered to aim at, controlling all movement of Bantu into, out of, or within, a specified area, at enforcing contractual relations, at maintaining order and at identifying the bearer. Also registered in the pass were all service contracts and tax receipts. The pass had to be produced on demand by certain specified persons, and failure to do so constituted a crime, for which imprisonment followed.[5] In the Cape the first introduction of passes dates back to 1760, in Natal to 1884 and in the Transvaal to 1860. These passes appear to have been aimed originally at ensuring the

P

unhindered movement of non-whites. However, they gradually came to be used in the service of the control of Bantu labour movements and of urban influx.

The Native (Urban Areas) Act, No. 21 of 1923 aimed at the adequate accommodation of Bantu in segregated sections of urban areas, and at ensuring the control of the movement of Bantu into towns. Until recently, however, its provisions were never fully enforced; accommodation was never adequately provided, nor was the townward flow of Bantu stemmed.

Subsequently, amendment followed amendment and enquiry followed enquiry, while various laws controlling the movement of Bantu became ever more complex and opposition to the 'pass laws' ever stronger, until the Natives (Urban Areas) Consolidation Act of 1945 confirmed, simplified and tightened all provisions. In spite of all efforts, however, the urban Bantu population had by 1960, the year of our field research, increased to more than 30 per cent of all Bantu in South Africa.[6]

In later years, the direction of developments has been towards ever stricter control of the movement of labour, and even further curtailment of the rights of residence and of the acquisition of land in (white) urban areas, culminating in the Bantu Laws Amendment Act of 1964. In addition, the previously-accorded exemptions have been progressively restricted.

These exemptions are what concern us here, and must be explained. Under Proclamation 150 of 1934, certain categories of persons had been exempted from the so-called travelling pass, as well as from the passes created under the Urban Areas Act. These were, as far as relevant to our elite's job history: policemen and government messengers; natives accompanying their European masters; chiefs and headmen; members of the various Native administrative and advisory bodies; clerks and interpreters in the public service, or in the service of the local authority; ministers of approved churches; teachers in state and state-aided schools; university students and lecturers; members of the various learned professions, such as doctors and lawyers; employees of the Department of Native Affairs, and finally 'any native of good character and repute certified by a Native commissioner or magistrate as a fit and proper person to be exempted'. Also exempted were registered owners and purchasers of land. The result was that up to the end of 1946 nearly 10 per cent of the total Bantu population of Johannesburg had received exemption.

But of special importance in our context was the fact that also exempted from Influx Control, and not mentioned in the above, were the Mines and certain further agencies connected with the Mines. In our records were mentioned, for instance, the Modderfontein Dynamite Factory, the Witwatersrand Native Labour Association and the

188

Native Recruiting Corporation. And it was here that the South African Bantu, as well as many so-called 'Foreign Natives' found a loophole in the tight and ever tightening net which was drawn around the big cities.

It had become a well-known fact that if only one could get oneself recruited to the Mines, all could be arranged. (And if one allowed oneself to be recruited in the country, one could even obtain free transport by plane!)

'When I came in 1936 I had no urban pass. You just said you were visiting a friend in Johannesburg, and you got what they call a "visiting pass", and then you just stayed. I tried hard but I could not get a pass. I was six months looking for work. Then I met a schoolmate who told me of work at the Modderfontein Dynamite factory. This counted as a mine and was not subject to restrictions. And then, well, you're in and you got to know people and things, everything was quite easy. . . .'

Another one related his experiences as follows:

'All those urban permits, it did not work at all. They tried to round them up and took them back by lorries. But they all came back again from the country, the very next day. Or better still they learned how to do it. They had themselves recruited for the mines and as soon as they could they returned to the location and to the old boss. "Here I am again, baas." '

Hence, we found in our sample that, with only two exceptions, all the present clerks, ministers and traders who were not already in town and who were, at that stage, not qualified teachers (except teachers who did not want to teach) passed through the mines to get to town. To be precise: 11 of the 17 clerks (6 were already urban by the time they started work); 3 of the 6 ministers (the other 3 only came to town after they had become professionals); and 4 of the 10 traders and salesmen (4 were already in town when they started working and 2 were the exceptions). This was an interesting finding, for, although these eighteen individuals represented only 30 per cent of the total elite, the figure assumes significance if it is realized that they constituted 90 per cent of the not-urban-reared non-professionals.[7]

All jobs

Extent and nature of the job changes

In the subsequent occupational history of the elite there has been a great deal of change and movement. (See Table II 4:3.) Calculating

Table II 4:3 Showing the average number of working years
of jobs per person and of years per job of the elite by occupations

N = 59*

Occupational	Average number of years worked†	Average number of jobs held‡	Average number of years per job
Higher Teachers	19·50	5·74	3·40
Clerks:	27·12	7·88	3·47
Government	34·35	6·75	5·08
Municipal	27·11	8·50	3·19
Private	17·33	7·33	2·36
New Professions	11·50	5·50	2·09
Doctors	9·83	5·67	1·73
Ministers	30·08	7·83	3·84
Businessmen	21·63	5·88	3·68
Total	21·75	6·56	3·38

* One was unknown in detail.
† The 'years worked' or 'working years' are the actual periods in which
jobs were held. Prolonged interruptions, when jobs were left for study
purposes or to go home, have not been included.
‡ As 'odd jobs' had generally to be taken as one job only, the rate of
job change was probably slightly higher.

the extent of this job mobility, it was found that, in an average
number of 21·75 working years, they held an average of 6·56 jobs
per person, which means that the leading citizens of Reeftown had
a new job at least once every 3·38 years. This new job included, in the
definition given earlier, a change in place or type of job under the
same employer, as well as a change of employer. It applied to promotions as well as to stages of self-employment. This beat in the general
rhythm of the job changes was maintained during the greater part of
the working years. It was partly the result of their own restless search
for improvement (see Table II 4:2) and partly due to the general
fluidity of the living conditions of the African people.

In Fig. 3, the number of jobs held has been related to the number
of working years (not ages) and this comparison shows a fairly
marked positive correlation trend (corr. coeff. is 0·746) which
demonstrates the job mobility of the sample. In spite of this common
rhythm, however, there were some differences between the occupational groups which make generalizations somewhat misleading. The
teachers, the clerks, the ministers and the businessmen had changed
their jobs more or less every three years, but the younger professionals
had changed theirs more often, usually every two years, but most of
these were still in the earlier stages of their careers when job changes

190

were more frequent. The older professional groups had all worked an average of between twenty and thirty years, and the patterns here were more developed. Of all the groups, the teachers appeared to have conformed most closely to the general pattern of about two to four years per job. Within the clerical group there were, as always, wide divergencies. The Government clerks had worked by far the longest (34·35 years), had held fewer jobs, and each job on an average for over five years. The private clerks appeared to be the most unstable in this respect; they had changed their jobs every 2·36 years. The municipal clerks stood between these two groups: in working lives, which were considerably shorter than those of the Government clerks, they had held an average of two jobs more than the latter; but they had held these jobs somewhat longer than the private clerks. These municipal clerks had held more jobs than any other group, but although their average job duration was just below the general average, this does not say much because there were such great variations among them.

The ministers had worked only a slightly shorter time than the Government clerks, while they had held on an average one job more, and worked for a considerably shorter period in each job, whereas the traders and salesmen, apart from one isolated case, had all held their jobs an average length of time, and worked an average number of years.

This general rhythm applied both to 'bureaucratic' and to 'free-enterprise' mobility. But the careers of our elite cannot show their true dynamism when they are merely considered in terms of averages and rates of job change, because many different types of jobs and professions, each with its own mobility imperatives, were hidden in a classification according to present occupations.

At one time or another during their working lives, three-quarters of the elite had held types of jobs other than those held at the time of the field research. (See Table II 4 : 4. This excluded holiday jobs as well as pastoral and agricultural jobs.) Among them they had held most types of occupations which, in their days, were usual for Africans – jobs such as 'general labourer' and 'boy', 'police constable' and 'underground miner', as well as clerical jobs in public, private or mine employment. Sixteen of the present non-teachers had once taught; nearly two-thirds of the whole group had once worked as clerks either for the Government or the Local Authority or in one of the Mines.

More than one-third had spent some part of their working lives on the Mines, although only eight had been underground miners. About one-quarter had spent some time in a police uniform, whether with the S.A. Police Force, the Native Affairs Department or with one of the local non-European Affairs Departments. Some 25 per cent had

Figure 3 Comparison of the number of jobs in a man's working life with the number of years that he has worked

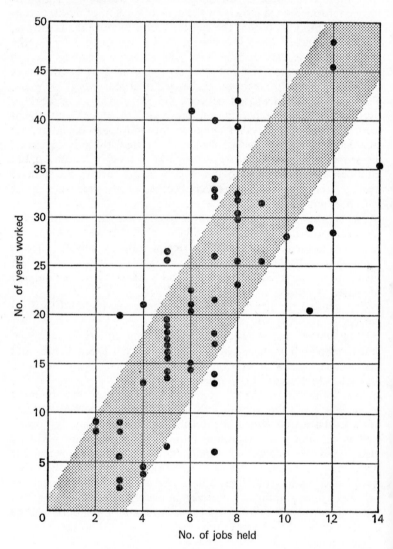

Figure 4 The relationship between number of years worked and average duration of each job

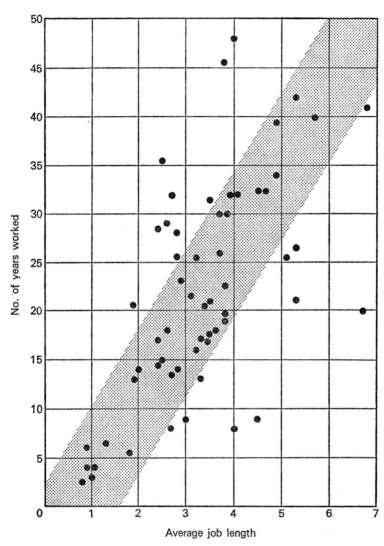

Table II 4:4 Showing the number of those who had worked in occupations other than the present, by present occupation

N = 59

Present occupation	General labourer	'Boy'	Uniformed		Mines		Clerical		Teaching	Other	Total
			SAP*	NEAD†/NAD‡	Under-ground	Clerical	Public	Private			
Higher Teachers N = 9	2	2	—	1	—	—	1	1	—	—	5
Principals N = 10	—	—	—	—	2	—	2	—	1	—	4
Government Clerks N = 4	2	—	1	4	1	3	—	2	1	—	4
Municipal Clerks N = 10	3	4	1	1	2	6	1	4	3	2	10
Private Clerks N = 3	—	1	—	—	—	2	2	—	2	—	3
Newer Professions N = 6	—	1	—	1	—	1	—	2	3	—	5
Doctors N = 3	—	1	—	—	—	—	—	—	1	—	1
Ministers N = 6	2	2	—	1	1	2	—	—	4	1	5
Traders N = 3	2	1	1	1	—	1	—	2	—	1	3
Salesmen N = 5	1	2	2	1	2	2	1	3	1	1	5
Total	12	14	5	10	8	17	7	14	16	4	45

* South African Police.
† Non-European Affairs Department (Municipal).
‡ Native Affairs Department (Government).

spent part of their working lives as 'boys' while 20 per cent had begun their careers as 'labourers'.

However, taken as a whole, the elite did not spend a long time in other types of occupations or with other kinds of employers. The actual time spent was only two-fifths, or 40 per cent of their total working lives. (See Table II 4:5.) And by far the longest period, indeed more than half of this percentage, was spent in clerical occupations, mostly in private and mining jobs, as well as in teaching. While twenty-six members of our elite had once worked as 'miners', 'boys' or 'labourers', the actual time spent in these occupations was short. In fact, and with only few exceptions, it was never longer than three years and generally less. The underground miners stayed an average of one year before they either entered a clerical mine job or left the mine for good. Actually, more time was spent in the police uniform than in the miner's helmet.

But there were great differences between occupational groups, as well as between individuals. As we have come to expect by now, the three clerical groups also differed considerably in this respect. The Government clerks spent nearly one-quarter of their working lives in uniform; but if the uniformed job in the Native Affairs Department is considered as the normal preparatory stage for their present jobs (and we shall see that it was), then, except for the teachers, the Government clerks have had the most homogeneous job experience of all. The municipal clerks spent almost double the time in jobs and with employers other than the present, mainly as mine clerks and teachers. They have had the most heterogenous job experience, having held all the types of occupations ever held by our group, including those of industrial and factory workers, and of semi- or absolute self-employment.

The private clerks had spent the longest time of all in jobs other than the present one, and the relatively smallest period in semi-manual jobs. They were longest in the public service, whence all of them came to their present jobs. With regard to time spent in other occupations, the private clerks were closely followed by the salesmen, who also came from a very varied occupational background.

The longest time spent as general labourers was recorded by the traders and the municipal clerks, and the longest time spent as 'boy' was found among the doctors (this refers only to one of the three) and the salesmen.

As could be expected, the greatest homogeneity was found among the teachers, about half of whom never did anything but teach, while those who did something else for a while did so for a short time only. Again, as in so many other respects, it was found that the teachers were the lucky ones; they had had a viable profession right from the start of their careers. Except for the Roman Catholic priest, the

195

Table II 4:5 Showing the percentage of time spent* in occupations other than the present, by present occupation

N = 59

Present occupation	General labourer	Uniformed				Mines		Clerical		Teaching	Other	Total
		'Boy'	SAP†	NAD‡	NEAD§	Under-ground	Clerical	Public	Private			
Higher Teachers	1·42	1·99	—	1·43	—	—	—	2·43	0·28	—	—	7·56
Principals	—	—	—	—	—	0·51	—	2·67	—	6·59††	—	9·77
Government Clerks	1·09	—	1·81	23·80	—	1·45	4·54	—	2·91	0·72	—	36·36
Municipal Clerks	7·31	2·68	4·77	—	—	1·64	28·06	0·89‡‡	12·83	24·18	11·64	61·75
Private Clerks	—	2·88	—	—	1·49	—	27·88	45·67	—	5·28	—	81·73
Newer Professions	—	1·42	—	—	6·38	—	8·51	—	14·53	15·60	—	46·45
Doctors‖	—	11·86	—	—	—	0·55	0·41	—	—	1·69	—	13·56
Ministers**	3·87	6·23	—	2·22	—	—	—	—	—	15·78	3·88	32·96
Traders	6·44	0·43	2·57	24·03	—	—	2·57	—	14·59	—	—	50·64
Salesmen	1·74	10·02	3·05	8·28	—	1·02	12·20	0·87	24·62	7·84	7·84	77·56
Total	2·25	2·85	1·20	4·87	0·54	0·62	6·99	2·77	5·67	8·25	2·76	39·42

* The total number of years spent in the occupation has been expressed as a percentage of the total number of working years; times have been rounded off to nearest quarter year.

† The South African Police.

‡ The Native Affairs Department (Government), now called B.A.D. (Bantu Affairs Department).

§ The Non-European Affairs Department (Local Authority).

‖ Housemanship and Probationship have been included in the total working years and not as jobs other than the present.

** One minister taught after he had been ordained. This has not been included in jobs other than the present.

†† This refers to one of the two teachers employed as clerks by the Bantu Education Department, who had originally taught. The other one never taught.

‡‡ The one police sergeant.

ministers, by contrast, had had quite varied careers before they finally decided to choose their professions.

Of the ministers, only the Roman Catholic priest had never had another type of job before entering the Church. Only one of the doctors, Dr L., had had other jobs. None of the traders, although two had been to Teacher Training College, had ever taught. The one, Mr O., did not like teaching; and the other entered his father's business at an early age and went on from there. As can be seen ex-teachers are to be found among all occupational groups.

However, all this mobility took place among only a limited number of various jobs and employers which, even in a detailed classification, can be exhausted by nine categories. Only three individuals, who are not at present traders or salesmen, had worked during a certain period as full-time salesmen or had attempted to live entirely from the proceeds of an independent business. Only one person who is at present a salesman had spent about one-fifth of his working years in a skilled manual capacity. His story is told on pp. 225–7. In addition, our sample contained one individual who had worked for a short time as an industrial worker, a category which otherwise hardly occurred. This same person also worked later for a private employer in an unusual capacity.

With these few exceptions, however, the elite's past mobility followed certain stereotyped patterns which will now be explored.

Occupational mobility

In the career histories of our elite certain clear patterns of mobility can be traced. As these constituted the channels through which their occupational mobility upwards was effected; they make sense of the merely static and quantitative analysis of the rate and nature of the job changes.

There was first of all the pattern of the bureaucratic mobility of the teachers and Government clerks. Something of that of the teachers was shown in the career history of Mr Y.Z. (See pp. 183–4.) This type of mobility upwards implied job changes under the same employer, generally representing promotions or transfers with increased salaries, to ever larger schools with an ever greater number of pupils, more authority and greater responsibility; job changes from that of simple teacher in a village school (a 'one-teacher school' as these were often called) to a principalship of a large city school, and finally, to a supervisory position; job changes from a lower primary to a higher primary, and thence to a secondary and high school. In a few cases there was a sudden demotion either explained away or fully discussed with the investigator. The reason may have been a professional or personal mishap or transgression, and the result a missed promotion, a lost seniority or even a straightforward reappointment at a lower salary. Or also a drop in salary was due to preference for a smaller post in a preferred place where the teacher could live with a relative or where he hoped to get a better position later, where his transport costs were negligible, or his wife already had a good job. But generally, the successive jobs, accompanied by educational progress, represented a continuous series of improvements.

The Public Service, and particularly Government Service, was entered via the police uniform, either the khaki uniform of the S.A. Police or the dark uniform of the Municipal Police Force. In Government Service the pattern then was as follows. From uniformed police constable promotion to uniformed record taker, which meant an increase in status and pay; this offered a good chance of becoming interpreter–clerk, first in uniform, though later this was no longer necessary. The position of interpreter–clerk was much sought after – it had semi-professional status; it had legal associations; and above all else, it gave ample opportunities for additional earnings; it gave real power. 'All police were keen to do that,' we were told. Many individuals had seen such persons in their home district and now wanted to imitate their example. Subsequently, one passed through the various grades: from Interpreter–Clerk Grade III through Interpreter–Clerk Grade II to Grade I or, at a certain stage, one was promoted to Clerk Grade II with the hope of ultimately becoming Native Clerk Grade I.

It was not only the role, the discipline, the power and the uniform which appealed to many of our respondents. Four of our elite became policemen because there had been talk that, as and when Africans were given greater responsibilities over their own affairs, they would soon be given the jobs of station commanders. But the main reason why so many of our elite donned the police uniform was because it was the only way to enter the coveted Government Service, and this is still today the supreme goal of large numbers of Bantu in South Africa, as it is in other countries of Africa. But also in this field promotion could only follow upon increased educational qualifications, and most assistant Government clerks became bogged down by examination failures. They then remembered that they 'had never really liked the job of policeman'. These seven appear on Table II 4:2.

There were in our sample three marked movements away from something. The one was away from the teaching profession, mainly into clerical occupations or into other professions. The second was the movement away from the Mines. Most of the eight persons who began their urban careers as underground miners left as soon as their contracts were completed. In a rare case there was promotion from mine labourer to mine clerk, but in the Mines mobility was usually from one clerical job to the other, particularly in the case of those individuals who were 'good at sports', for then 'all the Mines wanted you and offered you good clerical posts', which were really sinecures. Apparently, as a sportsman, you 'had an easy life and not a worry in the world'. But for persons with initiative and drive, the Mines offered no prospects, and it was essential to move out and into real urban life, before one would 'fall asleep' or 'become stupid'.[8] 'Of course, that's what they wanted you to be!' Some discovered in time that 'although you had free accommodation with your family, when you die your family has to leave. There is no security in the Mines,' they said. 'Government service is much safer.' And in fact, the biggest stream away from the Mines was into the Public Service. This move was usually direct, but sometimes it was effected via an attempt at improvement by means of a job in private employment.

The movement away from private employment was the third of these. If the Mines were already considered to be lacking in prospects, this was even more so in other types of private employment. We recall that even the three private clerks in our sample were really employed by semi-public bodies with branches all over the country and particularly with potential branches in the African territories. There was no hope of promotion to executive positions for the African clerk or salesman, and sooner or later he would come up against the colour bar. We have in our sample only one case of promotion to a better-paid and higher-status job in the private sector. Not unexpectedly, the employer was a large Corporation with many branches all over Southern Africa.

There were, as there are today, many changes between the occupations of teacher, clerk and salesman, often as a result of the conflict between a man's own inclinations and the wishes of his parents. Mr. N.D., for instance, the earliest case in our sample of a life insurance agent ('It paid well because there was a 'flu epidemic on!') was forced by a strong-willed father to return to teaching. He escaped once more, now to the Mines, because his brother had come back with glamorous stories of money in Johannesburg, 'and I wanted money most'. But his parents thought 'my life was too free', and his father provided him with a principalship as a bait. In two cases, again both concerning teachers, unwilling teachers escaped over the border, the one into Mozambique and the other into Rhodesia, where the one continued teaching but on a higher salary, and the other became a clerk, also with a better income. Both, however, had to come back; the one because his father said: 'What if you should die so far away, and I would not see your grave?!', and the other because: 'I could not bear to see my mother in tears.' In those days parents still wanted their sons to enjoy the status and security of teachers and ministers, and they looked down upon mere clerks and salesmen. Now this has changed.

199

There were also many job changes between the private and public sectors, as well as between the three authorities: the Government, the Province and the Local Authority. The persons concerned were frequently the less stable elements. They were ambitious and restless, generally intelligent but not highly educated. 'Live wires', they were called by the Reeftowners. Their careers do not show the steady improvement from job to job, but rather a ceaseless and generally useless search to reach the top. And in this they succeeded in their present jobs, but in some cases one had the feeling it would not last. In ranking tests they showed a wide scatter because the more securely established elite were loath to admit them to their ranks. They represented, in our sample, the nearest approach to the self-made man.

Two examples should here be given to complete the picture, for there must be many in Reeftown who, unlike these two, did not make the grade.

Mr I.P. began to teach in a farm school, but 'saw no money in it'. He did his J.C. by private study and became a despatch clerk in a grocery shop in a nearby town. Though better paid than teaching, the job had no prospects, so he wanted to enter Government Service.

Towards this end he obtained a male nurse certificate and he got the job of Dispensary Clerk at the Mental Hospital, with a salary almost double that of his previous job, and there were free rations. After almost seven years in the Hospital, 'Johannesburg came to my mind', and he became a Safety Supervisor in one of the Mines. He had two quick transfers or promotions within a year, then left for a clerical job in the Casualty Department of the General Hospital 'because the working conditions were better there'.

After five years he applied for and obtained a job as Interpreter–Clerk Grade II at the Magistrate's Court in a Reef town.

After four years something must have happened; he left because 'the pay was poor', yet he took a job as Chief Clerk, again in one of the mines, for less than half the pay. However, after six months at the mine, the Court 'took me back', again as Interpreter–Clerk Grade II.

Although, as he explained, 'I was earmarked for promotion', he did not get it. (The sad truth was that he never passed the required Matric.)

He then accepted his present job because he saw in it new and undreamt-of prospects, and in this he was right.

As anywhere else in the world, intelligence and personality were rarer than educational qualifications, and many employers were probably quite willing to forgive much in order to keep someone who had the rarer commodity.

As it was the 'only way to come to the Reef; you could only come via the Mines', Mr Y. M. went to the Mines and then took a job as a 'boy' in private employment as soon as he had secured himself a pass. But the only clerical job he could get with his qualifications (he only had J.C.) brought him back to the Mines for a further couple of years until he succeeded in pushing himself into the public service of a Reef town in a non-manual capacity. 'Trouble' made him then take on a clerical job in private employment. Again he had 'trouble' and he left to take up a job in the Native Affairs Department. 'Trouble again', and the N.E.A.D. in his own Reeftown, who had employed him before, took him back in another of their departments. At the end of 1960 he had to be dismissed but his own Township Administration found him another excellent job in another of the Public Services, where his undeniable gifts could be used to his advantage.

Such patterns occurred not infrequently. Once an individual had settled in a township, had bought or built himself a house and had become active in various organizations; once his wife had also found employment and become an asset in community functions; once his children were in local schools and had joined in the sports and music, a well-meaning Administration felt, in a sense, responsible for the family's welfare and tried to be of assistance. They often covered up the reasons for a sudden departure from their services; and quite often they were instrumental in finding employment with another public body or with another department of their own service. This was one of the many reasons why public service was preferred to private employment. The protection of a benevolent Local Authority was invaluable and could often put a man again on the right road.

Finally, there was the move into semi-self-employment and self-employment, and some mobility between the two. Of the nine persons in our elite who were semi- and entirely self-employed in 1960, all except one, who had inherited his father's business, had come from the police or from private clerical employment, and among them we found the greatest number of those who had spent the largest proportion of their working years in manual or semi-manual employment.[9]

It has been asserted that the first job is an excellent predictor of the subsequent career, and that the degree of social mobility can be described in terms of the occupational distance between the first and the current job.[10] Both of these assertions would apply in the

201

Republic only with great reservations. Yet it has become quite clear that the people studied here have made phenomenal progress. From a beginning in manual or semi-manual jobs, or at best in jobs as assistant teachers in small village schools or as minor clerks they now occupy the highest professional public service and commercial jobs available to South African Bantu as represented in the township of Reeftown. There is also not one among them who is not educationally and occupationally higher than his father.

Yet whether this social mobility upwards can be expressed by comparing the first and the last salary is doubtful. The usual difficulties in establishing real wages, in view of the decreasing value of money and the rising price level, were here complicated by the changing needs of people gripped in the process of the most far-reaching modifications in their way of life. Moreover, the differences in social origin and age of these individuals all in uneven stages of advancement made any precise analysis impossible. Added to this a higher salary in the next job was no unequivocal indication of a higher income. Ever-increasing costs of transport, which have always weighed heavily in Bantu wages, may have been such as to negate the increase in pay. Fringe benefits, and especially opportunities for earning 'on the side', may have offset a lower salary. The same applies if the new job offered better prospects in the long run, or could be used as a 'stepping stone' to the next stage, or brought one to an area where one wanted to be. Residential or geographical changes, either as a result of the policy of successive governments or as a result of the uneven economic development of the country, have always played a large part in Bantu job histories. There was, even at present, a definite migratory movement among the younger professionals from the West Rand (which was said to show less development: 'All the main jobs have been given to the well-known older residents, and newcomers or younger people haven't a chance') to the East Rand where there were more industries and jobs and where the new townships were enlarging faster and people believed there were more openings in the public service. It should, moreover, be recalled that the total African income (calculated after due adjustment for the upward trend in prices) had more than doubled in the twenty-year period between 1938–9 and 1959;[11] that during the years 1963–5 (i.e. after our own calculations were made) most public-servant salaries had been increased (which included the teachers, the clerks and professionals employed by Government and Local Authority in our sample); and that some of the highest earners (ministers, doctors, salesmen and traders) who constituted almost one-third of the elite, were not included in our calculations.

While cautioning therefore against any rash conclusions, we are giving in Table II 4:6, the first and present average salaries of all

Table II 4:6 Showing average earnings in their first and current jobs of all salaried respondents, by present occupation

N = 42

Occupation	Earnings in Rands	
	First job	Current job
Higher Teachers	16·12	119·66
Principals	17·86	95·16
Clerks:		
Government	9·50	109·00
Municipal	12·66	69·00
Private	15·34	71·34
New Professionals	29·84	86·34
Total	17·00	92·54

those employed, by present occupation, without any further comment.

Future mobility trends

Having arrived in the higher levels of the occupational field, little purpose was served by changing yet again. Thus, one would expect a gradual slowing-down of the general rate of job mobility. And, indeed, it was found that as the elite grew older, the average duration of their jobs increased. In Fig. 4, the number of years worked has been related to the average job length; this comparison shows a positive correlation trend, though not as marked as that of Fig. 2 (corr. coeff. is only 0·599). With some this job stabilization was very marked, with others less so. It depended on a great many factors.

It may be that as people become older and more established, they do not risk losing their jobs so lightly, with the attendant worry of having to find new ones. It may be that people grow tired, and that a certain inertia militating against the very idea of change develops; but knowing the precise job histories of all individuals, we can say with confidence that other factors were involved in this gradual slowing-down of the earlier job mobility.

In studying the material for the potential future mobility trends it adumbrated, we were concerned mainly with the rate of mobility, i.e. with the changes in the duration of successive jobs; but these were inevitably connected with the nature of the job changes and, therefore, with the types of jobs to be changed from and to.

For surely, with our people, the main reason for remaining longer in their jobs was that it became increasingly more difficult to find still better ones. They were approaching the ceiling, either of their own capacities or of the present opportunities for Africans.

Q

From a study of the job histories of our elite, and a precise analysis of the duration of the first, the previous and the current jobs, and from what was known about later developments up till recently, two main patterns emerged which appeared as two different and opposite mobility trends: the one towards stabilization, and the other towards continued mobility, though at a slower rate.

Whichever of these two trends obtained depended, of course, on a great many factors besides age. Among these we would single out mainly the type of occupation/profession and the extent to which any new job could be combined with residence in Reeftown.

As to the first factor, it needs no explanation, because, as everywhere else, it was mainly the group of the self-employed – in our sample represented by the doctors and the shop owners – who tended towards stabilization, whereas, also as everywhere else, the group of civil servants and (potential) managers had to be prepared for the fact that any occupational mobility upwards would necessitate residential mobility.[12]

The pattern of **the self-employed** would be seen clearly in the job history of the doctors. Whereas the eldest of the three moved almost automatically together with the population from the old location to the new township, the second doctor came to join him during the early years of our field research. After having tried out two other towns in each of which he practised for some two to three years, and not finding the conditions to his taste, he then chose Reeftown for final settlement. At that time our third doctor, the youngest and most recently qualified, was in his turn using Reeftown for a first 'scouting around' period. He then lived in a hired municipal house and practised in temporary consulting rooms. Towards the end of 1961 he decided that there was 'too much competition' in our township, and moved to a neighbouring township which still seemed virgin ground. There he has since built himself his own large residence.

In this pattern of early stabilization after a brief experimental period, the job histories of the independent entrepreneurs from the moment that they became self-employed (most of them had had other jobs before) were similar, whether they were doctors or traders. They represented the stability which was the hallmark of an earlier, mainly pre-twentieth century, western-type middle class.

Looking now at the job histories of the representatives of a **(potential) managerial class,** it was found by contrast that the past mobility as well as the future mobility trends of the semi-self-employed and the privately-employed clerks in our sample were similar. The occupational background of both groups showed great variations. They had held first jobs which lasted just under or just over one year, their careers seemed to have taken a long time to get under way, and even now did not show a definite pattern. Even in their penultimate jobs they still had not yet exceeded the average job length.

In their current jobs both these groups had similar types of employers – large corporations, semi-public bodies, with branches all over the Republic, in the towns as well as in the country, in white as well as in black areas, corporations eager to capture the growing African market and, towards this purpose, to train and employ Africans.

With regard to the sales representatives, they had already been longer than average in their current jobs – $4\frac{1}{2}$ years. There were, however, considerable variations; and, on closer inspection it became manifest that the older ones had stayed already longer than these $4\frac{1}{2}$ years in their present jobs, showing that some satisfaction and, therefore, some job stabilization had been reached. (See, for example, Mr M. K. whose job history is told on pp. 225–7.) But the younger ones were becoming fidgety and it was easy to predict that they would soon move to jobs with better prospects, or, at least, to jobs where similar promises of managerial posts seemed to them more likely to materialize. In the relatively new field of salesmanship, there was considerable job mobility from one European importer or manufacturer to another, and the continued mobility of most of the salesmen in our sample can be confidently predicted for the future.

In contrast, the privately-employed clerks had in this same year of 1961 not yet been long in their present employment, which they had accepted in anticipation of promotion to managerial positions, if not in town then in the country. However, if these promotions would not materialize after an expected period of training and of gaining experience, as would appear likely, no one could doubt that these 'failed managers' would move on again, frustrated and embittered.

Everywhere in the African states, black matriculants were becoming managers, and black graduates Company directors. It is not the aim of this study to investigate why this was not happening in South Africa, whether, that is, the reason was inadequacy of the African incumbents or unwillingness on the part of the whites to accept Africans in managerial positions equal to, and on a par and in natural competition with, their own. The important point was that most educated Africans believed themselves capable of taking up executive posts.

There were, thirdly, **the public servants.** In the public service, whether in professional or clerical jobs, occupational mobility could as a rule not occur without residential mobility. Among the professional public servants were some of the youngest members of the elite, who would still have to move around to different areas in a succession of jobs lasting between two to four years before the rate

205

of job change would show signs of slowing down to more than the average job duration, when they would occupy the senior posts in their profession.

The pattern of the older public servants could be seen in the Government clerks, in some municipal clerks and in the teachers. Their job mobility and/or promotions at first followed a fairly regular rhythm of some two to four years, slowing down gradually until, in their previous jobs, they had stayed twice as long. In their present jobs the clerks and interpreters had been already a considerable time, whereas most teachers had only as recently as three or four years ago attained their present positions. In other Government departments, there had been no new promotional opportunities opened up for African clerks comparable to those which had been created for African teachers in the Department of Bantu Education. Our teachers owed their present jobs to two developments: the gradual growth and expansion of the school system in Reeftown, and the sudden Africanization of the administration and supervision of African education. These developments probably caused considerable job mobility at first, not only because some moved into higher positions and others moved into the positions vacated, but also because of the increase in transfers and dismissals, as well as in the number of teachers who left the profession or the country. This very Africanization, however, may tend later to stabilize job mobility, particularly in the lower educational levels, because transfers, now largely in the hands of Africans themselves, were becoming more cumbersome and expensive to arrange as 'tribal' and kinship affiliations were replacing the previous religious considerations as a major inducement for appointments and promotions.

However, some of the older public servants, professional or clerical, in our sample had gone as far as was possible for persons with their qualifications, considering the job opportunities currently available for Africans. If further promotion meant making yet another educational effort, they were unlikely to obtain it.

Another point was that if promotion meant moving away from the neighbourhood of Reeftown, which it almost certainly would, then these older public servants would probably think twice. For a very important factor in slowing down mobility was formed by the family, the house and other possessions.

If the wife was working satisfactorily in the place, a job change meant temporary or prolonged separation from her, depending on how soon she could find a similar or better job in the new district; and if the children had settled into schools or jobs, it meant separation from the children also. In a few cases in which a member of the elite had newly arrived in Reeftown, the wife had remained in the old place, either alone or with the children, either until a new job was found or the previous house was sold. And in this last was the snag. For family separations had happened before in these people's mobile past, but the house was a different matter.

Most of these individuals were, as we have seen, owners of better-type, more expensive and often self-built houses; even some whose occupational field was not, or not primarily in Reeftown, had chosen to live there because of the favourable housing conditions. And it was these houses which now tied them to their present jobs. For these houses were very difficult, if not impossible to sell. There were a number of reasons for this. People who could afford to pay cash for a house (and in the present fluidity of these Bantu communities only cash payment was acceptable) were few and far between. Private housing bonds were not available to Africans in the new housing estates where they did not enjoy freehold rights; and commercial loans were, considering the risks, in any case not profitable propositions. Some employers lent money to their employees to buy their own houses; sometimes European friends, particularly co-religionists, gave loans, but if money was lent privately on a purely commercial basis exorbitant rates of interest were demanded. Ethnic grouping further restricted the number of buyers.

Moreover, people who could afford to pay cash for a house preferred to build their own houses according to their own tastes and requirements. There was a curious resistance in the township to buying a house which had been owned and occupied by strangers who had possibly died there. Yet unless the house could be sold, a move was not desirable; capital needed for the new establishment remained tied up in the old place.

It was almost impossible to let the house, and in any case not advisable. Tenants were said to be unreliable and generally ruinous; while separate tenants for each room could possibly be found, a tenant to pay a reasonable rent for a five- or six-roomed house was almost non-existent. We were frequently told of losses incurred by having to leave one's previous house in the hands of African lawyers or estate agents and finally, having to sell at a loss. Property buying and selling were still rather new activities and the appropriate attitudes had not been formed.

In view of all this, it was often considered not worth while to move elsewhere, even for a better job. Thus the house, far more than the family, acted both as a stabilizer in the flux, and as a brake on upward mobility. (Here there was no difference between houses held in freehold or leasehold. The question of freehold *versus* leasehold for Africans in the urban, i.e. white, areas was a political principle, not a social problem. The right of freehold had meaning only as a symbol; time and time again, in the past, it had not prevented removals.) Some members of the elite went so far as to express their regret at

207

having built themselves their large, expensive residences, as these now literally immobilized their further careers.

There was, at present, a growing number of higher public servants as well as higher teachers who, having become wise to this fact, preferred to live in rented houses in order to preserve their freedom of movement; or who, conversely, searched for ways and means towards an independent livelihood in Reeftown.

In this increasing interdependence between occupational and residential mobility one could recognize the beginnings of a new migratory elite of educated and professionals, who must move about in order to move up. Sooner or later the local authorities would have to provide for the specific housing needs of this new migratory elite.

Two completely successful careers

These careers have much in common, though in other respects they differ greatly. Both persons were ambitious and endowed with gifts of personality and character. Both came from good homes, and had parental encouragement. Both had mothers who were aristocrats in the old order. Both also had a background of inter-'tribal' mobility.

Both were, in a sense, self-made; they came up the hard way and were brought up in relatively poor circumstances. Both only gradually acquired, by dint of planning and application, the qualifications on which their present positions were based. Both have since moved away from Reeftown.

However, the one came up within the professional framework of his original training and under the approving eye of his superiors; the other left his original profession and had to move through many different jobs and employers until he too found his vocation. Both represented an earlier type of professional, and were in many ways untypical of the younger generation with its narrow professionalism. For both loved their chosen professions, and meant to help their less-favoured countrymen.

However, in other respects, such as the more private domestic side of their lives and careers, they represented complete contrasts.

Having reached what was so far the highest rung on their respective professional ladders, both Mr S.K. and Mr P.Q. enjoyed wide esteem. They not only occupied positions of authority, and were regularly in contact with Europeans, but they were sincerely interested in European art and culture – the one in European visual arts, the other in classical western music; and both actually read books!

Mr P. Q.

Mr P.Q. started his teaching career at the age of 23 in one of the schools belonging to his own Church and at a salary of R6 per month. It was, as he explained, the period of the depression and teachers' salaries were reduced to the level of those of the unqualified teacher. In 1934 salaries were restored to their former level, which was R11 for NPL-qualified teachers. 'Teachers' salaries have always been bad,' said Mr P. Q. From as early as 1916 onwards, resolutions asking for improved salaries were adopted at every single conference of all the provincial African Teachers' Associations.

After he had passed his J.C. two years later, he wanted to leave his job. 'That was not difficult. I was always in demand.' When the Inspector came for the oral examination of his school, he gave him a recommendation for a vacancy at Sch. He wanted to go to Sch. because his mother's younger sister, whom he dearly loved, lived on the other side of the river, which meant that he could stay with her. But when he arrived at Sch., he was taken to R., to another school belonging to the same mission. There his salary was increased to R13 per month. But he only stayed about one year, until he got his appointment at Sch.

This was to be promotion, for now he would be a principal. Just after his appointment, that was, 'just after she had had the joy of seeing her son appointed principal', his mother died.

When he arrived at school, 'the place was being cleared'. As so often happened, the location had grown to such an extent that it now almost touched the white town. Instead of taking up his new post, he had to watch the removal of his school, together with the removal of the entire location, to L.S. In that school he remained principal from the middle of 1935 to the end of 1943. During this period he passed Matric.

That had been an uphill climb, he told us. 'I had always been handicapped by the fact that in J.C. a second language had not been compulsory, and I had no second language. My first had been English. I had already tried to catch up with Afrikaans as early as in 1934–5, but not seriously. Then, in 1936, I began to think seriously of doing my Matric in two years. But I failed several times, mainly because of my Afrikaans. Then, finally in 1939 I passed, mainly because of the help of a European woman who improved my construction.' In January 1940 he married. His wife had N.P.L.

When the family increased, he 'sent her to school' to get her kindergarten diploma which she achieved in one year. One day, while she was away on her training, Dr Eiselen came to Mr P. Q.'s school and said that the school had too many children. 'He said that there was not enough room for all those children and that I was breaking the regulations. He said that he could not understand that I, as a responsible person (I was then Secretary of the Transvaal Teachers' Association) could do such a thing. I ought to be dismissed. But by the way, why was I still teaching in a primary school? I should work in a secondary school. I protested that I was not a graduate, but Dr Eiselen said that was nonsense, you are more competent than many graduates. You must take the first advertised post in a high school.' [This is Dr W. W. M. Eiselen whose appointment as Chief Inspector of Native Education in the Transvaal was an important event in the history of African education. Dr Eiselen's name occurred in many career histories of our teachers as a benevolent figure, helping and advising; he is without exception gratefully remembered.]

This started P. Q. thinking – and calculating.

Fort Hare University then cost R90 per annum. (Later this was increased to R110.) But the Fort Hare bursaries were still for R60 only – a sum fixed in earlier days when the costs were lower. And Mr P. Q. had no money to supplement the difference. What to do?

He applied to the Superintendent of his township but to no avail. He then contacted Mr Rheinallt-Jones for the missing R30, and was told that he should apply for a bigger bursary. [This is J. D. Rheinallt-Jones, who was a.o. Founder and Director of the S.A. Institute of Race Relations (1930–47), Senator representing the Transvaal and Orange Free State under the Representation of Natives Act (1937–42), etc.] But even before he could do this, something extraordinary happened. He received a letter from the Department which said that 'in reply to your letter' he had been granted a bursary. Dr Eiselen was responsible.

'You know, Mrs Brandel, in those days bursaries were few and difficult to get. Nowadays everybody can get a bursary of some kind.'

Now, impatient to start, Mr P. Q. had already begun studying for his B.A. with the University of South Africa which, at that time, controlled the Fort Hare examinations. And in 1943 he had already written three subjects on his own. So when he finally obtained his bursary and went to Fort Hare, this counted as his first-year B.A. He then passed his second and third year at Fort Hare.

During these years his wife supported the family, for she was now a qualified kindergarten teacher.

As a graduate he returned to a Principalship in the newly-founded High School of L.S. township where he had previously taught. During the ten years of his principalship he became one of the most esteemed personalities in African education, fearlessly speaking up for what he thought right and sensible against a restrictive Government on the one hand, and an irresponsible, confused and demanding younger generation of teachers on the other.

In 1956 he applied for a post as Sub-inspector. He described the sequence of events as follows:

'With the first Sub-inspectors, there had been no question of applications. They were simply nominated. Probably the Department was afraid that what with all the opposition to the Bantu Education Act no Africans would come forward for the new higher posts. Some of those first Sub-inspectors were not even graduates. That was a big mistake. It now holds up our salaries. When a second group of Sub-inspectors was required, all the principals of the secondary schools were expected to apply. I had been in the forefront of the struggle against Bantu Education – in the right way and for the right reasons, not like those politicians. Some statements of mine had even appeared in the Press. But when my inspector's clerk advised me to apply, I decided to do it. I had already for some time felt over-strained; I was working too hard. My health was affected. A principal's job demands much work and all very intensive. But a supervisor's job, although the work involves much running around, is less intensive. So I was part of the second batch of sub-inspectors.'

Mr S.K.

No sooner had Mr S.K. obtained his NPL than he became principal of the farm mission school which had been founded by his father (who had been a migrant labourer while the family lived on a large European farm. He was literate and very Christian so that he became a Church elder and later an evangelist in his Mission), and where he had himself gone to school.

'Those people there were raw,' he said. 'They were twenty years and older when they started school.' The idea was mainly to give them religious instruction and, of course, they learned to read and write. 'You were taught not much in those days, but that little well.' However as it now had, in Mr S.K., a qualified principal, the school was taken over and subsidized by Government and considerably modernized. 'My father was kicked out and even privies were made.' His salary then was R13 'and that was a lot'. The (European) minister apparently could not believe 'that this high salary for a native could be true'.

S.K. worked hard, but then got bored staying at home. His

father was too strict. His beloved sister was also teaching at the same school, and every month father took all his sister's money away from her. 'That was of course normal in those days and even now.' All this explains his background, and why he wanted to get away to the Reef.

He had a friend who was then running the Bantu Men's Social Centre in Johannesburg. 'Oh, that's a long story. . .' Mr S.K. hoped to get a job there but the friend did not like it. He was afraid that Mr S.K. would oust him from the job, so he always got him jobs as far away as possible to get him out of the way. 'He feared my intelligence. . .'

Nevertheless, all went well and Mr S.K. started work in the time-office of one of the mines, though far away from Johannesburg. 'That's where you calculate the wages,' he explained. Although his father did not want him to leave and they 'had some misunderstanding', he left. The pay was around R10 per month. He calculated the wages and decided 'they rob their labour on those mines you know!' However, in the short space of three months he became 'a big *mampara*'. He was put to time-office plus compound records. 'I was quick and efficient.' Another three months and he was made a second senior. 'You see, Mrs Brandel, all my friends were drinking. That's the trouble with us Africans. I did not. So I got on. I then got R16 per month. That was more than I could have got with teaching.'

He then began to think of marriage, but that is another story.

Then a friend, yes, the same one, told him that at the B. Municipality (again far away) they wanted African clerks in the old location. 'That was something new then, and I thought here might be a chance to move forward, as I wanted to leave teaching for good.'

He then found that he was wanted, not as a clerk but as a policeman. At that time urban permits and influx control were being introduced and according to Mr S.K. intelligent people were wanted as police. This was in 1935. He obtained a senior job but was thoroughly disappointed. He had to be in a black uniform, and the pay was only R8 per month all told, but there was free board and lodging and lots of free meat. After six months he was promoted to clerk in the Immigration Department, and here he stayed throughout 1936. He then earned R20, which with all allowances, was 'a lot of money'. The job then came to an end and Mr S.K. went back to the police but with promotion and 'in charge of things'. Pay, however, was once again lower, only R15. 'Actually I was happy in that job as sergeant. People liked me. I caught them in a decent way. And I had a very good European boss. He liked me so much that when I left he gave me a fountain pen.'

At this time he began studying 'Health'. A certain Dr E. became Medical Officer of Health in B. and started lessons in Public Health, and that was when the idea of health as a career came to him. He did not take the usual course, but immediately went for the National Technical Certificate Part II, which was done through the Technical College, where there was no colour bar. It was a one-year course; and with only two others he passed the examination at the first attempt. He then took the Health Inspector's course of the Royal Sanitary Institute, which normally takes two years. But it took him a long time, five years in fact, as he failed a few times. Everything was new to him, he explained. 'Today you do your Matric first with a science subject,' but 'We, Mrs Brandel, we were pioneers!' Mr S. K. was the third African in the whole of South Africa to complete the course.

Earlier, however, two years after he first began studying Public Health, he learned that one of the Rand Mines wanted a person with Public Health qualifications. He applied and was accepted. He was really glad to have a profession again. His friends had told him all the time that chasing people and arresting them did not suit him, though he liked the job. As Health Induna on the mine he now got R17 plus a house and full rations. 'I must say my father was happy with so much meat!' During the five years he remained in that job, his pay was increased to R20 after he had passed the Royal Sanitary Institute exam.

'Another Reef town then advertised a job as Milk Depot Supervisor, which included looking after the vegetable market,' Mr S. K. continued. He obtained that job, which he kept for about one and a half years at a salary of R36 per month. What with oversales and odds and ends he earned R72 per month. This was certainly a big jump. But he had an 'expensive wife, and everything cost a lot of money'.

'Oversales? That is when you sell milk in a hurry, and you are expected to show an oversale, the foam on top. The difference is then yours. I did very well in that job. But it was not health work, it was really looking after the money and general cleanliness. There was no scope. Then also, there was a European inspector who did not like native inspectors. You see there was no native name for a health inspector. They just called you "Oespektor" and the Europeans were also called "Oespektor".' He did not like that. That was the only bad one, the others were all right. He is still there now.

It wasn't his type of job though. His wife was annoyed; but nevertheless he left, but not before he had secured the job for his brother and 'it made him rich in a few years'. He now has a shop in that township from the money earned at the milk depot. What happened was that he only did it for a short time, because the Council then stopped the milk subsidy, and so his brother was forced to start on his own on a real business basis. He began as a milk purveyor, then became a general dealer and he now also sells fruit. 'He is rich now.'

Mr S.K. then went to a township near Johannesburg which occupied a somewhat exceptional position among the African townships and locations, and was first an ordinary health inspector, starting with R48 per month. About five years later, after he had successfully passed yet another certificate (this time one termed 'Meat and Other Foods') his pay rose to R100.

'This Township was run by the Africans themselves. We had a Health Committee and it was run by us. An African Doctor was MOH. I got on well with him. Then, when *apartheid* came we said we wanted to run ourselves entirely, and we needed an African Chief Health Inspector and that's what I became.' In this position Mr S.K. earned R162 per month. In addition, he had a travelling allowance of some R40 to R60 per month. He had a large brand new Chevrolet. 'We Africans do ourselves well, when we can run ourselves.' He had eight or nine African inspectors under him, and says proudly: 'I am the only African who has ever been a Chief Health Inspector.'

'We in that Health Committee ran the Township. We were like a Town Council, but we had no borrowing rights and that is why we failed.' But before the Township was taken over by the Peri Urban Health Board of the big city, Mr S.K., who had seen the end coming, had already found something else . . .

Now Mr S.K. was one of the leading figures in Reeftown.

Black careers and white colour prejudice

Manual labour and the colour bar

In a study of the careers of a group of successful South African Bantu, the question which inevitably arises is in how far the careers of these professional, educated Africans have been adversely affected, or affected at all, by racial discrimination or the official colour bar. Our records can give us some specific information on certain well-defined and limited points bearing on this question.

First, we saw that quite a number of our elite did some form of

214

manual labour in the course of their careers. In how far was this due to the colour bar?

In order to give a precise and responsible reply it is advisable to make the usual distinction between manual and semi-manual work, but, in order to avoid any semblance of bias, to classify both as manual labour. Towards this purpose, all jobs as 'boys' and 'policemen' have been categorized as manual labour, together with the 'labourers' and, of course, all underground miners, called so by our elite themselves, as well as those who were said to have done 'pick-and-shovel' work. The 'boys' thus classified as 'manual' included minor clerks, a 'canteen manager', 'a laboratory assistant' as well as three men who did printing and developing in a photographic studio. The policemen included all constables and uniformed record takers. (See Table II 4:7.)

Yet, despite our deliberate attempt to boost the figure for manual work, only 50 per cent of our elite had apparently done some form of manual labour. This seems rather low in comparison with the 62 per cent found by Lipset and Bendix, for instance, in their sample of 935 Americans now in non-manual and professional occupation.[13] These authors do not explain which type of work was included in their term 'manual'; neither do they give any reasons why this manual labour was done. One can think up reasons, such as that this

Table II 4:7 Numerical distribution of all respondents by present occupation according to manual, semi-manual, or both kinds of jobs held during the course of their careers

Present occupation	Manual jobs only*	Semi-Manual jobs only	Both	Total
Higher Teachers	1	1	1	3
Principals	2	—	—	2
Government Clerks	—	1	3	4
Municipal Clerks	—	4	3	7
Private Clerks	—	1	—	1
New Professions	1	1	—	2
Doctors	1	1	—	1
Ministers	—	—	2	2
Traders	1	1	1	3
Salesmen	—	2	3	5
Total	6	12†	13	30

* 'Odd jobs' mentioned at the start of a career have been taken as one job and as manual labour.

† Four of these individuals never did any other manual or semi-manual jobs except those of uniformed policemen.

was the normal start of a career with the lack of qualifications and family connections they had at the time; that they had to have jobs and earn while they were waiting for a suitable job in their own profession, or perhaps because of sheer rebellious bravado and desire for adventure, freedom and travel. All these reasons also applied to our sample of educated Africans.

It is almost impossible to pinpoint exactly how far colour restrictions were responsible for the manual labour of our elite. Influx Control Regulations, for instance, which in themselves were a colour-discriminatory measure, determined with *whom* jobs had to be taken in town, but not *what* sort of jobs they had to take. Many of our elite obtained clerical mine jobs. It is, therefore, only by a process of elimination that one can arrive at an acceptable answer.

A desire for adventure, and not the colour bar, was definitely instrumental in the case of seven individuals who expressed this in terms of 'naughtiness' and 'to be a man'. There was no reason for taking up a job at all. Further schooling was not only possible, but desired by parents or rearers. Some of the policemen's jobs can be considered as having been taken up in the normal course of a desired career, such as those four cases who became policemen in the hope of becoming station commanders, and who, when this did not materialize, went back to clerical jobs.

Two further cases of manual labour in semi-manual jobs can be eliminated. They were taken up because of a sudden family crisis, and were normal jobs based on an education no higher than primary school. When the family finances were straightened out, both incumbents returned to school.

Having eliminated the seven manual and six semi-manual jobs of 13 individuals, 17 persons remained who may have been compelled by colour restrictions to do, at least for a while, manual labour in manual or semi-manual jobs. It is, however, impossible to decide whether these men were unable to obtain non-manual jobs because they were black or because they lacked experience, competence or qualifications.

It is, however, safe to assume that the pull towards non-manual jobs had been stronger in those days in South Africa than in America, for instance, for two reasons. First, in the period of their earlier job histories, the elite with only J.C. or even Std. VI, had higher status rating than they would obtain at present or in other countries; and they therefore believed themselves capable of holding any clerical position. Secondly, they had by that time already fully adopted from their white compatriots a generally contemptuous attitude towards manual labour. After all they grew up in a social environment in which all manual labour and unskilled work was called and regarded as 'kaffir-work'.[14] Consequently, our elite would make a more

216

determined effort to avoid manual labour than, for instance, their American colleagues.

Summing up, we may conclude from this careful analysis that, as against 62 per cent in a comparable American sample, only 50 per cent of our elite did manual work in manual and semi-manual jobs during the earlier stages of their careers and/or their urbanization. In just under half (43 per cent) of these instances, this was definitely not the result of colour discriminatory restrictions or practices, but in just over half (57 per cent) of the cases the colour bar may have been partly or wholly responsible. However, this applied almost exclusively to non-professionals.

Interracial and intraracial conflicts

In how far did racial discrimination or racial prejudice enter into the relatively few cases of demotions and dismissals which came to our notice?

To find the answer to this important question two sets of reasons for leaving a job must be carefully examined. These were the thirteen occasions when a job had been left for reasons classified as 'Technical or External Circumstances', and the twenty-five instances in which the reasons for leaving a job had been stated in terms of personalities and personal conflicts – reasons classified as 'Human Considerations'. (See Table II 4:2.)

The 'External Circumstances' included five cases of redundancy, and one case in which the employee had reached the age of retirement in his profession, when he took on a non-professional job. In the remaining seven cases racial discrimination in one form or another, whether directly or indirectly, may have occurred or contributed.

Two jobs had been in welfare organizations in Alexandra Township; when the status of Alexandra was changed, both persons became uncertain as to whether and in how far their jobs might be affected by the total reorganization entailed; and, therefore, they applied in advance for posts elsewhere. Another job, in a foreign country, was lost because of immigration difficulties. The job was in the Congo and the Belgian authorities refused permission for the immigration of the wife and children of the incumbent. One reason was a clear-cut question of colour bar. (See the full story of Mr M. K. on pp. 226–7.) Further, in the loss of two successive jobs held by another individual, the indirect consequences of discriminatory legislation could be seen. In the first job, dismissal followed an attempt to organize a strike, and in the next job an anticipated dismissal for the same reason was foreseen by the strike organizer. (European workers' strikes are not illegal, though strike leaders may still be threatened with dismissal.)

217

There was a possible colour-bar case in Mr. O. A.'s loss of an excellent job, with bonus and commission, in a firm of dry cleaners, although he himself did not report it in terms of colour discrimination.

Thus, redundancy and certain direct or indirect effects of colour discrimination were the main external reasons for a set-back in their occupational careers as reported by the elite themselves. Two interesting observations can be made. First, in most of the cases in which the colour bar in one form or another could be spotted, discriminatory *usus* aggravated the consequences of discriminatory laws. Secondly, all these jobs were held in private employment with private firms. Thus it becomes understandable why the general aim of the elite was directed to entering the public service and semi- or total self-employment. In the former bureaucratic machinery protects against redundancy, while in the latter separate development shields against the economic colour bar; and in both kinds of occupation the individual operates in the African sector of the population, thus minimizing the risks of interracial conflict.

Examining the reasons for leaving a job in which personalities were involved, and which were almost always mentioned in terms of a 'tiff', a 'quarrel', 'trouble', or a 'misunderstanding', it was found that in eight cases these persons were fellow-Africans, in sixteen cases they were Europeans, and in one case they were both.

Looking first at the reasons in which Europeans were involved we found that in eight cases dismissal had followed certain financial, marital or professional irregularities or acts of public misbehaviour in which drink and assault figured most frequently. In six of these, this was explicitly mentioned by the respondent himself, and in the two remaining instances the misdemeanour occurred during the period of the field research.

Of the eight further cases in which individual Europeans were involved, in five cases the employee decided to leave and in three he was given notice.

In four of the five first-mentioned cases the personality conflicts (two blamed on the European Senior's 'un-African', i.e. inhuman or unforgiving ways, and two on the obvious colour prejudices of a European in charge) had not in themselves been enough to cause the individuals to leave, but had merely precipitated or justified a job change already contemplated for other reasons, such as that the job had insufficient pay or prospects, or that an avenue leading to a better job or a new profession offered itself. For example, the policemen who only after they had found the job lacked prospects remembered that they did not like being policemen.

Such experiences, called by the African co-researcher 'status wrangles', appeared to us to have occurred frequently. They concerned minor matters of common courtesy, frequently related to no more than modes of address (see Mr D. H.'s story, for instance, on pp. 223–4). But when the African had a stake in the job, such matters were not allowed to interfere with his career. The African superior wisdom in dealing with human relationships often succeeded in 'teaching the European a lesson', or he would appeal to a more senior European to smooth over hurt feelings or see to the wrong being redressed. Only when the job had already failed to satisfy the individual's aspirations, did colour-discriminatory practices become all-important. The influence of the Bantu Education Act in some of the cases in which teachers left the profession seems often to have worked similarly (cf. p. 164).

The fifth case in which a respondent decided to leave his job after a 'row' with a European was not one of racial discrimination. Here is a verbatim quotation of Mr J.L.'s report; it shows that there was often more to black–white relations than mere colour discrimination:

'There was a misunderstanding. A new system had been introduced whereby the workers were paid according to the work done, in the form of a bonus. I got the underground reports about the miners' work. That was my job. There were other clerks who worked on boards with figures, writing down the number of trucks, etc. They got more pay than I did, and yet I was the one who checked their work. So I wanted to be transferred to that work. But the underground manager did not want to do this.

'He said: "That job only deals with figures, it's simple arithmetic, whereas your job needs understanding and judgment, and you carry greater responsibility."

'I said: "Who cares for more thinking? I work for more or less pay, not for more or less thinking."

'We then had a row and I left.'

From our subsequent discussion with Mr J.L. it appeared that although he did not consider this experience in terms of racial discrimination, he did give as his opinion that it showed the basic lack of understanding by the European of what the African really wanted.

Examining now the three cases in which the African was given notice, it was found that in only one case was there flagrant colour discrimination. In the two other cases this was not so certain. These can be briefly recounted as follows:

In one case, the African was employed with a local Reef newspaper. The owner had invited him to join as special correspondent for African news. After three months, the General Manager sent for him and said that the Europeans would boycott the paper if it were known that there was an African on the staff, and that there was in any case too much news of Africans in the paper. And so he left. This was in 1957.

In the other case, the job was that of 'clerk-accountant' in a large company. The salary was R11 per week. After the African had been there for six months 'a white female accountant was employed while I was on leave'. Asked whether he thought this had happened because he was black, he answered 'Judge for yourself. Not only that a white woman took my place but the boss who had me employed was dismissed.' This was in 1958.

In neither of these cases was it absolutely certain that the reason actually was colour prejudice. In the 1950s European newspaper readers had already become quite accustomed to reading articles about township affairs written by Africans, and the employer might have chosen colour as the minor hurt rather than, for instance, the reporter's incompetence. In the case of the 'clerk-accountant' there may have been the usual 'misunderstanding' about taking leave after only six months in a job.

The third case was a typical one in this colour-discriminating country, and should be quoted in full and *verbatim* as told by the individual concerned, again Mr J.L.:

> 'I was in charge of the till and my immediate European Chief was in the habit of asking me for "loans" against IOUs from the day's takings. He was building himself a house in the neighbourhood and would use our property and labour for this purpose. Then just before the auditor's regular visits, the European, funnily enough, would quickly pay back the sum he owed.
>
> 'But the amounts asked became bigger and bigger, until I began to refuse. The European then asked all his previous IOUs back but I again refused. There was a big row, and I finally went to my lawyer – an African – and gave him all the IOUs to do my case. But the lawyers were an unreliable lot just eager for my money and they did nothing.'
>
> Apparently, the case then came before a European Board and the African was suspended for three months while the case was heard. Although it would appear that the Board decided in his favour, he was given a month's notice to leave. He reluctantly accepted this. His wages had been R80 per month and, in addition, he gained about R600 'through the pension scheme' as he explained.

This story was told to and written up by the African investigator. As there were some points to be elucidated (for instance, the R600 from the pension scheme, gained during only two years in the job), we discussed the case. In her opinion, 'the European senior official had been standing by him all the time, and it was he who advised Mr J.L. to leave. You see, once you succeed in putting a European at a disadvantage, you must go. Because you have gained status, and the relationship must always be servile. The strained relationships would have reflected on the one friendly European. I think those R600 were some sort of compensation.'

Thus a very careful examination of those reasons for leaving a job in which European individuals were involved, with special reference to any possible signs of the operation of racial discrimination, showed that, although in some cases (possibly more than expressly mentioned), colour-discriminatory practices did strengthen an already contemplated intention to leave a job, it was in only one instance that a job certainly (and in two instances possibly) had been lost for reasons of colour only.

Concluding, it would appear that in a total of 312 reasons for leaving or losing a job mentioned by our respondents, racial discrimination operated in not more than ten cases certainly and a further three cases possibly, either as the only or as a contributory cause, either indirectly or directly. In many cases the job was left or lost, not as a result of actual colour-bar legislation, but of colour-bar convention – because of intra-European usage; the concealed or open European conspiracy against employing Africans in certain educated jobs; or because of European employers' fears for the consequences among their European staff or customers.

From the eight cases in which fellow Africans were involved some interesting facts emerged:

One case concerned an alleged slander by the colleagues of a successful clerk in the Native Affairs Department. 'I was popular with the Native Commissioner and he liked me and, of course, immediately you're up they try to pull you down . . . they informed on me to the Special Branch. I've never been really active in politics although I used to speak out when a thing was wrong . . . they even wrote anonymous letters about me . . . so I thought I'd better leave.' Many anonymous letters about (African) colleagues and seniors were regularly received in the office of the (European) inspector of Bantu Education.

Another case 'got into trouble with a girl', while he was the principal of a school belonging to an independent African church. 'The parents wrote to the Inspector, although I begged them to give me one year's chance to save money. The European inspector refused to dismiss me; but the African missionary superintendent decided to sack me. [It was the general experience of the (European) Inspectorate that African authorities were inclined to punish such transgressions with much greater severity than the Europeans.] So the Inspector offered me another job.'

221

In two cases the respondent, then assistant teacher, could not get on with the principal. 'He was jealous of me,' said one of them. 'I could discipline the children better than he could. The school had had a strike. The scholars were dagga-addicts and dice gamblers and the Std. VI classes were failing. I could uplift the boys and under me their results were improving.' In the other case, 'The principal refused to recommend me for a vacant principalship and we had a tiff; we came to blows.'

In four cases the trouble originated with the School Boards; either the individual concerned was an 'outsider' and, 'The School Board was keen to promote their own people', or the issue was 'tribal': 'For advancement the School Board would always give preference to teachers belonging to their own tribe, so I thought I'd better go.'

In one case of School-Board trouble Africans and a European were involved. This is what we were told:

'The School Board had the wrong type of men. All drank and came drunk to the meetings. You couldn't agree with their decisions and you felt very insecure. They wanted a principal who also drank, because then he could entertain them. But there was a strong inspector, a European, who could exercise some control over them. But when he left for Johannesburg the new inspector seemed to agree very well with the Board. He also drank every afternoon. After 4 p.m. you couldn't interview him.

'We felt it was against our principles and I was the first to decide to leave. After me three other teachers also gave notice. My previous inspector wrote to me to come to see him. He promised to recommend me for the first really good job vacant, and he did.'

These were then the cases in which human – all too human – factors were reported as the reasons for leaving a job. It may well be that more jobs were left because of alleged jealousy of colleagues, or because of black–white 'trouble', but in this respect the collaboration between a black and a white researcher who frequently both interviewed the same respondents during the years of the field research would have caught one or the other kind of conflict.

With regard to both kinds of conflict experienced by our elite, it is of particular interest to note that the interracial conflicts occurred notably more often in clerical jobs and the intraracial ones in professional jobs.

Summarizing, it would appear that in spite of the steady general advance which the series of job changes represented, certain demotions and dismissals occurred or good jobs had to be left. The circumstances under which these occurred, and as reported by our elite, can be arranged under three headings. First, there was the official colour-bar policy, but more often the unofficial colour discrimination and prejudice of the European individuals concerned; secondly, there were alleged jealousies or discriminatory practices on the part of fellow Africans; and thirdly, there was professional or personal misbehaviour on the part of the elite themselves. Among all reasons for job changes, as reported by our elite, these three types of circumstances occurred in very few jobs and in roughly equal proportions.

Racial discrimination as a negative stimulus

While it was impossible to pinpoint precisely the direct effect of colour discrimination, either officially or unofficially, on the considerations and circumstances which induced our elite to take on some of their lowly manual and semi-manual jobs during the earlier stages of their careers, we have some very telling instances in which the colour bar actually pushed them up and provided the stimulus to dare enterprises which would otherwise not have been attempted.

A typical case in point is that of Mr. L. O., who as a young man matriculated in a rural college and came to town full of expectations. He then discovered that he could not get a job other than in personal service, as this was the only work for which he could get a pass. The job was that of personal attendant/male nurse (classified as that of 'boy', although he himself referred to it as 'just a labourer') to a crippled European boy. As this was in 1955 when African matriculants were increasingly employed by private firms in the European sector in minor clerical jobs, the fact that he was and still is a rather shy and withdrawn young man may have also been a handicap in a very competitive market. However, after a year in this job he discovered through friends that some professions were for all practical purposes exempted from Influx Control Regulations, and as he 'did not like teaching' he applied for a bursary and entered upon the training for his present profession.

One wonders how many other individuals would never have entered their present profession but for the pass.

In a great many other cases this negative stimulus, while operating not quite so directly, was nevertheless equally definite. It was often hidden behind 'I had not enough pay' or 'No prospects', or behind the more positive reason for leaving a job, as 'I wanted more education'. Sometimes it became known to the European investigator only through more general conversations over a cup of tea, or after one had become friends. Our records show several cases in which it was rather more discriminatory *usus* than legislation which acted as a negative stimulus.

223

Here is an instance in which a European employer inflicted a wound which could only be healed by 'higher education'. Mr D.H. recounted:

'I was working in a chemist shop, and I began to think that I was wasting my time. I thought in this job I never get anywhere. But I would not have left so easily. The man in the shop was nice. He was like a liberal, a Jew, and I was very good friends with him. And then it happened.

'One day, it was raining, and I was just going home, I went through the back-door and stood for a moment waiting near the door. A European lady came in and bought something. My master said that it could be sent to her, and she said that she could easily take it with her. But my master insisted and I heard him say: "I shall send my kaffir boy to deliver it."

'I had never thought that he would do that behind my back. It happened on a Friday and on Saturday I sent a telegram to the college asking if I could come. On Monday morning I had the reply that I could come. I did not tell my master I was leaving. I just left, I was very hurt . . .'

Mr D.H. obtained his Matric and subsequently had a brilliant academic career. He has remained, as he told us, for ever wary of liberals, and it is interesting to speculate whether his former master's liberal attitude had also hardened somewhat because of the supposed faithless behaviour by a servant to whom he thought he had always been very kind. Race attitudes arise from such small happenings.[14]

While in the foregoing cases the negative stimulus drove a person into an academic career, in another case it led to a business career.

'I walked about for a while and then I got a job at . . .', Mr U. related. 'First as a labourer and then as a dispatch clerk. I was there about three years, till 1945. Although the people were Jewish, they were all right. The European in charge got R120 per month and, although I did most of the work, I got paid R6 a week. Then he left and what I had done before unofficially, I now did officially. All the invoicing and everything. I even did work at home.

'Then I asked for a rise and got R8 per week. It was still too little and I even had a greater output than before. I asked again for a rise and got R9. There was then a German chap, hard as nails. He was impossible, extremely exacting also for the European employees. He was the big influence in my life and it is he who started me in business. Yes, madam, because he made life a misery to me.

'If the manager had been nice, I would still have stayed.

224

The job itself was satisfactory, but it was a sheer reign of terror. Once I was late. I thought, "I'll only get a lecture so I'd better leave." But I didn't yet. I waited for one bad word. I wanted to leave dramatically and thought, "Let's wait and make a grand show of it." You know how one is when one is young.

'But the bad word did not come. He even became a little nicer. I ask you! So I finally had to leave without a drama. For I wanted to start my own business. But I tell you if the manager had been nice to me I might have stayed and I might now still have been there . . .'

This sort of negative stimulus can work on an ambitious person when it comes as a stroke of lightning, or it may work on a less ambitious and more easygoing type slowly wearing him down, or it may come 'as a last straw', but there is no doubt that it has stimulated many a black South African to greater achievement, 'just to show them'. Many a time were were told: 'We Africans in South Africa are kicked into growing up, or 'The Government (or the colour bar or the Europeans, whoever was blamed at that moment) beats us into developing ourselves'. (Noni Jabavu,[15] believes that it is exactly this which 'was precipitating me and mine into the twentieth century', while 'the geographically cut off tropical Lake region' [Uganda] had remained in so many respects backwards because it had been presented with everything for which the South African Bantu had to fight.)

The universal desire to have 'a job independent from Europeans' has often risen from a humiliating experience and a deeply wounded heart.

Mr M. K.'s job history

Unruffled persistence
Mr M.K. was a first-born son of a first-born son; he inherited his father's large and prosperous freehold farm which he ran from town.

In August 1914 Mr M.K. joined the Army, after spending nine months as an underground mineworker, and about a year and a half as a detective in the C.I.D. By that time he had passed his J.C.

What happened to him after peace was declared is told here by Mr M.K. himself:

'As a storeman with African Explosives, I had 175 Africans under me. After 15 years in that responsible position my top wages were R8 and never more. Yet I was entrusted with a stock of dynamite worth R3 million. I am not afraid to say that. I was licensed to handle explosives and was then the only African to have such a licence.

'Then early in 1934 I saw an advertisement; a Doornfontein dairy wanted a buttermaker. I applied and got the job. I knew

225

how to make butter from home; this was different, but I learned it nicely. I got R34 and free board and lodging. So that was a big improvement.

'After nine years in that job (i.e. in 1942) the Government made a colour law. The Government said that every man must be paid the same rate for the job, whether black or white. And so the Government forced the Dairy to pay me R70 per month. So they thought it fit rather to employ a European for those wages. They took an unqualified European, a Mr. N., and they wanted me to do the same job, but now under him and he would then supervise only. And I with all my qualifications!

'So I demoted myself. Rather work in the streets, I said to myself.

'A European friend of mine (I had got that buttermakers' job also through a European army friend) knew that the W.N.L.A. [The Witwatersrand Native Labour Association] wanted a reliable African, and he sent me a telegram to tell me about it. I applied and got the job. It was the best I could get. I was now a clerk, earning R40 per month with free board and lodging, uniform and transport.

'The W.N.L.A. is owned by the Transvaal Chamber of Mines. All the recruited mine-boys came there from the country, and raw they were! We washed them and registered them and gave them new clothes and new passes, and we distributed them to the various Gold Mines. Today it is still the same. After seven years I fell ill, pleurisy and inflammation of the lung. They took one lung away, and I have only one lung now. Upon recovery I did not want to go back. The mine dust, they say, and they said it might have been silicosis and even TB was suspected.

'In 1950 I then joined a large tobacco company. Another European friend, he was Influx Director of Non-European Affairs, brought them to me. He had heard that that Company was looking for a popular African and he thought of me. [Mr M.K. was widely known and esteemed; he was active in a number of important organizations. For instance, he was a distinguished member of one of the Regional Native Labour Committees, set up after the Native Labour (Settlement of Disputes) Act of 1953, to deal with complaints by African workers. He was also for many years a member of the Advisory Board in the location where he then lived.] He took the trouble to leave his office and bring those people to my house for an interview. They then wrote me to come for a final interview. I was the first African to be employed for the job.

'They wanted me as advertiser. A certain brand of cigarettes was then a new line among Africans. I went from township to township, carrying two suitcases, advertising the cigarette, telling everyone how good it was. It was then not yet on the market. The firm could not afford to pay me a wage. I had a commission only. 10 cents for every 1,000 cigarettes sold. I made at the most R3 to R4 per week.

'After six months the line was well in the market and I was employed as a salesman on a permanent basis with a fixed salary. R10·50 cents per week plus 5 per cent of the sales, and I was given a car with stock. In the best times I made some R24 to R28 per week and that was good.

'I did that for six and a half years and then the firm closed down. One European who was also employed in the firm knew it beforehand and he warned me. He knew of an English firm which sells all sorts of things, like floor polish, baby foods, shoe polish, etc., etc.

'On Friday I left my old firm and on Monday I started in this new job. I am doing very well now, on a fixed salary basis. I drive a van worth about R4,000 and am regularly carrying a stock worth R1,000.'

Thus did Mr M. K. relate his job history, and only by reproducing it in what were, to the best of our knowledge, the actual words used, is it possible to communicate to our readers not only its factual and moving simplicity, but also the exact circumstances of Mr M.K.'s demotion as butter-maker. As he had apparently understood it, and told it to us, he had lost this lucrative job not because of the Government policy of 'job reservation',[16] but because of the resistance from the European employers and/or co-employees against a policy called 'the rate for the job'.[17] Although Mr M. K. is probably one of the very few among our elite who experienced this particular form of colour discrimination in his career, it is not at all untypical as an experience in South African commerce and industry, generally. Neither is Mr M. K.'s occupational history untypical in other respects. It exemplifies the ruthlessness on the part of European employers and the kindness and helpfulness of individual Europeans – both so characteristic of South African race relations. Similarly Mr M. K.'s career is typical for the direction into semi- or self-employment towards which the occupational success story of any educated, non-professional urban African must eventually move, possibly as a consequence of both these European characteristics.

Summing up

An analysis of the job history of our elite showed their occupational mobility in the sense we defined in the Introduction, not so much by the rate as by the nature of job changes. With regard to the rate of this job mobility, whether inter- or intra-job mobility and whether bureaucratic or free-enterprise mobility, the elite of Reeftown had during an average number of working years of 21·75, a new job every two to four years; but, for obvious reasons, the first few jobs lasted for a shorter length of time than the later jobs. Consequently, there is in most occupational groups a marked lengthening of job duration, although, because of a continued mobility in other occupational groups, this does not show so clearly in a graph.

Particularly marked were the differences between the professional and the non-professional jobs, especially in the first jobs. The professionals fitted easily and smoothly, and from the start, into their occupational niche, whether in a rural, a semi-rural or an urban area, whereas the non-professionals (also those teachers who would not or could not teach) were considerably handicapped. Those who had already come to town at an earlier age with their parents or to stay with a relative, could find at best only any one of the jobs as 'boy', or at worst some job as 'labourer'. Those in the rural areas, with our elite the majority, were even worse off, for in the country there were hardly any jobs at all for J.C. or even for Matric-qualified persons. Hence an ambitious, courageous adolescent, or someone who simply had to leave the kinship system, had to come to town and face the Urban Influx Control Regulations. Hence 90 per cent of these men among our elite took jobs in the Mines. Eight worked as underground miners, and almost one-quarter had been a 'boy' in one or another capacity or status. About the same number had been policemen with the S.A. Police Force, a (municipal) Non-European Affairs Department, or the (Government) Native Affairs Department, in the expectation of becoming promoted to station commanders or Government clerks. But much more time had been spent in clerical occupations, and altogether only 40 per cent of the total working years had been spent in other than the present occupations/professions. The Government clerks had the highest number of working days, the longest average job duration and the most homogeneous job experience of all. The private clerks spent the longest time in jobs other than the present, and relatively shortest in semi-manual jobs. The municipal clerks were, as could be expected, somewhere in between. They and the traders spent longest as 'labourers' and they varied among themselves. Obviously, the Local Authority often had the occupational 'left-overs'. But then they had, it would appear, a somewhat more stable element than those that went in private employment as non-professionals. The private clerks and the salesmen had had the most heterogeneous job experience, as one would expect of 'failed managers'. The ministers had a far less homogeneous background than the teachers, who appeared throughout, with the Government clerks, as a privileged group.

228

We subsequently traced certain clearly marked patterns of job changes which have constituted the channels through which the elite's mobility upwards was effected. And here we saw the jobs as means to self-advancement, the careers almost entirely in the service of financial and social improvement, successive job changes determined by considerations of material benefit and social advance and sometimes by the desire to obtain power over other Africans. If in this steady search less satisfactory jobs sometimes had to be taken, these had to serve other needs and requirements which, for a while, seemed more important. Among these were family considerations and the need for a change, or for a more progressive area. Altogether professionals were, even in their first jobs, more kin-determined and kin-influenced, whereas the non-professionals were more dependent on the geographical area. However, as the family finances improved and other siblings started earning, and as the more progressive areas were being reached, both these reasons gradually decreased in importance.

A very careful scrutiny of the reasons for all the job changes showed that only in seven cases was a job taken to gain more experience or to test oneself, and in two cases a job was left because it did not give enough scope for self-development. In all other cases the idea of self-improvement was understood in terms of the acquisition of more educational and professional qualifications for the sake of advance in status and income. There appears here to be a similarity with the people in a small town in American mass society (Vidich, 1958, 50), for whom the idea of self-improvement was less connected with any idea of self-fulfilment than with the striving for the rewards offered by society. This should be expressly mentioned. However, there appeared no American parallel of our other finding that our elite apparently never took on a job for the sole reason that they liked that particular job, while in only seven cases a job was left because it was not liked. These almost always concerned police jobs, and the dislike was never the only or even the main reason for leaving. In view of the public stigma on black policemen, what appeared as personal dislikes of the job may have been in reality public-opinion, determined sentiments.

The almost entire absence of personal or emotional involvement in their jobs which was certainly the most important finding of a study of the occupational mobility of our elite, corresponds to the predominantly neutral attitudes in the choice and change of courses of study and professions which emerged from a study of their educational mobility.

Subsequently, and tentatively, we traced some future trends, and found two main ones. The one towards stabilization, followed by the self-employed and the aspirant self-employed, who in this respect would go the way of the typical pre-twentieth-century middle class in the western world. The other was the trend towards continued mobility, though at a slower rate, of the successful public servants, who represented in our sample the new mid-twentieth-century migratory elite of individuals who will always have to move on in order to move up. As an in-between, there were the 'failed managers' among our elite, the clerks and the salesmen employed by the big corporations and semi-public bodies, whose future fate will be a continued mobility in search of managerial positions; and the higher-graded municipal clerks who again represented complete residential stabilization in occupational culs de sac. For their promotional changes were, of necessity, somewhat restricted, bound up as they were with the development of Reeftown towards greater articulation and self-sufficiency.

In the light of the generally non-committal attitudes towards their jobs and professions, the influence of racial discrimination and the colour bar on these careers may be viewed. With regard to this complicated and basically intangible problem, our case records offered three areas in which a well-defined question could be precisely answered. First, in respect of the manual labour done by our elite in the course of their careers, it was found that not more, but less had done manual labour than a comparable group of white Americans, and in only just over half of these cases of manual labour it may have been the result of colour-bar restrictions and/or colour prejudices. Secondly, a very careful and precise scrutiny of each job which had been lost for what we classified as 'human' and 'technical' reasons, resulted in our conclusion that only few of these occupational setbacks had been reported as due to colour-bar *usus* and even fewer to colour-discriminatory laws. Furthermore, it was found that in most cases colour prejudice had not been the only or even the main reason why a job was left, but had entered as a further consideration after the job had been found unsatisfactory in other respects, or after a job with better pay or more prospects had offered itself.

Moreover, the careers of the elite showed some interesting cases in which racial discrimination had acted not to check aspirations or to curb ambitions, but, on the contrary, as a stimulus to try and reach a goal which otherwise might not have been achieved or even attempted, 'just to show them'.

part three

Figures in the background

5   Figures in the background

Introduction

Introduction

Throughout conversations with the members of the elite, and at almost every stage of the respondents' stories about their lives and careers, certain people were mentioned who had influenced particular decisions or encouraged specific courses of action: people who had provided general inspiration or particular assistance. There were those who, by advice and example, had fired certain ambitions, had opened new horizons and had made possible certain achievements. Indeed, by the time the complete educational and occupational histories had been unfolded, a fairly adequate picture had been obtained of all these people.

It was, then, more with a view to hearing the respondents' personal opinions on this matter that, at a later stage in the interviews, we asked a general question: 'Who was (were) the main influence(s) in your life?' The replies were sometimes both surprising and revealing. Probably because the question was always asked at the end of the educational and occupational histories, the answers seemed to emphasize the people who had been influential during the later stages of the careers rather than those who had helped them on their way during the earlier parts of their lives. Consequently, there was an over-emphasis on individuals who had influenced them more recently. There was too, at this stage in the interviews, a certain fatigue which affected the replies. Therefore they cannot all be taken as a careful review of all the people who at one stage or another and in one way or another had influenced the speakers' actions and attitudes, particularly as we could not enquire after particular individuals. Experience had taught us that these would then simply have been added to those already mentioned spontaneously. Respondents would have reacted with: 'Yes, of course, she did too!' or 'But naturally he

233

influenced me as well!' as if the omission were a lack of good manners or of enlightenment on the part of the speaker.

Nevertheless, the types of people mentioned (and some replies included two, three or even more different individuals or groups) gave some indication of their relative importance.

There were three broad categories of people. (See Table III 5:1.) These were, in order of frequency of mention (which need not necessarily have been the order of their qualitative importance): parents and relatives, who were mentioned in nearly half the replies; fellow Africans, mentioned in one-third of the replies; and, finally, Europeans, whose names appeared in 18 per cent of the answers. We propose now to review, in this order, the various persons who were said to have exerted some influence on the careers of our elite.

Table III 5:1 Numerical and percentage distribution of the elite by their replies to the question:
'Who was (were) the main influence(s) in your life?'

N = 60

Replies	Number	Percentage
Parents and Relatives	61	47·66
Mother	14	
Father	14	
Both Parents	13	
Wife	4	
Brother	3	
Other	13	
Africans	44	34·37
Missionaries	3	
Leading Personalities	14	
Primary-school Teachers	14	
Secondary-school Teachers	6	
Colleagues and Friends	4	
Other	3	
Europeans	23	17·97
Missionaries	7	
Secondary-school Teachers	7	
Other	3	
'Good Contacts'	6	
Total	128*	100·00

* Some individuals mentioned more than one person.

The importance of mother

Of all the members of the entire kin-group, mother proved to have been the strongest and most lasting influence.

From previous researches we had become convinced that in the descriptions of tribal kinship relations, as these can be read in anthropological literature, the role of the mother in African life had been under-estimated, probably because it was less institutionalized and therefore escaped the attention of social anthropologists concentrating on the study of institutions and institutionalized behaviour. But even if this had not been the case in traditional tribal society, the transitional situation manifested clearly the important position and the comprehensive function of the African mother.

In addition to this, our previous experience with the urban woman[1] had convinced us that she was a major figure in the break-up of tribal life and the main progressive force which pushed the next generation into modern twentieth-century life. In the meantime, Tardits established in his research in Porto-Novo that the women of Dahomey were in a statistically significant way possessed of a more progressive and pioneering spirit than the men. 'Conservative attitudes were found mainly among men and pioneering attitudes among the women', he wrote.[2]

Table III 5:2 Numerical and percentage distribution of the elite by their replies to the question: 'Who was the most important person for you?'

Most important person	No.	Percentage
Mother	31	51·67
Mother and Other	3	5
Father*	11	18·33
Father and Other	1	1·67
Both Parents	8	13·33
Other	6	10·00
Total	60	100·00

* In three cases father became a widower and remarried, and his main importance was that he defended the child against a 'bad' stepmother.

And now in this investigation we were able to confirm Tardits's findings. In so far as the elite of Reeftown were concerned, the importance of mother in their careers emerged strongly, completely and without question.[3] The mothers of our elite had not only been the most important persons for them, but they had also been the driving forces behind their education.

Clearly and unmistakably mother had been the most important person for our elite certainly during the early and formative years of their lives. (See Table III 5:2.) Mother was mentioned in 55 per cent of the replies, while in no more than 20 per cent was father mentioned.

Only eight individuals (13 per cent) considered that neither of the two could be singled out, and they considered both parents to have been of equal importance in their upbringing. Six individuals (10 per cent) mentioned other persons, generally a rearer or grandparent.

That the importance of one or other of the parents or relatives was, in many cases, measured by the active interest they took in the boy's education cannot be doubted. This is probably more definitely in the case of father than in the case of mother, as little else seemed to have been expected from father. In another context we saw that only one-third of the elite reported father as having taken an active interest in their education. (See p. 123.) Father then had acted either in collaboration with an equally interested mother or, occasionally, alone. That the other boys received any schooling at all, or that they remained in school long enough to become interested themselves, now appears to have been almost entirely due to mother's untiring efforts.

Both investigators, acting independently, carried out a careful and meticulous scrutiny of each individual's story; and, weighing all the data collected, came to certain conclusions as to who had been the main driving force behind the early education of our elite. (See Table III 5:3.) In only two cases the young lad himself seemed to

Table III 5:3 Numerical and percentage distribution of the elite by those who were the main driving forces behind their education

Main driving force	No.	Percentage
Both Parents	10	16·67
Father	12	20
Mother (Father alive)	17	28·33
Mother (Father dead)	13	21·67
Other Relatives	6	10
Ego	2	3·33
Total	60	100·00

have wanted and planned his own education, against opposition. In the one case he had had his mother's help (see Mr R. Z., Chapter 3, pp. 131–2); in the other case a teacher had helped. (See Mr J.O., Chapter 3, pp. 133–5.) In all other cases the initiative had come from others.

In thirty cases this was mother and in thirteen of these cases mother was a widow. Either father had died before *ego's* education became a matter of urgency, or mother could go ahead with the child's education only after father's death. In the other cases mother had prevailed upon an unwilling or indifferent father, and in half of these she also had had to control an unruly son. In only twelve instances had father been the main driving force behind the son's education. Most of these sons had simply obeyed, but in four cases father had had to compel unwilling sons.

There is no doubt that, if a father was truly interested, a son's education was assured; for father disposed of most resources, as Mr N. G.'s education history showed. (See Chapter 3, pp. 137–8.)

In no more than ten cases did we decide that both parents had collaborated in providing for their son's education, while in 10 per cent the main push had come from other relatives, mainly rearers.

Consequently, mother emerged as the greatest single force driving her children into an educated career and into a new way of life. Generally the elite were conscious of what they owed their mothers. Much comment was given on the subject, on which some telling quotations follow:

'My people were well off and believed in cattle. But it was mother who convinced father that I was worthy of education. Mother came from an educated family and she was more ambitious.'

'My mother was the most important person. She encouraged me more, though both were interested. I was never expected to go to school, but to do herding. But mother decided that education was more important than cattle.'

'Educationally my mother was the more important. I was given to my mother's sister, but she was the wife of a roving Evangelist and he was always *trekking*, and I was losing my chance of education. So my mother convinced my father that I should come back home.'

If it was possible, mother acted through father by incessantly working on her often reluctant and sometimes just indifferent husband, but if necessary she could also act on her own. We have already quoted cases in which mother simply overruled father and took the matter into her own hands. In the following cases, for instance:

'Father was a quiet person. Mother used to thrash me and she took me back to school when I played truant. I came to like her because she did not want me to do wrong.'

'I was brought up with mother's people, but mother pushed my education most of all. Both my parents were teachers, father retired before mother, and mother continued teaching. It was she who paid for my later education. Both were keen for me to be educated, but mother had higher aims. She did not want me

237

to teach. She wanted me to do a University degree at Fort Hare. She encouraged me very much. She would go all out to see that I got what was good for me. When I had a good report, I got a new suit. [A white boy would have wanted a football or a bicycle.] I used to work hard for that new suit! But if I was number two in class, I only got a pair of new shoes, and if I was number three I got nothing at all.'

The importance of mother was usually such a familiar thought that many of our elite generalized beyond their own personal experience:

'That mother is more interested in education than father is generally the case among us Africans. If mother is not interested then the children haven't much of a chance.'

With our elite, mother's pressure and discipline were most apparent during the primary school years. But these were exactly the crucial ones. If a child could be sent to school and, more important, could be made to remain at school until Std. VI was passed, the battle was won. (We described how rare this was in Chapter 3, p. 118.) For by that time the child itself had experienced the value of education and wanted to continue.

It is interesting to compare mother's preponderant influence on our elite's careers with similar findings about Negro mothers. Gist and Bennett[4] found that 'Negro mothers aspire higher for their children than Negro fathers and tend to be more intense in their attempts to exert influence over their children's decisions'. However, the authors added, 'the white control group . . . likewise showed evidence of pronounced maternal influence, though not as much'.[5]

As far as our elite were concerned, the importance of the African mothers in their careers, and the tremendous power they could exercise over the destinies of their sons, emerged from many smaller and larger instances in the life histories, and were recorded throughout this book. They do not need here any further examples.

The importance of the mother's attitude to education was most clearly manifest in those instances in which father had married more than one wife. In such cases there was almost always a striking difference in general educational level between the children of the different wives; and, at least in our sample, this difference could always be traced back to differences in the educational attitudes of the mothers.

In Mr H. L.'s case it was the first wife who was the more progressive, but in most cases in our sample the most progressive of the several wives tended to be the second or third wife. In such a situation the first wife's children would all be uneducated or less educated and sometimes had remained rural, while the second or third wife's children would become educated and often had become urban.

It was not always easy to arrive at the correct explanation, for respondents would avoid the issue as long as they could with evasive circumlocutions.

Similarly, to say in so many words that father had not been as important as mother went against centuries of traditionally instilled awe.

It would appear that, as a general rule, the father needed to be educated himself in order to be interested in his son's education; but, with the mother, whether she was educated or not was irrelevant to her decision that only by a complete break with tribal life could she become emancipated and released from her status of perennial minor, and that this could best happen through the education of her children.

'My mother was only an illiterate woman but she knew the value of education better than anyone. While father was alive she never succeeded in convincing him, but she always talked to me about education. Then father died when I was 13 years old. If father had not died I would never have been educated.

'Many of us owe our education only to the fact that father died and mother could do as she wished.'

We saw how immediately after father's death four widowed mothers packed up their children and other belongings and trekked to town, where schools were close, where the mothers could earn money to keep the family, and where they could escape the widow's inferior position as well as the bondage of the levirate which still prevailed in many 'tribes'.

Here perhaps lies the explanation of the large number of widows' sons among the elite.

But mother's important role was not confined only to her direct action and positive interference in her determination to set her son on the right educational path – it went deeper.

'I think both liked education but mother particularly. Mother liked the educated teachers and had teachers as boarders. She had big plans for me. I had to help her sometimes with her washing and ironing and she would then open her heart to me . . .

'You see with us Africans, you really have no direct contact with your father. There is that respect. So when you wanted something you went to mother and then she would tell father.

'You can't approach father. With my people the men were not in the kitchen, they had the kraal outside. In the daytime they were with the cattle and they spent their evenings together around the fire. We children were with mother. So if something was worrying me, she was the easiest to approach.

'Then, later when you grow up you suddenly have to be with the men and you are told not to be with the women. I often sneaked away to have a chance to be with mother. Those were precious moments and they made me very happy.'

In town today it is not so very different. There is, however, perhaps a new resentment on the part of the mothers – and of their sons.

'Father is the big *Mampara*, he sits in the lounge and entertains his friends. Mother has to be in the kitchen with the children . . .'

'Where the African parent fails is when his children are a little older, that is when they can't be given corporal punishment any longer. Then father has nothing more to do and he no longer has any influence over the child, with the result that you do not remember anything about your father except the thrashings . . .'

Considering the number of our respondents who described how much they had missed by the institutionalized social distance between father and son in traditional life, one can imagine how much they themselves planned to do better with their own children.

It may be recalled that despite all 'the respect', a certain irritation came through when we discussed the fact that so many father farmers had thought about their children only in terms of herding and farm-labour. Similarly, there was often a scarcely-veiled impatience with those fathers who had left the complete responsibility for the children in the hands of mother. 'Our father worked in Johannesburg and only came home occasionally, so he couldn't have moulded our character even if he had wanted to, but he couldn't have cared less.' But, even though fathers sometimes interested themselves in the education and general well-being of their sons, sufficiently anyway to provide for them and punish transgressions, and for that reason already alone assumed some importance in the careers of many of our elite, in another sense they probably had even less influence than most of our respondents cared to admit.

The following seems the best summing up and the most touching testimony of the enduring role of the African mother:

'It is very queer, Mrs Brandel. You can't really understand it. Why should it be mother? You see there was, and still is, that old custom of harshness to children, even when the parents were Christians. Now I was a naughty boy and father always beat me. But I did things for mother. For the love of her. She

240

talked nicely. Mother had a way of putting things so that they would stay in your mind forever. She was not an educated woman, but she had a fund of African proverbs and idioms. Native wisdom, you know. Even African custom had its own philosophy.

'And, then, later in your life, it is those things mother said and did which you remember . . .'

After one such conversation with a son, a minister, who also proudly wears a graduate's gown, I could not help saying: 'Look, you people, rather than worshipping Walter Sisulu or Chief Luthuli, why don't you Africans in South Africa put up a statue to the African mother, to whom it all is due?'

He looked at me uncomprehendingly. 'I'm afraid, Mrs Brandel, with us African people – we don't respect women . . .'

The contribution of the relatives

By the time the son had completed his primary education, mother was no longer so alone in her endeavours. First, in many cases father had veered round to other ideas (hers!). Perhaps the son had come home from school covered with the glory of a first-class pass; possibly father had at last had time to look around and see his friends' sons being honoured in the community; or maybe he was beginning to find the struggle to maintain the traditional way of life increasingly burdensome; or also the teachers and missionaries had finally succeeded in making him see the light. However this may be, half the fathers were now willing to provide the college fees. Mother had won her lonely struggle. Frequently also relatives, equally ambitious by this time, came forward with offers of financial assistance.

But already during the primary-school stage, the kin had often contributed their share not only as temporary rearers. One-quarter of the kin had been actively involved in the school moves. (See Table II 3:2.) In ten cases a child had been sent to relatives for proper schooling, which always meant that it had been 'naughty'. (Cf. p. 127). In three cases father took his son to another relative in order to protect him against a 'bad' stepmother. In other cases mother, feeling that her son was neglected, placed him in the hands of one of her own kin. In many cases, urban relatives gave the boy his first introduction to town life.

Thus in all manner of circumstances, but most of all in emergencies, there were always relatives both able and willing to undertake their customary responsibilities. While in the primary-school stage mother contributed funds probably as much as father, in the secondary-school stage the relatives replaced mother, and, after father, paid the largest percentage of the college fees. (See Table II 3:3.)

241

But also on the occupational careers of our elite did the relatives bring their influence to bear. They determined certain job moves; they secured almost one-third of the non-professional jobs for our elite; they contributed towards their further education by gifts of clothing and books. Finally, they provided the venue for free holidays for the elite and their children.

As time went by the kin began to expect their due compensation and, in later years, the elite found their relatives a great burden. They helped them whenever they were in need. Moreover, they were now in their turn paying for the education of one or more of these relatives' children. Nevertheless, and although some of our respondents could hardly suppress a sigh when talking about 'my relatives', it is true to say that to date very few of the elite would have been where they were now without those relatives.

During the course of such conversations, respondents would sometimes add that 'mother's people are generally more important than father's people'. No specific questions on this topic had been inserted in the schedules, but just to test the statement we gathered together all the relatives who had been spontaneously mentioned in one capacity or another during our conversations, and who had been recorded by the investigators on the schedules in the relevant contexts. In this way it was found that in 42 per cent of the cases mother's people had been mentioned and in no more than 25 per cent father's people. (See Table II 5:4.) While the issue merits further precise testing there seemed, therefore, some support for our elite's statements.

On this matter two points were worth considering. The first was that it would appear that the relatives' assistance had not come into play automatically. There seemed to have been some selection as to which kin were asked for their assistance, which relative lived in a place favourable for the child's upbringing, or had the required personal or social characteristics, resources or connections. Similarly, on the part of the relatives themselves, some choice was exercised as to which child they wanted to support or considered suitable to be brought up with their own children. Here one saw how the increasing differentiation in economic, social and residential circumstances and a more ready yielding to personal preferences brought about changes in an old tribal custom.

Secondly, and connected with the first point, those relationships which were not so institutionalized and more individually determined were often fostered whereas the more highly institutionalized, status-determined ones were avoided. In the modern world preference was often given to those relationships for which the need was greatest, which had higher emotional value and which carried the least binding and onerous obligations. Noni Jabavu[6] writes how as children they had always gone to their 'maternal home', 'to be indulged, fed on fresh liver by mother's people, treatment you traditionally don't get from your paternal people, who are supposed to discipline you and make you worthy of your line and clan'.[7]

And in fact, while the contribution of all relatives to their careers was duly and dutifully acknowledged by the elite, those most fondly remembered were 'mother's people', and in general, 'the women in the family'.

Table III 5:4 Numerical and percentage distribution of the elite by the relatives spontaneously mentioned by them as having actively contributed to their careers

	N = 59	
	Times mentioned	
Relatives mentioned	*No.*	*Percentage*
'*Mother's People*'		42·37
Mother's mother and mother's mother's sister	7	
Mother's sister	9	
Mother's brother	9	
'*Father's People*'		25·42
Father's parents and father's father's brother	6	
Father's brother(s)	5	
Father's sister	4	
Other		32·21
Eldest sister	7	
Eldest brother	4	
Half-brother's son	1	
'Relatives'*	3	
Friends†	4	
Total	59	100·00

* Not further specified.

† These may have been relatives, but this was not mentioned.

The assistance among the siblings

Sibling relationships

The difference between the institutionalized and other relationships and the greater importance attached to the latter in the insecurity of rapid culture change emerged once more when we studied the differential part which the siblings had played in the careers of the elite.[8]

Except in a few cases when a sibling had disappeared and all contact had ceased (in two families[9] one sibling had become 'coloured' ['coloured' in South Africa means of mixed blood] and had left the family circle) active relationships with other siblings and their children was maintained by regular visits, the exchange of correspondence, and by periodic family reunions in what was considered 'the family farm' or, in town, 'the family home', during Christmas or holidays or on special occasions. We were, however, again struck by the general formality, or rather the impersonal nature of the sibling relationships. We noticed a lack of intimacy, an absence of deep interest or loving curiosity about one another's thoughts and feelings, except in a few cases of a favourite sister. This was all the more striking as, of all kinship relations, those between brothers and sisters appeared to have remained closest and most continuous.

The maintenance of good relationships was a source of constant concern. Questions were often answered by giving the norm, not the practice, showing a desire to underplay misunderstandings and quarrels, and to stress the happier moments. We discerned the continuous effort, as well as the almost superhuman forbearance and repeated sacrifices, which this demanded of our elite, whose very success so often made them the target for petty jealousies and exacting demands. We could not but admire the readiness with which earlier wrongs had been forgiven and forgotten and they said 'Now I am happy to report that we are a united family again.' (See, for example, the sibling histories of Mr. N. K. and Mr A. J., pp. 248–50.)

We caught a glimpse of the colossal burden which these siblings and the need to remain on good terms must have represented and still did for the one among them who so often had 'come up highest' or 'gone further', and who was sometimes even the only one in the family to have 'come up' at all. They were in majority disappointed about the achievements of their brothers and sisters but dared not say so.[10] They blamed their fathers, the force of circumstances, their eldest brothers, anything. They would have liked to be able to say that all had been highly educated or successful in business. For that was what they cherished most in their hierarchy of values. If this could not be said, they comforted themselves with a second value: that the siblings could at least earn their living and did not come for assistance; that they were hard-working and self-supporting. And if they were not highly educated nor self-supporting then the third value came into play: 'We at least maintain contact and we have preserved harmonious relationships.' For everything was still all right, and there was no need to admit disillusionment with one's own family, as long as sibling cohesion was maintained and one's own elevation had not caused one's isolation from the group.

We had frequently occasion to notice that in a situation which was unsatisfactory in modern terms, our elite could and did fall back on traditional African values.[11] They did not only live *between* two worlds but also *in* two worlds and could appeal to either for the satisfaction of their emotional needs. And their deepest need was certainly to maintain the so vital group belonging in spite of their own elevation.

Yet relationships had often become strained because of the too uneven progress of the siblings. We sometimes had to listen to remarks like the following:

'They seem to resent the fact that I am educated . . .'

'When I went to high school, the two brothers just above me promised that they would give a hand and trouble started when they failed. Now all my brothers and sisters are full of petty jealousies that I succeeded. And they are particularly jealous of my older brother, because he could help me – not that he had any education beyond Std. VI, but he had a good job – and still feed his own family also.'

In the still strongly-preserved kinship system with its particularly binding obligations of mutual assistance and reciprocity among the siblings, no African desirous of preserving the vital link with his family, could afford to think of his own education alone. For a single sibling who would 'rise too high above the others' was strongly censured. It was necessary for the whole group to rise together to avoid the disunity and strife which would otherwise ensue. Many a respondent assured us that if his father or rearer were to be considered 'to have spent all the money' on the education of one child only, the other siblings would for ever reproach him for having been 'individualistic' and 'like a European', and would expect to be compensated for ever after with occasional gifts or regular maintenance.

Here the curtain was lifted slightly on the terrifying anxieties of successful individuals who have been rising up from a culture in which there was a traditional prohibition of individual excellence.

The system of mutual assistance

The most important way in which good relationships were expressed and maintained was by the exercise of certain traditional rights and obligations. Among these were most often mentioned the right to be consulted in important family matters such as marriages and the children's future, as well as the right to be asked to solve domestic conflicts or inheritance wrangles. But probably even more important was the right to ask for, and the duty to give, monetary assistance whenever this was needed.

245

Assistance was apparently given in the form of books and clothes, by the payment of school fees, by occasional 'presents', or by regular pocket-money or 'when in need'. Other siblings also contributed towards a brother's *lobolo*, a sister's wedding expenses, or towards the purchase of a house, a shop or furniture.

Just over half of our elite (numbering thirty-three individuals, who included three-quarters of the first-borns) declared that they had not been assisted by any of their siblings.[12] Some ventured to express their relief about this in terms such as: 'I am glad I owe nothing to anybody; later when you're well-to-do you've got to help them, and they're a real nuisance.' The rest (20 in all) acknowledged assistance. In thirteen cases sisters were mentioned and in eleven cases brothers, but always older sisters and older brothers, and usually the eldest of them. In one case mother's brother's son was mentioned.

Assistance given was, probably, more freely disclosed than assistance received. Three-quarters of the elite had assisted, or were assisting, one or several of their younger brothers and sisters. About ten of these were assisting or had assisted 'all of them', while in eight cases a younger brother had assisted or was currently also assisting his own eldest brother. While four cases were unknown, only eleven individuals among our elite were not assisting or had never assisted any one of their siblings.

The fact that three-quarters of our elite had, therefore, one or more dependents among their own siblings (besides the number or dependents which would have emerged had we enquired after other kin) confirmed what is already common knowledge: namely that this is one of the main problems of the educated African in town. Such conversations then often led to the subject of urban influx control, and although some elite had different ideas, the majority saw in this control their protection against poor and predatory relatives; 'If there were no influx control, I would have tomorrow twenty relatives in my kitchen, and no excuse to get rid of them. Now I can blame the government.' It must be said that most of our elite were bearing up manfully, particularly if their assistance had resulted in or promised to result in, a rising status of the whole sibling group.

Good relationships were often expressed in terms of 'co-operation'. This shows how the rise of the sibling group in the modern world was considered a joint responsibility, in which all brothers and sisters were expected to act as a group and in the best interest of all.

Here and there complaints were recorded, but these seemed to come mainly from siblings who had been left by the others to carry the whole burden alone. Mr N.K., whose full story appears on p. 250 was one of these.

'Generally, we advanced Africans have many dependants,'

Mr N.K. related. 'When they see you are better they hang on
to you. It makes progress slow. You have got to divide yourself.
It makes us enlightened Africans poorer and poorer.

'Once you are stiff, they consider you a bad man. Now I, for
instance, have spent more on my dependants than was spent on
my own education. And now, one of my father's sons died. He
lived on a farm. Now there is his wife with two young boys, and
it has now become part of my duties to see how they fare.'

It is doubtful, however, whether some of our upper-class Reeftowners would ever have made the grade had they not been assisted
by their own older siblings. For the most important assistance had,
of course, been educational. And in this we noticed a difference as
to the type of assistance and the manner in which it was given
between brothers and sisters. A brother's assistance was generally
formally invited, pledged and planned in detail beforehand in a
family council, when the various contributions were dovetailed together. But a sister's contribution was mostly informal and freely
given when there was a need.
Mr T.O. explained this clearly:

'Sisters help a lot, the older ones, that is, out of their own
wish, not like the men. Father would call all my brothers
together and say: "Brother so-and-so is keen on education", and
then each brother would say, "I finance this" and "I will finance
that". Our sisters would then be informed of the decisions.

'With me it went like that and when I had to go to college
my sisters, who were already married, out of their own free
will gave things like pocket-money and clothes. Voluntarily,
that is. They don't make a definite undertaking. But at the back
of it one knows that if a brother would fail to continue his help,
the sisters would always come in. It happened like that with me.

'But one's older sisters would all along give one something
just for the love. One could rely on one's sisters.'

The duty to assist the other siblings rested most heavily on the
shoulders of the first-born, of course, but he did not need to carry
the financial burden alone. His role could rather be compared with
that of a producer–actor whose job it was not only to act, but also
to co-ordinate the different roles which the actors are going to play.
He had to set the ball rolling by arranging, with or without the help
of father or mother or both, and often together with the eldest sister,
for the education of the second sibling, who then in his turn reci-
procated by undertaking the liability for the educational expenses of
the next brother or sister, and so on, from the eldest down to the
youngest. As in earlier days the cattle payment for the *lobolo*, so now

a more invisible exchange took place and bound the sibling group together, linking them in a chain of reciprocal rights and commitments extending from the older to the younger ones, and, as with the *lobolo* the obligations incurred were often continued into the next generation. Truly, it was in more senses than one that: 'Education is the cattle of tomorrow'.

Mr T. O.'s family furnished an excellent illustration of the manner in which the system of mutual assistance worked. (See p. 250.) As Mr T. O.'s father was not only keen on education but quite well-to-do, the siblings in his case entered in addition to and following upon his father's assistance. But this was by no means always the case. A variant of what was essentially the same pattern was shown by Mr O. A.'s family. (See pp. 251–2.) This time it was the eldest sister who helped a widowed mother with the education of Nos. 2 and 3, who then in their turn assisted with the education of the youngest ones.

In this system the key figure was the first-born and eldest brother who ideally set the example and triggered off the chain reaction of assistance linking the siblings. In those cases in which a first-born failed to shoulder his responsibilities, the operation came to pivot on the second brother. The ramifications of this network of assistance and reciprocity which were carried on into the next generation were not followed up in detail; but enough was learned to see that the network did indeed exist and to see the method of its working.[13] In this way many a respondent pays off assistance received earlier from mother's brother by now educating one of mother's brother's sons. Or 'Father's sister's son was brought up by me and he is now helping me with my youngest son.' Or 'Father's brother's son liked my father too much; my father looked after him. He always featured in the family. I also see a lot of him. He still likes the family and at one stage gave us assistance.'

Thus education now welded new economic links in the chain of sibling relationships which seemed to us to have weathered the storm of change better than any of the other relations. And again it was found that in these insecure times those relationships that were less institutionalized, more emotional and personal, such as that of the eldest sister with the other siblings, or that between a man and the sister nearest to him in age, had become more emphasized.

Some sibling histories

One who feared isolation

Mr A. J. had two older sisters who were educated to Stds. V and VI respectively. The eldest one never married and remained in the country, poor, until she died, while the younger one married a factory worker and achieved no more than an 'average' economic status. Then came A.J. himself who was the eldest son. In the meantime, the family had assimilated mother's eldest sister's son, who was older than A.J.; and mother, 'who was pushing hardest for education', helped him to pass Std. VI. He did not go any further, however, but became a chef in a hotel.

After A.J., mother had two more children, a son and a daughter, and then she died. Mother's eldest sister's son then felt it *his* duty to 'educate' A.J. 'instead', especially as father remarried and step-mother refused to allow father to spend so much money on A.J.'s education, saying it was a waste.

At that time, mother's eldest sister's son earned about R12 per month. He also grew beans, and bought cattle with the proceeds. He worked for years without taking leave. He even postponed marriage in order to educate A.J. He wanted to 'prove to our stepmother that I was worth educating'. When A.J. subsequently got a bursary to do N.P.H., he asked his mother's sister's son to stop 'educating him' [when the elite talked of 'to educate' someone it meant, to pay for his education], and to marry. He also did this because he did not want to alienate him any further from his parents, particularly his stepmother.

During holidays A.J. often stayed with his eldest sister, who always gave him pocket-money.

When he had completed his teacher-training and started working, he 'looked after' his younger brother and sister, as well as his step-mother's only son, who was irresponsible and made hardly any progress in spite of A.J.'s efforts. According to A.J. it was only his own laziness that prevented his education from going further than Std. VI.

Looking back now, he feels dissatisfied with the progress his family has made. 'They were not as ambitious as I,' he explained. 'All of them refused further education.' Not one became more than a factory worker, and the girls married factory workers. 'They are all lower than myself.' He is now very sorry that he sacrificed his own career and went into teacher-training for the sake of his younger brothers and sisters, instead of accepting the bursary he was offered for Matric.

When the African investigator asked him whether the attitude of his stepmother did not cause strained relations, A.J. replied that this was only so at first, but as she did not have to pay for his education, the burden was not felt by her. 'The only thing was that I was isolated,' he added.

However, 'We have now buried the hatchet,' he continued. 'Now that my father is late (the usual African expression for 'deceased' or 'dead') we are letting my stepmother own the farm and it will be her son's after she dies. But it seems as if she has sold all the cattle, for I now find myself also supporting her.'

A wronged second brother grants his pardon

Mr N.K. was the youngest of seven children. The first-born was a boy; he only did Std. VI and was 'just a labourer' and, in addition, 'sickly'. ['Sickly' is the African euphemism for being 'an alcoholic'.] The next brother and then a sister died young. After them came three girls and then N.K. He had no educational help from his eldest brother. His mother and his eldest surviving sister assisted him during his college years, as his eldest brother was a 'write-off'.

His sisters 'got nowhere'. They were barely literate, and married 'labourers'. His youngest sister married a member of another 'tribe' – 'That is why her marriage went wrong.' [This was the only case on record in which failure in marriage was blamed on tribal differences.]

During all these years, mother kept the link between N.K. and his eldest brother, and she sometimes asked her youngest son to help him. This he dutifully did.

Before their mother died they all came together. N.K. felt he had been the most wronged of all. He pointed this out to his eldest brother and 'told him to confess'. This his brother did; 'he agreed that he had made a mistake and asked pardon'.

Some time after that his eldest brother became very sick, and on his death-bed he asked his younger brother to do two things for him: educate his children and buy him his coffin and bury him, as there was no money left. So when he died, all was over and N.K. 'no longer felt any pressure'.

His brother's sons then depended entirely on him and he educated them all. He also educated a daughter of sister No. 4, and a son of sister No. 3.

He now sees them very often. When he is in town he is a bit far away, but during holidays he always goes home. All remember 'my brother's behaviour'.

Education as a joint sibling responsibility

Mr T.O. was the seventh child of nine. His eldest brother was Hendrik, the only son of father's first wife. Two years after her death, the father remarried and had a further eight children at regular two-year intervals. Father's educational level was Std. II, but he was interested in his children's education, and so was his second wife. She was better educated than the first, and even better educated than father himself.

Hendrik did not want to study. After Std. VI he went to Tigerkloof to be trained as a builder, but he did not complete his training. At present he is a police sergeant and of lower status than the other children, most of whom he helped to educate.

First there were three girls; the eldest daughter never went beyond Std. VI, then worked as a domestic servant and finally married 'just

250

an ordinary man', a driver. The next two girls both completed professional training after Std. VI. Nos. 5 and 6 were boys. The elder did Matric and teacher-training and is at present a high-grade clerk in the Non-European Affairs Department. He married a nurse, and 'is of the same status as I', said Mr T.O. The other boy died young. Then came T.O., the seventh child. After him were two sisters.

First father and later Hendrik paid for T.O.'s education. As there was quite an age difference between brother No. 5 and himself, this brother could, in his turn, take over and pay the school fees when T.O. went to college to do his Matric.

Every now and again, when money was tight, his eldest sister took over the responsibility, and she also gave her brother presents.

Ever since Mr T.O. completed his professional training and began working, he, in his turn, contributed to the education of his two younger sisters. No. 8 reached Matric, and then became a nurse; she married a clerk and her situation is satisfactory, though not quite up to the level of her brothers, Nos. 5 and 7.

The youngest sister failed her J.C. and became a nursery-school teacher. She 'got involved with an ordinary labourer and finally married him'. But her economic situation was nevertheless satisfactory. T.O. contributed to her wedding when he gave her a present of R10 and a costume worth R30.

Educated by the elder and educating the younger siblings
Mr O.A. was the eldest son and the third of five children, all of whom reached J.C.-plus, with the exception of the eldest sister. She had been born, as was the custom, with mother's parents, while all the other children had been born in the small provincial town to which their father had been transferred on his mission work. However, she went into domestic service, became good at needlework and obtained a good job in a factory. Although she married 'a common labourer', her general economic situation was not bad.

The second sister, as well as *ego*, held a Higher Teachers' Certificate, and both married professionals and did well.

O.A.'s father died when O.A. was eight years old, and, although he once had a bursary, his mother paid for most of his education, while his eldest sister helped him along with the extras such as clothes and books.

From the moment he started working he helped his mother with his two younger siblings; his four-years younger brother did carpentry after J.C., and his eight-years younger brother did tailoring after J.C. Although neither of them wanted any further education, they are not doing badly. At the ages of 32 and 28 both are still unmarried. But Mr O.A. is not dissatisfied, as they are all self-supporting.

All the siblings live on the Reef. All are 'lower' than *ego*, but relationships are good. They do not visit each other regularly, but the two younger brothers always come to see O.A. at Christmas and Easter, when he is generally 'somewhat the poorer afterwards'.

The example of fellow Africans

Help in securing jobs

In reply to the question as to who had been the main influence(s) in the lives of our elite, fellow Africans were mentioned in 35 per cent of the responses (See Table III 5 : 1). These fellow Africans represented the second largest category of persons mentioned. Among them the two groups of persons who were most often indicated were primary-school teachers and leading personalities, and these persons were usually mentioned by name. However, a number of secondary-school teachers were also listed, both missionary persons and laymen; and finally, some respondents gave particulars about certain colleagues and friends.

All these persons were influential in various ways: they gave recommendations for jobs, or advice in a crisis, or they uttered certain words which had impressed youthful minds. They furnished the necessary inspiration to determine the choice of particular courses of action, they sparked an ambition or pointed the way to success; and they did so either at a crucial period in a life or as a constant source of encouragement. Their influence was exerted by word and deed, and particularly by their example, as we shall see. Probably the most direct and concrete contribution which other Africans made to the careers of our elite was in the sphere of jobs and employment. In the present situation in South Africa very few Africans are, as yet, employers of other Africans, and in the past history of our elite there are only one or two instances in which they worked for a while for an African employer. Yet Africans played their part in securing jobs for our elite by telling them of vacancies, and by recommending them to their own employers for jobs in the same organization. In about two-thirds of all the jobs about which data were collected, certain persons were mentioned as having been instrumental in helping to obtain employment. In again about two-thirds of the jobs, these persons were Europeans, while in about one-third they were Africans.

Understandably, the professionals were normally recommended or invited to a particular post by a European official in the same department, an official who had already known them for some time and was able to watch their performance in an earlier job or at college. If Africans were instrumental in finding professional jobs for our elite, these were most often their former school principals or teachers. Non-professionals had to rely more often on their own relatives, and particularly on their own African friends to help them find a job. While, therefore, non-professionals were forced to depend on fellow Africans more often than professionals, on the other hand most non-professional jobs were acquired on simple application – an applicant would just present himself, sometimes after reading an advertisement, but more often simply trying his luck. As respondents explained, 'I just happened to pass', or 'I thought I'd walk in and see.' One may safely assume, however, that even in these cases there was often a friend who suggested trying a certain firm or who had read the advertisement first.

The general conclusion to be drawn is that up to the present time at least professional jobs – and normally the most important ones – had to be obtained through European recommendation, while, for the non-professional, and usually lower type of job, our respondents had more often to depend on the goodwill of members of their own community, either friends or relatives.

This situation, however, began to change after the creation of African School Boards. Here, for the first time, Africans became the direct employers of what had always been and still was the largest professional group: the teachers. Whereas originally a teacher's job chances depended almost exclusively upon European educational authorities (and if on African colleagues, these were still people of the same profession), now their appointments, promotions and transfers were increasingly dependent on the recommendations and/or appointments made by fellow Africans outside the profession. As this movement continues and spreads to other departments, more and more Africans will depend on other Africans for their jobs, and more and more professionals will have to follow the teachers and pay more attention to African public opinion and the community's assessment of their professional merits. It is worth noting that although the two professional groups of the health inspectors and the social workers both worked under the supervision of a white Chief Official, there was in both groups a black Senior official in immediate control, and it was the policy to give this official gradually more responsibility.

With this 'return' of the educated and professional to his own community, important changes are likely to occur in occupational behaviour patterns and in job attitudes, and the consequences may reverberate through a wider range of intraracial relationships.

The primary-school teacher

However, the more important influences of fellow Africans on the elite had apparently been of a moral nature, and here the place of honour goes to the primary-school teacher, who seems to have been such a lasting inspiration to many of our respondents that his influence emerges from the education histories far more frequently than he was actually singled out in the replies to our specific question.

Statements about the primary-school teacher abound:

'My teacher, although he was an incapable teacher, was morally influential.'

'The primary-school principal instilled in us the love of education.'

'It was one primary-school teacher particularly who directed my ambitions on to the higher things in life.'

'It was my school teacher in the village who built me up; it was he who convinced my father that I was worthy of more education.'

In spite of qualifications that were often pitifully low and professional methods that were utterly inadequate, these teachers of an earlier generation seem to have had something which their modern colleagues with their higher qualifications and better educational backgrounds were said to lack: high ideals, seriousness of purpose, and awareness of the moral obligations which the privileges of education brought. Noni Jabavu[14] writes: ' . . . how those earlier generations had made conscious and constant efforts to measure up to the new requirements, the higher standards of life: to stretch the intellect to try and meet the new ideas. We young people . . . of this century listen and shudder to think how unbearable life must have been in such a hive of puritanism, of perpetual endeavour.' They believed in the importance and the responsibilities of their profession. It was with pride that they carried the green pass, the exemption from the pass laws to which their high status entitled them. These early knights of a new aristocracy knew the meaning of *noblesse oblige*, or, as Africans always put it, 'In those days a teacher behaved like a teacher'. For, in African eyes, there is no status which does not carry with it its own particular form of status behaviour – and this is a moral notion.

It was the behaviour of these early teachers who were, in the African sense, 'true', that inspired our elite to imitation, which helped them in later life probably more than mere school learning. The teacher's manners and dress invited hero-worship, and the scholars became imbued with the spirit of high-minded seriousness and the wish to be pioneers in their own community.

Let me quote my friend P. Q., a devoted educationist:

254

'The older type of teacher was held up by the high esteem
he enjoyed in the community. He had to live up to it. . . . It was
a revelation to me when I began entering the schools in my
supervisory capacity and when I saw for the first time what I
had never known: the low moral level of the modern teachers.
. . . The old ones may not have read much, but they did read
the teachers' magazine, and they discussed the articles among
themselves. And they were inspired in their endeavours by all
those teachers, many of them famous names, who wrote in the
magazine. And every year they went to the General Conference
of the Teachers' Association and they saw and heard their
teacher heroes, and this inspired them to a big effort.

'Nowadays the Teachers' Association does not give much
serious moral or intellectual inspiration to the teachers. It's all
politics now, and who can shout loudest . . . and wanting more
money. And then there's drink – and it does not remain with
one tot only. And then, running away quickly after class to earn
some money. They run taxis and sell insurances . . .'

'No wonder,' Mr P. Q. concluded, 'that the modern teacher has
lost prestige.' Many Africans blame the Bantu teachers' loss of
prestige on their low salaries. Among these is also Mphahlele.[15] However, there is more to it than that, and Noni Jabavu seems nearer the
truth, while Mr P. Q. explains it very clearly. It cannot often enough
be said: most Africans expect status to be expressed in behaviour to
which they then will respond with respect. Inappropriate behaviour
invites censure and ridicule.

It remained for the secondary-school teacher to make up the
educational back-log, but as a personal inspiration, his role
paled into insignificance compared with that of the simple village
schoolmaster who taught in the one true manner, by his own
example.

Among those early teachers some names were mentioned – they
were of Africans who had since become leading figures in the educational field, in the literary and art world, in business or politics. They
were the first Africans who 'made good', and who later occupied
leading positions in their communities and even in national Bantu
society. 'I know all those early big men,' we were frequently told.
'They were our first teachers.'

It was not always easy to find out whether these pioneers had
inspired a respondent while he was still at school and they were still
simple and unknown teachers, or whether this came afterwards when
they had become leading African figures, which sometimes did not
happen until they had left the teaching profession. Like Noni
Jabavu's own ancestors, many of these early pioneering families, and

particularly those of the Eastern Cape, had intermarried with non-Africans: coloureds of different racial origin as well as whites. Many were not of pure Bantu stock. Our own respondents appeared to be conscious of this and always added some remark about the mixed racial descent of this first elite. We noticed a definite tendency in our respondents to mention mainly those leading families (less well known to Europeans) who had been of pure Bantu descent, as having been influential in their careers.

Certainly many of our elite were proud to associate themselves with those whom they considered to be the pioneers of an earlier era. Those were the true pioneers in the sense that they had been the first to decide upon what was an entirely new venture: a response to the challenge of European contact. Our elite were merely those to whom the pioneers showed the way, and who followed after them.

The example of leading personalities

The tremendous importance of personal example or, sociologically speaking, the force of *mimesis* in social change (Tardé wrote *La societé c'est l'imitation*) was well illustrated in the careers of our elite when we asked them how and when the idea of their present profession or kind of occupation had for the first time occurred to them.

As early as 1953, in an investigation among the nurses of a large non-European hospital on the Reef, we wanted to find out why they had chosen the profession, and in order to avoid the stereotyped reply, 'I wanted to serve my own people', the question was phrased thus: 'How did you get the idea of becoming a nurse?'

Two kinds of answers were received. One was that they had been persuaded, or simply ordered, to apply by a relative or a parent, or that the idea had been suggested by a European friend or missionary, and in these cases they had therefore not actually exercised their own choice at all. In the other group of replies, they all mentioned that they had *seen* other nurses who 'were smart', 'looked important', 'apparently earned a lot of money', or who had, in other ways, impressed them and had made them desire to become like them. Typical statements were: 'Nurses looked so smart in their uniform', 'I also wanted to carry a briefcase', 'I saw schoolmates going nursing and they looked so gay', 'They obviously had more money than the teachers', 'A nurse came to our house and attended my aunt and she impressed me', and 'Our whole class wanted to do nursing'.

This time, in submitting the same question to our elite, we collected the same kind of replies. Here the interesting point was not that the reasons why the nurses and our elite had wanted to enter upon their respective professions were similar, but that with both groups it had been *seeing* others in a desirable role which had inspired their choice of profession.

Again with our elite the operative word was *seeing*; those who had 'seen' others in a certain profession or occupation and had decided that they wanted to become like them, formed the largest single category.

The following are some examples of such statements:

A health inspector:

'I was working in the administrative offices of B. . . . Opposite was the clinic. I saw health assistant students going into the clinic. They looked inferior to myself, and I felt if *they* can do it, *I* can certainly do it.'

A trader:

'You want to know what really decided me? I'll tell you. I think it was when I saw a man, someone in the same kind of business, receive a cheque for R160. I thought: My! So much! I must do that too.'

Teachers:

'I saw that lots of authority went with teaching. Teachers were high people. They had real salaries and holidays.'

'I saw that teachers were well-mannered and well-dressed, and I hero-worshipped them.'

'I never saw any enlightened people other than teachers and ministers. There were no businessmen in those days. I hated prayers and ministers, so I got the idea of becoming a teacher.'

'I noticed quite early in life that as a teacher you did not need to get up when our fathers got up, and you had certain other privileges.'

Clerks:

'I saw a man in H. He looked good to me. He was a Pass Office clerk and so I wanted to be like him.'

'The Native Recruiting Clerk was the big shot where I was born. He was wearing a suit. And I made up my mind that I would do the same.'

Thus, in choosing their present professions or kinds of occupation, the majority of the elite had followed the example of certain seen and admired persons, who were in all cases Africans. 'He was an African like me', 'He was no better than me'.

Sometimes such an admired person was an older member of the family, either a paternal or a maternal relative, who had occupied a leading position; or an uncle had been the first secondary-school principal or a first court interpreter, or even the first Bantu clerk in the local Post Office; or an aunt had been the first trained nurse in the district, or the first social worker. Our respondents had heard their praises sung at weddings and funerals; they had seen the reverence with which the community or clan had treated them, and they had made up their minds to be like them. The common thought was: 'If *he* can do it, *I* can do it too!'

Apparently, this thought did not come so easily merely through seeing a European in that profession or occupation. Certainly, there was, as is well known to all in contact with Africans, a general desire to be like Europeans in respect of certain material possessions and external characteristics, but it may be that this was too vague and suffused a sentiment to lead to well-defined concrete action. All we can say here is that with our elite, when the desire to imitate was focused and became the incentive for planning a specific course of action, namely the entry upon a profession or the application for a particular kind of job, the direct inspiration seems to have come from seeing another African in that job (the only exception may possibly be Dr R.) and never a European.

It is possible, even probable, that if a similar question about their professions had been asked of those earlier pioneers whom we mentioned before, the replies would have been different. To dare to think of imitating persons seen as being of an entirely different cultural fibre (and in this case even of an entirely different physical appearance); to be capable of imagining oneself in the role of persons so obviously foreign as Europeans were felt to be (certainly in the earlier stages of black–white contact) needed certain imaginative and creative qualities, which those earlier pioneers must have had, but which our elite obviously did not possess. Our elite were no original cultural innovators and explorers of hitherto unknown cultural areas. They did not cut a first road in a hitherto unknown cultural land. They simply followed upon a path already opened up by members of their own society. At least in one well-defined detail of their careers, specially investigated in this study, they followed westernized Bantu rather than westerners.[16]

As far as we know, the role of *mimesis* in cultural change has not yet had the attention of social scientists which its study would deserve and it is hoped that these tentative findings from a very partial investigation will induce someone to inaugurate such a study. However, time is running out, for the original pioneers are becoming older and dying out.

With a view to such a study, another point should be mentioned. According to our own general observation a change in chosen leaders and in preferred examples was taking place at present. The heroes worshipped by the younger generation were no longer the educated, and what were called 'the enlightened', but nowadays they were the pop singers and jazz players, the get-rich-quick gangsters and, particularly, the professional politicians – all those representatives of a new and supposedly easier way of achieving recognition and wealth. (See P. Q.'s statement, p. 118.) Among the younger members of the elite we could notice already the first stirrings of this change. In spite of their youth some could scarcely remember the humble village school-teacher, and the ponderous and dignified principal who had inspired their earliest years. Nor were they any longer awed by the first African doctors and university professors.

One of the younger members of our group said it for all of them:

'I am somewhat confused about it now. Lately I have new aspirations, seeing that I could not achieve a B.A. [he failed Matric]. Earlier on I was inspired by the teachers and ministers; they made me long for the higher things. Today there is a drastic change in me. Now I am turning more and more to Africans and to political leaders. I wondered about it myself. . . .' [Note that the change happened after he failed all chances to become a University graduate.]

Consequently, we would suggest that a twofold change has been taking place during the last few years. The one change was a movement away from the teachings and examples of the Europeans to those of fellow Africans; and the other change was a turning of the *mimesis* away from the educated Africans to the African political leaders and successful gang-leaders.

The role of the European

The influence of the missionaries

In reply to our leading question as to who had been the main influence(s) in their lives, the smallest group mentioned by the elite was that of the Europeans. Whereas Africans, whether relatives or friends, were mentioned in more than 80 per cent of the replies, Europeans figured in less than 20 per cent of the answers. (See Table III 5:1.)

At first, this seems surprising, considering the historic role of the European in this country. But as individual persons, Europeans have obviously made far less impact on our elite than individual members of their own race and kin. This confirmed an earlier impression which we formed after our first researches, i.e. that Europeans were inclined to overrate the impression they made on the Bantu.

With the exception of some individual Europeans, mentioned by a few respondents, with whom they had apparently had some personal contact of a kind which can be described as 'social', or in one exceptional case as 'political', white individuals had entered the lives of our elite mainly in two roles: as secondary-school teachers (mainly missionaries) and as employers.

In spite of the fact that 80 per cent of their primary education and about 77 per cent of their post-primary education (not university education) was received from white missionaries, it was the African primary-school teacher who was felt to be the most important influence. In those early days, the white missionary was probably a rather shadowy, impersonal presence in the background, too far removed from the mental vision of a young black boy to have any direct, personal impact. It was not until he reached college that the black youth began to perceive the white missionary and teacher as a particular person, and it was only then that the type of contact was sometimes established which could presumably influence the black youth's actions and attitudes. At the secondary-school level, some missionary personalities began to be mentioned by name in the educational histories. But we have seen in the previous section how this influence was such that it was felt mainly as concrete assistance or verbal admonishment rather than as personal example.

Naturally, the influence of the missionaries has, in South Africa, mainly operated through education and the school system.

Almost two-thirds of the elite belonged to the two largest missions in the Transvaal (see Table III 5:5) and three-quarters to the three mission churches that had the best-known teacher-training colleges and high schools in the province, namely, St Peter's (the Church of the Province), Kilnerton (the Methodist Church of South Africa) and Bochabelo (the Berlin Lutheran Mission). Whereas the indigenous churches constituted the largest religious group among Africans in South Africa as a whole, only 13 per cent of the elite belonged to an Independent African church, in this case the African Methodist Episcopal Church, the Bantu Methodists and the Bantu Presbyterians. With the exception of the A.M.E., however, these African churches had few institutions of learning and none of post-primary level. So, if an African desired education beyond Std. VI, he almost inevitably came within the orbit of one of the European school missions.

Some eight different Christian denominations had been involved in the primary education of the elite. The Methodists were the most important numerically: 45 per cent of the mission schools attended belonged to them. About 20 per cent belonged to the Church of the Province. A further 10 per cent and 7 per cent were run by the Lutherans and the Roman Catholics respectively.

On the secondary-school level, almost the same missions contributed, but the Nederduits Gereformeerde Kerk was absent and the A.M.E. Church now added its influence. The relative contribution of the mission churches was similar, except that the roles of the two main churches were reversed. Now the colleges of the Anglicans (a.o. Khaiso and St Matthew's, but particularly St Peter's of Johannesburg) represented 35 per cent of the total, and the Methodist colleges (Kilnerton, Clarkbury and Healdtown, etc.) only 23 per cent. Important contributions to our elite's post-primary education were also made by Lovedale (Presbyterian), Adam's (American Board Mission), Wilberforce, Evaton (A.M.E.) and some of the well-known Roman Catholic colleges.

Of the Government High schools, Orlando High in Johannesburg was most often mentioned, while some respondents had been to Madebane High also in Johannesburg, and to Langa High, near Cape Town.

Almost half of the 52 bursaries received by our elite had been directly given by mission churches. Of these the Church of the Province formed the largest single religious group with no less than ten bursaries to their credit. However, it may be assumed that in those days most bursaries and scholarships were obtained through missionary recommendations, even if not always from missionary funds.

Table III 5:5 Numerical distribution of the elite and their fathers by their last religious adherence

Christian denomination	Elite	Fathers
Anglican	24	12
Methodist	15	21
Lutheran	6	11
A.M.E.	4	2
Roman Catholic	4	2
Dutch Reformed Church	3	3
Bantu Methodist	3	3
Bantu Presbyterian	1	3
Bantu Catholic	—	1
Paris Evangelican Mission	—	1
Nil	—	1
Total	60	60

The reversal of the Methodists' and Anglicans' share in the education of our elite between the primary and the secondary level appeared to correspond with the changes in denominational adherence between the parents and the sons. (See Table III 5:5.) This raises the interesting question of the relationship between the denominations of the people and those of their schools. Some of our data regarding denominational changes may throw light on this interesting question.

Seven fathers changed denomination and although there was no first-hand knowledge about the exact circumstances which induced them to do so, their sons' reports seemed to suggest that the reasons were throughout of a practical nature (see, for instance, the denominational change of Dr R.'s father, p. 167) and mainly educational. Therefore, those missions that ran the best-developed school systems exerted the greatest attraction. In one case the reason was as narrated here:

'The family had belonged to the A.M.E. Church, but there had been a quarrel and they had been "sitting down" for a while. Father's father suffered many misfortunes, and as if all this had not been enough, his youngest son Solomon was blind. He tried various witch-doctors without result, and then he heard that "the Romans were interested in orphans", and he thought that upon his death the Roman Catholics would look after his blind son. So the whole family joined the R.C. religion, with the exeption of the first-born.'

We also concluded that scarcely any of the school changes had been determined by purely religious considerations. (See Table II 3:2.) There was, therefore, little evidence to suppose that the religion of the parents had in any way determined the choice or change of primary schools. If there was a casual relationship between the denomination of the parents and that of the primary schools attended by their children, it would be due rather to the circumstances which had brought a particular mission to the district so that its church converted the parents and its school educated the children.

In four cases the rearers (two widowed mothers and two fathers' sisters) became responsible for the boys' denominational change by sending them to primary schools of different denominations from those of their fathers. This was reported, for instance, as follows:

'My father's brothers all had different churches, because of their professions mainly. When you got a post at a particular mission school, you became that denomination. My mother became an Anglican because she taught in an Anglican school, but she was baptized Presbyterian.'

'Father's sister herself belonged to the Assemblies of God, but she choose for us R.C. schools because they were strict.'

[Roman Catholic schools were considered 'very strict', and therefore generally preferred by the parents and rearers. Anglican schools were considered 'more free', and therefore usually preferred by the sons.]

262

It would appear, therefore, that educational and occupational considerations were the main inducements for such changes.

With regard to the denominational influence of the primary school on the pupils themselves, our records do not show one single case of this among our elite, unless the influence was continued on the post-primary level, as was the case with all the four rearer-fostered children mentioned above.

Nineteen respondents changed their original denominational adherence as and when they grew up. Eleven of these changed to the Church of the Province, while three became Roman Catholic, two Methodist, two A.M.E., and one a member of a Bantu Methodist Church.

A careful scrutiny of the reasons for these conversions revealed that, besides the four above-mentioned cases, nine were almost entirely the result, not of religious, but of educational and occupational considerations. With regard to the Anglican Church, there was the added attraction, first, of the considerable snob-appeal of St Peter's, 'the Eton of the Reef' and, second, of the open anti-Government involvement of some of the priests of the Church of the Province. However, these two attractions could not always be clearly distinguished in the reports of our spokesmen.

By and large, the two Catholic churches seem to have exerted a greater persuasion and pressure towards conversion than the other denominations; facilities appear more often to have been offered with religious strings attached: with the Romans more openly, with the Anglicans more hidden. About this our elite were quite outspoken.

Three cases of conversion were unexplained, and here the motives may have been of a more purely religious or spiritual nature, and possibly for that reason incommunicable.

As to the Independent African churches, however, neither schools nor colleges appear to have had much religious influence – if we judge, for instance, by the fact that not one of our A.M.E. respondents went to Wilberforce (the A.M.E. college), and that the two A.M.E. converts had not received their post-primary education there. The circumstances leading to a conversion to an Independent African church had little to do with educational or occupational advantages; they were of an entirely different nature. The following illustrates these motives rather well (the italics are ours):

'My parents were Berlin Lutheran, but as a young man I never used to attend the Church. [This was how Mr Y. began his explanation. He had been helped by the Lutherans with a part bursary, and then he failed, which may have been the reason that no further educational assistance was offered him.]

'But in G. where my brother-in-law lived who had found me the job, my Lutheran Church was far away. Moreover, *I wanted to stand on my own. I felt with my education I am entitled to my own church. Now my brother-in-law was Bantu Methodist,* and I sometimes went with him to his church. People took it for granted that I belonged.

'Then I wanted to get married. The Lutherans asked me to undergo a process of purification. *A lot of religion I had to do!* That was too much for me. I had already quite enough trouble, what with my future mother-in-law and the *lobolo*. (My father-in-law did not care but she wanted it.) Then when the Bantu Methodists heard that I was Lutheran and had been Lutheran all the time, they were astonished.

'But then they said they were willing to accept me whole-heartedly and to marry me quickly.'

From previous research, we would suggest that the reasons for Mr Y.'s conversion to a Bantu church were not untypical. The desire to be emancipated from missionary tutelage and the resistance against the intellectual effort demanded by European Christianity appear to be two very important considerations in bringing South African Bantu to their own churches.

Summarizing the role of the European missionaries, it would appear that the schools, and particularly the colleges, were the great centres of missionary influence in South Africa, not so much because of the education they provided, but because of all that went with it: missionary contacts and recommendations, bursaries and other forms of financial assistance, and, last but not least jobs, especially in the days when teaching and the ministry were about the only professions for the educated Africans, and well-nigh the only channels for the attainment of superior status.

The consequences of the removal of the missionaries from their almost exclusive dominion over the educational and occupational field cannot yet be foreseen although one consequence has already become manifest. In an attempt to find a substitute for their lost educational influence, some missions have been throwing themselves more actively and openly into the battle against racial discrimination.

The attitude to Europeans generally

The elite themselves were only too conscious of the benevolent attention they had received from Europeans during the greater part of their lives, and the majority did not hesitate to admit this indebtedness. Some of our respondents only talked about Europeans generally, but a few mentioned particular white individuals, and quite a number quoted particular instances of either help or hindrance.

As many as almost 70 per cent frankly and often gratefully admitted that to such a question they would have to reply that Europeans had been more often helpful as far as their education was concerned, and an equal percentage gave a similar answer with regard to help received from Europeans in the matter of jobs and employment. (See Table III 5:6.) Quite a number added to this the exclamation: 'Definitely!' 'All through!' 'A great deal even!' 'Certainly!' or 'Indeed!'

General educational help received from Europeans was described in terms of European interest in African education generally. 'After all, it was the Europeans who brought education to Africans by opening schools and training teachers.' Some spoke in the name of all Africans and said, for example, 'It is due to the Europeans that we no longer live as our poor unfortunate illiterate brethren are living,' or 'They helped us change our lives.'

Table III 5:6 Numerical and percentage distribution of all respondents by their replies to the question
'Would you say: Europeans have helped or hindered me in my education/employments?'

Help or hindrance from Europeans	Education		Employment	
	No.	Percentage	No.	Percentage
Helped generally	16	26·67	21	35·00
Helped in specific instances	26	43·33	20	33·33
Generally helped, but hindered in specific instances	1	1·67	4	6·67
Hindered generally	2	3·33	4	6·67
Hindered in specific instances	—	—	3	5·00
Generally hindered, but helped in specific instances	1	1·66	—	—
No influence; neither helped nor hindered	12	20·00	6	10·00
Helped and hindered in specific instances	1	1·67	1	1·66
Unknown	1	1·67	1	1·67
Totals	60	100·00	60	100·00

Specific instances of such educational help were recounted in some two-thirds of these replies. Europeans had helped by giving bursaries or recommendations for bursaries, and also by educational guidance and personal coaching. But, all the same, as many as one-fifth of our respondents replied that they had not felt any educational influence from Europeans. 'They neither hindered nor helped me,' these stated. Or, 'They had no influence on my education.' That most of them, however, understood this help in a material, mainly financial, sense, was clear from such replies as these: 'They had no influence. I had to struggle on my own,' or 'No, my parents could afford to educate me.' (This was one of the ministers who received his professional training entirely free. But we are here investigating the subjective, not the objective situation.)

On the whole, these people did not feel they had any axe to grind. From their achieved educational success they could look back and 'view it broadly', as was generously told us by a school principal after due consideration: 'Yes, viewing it broadly, I must say Europeans greatly helped me, particularly the missionaries.'

That such admissions, however, did not always come easily was manifestly clear. One speaker said: 'I could never truthfully say that they hindered me. But you know, Mrs Brandel, we Africans do not appreciate much.'

With regard to the help or hindrance received from Europeans in the sphere of employment, the replies were not very different, except that there was a tendency to talk more generally and mention less specific cases of help, less 'no influence', but more cases of specific hindrance. Help was seen in terms of having been recommended for vacancies or having been promoted. Professionals felt it was due to certain Europeans that they now enjoyed their present professional status. Businessmen felt that they had been helped by Europeans who had recommended them for business sites and licences, who had given them loans, or advised them in commercial and technical problems. General help with jobs was seen, particularly, in terms of the present widening of occupational opportunities and the raising of the occupational ceiling.

In spite of this general recognition of the European's contribution to their present careers by a majority, the satisfaction of being no longer dependent on any European help, or of having jobs in which whites no longer have much to say, emerged clearly from some replies. 'I am happy to be away from working with whites', or 'Thank God, I am independent from European employers now!' The resentment felt about past or present dependence on European employers is clearly shown in such replies as: 'It did not fall within the scope of the Europeans either to help or hinder me,' or 'It is not for them to help or hinder me.'

Generally, however, European assistance was gratefully accepted and acknowledged by people who were happy that the need for such assistance had passed. It is only those who have achieved their emancipation (or feel that they have achieved it) from European patronage who can afford to acknowledge indebtedness.

266

Afrikaans- or English-speaking whites?

Because our findings about the attitudes of our elite to the English-speaking and Afrikaans-speaking whites were so different as to be almost the opposite of those established by other researchers studying similar groups of Africans,[17] we shall begin with a brief description of the manner in which we approached the subject and of the general context in which our question was asked.

The subject was usually raised after the whole educational history had been passed in review, and in a discussion on the respondent's jobs and of what he had liked and disliked in them. The conversation then dealt with European employers, supervisors, Department Seniors, and subsequently drifted on to Europeans generally. After this the question which we discussed in the previous section was asked first. And the conversation then proceeded from employers and teachers to shop assistants and salesmen, co-religionists, co-members on committees or in organizations – the types of Europeans usually encountered by educated Africans. Generally at this stage the words 'Afrikaners', 'English', 'Jews', had been dropped and then the question was put: 'You know as a foreigner in this country, I am myself interested. Tell me what is the difference between them? Can you characterize them for me?' Care was taken that the question appeared as an aside, because I myself was interested in it.

The majority of our respondents would then begin talking from their own personal experience, and they were encouraged to do so, for it is only in this way that one could be sure that the question had meaning for them. A small minority said that they had not had much experience with either Afrikaners or Englishmen. Or they said: 'At first I only knew the English, and it is only in the last few years that I came in contact with Afrikaners,' or the reverse. (No specific questions were asked about the Jews, though if they were mentioned at all, it was always as a category apart. What was said, however, was noted.)

A number of respondents asked first: 'You mean their attitude towards us?' or 'You mean their treatment of the African?' Upon this we then replied: 'Yes, if you like to begin with that. But I also mean it more generally.' And, in fact, for people who saw the world almost exclusively in relation to themselves, our elite surprised us by frequently including more general characteristics.

If, as sometimes happened, there was some difficulty with the word 'characterize', an example was given – always the same example: 'Well, you know, like the saying that all Germans are efficient and all Italians can sing.' This had been carefully planned beforehand, and chosen because both characterizations were considered to be 'good things' and not opposites. All through we avoided a

U   267 confrontation of the two groups, which, if the one was 'good' would make the other one inevitably 'bad'. In many replies, as we shall see, a number of general characteristics were given as well as more specific differences between the two groups. But in an astonishingly large number of conversations, both the pros and cons, the 'good' and the 'bad' characteristics of each group were discussed.

In a large majority of the interviews, however, the characterizations were at once forthcoming, as if this was a much-discussed subject about which there was no longer much disagreement. Sometimes opinions were brought forward with the addition: 'I am not alone in thinking this', or 'This is what all Africans think.'

Most respondents showed that they knew of the bitter cultural antagonism between the two white groups. Some said: 'But I am not interested in their quarrel,' or 'That doesn't concern me.' Another said: 'There is too much emotion between them. They're worried by the political situation, and instead of progressing together, they built safety camps against each other.'

Most often, however, this Afrikaans–English disunity was seen in terms of its effect on the African. Many respondents seemed to know that the African was used as a pawn in the white rivalries. With a touch of malice: 'There's competition between them. Each is trying to show the African how kind he is.' Ironically: 'The English are beginning to be very worried, and they try to use the African against the Afrikaner,' or 'They now want to hear our grievances only if they are against the Afrikaners.'

A distinction was sometimes made between 'before' and 'now'. 'Now' could refer to the situation which has arisen since the Afrikaans-speaking group assumed the government of the country, and *apartheid* became the official policy. 'Before' could also refer to the time 'when we were still on the land with our cattle'. The changes remarked upon between 'before' and 'now' were for the better or the worse, depending on the respondents' views. One would say: 'Before, there was a difference, now there is no longer any difference between them.' This was then amplified by: 'First we were together with the Afrikaner; now they are just as bad as the English,' or the opposite: 'First the English were very good; then they had to fall in line with the Afrikaner way of thinking for their own survival, and now the English are just as bad as the Afrikaners.'

There was often a surprising measure of agreement in the broad characterizations about the two groups, yet the conclusions drawn by respondents could not always be predicted. Respondents gave different emotional evaluations to similar happenings or patterns of behaviour. They would say: 'But in spite of all this, I still prefer . . . '.

However, there was no doubt that when the crucial question was asked, the preference referred to the actual contact situation in the personally experienced role-relationship between the black respondent and the whites. Here the European is seen either as helper, adviser, teacher and educator or as punisher and judge, exploiter and suppressor. But in whatever role the white man appears, he is always in the stronger position. He is the more resourceful, knowledgeable, experienced and powerful. In him the African sees the potential source of assistance, a dispenser of favours or a cause of misfortune and humiliation. Unlike the African's relationship with fellow Africans (or even with Coloureds or Indians) his contact with a European is almost never on a footing of true equality, even though both Europeans and Africans may prefer to make it appear so. There is in South Africa a qualitative difference between the relationship of the African with a European and with a non-European, which makes nonsense of all quantitative comparisons between these different relationships. The same measuring rod can simply not be applied. Yet this has been done in some previous researches which aimed at measuring and comparing the so-called 'social distance' between Africans and other ethnic groups including whites and non-whites.

Table III 5:7   Numerical and percentage distribution of the elite by their replies to the question: 'Of the two, whom do you prefer to deal with?'

Replies	No.	Percentage
The Afrikaner	25	41·67
No preference	10	16·67
The English	7	11·67
Doesn't want to say	6	10·00
Neither	4	6·67
It depends	3	5·00
Question not asked	5	8·32
Total	60	100·00

Furthermore in the real-life situation, preferences are far from absolute; on the contrary, they are usually relative to a number of provisos and qualifications. A very good illustration can be given by quoting the following reply: 'I prefer a good Afrikaner to any Englishman, but I'd rather have any kind of Englishman than a bad Afrikaner.' Also, although one may prefer to deal with one person rather than with the other, one may admire the other more; or one may not always like to associate most frequently with someone to whom one feels closest; or again one may prefer to deal with one person in one situation and with another person in another situation. All three persons, who replied to our question with: 'It depends' (see Table III 5:7), said that in their work they preferred the Afrikaner, but 'for social contacts' and as social friends they would definitely prefer the English. One of these enlarged on this by saying, 'You can also say that if I am educated and can have social contacts with Europeans then I prefer the English; but if I am not educated I would definitely prefer the Afrikaner.'

We would suggest that this was the kind of information which gave the best insight into the race relations prevailing in this country. It also taught us more about our elite than the superficial search for racial group stereotypes[18] and was, therefore, the kind of information required in our context.

An analysis of the replies to our question showed that those who preferred to deal with the Afrikaner formed the largest group of 42 per cent, and just over one-quarter of this number, i.e., only 12 per cent, preferred to deal with the English-speaking South Africans. As many as 17 per cent had no special preferences; there were good and bad ones among both groups. Those who did not want to say with whom they preferred to deal formed 10 per cent, and 7 per cent preferred to deal with neither. These wanted as little as possible to do with Europeans. 'I do not like to be bossed around', was one respondent's reason. Another replied: 'Neither, but if I have to deal with Europeans, I prefer the Afrikaner.' Yet another one said: 'Neither, I prefer the Jews. There are lots of bad ones, but once they're your friend, they are at least sincere.'

We collected all the statements and adjectives used by our elite to characterize the two white groups of South Africans. There were 200 such descriptive statements about the English and 174 about the Afrikaners.

In the following we present a selection:

About the English-speaking South Africans

'Very diplomatic', 'Hypocritical',[19] 'You can never trust an Englishman', 'Very tactful', 'The sugar-coated pill', 'He bluffs you all the time', 'Beating about the bush', 'A bit tricky', 'Sly', etc. (62 times)

'You never know what he thinks or means', 'He doesn't show his true colours', 'He hides his feelings', 'He always keeps you at arm's length', etc. (31 times)

'Kind', 'More cultured', 'More liberal', 'They appear humanitarian', 'More generally educated', 'More civilized', etc. (26 times)

'Efficient', 'Not human', 'More logical', 'Patient', 'Prepared to listen to your reasons', 'Tries to convince you by arguments', 'Prefers an educated person', etc. (23 times)

270

'Disciplinarian', 'Sticks to the rules and regulations', 'Never forgives a mistake', 'Always follows procedure', *etc.* (16 times)

'Hard', 'Harsh', 'Cruel', 'Vicious', *etc.* (11 times)

'They tried to work for our welfare', 'Did a lot for Africans as to education', 'They gave us education but what really benefited us was accidental', *etc.* (11 times)

'Says he has no colour bar but . . . ', 'They oppress you in a nice way', 'More experience in ruling people', *etc.* (10 times)

'They make you believe they sympathize with you and then when he has won you over, he's only out to better himself', *or* ' . . . to use you against the Afrikaner', *etc.* (6 times)

'Stingy', (4 times)

About the Afrikaans-speaking South Africans

'If he likes you he says so, and if he does not like you, he tells you also', 'If he likes you or knows you, he will always help you', *or* 'He can be a real friend', *or* 'He treats you like a human being', 'If he does not like you or know you, he thinks of all the Africans he does not know or like', *or* 'His prejudice against you is too strong', *etc.* (33 times)

'Very open', 'You know where you are', 'Does not hide his feelings', 'Understands us better', 'Very candid, even blunt', 'Easier to understand', *etc.* (31 times)

'Definitely straightforward', 'Very sincere', 'Doesn't bluff me', 'Won't smile if he hates you', 'Very undiplomatic', 'Tactless', *etc.* (30 times)

'More human', 'If I am at fault I would rather have to do with an Afrikaner', 'Always gives you a second chance', 'Lacks discipline', 'Makes exceptions for human reasons', *etc.* (14 times)

'More kind', 'Very sympathetic', 'Very considerate', 'Co-operative', 'Forgiving', *etc.* (14 times)

'Hard', 'Harsh', 'Crude', 'Arrogant', 'Obstinate', *etc.* (14 times)

'More emotional', 'Acts on his feelings', 'If you are obedient and honest I can plead and he will understand', 'Behaves to you like a father to his child', *etc.* (13 times)

'Never did anything for our education', 'Brought us Bantu education', 'Have given the Africans positions they never had before', 'They opened up more avenues, but the benefits were accidental', *etc.* (11 times)

271

'Has a colour bar', 'They don't like us', 'Suffers from an inferiority complex', *etc.* (8 times)

'Very generous', (6 times)

Such a list of adjectival characterizations and an enumeration of statements out of context cannot reproduce the reasoning underlying the preferences. We now give here some complete *verbatim* quotations which seemed rather typical.

Prefers to deal with the English 'in spite of':

'Well . . . I think . . . they are . . . I should say . . . It looks to me that the English are more liberal, I seem to be more attached to them, although the Afrikaners having been here earlier are nearer to us Africans. But they have had so much trouble with us, in a way they know us better. But they can't forget.

'The black man is more inclined towards the English. Then another thing, these English people started to educate the black man earlier through English, which is liked by the black people as an international language.

'Then the English are a more civilized and cultured people.

'The English, general speaking, have no capacity to tolerate weaknesses or failings. He does not show his dislikes though. Not like the Afrikaner, who will tell you at once "I don't like you or I do like you".

'In spite of all this I prefer to deal with the English, yes, but it is not that I understand the English better, I don't. The Englishman is more diplomatic, the Afrikaner is easier to understand. But it is better for social harmony to consider other people's feelings, don't you agree with me, Mrs Brandel?'

Prefers to deal with Afrikaners 'in spite of':

'I think there is a difference, especially towards us. The English – they did a lot for Africans as to education, specially in the north where I come from. But with an Englishman, even if he is doing you down, he always remains friendly, he never shows it to you, always speaks good to you and you tend to forget the wrong done. In fact, he bluffs you all the time. He's a hypocrite.

'The Afrikaner regards us as "hewers and drawers"; they associate us with labour. They've done little for our advancement. They hate the idea of the Africans progressing socially and economically. An Afrikaner will tell you exactly what you are.

'Which one do I prefer to deal with? The Afrikaner.
Although in the past they've done so little for us, they're
straightforward. They don't hide. You know what he thinks of
you and it is easier to deal with such a person.'

Prefers the English socially, the Afrikaner in work:

'The English pretend; they never tell you when they don't
like a thing. The Afrikaner always tells you, at once. "Don't
behave like that", he says. He warns you of your mistakes. The
English wait – they say nothing, and your mistakes pile up and,
then suddenly, you're dismissed. An Afrikaner might spank you,
but he wouldn't send you away.

'The Afrikaner, when he knows you, you get a wonderful
reception; he's nice and co-operative. But when they do not
know you, they're harsh.

'The Afrikaners just miss a little touch that would make
them wonderful people, some little etiquette. In any case, they're
more human than the English. The English always come to you
friendly. You're the ladder on which they climb. Then when
they get you where they want you, they do away with you.
When they get to the top they kick you away.

'The Afrikaner is much better to work for.

'They say they know the African, but they only know the
older type of African. Not the present one in town.

'That's why I say, I prefer the English in social life, but the
Afrikaner in work.'

Prefers the Afrikaner:

'We Africans find, as we look around, that the Afrikaner
either hates you or loves you, he's more open, even blunt.
Whereas with the Englishman, there's a lot of dishonesty. You
can never be too sure of an Englishman. He will be nice to you
and then he will use you to oppress your fellow-men.

'Today, lots of Afrikaners who don't know their jobs get
into jobs, but when the Englishman takes a job he knows it.

'The Afrikaner lacks discipline, but the Englishman is too
much of a disciplinarian; he's strict, really rigid. But that's
the English way of doing things. You must keep your distance.
If you're in charge of other Africans he does not like you to
mix with your own co-workers. But in loyalty they beat the
Afrikaner, they do not stand disloyalty, not in words at least,
but the Afrikaner encourages it.

273

'But really, they're hypocrites, the English. We want to know whether the English are going to give us freedom or not, or whether they're forced to do so by overseas opinion, or from fear that the Afrikaners will otherwise swamp them. . . . Take Rhodesia where the English are in charge.

'Of course, nowadays there are also clever Afrikaners, even cleverer than the English.

'Whom do I prefer to deal with? I unfortunately grew up with the English, so I got more used to them. But a properly educated Afrikaner is better. I am beginning to like these Dutch boys now. They're more human than the English, they get more attached to you personally.

'Even on the farms. The real farmer is a good fellow. If you were loyal to him, he'd never worry you. You stayed on his farm and you could grow wealthy. Of course with the English we got education but education does not pay . . . Now with the Afrikaners we are getting rich again. . . . Oh no, give me the Afrikaner any time.'

[The recurrent saying was: 'Before, under the Afrikaners, we got rich; then the English brought us education; and now, with the Afrikaners, we become rich again.']

An (Anglican) minister who changed his opinion:

'When I met the English first, I found them more interested in educating people and in culture. When I came across the Afrikaners they detested to see an educated African. They used to say: "You're making yourself a black Englishman." They called us: *Bobbejaan sonder stert.* "A Kaffir is not meant for education," they said. You see they hated the educated African.

'But today . . . I don't know. . . . Things have changed quite a bit. . . . Now the Afrikaner would like to see you enlightened, and speak the Afrikaans language, not in the English line. Afrikaners are not happy when you speak English; but if you speak Afrikaans, you're accepted. But with the English you're never accepted. This I found out.

'Now I prefer the Afrikaner.'

Prefers the Afrikaner:

'The English on the *platteland*, they are still regarded as . . . all Africans feel that an Englishman, wherever you put him, is cultural, a gentleman, he does not lose his temper although he can be merciless. One thing, however, if he punishes you, he wants others to see it, to make an example of it. He beats you hard, so you cry so that the others can hear you. An Englishman can be vicious in punishing you. He's ruthless. If he gets you in a corner he hits you again so that you never rise. For once you fall out with him, you're gone for good. He'll never accept you again in the same light.

'He's hard and uncompromising. He has no emotions, he is not emotionally inclined, never shows his emotions. But he does not begrudge you your progress.

'The Afrikaner, he is forgiving if you make him understand that it was all your folly, that you were too arrogant. He will always forgive you. If you work for an Englishman and you do wrong he has a fixed punishment – he has fixed rules for everything – but he will never accept you again. But an Afrikaner, if you come to him suffering, will always give you a second chance.

'Africans feel, the Afrikaner – he's like themselves, not systematic at all. The only thing is you must accept his baasskap and all is well. You can get to the highest top then, as long as he is baas.

'I give you an example from what I know. If you work for an Englishman, for instance, he is on horseback and goes to a shop, and you help looking after his horse, he then comes back and he gives you money. And if he does something for you, then you must give him money. Now an Afrikaner, if you held his horse for him, he would say, "Thank you very much", but give you no money. And then, if you go to him later, when you are hungry for instance, he gives you whatever you need without any payment. He's generous, and the English are stingy and calculating.

'An Englishman, and this is true, estranges the African from the Afrikaner. Before the English came the African and the Afrikaner worked together as brothers – man to man . . .'

Although as we mentioned above, we did not encourage our respondents to speak of the two groups in direct contrasts and by opposite characterizations, precise differences were nevertheless frequently brought forward. Here are some of those collected from the conversations. They are very revealing.

'An Englishman will always take you to his boss when a decision must be made, but an Afrikaner acts on his own.'

'The English are more the office people, they do more mental work. The Afrikaners like more hard work, they're men of the fields, they're more the manual workers.'

'They differ in education. The Afrikaner is one-sided in his education. He may be very highly educated, but they don't fuse things together. Whereas the English, they have a more general education.'

'An African can enjoy real, genuine friendship with an Afrikaner, but never with an Englishman. He will always keep you at arm's length.'

'The English do not credit you with any ability to get where they are. That's why they have no fear of us. The Afrikaner knows that we can get up where he is – after all he also was backward before. That's why he is afraid of us. The English think they're the only people who can get anywhere and do everything always better than everybody else. They're up in the air.' [In the many writings on racial prejudice it has sometimes been forgotten that racial tolerance can be humiliating and racial discrimination complimentary.]

'An Englishman will never forgive a mistake, he has no patience with weaknesses. But an Afrikaner will always give you a second chance.'

'An Englishman will always stick to the rules and regulations, but an Afrikaner considers human factors, and will always make exceptions to any rule for human considerations.'

'You ask an Afrikaner for a day off, and you get it. You ask an Englishman for a day off, and he will say: "the rule is so-and-so".'

'An Englishman may be a member of a system while not subscribing to it. He can execute a policy even though he does not agree with it. He always carries on the job whether he believes in it or not. An Afrikaner, if he does not believe in it, would sabotage it. Because an Afrikaner thinks independently, an Englishman thinks always as a member of a group.'

'An Englishman wants you to behave like an Englishman; an Afrikaner behaves to you like a father to his child.'

'An Englishman, when you make a mistake, won't say anything. He lets you go on and then he discharges you without warning. An Afrikaner will tell you at once when you've made a mistake. He will warn you several times. He will always talk with you.'

'The English brought us education – it was good education. It was the same education as the whites had. The Afrikaner brought us Bantu education, that is inferior education.'

'The education the English brought us has not been proper education. It has made us servile. It only taught us how to serve the white man. We have learned the habit of acceptance and subordination.

'But now with the Afrikaners we learn to stand on our own legs, and not to blame others for our failures, and use the European as scapegoat. If we learn that lesson well, then we'll get somewhere. You see, the Afrikaner is now kicking us into growing up.'

'An Afrikaner, once he knows you, you can drink out of the same cup with him. An Englishman will give you another cup, and then washes it quickly – and secretly.'

Of both the Englishman and the Afrikaner, it is said that he may be your friend in the location, but in town you must not pose as his friend. 'But the difference is that the Afrikaner tells you so beforehand. I had a nice master. He liked me and I liked him. Then he said: "But when you see me in town, you pretend that you don't see me. You understand?"'

Thus our elite have watched the whites, on the farms, in the small towns and in the cities. They have observed them mainly as employers, but also as co-workers and co-organizers. Little seems to have escaped them, and they have drawn their own conclusions, sometimes startling and sometimes easily understood by, and even familiar to, the Continental observer.

Obviously there was much to say on the subject and much had been said already among themselves – it was a subject of unceasing interest as well as of considerable importance, for they felt that so much depended on their understanding of the whites and on their skill in handling them.

Many jokes and riddles about the difference between an Englishman and an Afrikaner did the rounds in Reeftown. Among these we quote here are two which seem to illustrate – as such stories often do – the various points made:

Question: 'Do you know the difference between an Englishman and an Afrikaner?

'No? I shall tell you.

'There's a rat; he comes while you're asleep and bites your toes. Now if he's an Englishman he nibbles very softly, each time blowing on it, so you don't feel any pain and when you wake up in the morning, your toes are gone.

'If it's an Afrikaner rat, he bites hard. It hurts and you shake him off. So you still have your toes the next morning.'

Question: 'What is the difference between an Englishman and an Afrikaner?'

'I'll tell you the difference.

'Say I've just bought a second-hand car and come with it to the office. My Afrikaans employer sees it and says something like this: "My! What a beautiful car! Too good for a kaffir. What did you pay for it? Let me have a look, I'm sure you've been cheated."

'He then goes out and inspects the car, lifts the bonnet. He then finds something wrong and says something like this: "Look at this! I knew it! Och, man, you know what you do? You'd better go to my garage. They won't do you in. I'll phone them."

'Fine. And now what would an English employer do?

'An English employer? He wouldn't have noticed that I had just bought a second-hand car . . .'

Question: 'What's the difference between an Englishman and an Afrikaner?'

'The Englishman in a group is all right, but as an individual he's no good. The Afrikaner in a group is bad, but all by himself he is first-class.'

Regarding the difference between the Englishman as member of a group and the Englishman as an individual, or the English in theory and in practice, Michael Banton in the preface to *White and Coloured*, remarked: 'Why should Britons be strongly opposed to any discrimination in the public treatment of coloured people and, at the same time, be so hesitant about treating them equally in private relations?' This is cited with approval by Mphahlele[20] as follows: 'It *is* difficult to reconcile the willingness on the part of the British to accept a group and not the individuals in the group. . . . The Afrikaner can, in a very paternalistic fashion, treat his servant very well as long as the latter "keeps his place". But the Afrikaner loathes the black people as a group. The Englishman can say quite glibly, "A wonderful tribe those people are – so well behaved, so humble..." and yet he is a difficult man to get at from this side of the colour-line and keeps up a tacitly superior pose in his dealings with me as an individual. I think he despises and distrusts me.'

Leaving this subject to the social psychologists, we shall make two final and related observations – observations of no mean importance.

A recurrent thought, not included in the list already given, described the Afrikaner, as 'like us', 'more like us', 'Their culture is not so far from ours', or 'Like us they . . . '. This was remarked only once of an Englishman. Scrutinizing again all that was said by respondents and selecting all the statements in which the Afrikaner was said to be 'like us', or the African 'like them', the following characteristics emerged:

The Afrikaner(s) is(are) similar to Africans in so far as he(they):

– is not systematic at all. He's more emotional.

– is not strict. They are easygoing people. They always make allowances. They can always deviate from the rules for human reasons. They always make exceptions to the laws because of human considerations.

– settles things there and then; acts more independently. The English refer to authority.

– gives you a present in return for a service rendered. The English just pay you for work done.

– are also hospitable; the English keep their doors shut.

– is in his thinking also dominated by politics.

– are nationalistic and racialistic, like us.

– are religious-minded. They take their religion very seriously.

– go for education because of the money and status you can earn with it, not like the English for education's sake.

– have only very few educated people. The rank and file is nowhere educationally. Just like us.

– if he's educated, does not like the uneducated ones.

– were also backward not so long ago, or just did not count at first. Like us they are now coming up. They show us the way.

In all the characteristics, explicitly mentioned, or implied in these quotations, the Afrikaners are considered to be very similar to the Africans.

Such statements make one wonder what the authors of the researches quoted on p. 267 mean when they write that the 'social distance' between the African and the English-speaking South African is so much smaller than that between the African and the Afrikaner. Possibly the concept of 'social distance',[21] like the notion of 'preference', needs more careful definition. Moreover, the hidden assumption that it is inversely related to 'preference' may be unsound.

People who do not have a very high opinion of themselves may prefer those whom they consider furthest removed from themselves, i.e., those whom they find most unlike themselves.

This leads to a second and very important finding. This concerns the general mood which could be sensed from a great many of the sometimes very long conversations and which frequently emerged more strongly after the spokesmen had been relieved of their anxiety that it might be considered rather 'low-class' and 'primitive' to find something good in the Afrikaners.

It was a mood not readily amenable to quantitative presentation and hardly communicable in objective form. It was a general feeling of what is best expressed by the German word *Schicksalsgemeinschaft* ('community of destiny'). De Kiewiet[22] expressed it in economic terms: 'The search for water and grass was the first principle in the life of Boer and Bantu, for it was in their herds that both counted their wealth' and, 'Actually, the conflict of black and white was fed more by their similarities than by their differences'. It underlay much of what was told us, and came to the surface only in a few instances.

'Before the English came, the African and the Afrikaner worked together as brothers – man to man.'

'This country is the Afrikaner's permanent home, as it is mine.'

'The Afrikaners were here with us before . . .'

'We belong together. Our history has united us.'

'This is our country. The English came as foreign intruders, and conquered us all.'

'Those who grew up with the Afrikaner feel we are all together, and similar.'

'The English did not grow from our soil. They followed laws made in England. Look at de Villiers Graaff, he just runs over to England to get advised.'

It is the ever-recurring refrain: 'We were together with our cattle on the land . . . '. Here is a deep sense of community through a common history and the memory of a shared experience. 'When Chief Justice Beyers went courting his present wife, he borrowed my father's most beautiful black stallion, for our horses were better than those of the Boers . . . ', 'When the State President, Mr Swart, was a young man, my mother . . . '.

Of course, the English are superior people; they are more advanced; they have a longer civilization behind them, and with their international language and their overseas connections, they afford a valuable window on a larger world. But in this country they often complicate matters with their foreignness.

The English represent the glamour and the glistening appeal of the new way of life, the modern world of the west – all that is exciting, foreign and exotic, but they also represent the growing unease, the insecurity and the self-doubt which the western world brings, whereas the Afrikaners are what is familiar and trusted, and what ultimately is 'home'.

Finally, the reaction of some English and Afrikaans friends, when hearing the results of this investigation, also belongs to the general race-relational picture.

My English friends were shocked. Without exception, they had taken it for granted that the general African preference, certainly the educated African preference, was for them, and if not always in their favour, then at least for reasons which were nevertheless flattering to the English sense of superiority and the English belief in the importance of their own fair play and reasonableness.

My Afrikaans-speaking friends showed themselves pleasantly surprised; they had never expected this; and so influenced are they by the English self-picture, that they would never have believed it.

Among my English-speaking acquaintances, however, were an experienced journalist and two civil servants, the one employed in the local non-European administration, the other in Bantu education. None of these persons showed the least surprise. 'I've always known this,' they said. And when I pointed out to the two civil servants that this was contrary to as many as three previous researches, they just shrugged their shoulders. (It is a fact well known to white administrators in non-European departments, as well as to white practical workers among Africans, that they rarely agree with the findings of the social scientists engaged in urban African research.)

Summing up

'Culture,' says Dollard, 'is always presented to the individual in the form of concrete persons.'[23] This chapter has been devoted to the exploration of precisely this dictum: How far were persons and personal influences behind the careers of our elite, and who were these persons? The replies to a direct question showed that these were, in order of importance: parents and relatives (47·66 per cent), other Africans (34·37 per cent) and Europeans (17·97 per cent).

There was first of all **Mother**. More than half of our elite considered that, among the parents and rearers, their mother had been the most important person for them all during their childhood, and well beyond into manhood. Only one-fifth mentioned their father. Father's prolonged and frequent absences from home and the traditional respect which showed itself mainly in the social distance maintained between father and children, generally put the main responsibility for the children's upbringing on mother and made her the nearest friend and confidante. But her influence was possibly even more important for the careers of our elite because of her interest in her children's education. While father was inclined to take it easy, or to prefer cattle to education, mother realized that 'education was tomorrow's cattle', and that her own future security and her own emancipation was not with those sons who continued tribal traditions, but with those who could enter, fully equipped, upon the new way of life. Thus, a careful scrutiny of the life histories showed that the initial driving force behind our elite's education had been mother, whose influence was brought to bear either through father, or independently.

As for the **other relatives**, we found that they figured as important influences throughout the elite's childhood and adolescence as well as in their later lives. They provided alternative accommodation, they gave financial assistance with education and they helped in securing jobs. Most of all, they were ever willing to help in times of crisis and emergency. Our evidence suggested that generally speaking the maternal kin were more important than the paternal kin, and we assumed that, in times of uncertainty and rapid change, the emphasis changes from the more strictly institutionalized relationships to those of a more informal, spontaneous and affective nature.

The importance of the women in the family, epitomized by the importance of mother, mother's mother, and mother's sisters, was again confirmed when we investigated the siblings and found that the more personally orientated pattern of behaviour of the eldest sister had been better able to withstand the dispersal and differentiation which had taken place among the siblings than the more status-determined pattern of rights and obligations of the eldest brother.

Generally speaking, our elite owed much to the assistance given by **the siblings**. Thus 42 per cent acknowledged receiving help from older brothers and sisters; and 75 per cent had, in their turn, assisted or were assisting younger brothers and sisters. Some ten respondents were assisting, or had assisted, all their brothers and sisters. Assistance could take many forms but the most important for their careers had been the help with the payment of school and college fees.

In this, the siblings acted as in the payment of the traditional *lobolo* – as a closely-knit group who were collectively responsible, so that the advance of each was the concern of all, and each had his or her own allotted role to play. It was the first-born's task, with or without the help, sometimes only initially and sometimes continuously, of one or both parents or rearers, to set the ball rolling by paying or helping to pay for the education of a younger sibling who then, in his turn, had to reciprocate by paying or helping to pay for the education of a younger one, and so on down the line of siblings and assimilated siblings from the oldest to the youngest.

In those many cases in which the eldest brother failed to fulfil his traditional obligations, his function as key figure in this system of mutual assistance was taken over by the second brother, and it was then due to him that the younger siblings had their educational opportunities.

About 35 per cent of the replies mentioned the influence from **fellow Africans**, and among these were colleagues and friends who often sparked off an ambition, and also helped in securing jobs for our elite, particularly non-professional jobs. Primary-school teachers and principals also gave recommendations to ex-pupils, mainly professionals; but the main influence of the primary-school teacher of those days was of a moral nature. He stood not only for the material advantages which education could bring, but also for the dignity of learning. And many a young boy was inspired to persevere along the road by his example. Some of these early teachers have now reached fame and fortune outside the profession, and, like any African who has made a name for himself, they now inspired the next generation to follow in their footsteps.

Studying the function of *mimesis* as it operated in the careers of our elite in just one small field, namely, how the idea of their present type of job or profession had come to them, we found that it had occurred to them first through seeing other people. For as many as three-quarters of our elite, the vital decision had been taken upon the inspiration of other people – actual living and concrete persons, whether Europeans or Africans, relatives or strangers, persons who had influenced them by persuasion or by pressure, by actual assistance or simple suggestion, but most often by example. Furthermore, it was found that whenever the idea of entering their present profession or type of occupation had come to them by the example of other individuals, these had in all but possibly one case been fellow Africans, and not Europeans.

While much more research would certainly be necessary, we may conclude that in our sample and in only one aspect of their careers, although it was an important aspect, *mimesis* had been directed towards their own leaders. On this point, however, we noticed a change in orientation, particularly among the younger members of the elite. These no longer looked for their examples towards the highly educated and respected African figures of an earlier generation, but they were turning their hero worship increasingly to the pop singers and jazz players, the successful gangsters and professional politicians. Some social researcher should find here a rewarding subject of study.

A subsequent discussion of the role of *the European* in the careers of our elite showed that, apart from a few social and political contacts, individual Europeans had been important mainly as secondary-school teachers and employers. In the estimation of our respondents themselves, the European had contributed as job-giver, bursary-provider, favour-dispenser – in sum, he had contributed far more with the material necessities than as a moral influence. However, European individuals were mentioned in only 18 per cent of the answers.

As much as 80 per cent of the primary education and 77 per cent of the post-primary education had been provided by some nine different Christian denominations, and this led to a study of the denominational (as distinct from the general Christian-religious) influence of the schools, by a scrutiny of the reasons why seven fathers and nineteen sons had changed their denominational adherence. Our conclusion was that missionary influence had been exerted through the school system and particularly through the post-primary 'colleges', through the educational facilities and occupational opportunities which, in those days, could come only through missionaries and missionary recommendations. By contrast, the reasons for joining one of the independent African churches seemed to be of another nature altogether.

While individual Europeans did not seem to have made as great an impression on our elite as one would have expected, the elite was nevertheless conscious of having received throughout the greater part of their lives the benevolent attention of Europeans generally and they did not hesitate to admit the European contribution to their educational and occupational achievements. But underneath these replies there was the scarcely hidden and only rarely expressed satisfaction in having become emancipated from European tutelage, or the desire to achieve this emancipation as soon as possible.

While the attitude of the majority of our elite towards Europeans was, therefore, favourable – (in fact, about 70 per cent aknowledged receiving help rather than hindrance from Europeans in their educational as well as in their occupational advance) – they were aware of considerable differences within the European group itself.

Taking everything into account, and in spite of a number of characteristics which were thoroughly disliked in them, our elite preferred to deal with the Afrikaans-speaking whites and, most of all with the so-called 'good' or 'educated' Afrikaner, rather than with any type of English-speaking European. In fact, 42 per cent preferred to deal with the Afrikaners and only 12 per cent preferred to deal with the English. As our findings on this matter differed so completely from those arrived at in three previous researches, considerable space was given to a detailed description of the way in which we

284

approached the subject-matter and asked our questions, as well as to an objective and full presentation of our data.

The main reasons for our elite's possibly surprising preferences were fully set out. The Afrikaners were considered more open, more sincere and more human. They were easier to understand, and 'you know where you are with them'. An Englishman is too diplomatic and subtle. With regard to their colour prejudices, most Afrikaners had them and did not try and hide the fact. With the English, 'One never knows for sure, but they pretend to have none'. Nevertheless, one can never get close to them, and one can never really trust an Englishman.

The English were considered to be more civilized and more generally educated, but they were too impersonal and too aloof. Their love for ceremonies and procedure, their adherence to rules and regulations leaves no room for the spontaneous gesture, the personal approach. Whereas with an Afrikaner: 'Once he gets to know and like you, he makes an exception for you as he always makes exceptions for human reasons to any law or rule, even to the colour bar, and you can have a real personal relationship with him.' All the good qualities of the English did not appear to be able to compensate for their failure in personal relationships.

In addition, we noticed in our elite the awareness of an affinity between the Afrikaners and themselves, a sense of belonging together formed through a long common history and a shared experience in a rural past, from which the Afrikaners had emerged only a little earlier than the Bantu.

Conclusion: Social mobility in a changing society

In this study of social mobility, the life and career history proved an eminently useful tool, perfectly suited to the purpose. For one way of studying a changing society is to study the changing individuals within that society, and to observe the changing relationships between them and their changing environments. When social anthropology examines a changing society, it inevitably draws nearer to certain kinds of history; the appropriate approach, therefore, to the life and career history is as an event in time. Hence the manner in which we presented our data and their interpretation was as an historical narrative.

We went back in the history of each individual and retraced the successive stages through which he had passed before his arrival in Reeftown and at the top of the local social ladder. Naturally, the life and career history reveals the important influence on historical developments and individual destinies of accidental happenings, generally called good or bad luck, or also just chance. Moreover, and related to this, the life history emphasizes the role of the individual in culture change, and particularly the differential responses of the individuals to similar circumstances. The life history thus loosens the rigid determinism of the sociological hypothesis and restores to the individual his rightful place as a self-active, creative agent in his exchange with never entirely predictable historical forces and social environments. However, this investigation was purposely limited to the sociological viewpoint.

What had our subjects in common as a group?

They belonged to a society that had been shaken out of its customary ways of life and thought by the arrival on the scene of another ethnic group; and, in its development from a traditional to a modern

286

way of life, this society was undergoing such revolutionary and massive changes in its social structure as must inevitably lead to social mobility. On the other hand, the profound changes which were taking place in the country as a whole were giving rise to changes in the place and function of this black group in the National (European-dominated) economy of the country, and these, acting both as cause and effect, had again induced changes in the social structure of African society, and hence in the constitution of its newly emerging elite.

We saw how the establishment alongside the white cities of South Africa of subsidized housing estates such as Reeftown hastened the rise of this elite; how these black towns on the one hand confirmed the traditional policy of residential and social separation, and on the other hand expressed the increasing economic integration and inter-dependence between the two main racial groups; and how this dual orientation, which influenced all developments, also affected this new elite, which consisted of independent professionals *and* public servants, individual entrepreneurs *and* (potential) managers.

Undoubtedly, the so-called 'spirit of the age' was with them. When listening to the stories as told us by the elite themselves, and later when analysing and interpreting them, with all the human fluidities and imponderables, with the tangle of motives, the perplexity of family circumstances and physical environments, with the often contradictory influences at work, and with the continuously changing social scene, we were most struck by the tremendous mobility of the individuals concerned. And indeed, the first requirement for indi-vidual success in a rapidly changing society is, of course, the very capacity for change as such. Coming from parents who were highly mobile, the elite themselves were highly mobile.

This residential, occupational and educational mobility, which was the most typical characteristic of the elite, was forced upon them by the peculiar conditions of the time. With few exceptions they had originally started their working lives with far lower qualifications than they had at present – qualifications, whether academic or pro-fessional, which would never have allowed them to reach the top and remain at the top. This was due to several inter-connected factors. First, in their younger days (most of the elite completed their Std. VI between the years 1927 and 1939) educational opportunities had been very limited. Second, most of them had, at the time, lacked the money, the bursaries, the capacity or the desire for further education beyond a Lower Teacher's Diploma or a Junior Certificate. Third, a greater range of educational and professional opportunities and higher education had been made available only by slow degrees; and finally, the elite themselves had only gradually become aware of the widening opportunities as they saw other, younger fellow Africans taking them, and their own aspirations increased only after they had already been working several years and their needs had begun to increase.

In the attempt to make up for earlier educational deficiencies and the wrong vocational choices, and to keep abreast of the times, they had to return to college or subscribe to correspondence courses. And so they alternated between college and job; between correspondence courses and university scholarships. They moved from one educational institution, from one course of study and from one form of tuition to another. Searching tirelessly for new openings, they changed patrons and bursary givers as easily as they changed employers and employments. As in their younger days they had been moved from primary school to primary school, from rural to urban and back to rural areas, and from parents to rearers and other rearers, so now and with the same unruffled placidity and easy adaptability, they abandoned one educational aim for another and one profession for another, changing their educational aspirations according to their changing occupational orientations.

Thus, on the vast shores of human knowledge and achievement, the elite picked up here and there a pebble; the choice and sequence were only in rare cases determined by natural leanings, personal interests and special talents. For education was throughout the handmaiden of occupation, and jobs and professions were chosen and abandoned mainly with the aim of increasing in status and wealth.

They rarely had any definite preferences or personal likes or dislikes. Their decisions were made for them by relatives and European friends, by circumstances and chance occurrences, by family considerations and sporadic desires for 'pastures new'. Hardly any one of their achievements was the result of deliberate planning or choice. Neutral attitudes prevailed both in their educational and their job choices. Typical terms were: 'a vacancy', 'nothing better', 'anything which', 'I was told to', 'at least something', 'a stepping stone to . . .'. Everything was always provisional, until something better turned up. And even further, whenever a new plan or undertaking entailed a change in religious adherence, or a turnabout in political views or racial attitudes, it was no matter; for the elite's beliefs and values, their moods and biases were as liable to change as the changing opportunities, environmental influences and human contacts which they met in their advance.

This general mobility and the concomitant lack of personal involvement arose as much from the general uprooting of people perilously poised between two worlds – people who were growing up in an environment so incoherent and unpredictable that the individual could not possibly define himself against it – as from the cultural immaturity of individuals who were, despite all outward

288

appearances, still only at the beginning of a long process. But without doubt, these attitudes were entirely suited to the muddled and puny manner in which the South African whites were, always belatedly, preparing the ground for African advance. For it is our firm opinion that it was exactly this flexibility with which they could take advantage of whatever opportunities came their way; the changeability with which they could perform an immediate *volte face*; the ease with which they adapted themselves to any circumstances; the resilience with which they could bounce back when things were difficult or painful; and the happy expectancy with which each new venture was attempted – it was, in sum, this very capacity for change which was at the root of their successful progress in a changing society.

The conditions of the time and South African developments favoured their advance. The elite came up in a world desperately in need of them. The increasing industrialization and urbanization of the white population brought as its natural consequence and prerequisite, the increasing industrialization and urbanization of the black population. Here a whole new society was developing, a society ever expanding and becoming more articulated, and it became essential to give some thought to the creation of the cadres of this new society's future leaders. Thus, any African who succeeded in reaching Std. VI and could possibly be expected to be able to profit from a secondary education, was, first by the missionaries, then increasingly by the successive South African Governments and a great number of private institutions, carefully tended and nurtured and prepared for his future responsibilities as a leader of his people.

Far from having been thwarted in their educational ambitions, which, in those earlier days and even to a large extent up to this day, hardly ever ventured beyond the possibilities offered, they were aided and encouraged at every turn, and placed in positions in which well-meaning members of the white group promoted them, frequently prematurely and often even before they had acquired the necessary qualifications or experience.

Whereas at first this happened as a natural historical development, the tempo was greatly accelerated when this became official Government policy, and when the whites had to vacate leading positions with the express purpose that, whatever kind of man should take their place, it had to be a black man. Consequently, our elite hardly knew competition from the white man or from the other more advanced ethnic groups. On the contrary, either by intent or chance, their careers had moved along channels in which the South African race-discriminatory legislations or conventions had rarely exercised their restrictive effects. Maybe a few good jobs had been lost because of colour, but many more good jobs had been gained because of it.

Inevitably any African's life, wherever he is in the world of today, was coloured by the effects of racial discrimination, whether in the political, economic or social field, and in South Africa particularly by the many smaller expressions of *apartheid* in all its more painful aspects. And no doubt our educated elite felt wounded by all the small pinpricks received in even the most benevolent interracial contact. But in their careers, our elite had encountered only a few setbacks because of colour. On the contrary, their colour had rather favoured their careers. In reality, and the truth should for once be told, separate development gave them opportunities which they might not otherwise have had. This the elite knows although they would not so easily, unless taken unawares, admit that separate development has served them well. There was a general tendency in Reeftown, to ascribe all job and study failures in terms of human relationships, and all such failings in terms of black–white relationships. Our elite were definitely inclined to the former, yet refreshingly free from the latter.

Briefly then, the elite arose in a vacuum and naturally filled it.

Moreover, they were, by and large, a socially privileged group. First of all, most of them had the right parental background and were born in favourable family circumstances. In addition, they had the required disposition or the necessary personal endowments or both. In a time when African parents were only just beginning to wake up to the economic advantages of education, and the missionaries had to use every possible argument to obtain their co-operation, the elite grew up in homes and families which had already accepted some of the western customs associated with a conversion to Christianity. They had already successfully adapted themselves to various economic aspects of the modern way of life. Consequently, some educated and professional members could generally already be counted among the closest kin.

Not that our elite were particularly distinguished by any early enthusiasm for school and education. This is an interesting point because it runs contrary to the common belief in the west, and which derives from a generalization of a few isolated cases, the belief that Africans are, and have always been, hungering for education. Nothing is further from the truth even today. Most children went to school, and still do so, in simple obedience to parental wishes, and quite a number (and among these some of the most gifted) needed strict disciplining and constant watchfulness to keep them at school. Here the fact that most of our elite grew up in the country was of importance, for country children – so it is said – are and have always been more amenable to parental control than town children.

It was mainly at this point in the elite's careers that their parents played their decisive role. As most fathers were, like their sons, either indifferent or entirely opposed to education, it was here that our elite owed their biggest debt to their mothers. And this, we suggest, may be the reason that so many of them were widow's sons. For once mother had succeeded in getting her son to school and in keeping him there until Std. VI, the battle was almost won. By then, the sons themselves had begun to realize the advantages of education. It could bring unheard-of prestige, security of employment, and a more stable income; a release from manual labour and, as we have already emphasized, an escape from some of the worst effects of racial discrimination. Moreover, their ambitions had been kindled by their teachers, and quite a few had been told, or had discovered themselves, that they were, as they called it, 'bright' or 'brilliant'. In this aptitude for school learning they were very fortunate, for school learning does not come easily to Africans, and African education has always been characterized by excessive and progressive retardation.

Thus, with regard to family circumstances and personal endowments, our elite proved in majority so exceptional among their fellows that one could already at this stage confidently predict their continued ascent upwards.

Interesting, but understandable in view of what was explained above, was that our elite were, strictly speaking, not self-made men. With the exception of two individuals only, two individuals who were truly self-made (both non-professionals), in so far as they went to school because they wanted education above everything else and despite the greatest resistance from the whole kinship system, and continued their education against the greatest odds and with no help from anyone, all the elite were to a large extent made by others. For a great many persons contributed to the success of these careers.

There was, first of all, mother – life-size and fondly remembered – almost always progressive whether educated or not; she was the driving force behind the education of the elite, and the most enduring influence in their lives. There was also sometimes a very strict father who on occasions did not spare the rod, but who was generally a more shadowy figure. There were in four cases rearers to whom the boys owed their start in life. There were other members of the kin. They played their part in the occupational but particularly in the educational advance of the youngsters, by giving financial assistance and by offering accommodation. There were particularly the siblings, and we found that the sibling relations had withstood the changes better than any of the other kinship relations, and that the collective responsibilities and the reciprocity which had operated in the *lobolo* exchanges now also operated in the matter of educational assistance.

Against the generally rural background of the elite, the simple village schoolmaster loomed large. He was the most profound moral influence, and by his example and his admonition he imbued our elite with noble ambitions and high-minded purpose. There were the

291

colleagues and peers whose competition was a constant incitement to further progress; there were those first pioneers of African advance – those earliest educated Africans – who inspired our elite by their example, and whose achievements strengthened their self-confidence; there were the members of a younger generation who, coming up with again more opportunities and better openings, threatened to pass the older ones by, and who were a spur towards ever greater efforts in order to remain in the lead.

There were finally the Europeans; the white missionary at first only dimly perceived but assuming more importance as education advanced to the secondary level; then all the other whites – teachers, employers and supervisors, friends and co-religionists, patrons and mentors – who gave advice and assistance, encouragement and recommendations, and to whose benevolent presence the elite owes so much. The assistance of Europeans generally – Europeans who after all had launched them on their socio-cultural mobility – as well as in particular instances, was readily acknowledged, and even though our elite had sometimes been hurt by race-discriminatory conventions and colour-bar behaviour, they had on the other hand received much personal help from individual Europeans, while in some cases racial restrictions and humiliations had acted as an added stimulus to gain emancipation from the white man. Although they bore the European no grudge, they would now have liked to forget him and be able to do without him. But this was not so easy, for partly through the old habit of dependence and partly through continued need, they did not cease to lean heavily upon him. Prolonged conversations showed that the better-understood Afrikaner was felt to be a little closer to them than the more aloof and foreign Englishman.

However, not all had been equally privileged. As and when the life histories became revealed many inequalities showed themselves. These were inequalities of opportunity; varying degrees of help received through European contacts and family circumstances; inequalities arising from differences in endowment and disposition, in character and temperament. Such fundamental differences gave rise to variations in achievement and in the level of progress, and hence also in the differences among the occupational groups. But there were two main areas in which these inequalities were most apparent.

The first was the inequality in opportunity between the professionals and the non-professionals. The professionals had had throughout more protection, easier conditions and better opportunities. Vacancies in the professions were plentiful and this group, therefore, settled easily into their professional niche, usually first in a country area or in a small provincial town. After this they moved, by gradually improving their educational qualifications, to the bigger cities

292

and the better jobs through successive promotions and without being in any way adversely affected by the colour-bar restrictions in their successive job changes, by job reservation or by Influx Control Regulations. In fact, they were more handicapped in their social mobility upwards by family obligations, by the jealousy of African colleagues and seniors and by their own behavioural and professional lapses, than by any race-discriminatory restrictions.

With the non-professionals, it was at first almost the opposite. Already in their first jobs they came up against the general backwardness and the economic underdevelopment of the rural areas in South Africa where there were hardly any prospects for ambitious holders of J.C. or Matric; and when this almost entire lack of any but pick-and-shovel jobs forced them to come to town they were up against the Influx Control Regulations. When subsequently they succeeded, via the Mines, in obtaining an urban work permit and a city job, they had to move from job to job and work under many different employers and in many posts until they also found a job in the lee of racial discrimination. This generally meant leaving employment in the private sector of the economy where the chances of promotion to managerial positions were minimal, and entering the public service in the African sector where there was a chance of promotion to jobs carrying greater authority, higher prestige and more pay. These two main patterns of social mobility upwards are well illustrated by the two completely successful careers of P.Q. and S.K.

There were two other patterns. Here the differences in opportunities were the result of differences in provincial origin and age. With regard to the first, the elite from the Eastern Cape had definitely a start on the others, and with regard to the second, there were flagrant differences in the general educational and occupational conditions between the younger and the older members of the elite; the inevitable inequalities in opportunities of a rapidly changing society in which each year brings new openings, more choices and easier circumstances. This is well illustrated in the career histories of the three doctors.

But whether by means of the inter-job mobility of the non-professionals or by means of the intra-job mobility of the professionals, promotion could be achieved only by educational improvement, for education was still almost the only vehicle for social and cultural mobility. And it was during these later stages of their careers that the elite showed their mettle. For they were no 'scholarship' boys. The total bursaries received did not cover more than one-quarter of the principal post-Std. VI courses of study attempted. So more than two-thirds of the elite tried to pass one or more of their exams by correspondence course while earning a living in a full-time job. As many as four of them (and among these some of the most successful ones) attempted to pass as many as three successive examinations by private study.

Thus, with the exception of a few thoroughly lucky people (for instance, Mr. N. G., an only son, pushed and supported throughout by his father), many of the elite owed the final phases of their social mobility upwards mainly to their own efforts. Their achievement becomes all the more praiseworthy if one considers that it was accomplished at a stage when they were already married and had to provide for their families and educate their children; that their help was required for the education and careers of their siblings and other kin; and that the parents and older relatives now expected some repayment for their earlier assistance.

Thus to the factors mentioned in the above, must be added stead-fastness of purpose, ambition and dogged persistence. 'My people,' said the African research assistant proudly, 'never say die'.

By and large, our elite achieved their success rather late in life. When we found them together in Reeftown as the township's emerging social elite, their average age was 44·3 years. For most of them their present job had been again a general improvement on the previous job, and they were now at the height of their careers. They occupied the top positions in the various institutional hierarchies; in education and in Government, provincial or local administration; in health and hygiene, law and order, Church and religion, banking and business, sales promotion and selling.

The majority of their wives were professionals although many did not work. Most of them were home-owners and some had built their own spacious residences. They were beginning to congregate in the higher-status areas of the township. They were well known to each other and some of the wives were the leading Reeftown hostesses. They were socially inter-acting in a number of different situations in which they were performing the role of a local upper class. Consequently, each could measure his status against that of the others and so a distinct 'upper crust' had formed, while others were definitely at the lower end of the upper class and some were border cases. These last were those whose educational or occupational status would place them in the upper class, but whose social activities were below ex-pectations, or, conversely, those whose social activities had achieved such a degree of enlightenment that they compensated for any educational or occupational deficiencies.

For upper-class status had not only to be shown in the houses and furniture, in residential habits and domestic ways of living, in daily activities and leisure-time preferences, in authority and power, but it had also to be displayed by the elite in the daily exercise of their occupations and professions and in the manner in which they catered for the educational, health, welfare and other vital needs of the community, as well as in certain social activities such as their patronage of and honoured attendance at community functions and family occasions, their leadership in organizations and their membership of the main status boards and committees of the township and beyond. For social behaviour in the widest sense of the word was the main criterion of social status. It was precisely thanks to their occupational and social activities, in which they themselves and all Reeftowners considered that they used their status for the benefit of the community, that they had originally earned the people's respect. For, although the new social inequalities which inevitably developed from the foundation and settlement of these new urban housing estates, caused much bad blood in the community, and although Reeftowners were often resentful of the wealth and power displayed by the elite, on the other hand such display was entirely in conformity with the traditional expectations with regard to high status.

During the years of our field research they were beginning to lose the respect of the people. This was not entirely due to their western aspirations, even though what the elite considered a socially correct and enlightened way of life was sometimes diametrically opposed to the traditionally laid-down patterns of proper behaviour. It was not so much the new patterns in themselves which were resented. Although the masses often ridiculed the elite's social aspirations as 'merely aping the Europeans and that badly', and although the middle classes in their bread-and-butter preoccupations talked critically of the elite's social pretensions as a waste of time, many Reeftowners greatly admired and assiduously tried to imitate the elite. In the eyes of most ambitious Reeftowners, the elite represented the ultimate goal of all endeavours; they showed everyone not only *that* Africans *could* 'do it', but *how* Africans *should* 'do it'.

It was in this sense that the elite were the social leaders of the township, but in another sense they were beginning to relinquish social leadership, and it was this which was losing them the respect of their own people. During the years of our participant observation in Reeftown, we witnessed the growth of a new social aloofness. We observed how a top stratum of the elite was beginning to withdraw from social participation and organizational leadership into a new social exclusiveness. Breaking with the tradition of community service, established and maintained by an earlier generation of educated Africans – those first pioneers of education who had seen the emancipation of the African people as a whole, as their most important task – they now were beginning to turn away from their own people; and, utterly preoccupied with their own personal ambitions, the higher professionals and the university graduates of Reeftown were increasingly neglecting their communal responsibilities.

What were these ambitions and how could these be realized? New

295

occupational opportunities, higher executive positions and more job choices, bigger markets for the self-employed and extension of authority could come about only in two ways. The first would be the way of further changes in the social structure of African society. It was as yet relatively simply structured, and few institutions had developed. The positions at the top were, therefore, few and far between. Only by further expansion and articulation of its institutions as a consequence of increasing self-sufficiency and independent development could more and higher positions be made available. This would necessitate speeding up the Africanization of other Government departments besides that of Education, and the creation of a civil servant class of professional status in no way inferior to that of the established professions. The second way would be the way of increasing real assimilation, i.e. assimilation extending over all socio-economic, educational and administrative fields and all social and political levels into the national structure; in the private as well as the public sectors of the country as a whole. This would require not only a change in the attitude of the whites, but also a change in the requirements of certain jobs and positions.

Probably, and in view of the dual orientation of African society, these two changes would take place simultaneously, although the former would probably happen more quickly and more fully than the latter, which would encounter increasing resistance from the whites. Hence, for the immediate future, most educated and professional Africans could look forward to a further expansion of their occupational field only in the direction of the homelands.

However, in the meantime, the elite were alienating themselves more and more from the mass of Reeftowners. A similar alienation, but now on a larger scale, of the emergent elites all over Africa, has been commented upon by experts on the subject. (Recently in Lloyd, 1966.) But, unlike these other African countries, South Africa as a whole, and Reeftown in particular, showed the development of a reasonably large and lively middle class, a middle class in the true positional sense of the term, acting as a bridge over the widening chasm and as a buffer between the top few and the broad masses. It was from these new middle classes that the strongest critics of the elite were arising, and it is from their ranks that the new leaders were emerging.

Appendices: The fieldwork

In the middle of 1958 I began the general community research which provided the background for the more specific elite research which was conducted intensively during the years 1960 and 1961, and with decreasing intensity during some years after. At first I found myself going to the township about four days a week and almost every week-end as this is the time that the important events occurred. During the years of writing up the material I kept in contact with my subject-matter, and followed closely the developments in the township and in the careers of the individuals. Before definitely completing the typescript I made a final survey of the position in 1967.

In order to straighten the crooked picture painted overseas about the impossibility of urban African research in South Africa, I shall describe in some detail the way in which I established *rapport* and collected my facts.

I started with a courtesy call on the township manager, to thank him for his hospitality and to assure him of my intention to do my utmost not to upset the normal routine of township life. I explained to him what I was going to do and how I intended going about it, and asked him to help me as much as possible and allow me to benefit from his long experience and intimate knowledge of Reeftown and the Reeftowners. Mr Jones took me at once round the administrative buildings, introducing me to the white and black members of his staff and offered me the first of the great many cups of tea that I would be drinking in his office! He then took me personally round Reeftown in his own car, pointing out the various features and giving me a brief historical sketch of his people and their township. From then onwards I never had anything but kindness, encouragement and assistance from Mr Jones and his staff. It would appear of some importance to mention this, as there is a difference of opinion among social scientists as to whether, in South Africa, friendly and open relationships with the township officials are a help or a hindrance in research on urban Bantu. Reeftown was left in no doubt that I was 'true' to my own racial origin – an attitude which Africans of all people fully appreciate. I then began my fieldwork by just looking up old acquaintances, for I knew already some Reeftowners – mainly women, but also some men – through the multiracial functions and organizations in which I had been participating for many years and through my previous investigations into women's needs and women's organizations.

From the very first day, mine was a rather unofficial kind of research and it remained so up to the end.

The data were gathered by means of participant observation and guided conversations, which consisted actually of a mixture of free association and an 'active' technique. Participant observation cannot have a precise meaning in a situation dominated by the colour bar. This is, I believe, the main reason for the atmosphere of unreality which so often permeates urban African research done by Europeans; the group studied seems to float in a vacuum instead of being rooted in its social environment, and the particular aspect studied is often seen in isolation – and worse, in ignorance – of its context. However, until Africans themselves are capable of and disposed towards creative observation and unbiased reporting, and thus can do more than merely find what the European tells them to look for, participant observation cannot but mean something rather unsystematic and discontinuous. It meant dropping in on individuals for a cup of tea, a bit of lunch, or if I had to appear spick-and-span at evening functions, a wash and change. It meant having cold drinks in any one of the neat little restaurants of the township, talking with the waitresses, the owners and the other guests; taking my respondents and informants out to lunch; smoking a cigarette over the counter of a friend's shop or in his back office sitting on a packing case; in short, visiting people in their homes, their offices, their workshops, their schools and clinics; accompanying them on their professional rounds; giving them lifts to meetings, concerts and dances; attending weddings and funerals, upper-class ladies' tea parties and large township functions. It also meant having my Reeftown friends for drinks and dinner in my own home; showing them how I arranged my household; taking them to have a look inside new European houses under construction; and many other things in which they were interested. I remember once when I wanted to do a group ranking with a group of young upper-middle class men and women, I invited them to my home and, to be sure that they would definitely come, I promised them a demonstration on 'The Etiquette of European drinking'! It was a great success.

Gradually I began to know people, and by the end of the first year my address book contained some 600 names of Reeftowners. I knew their homes, their families and jobs; I knew their problems and circumstances, their frustrations and aspirations, their habits, hobbies and leisure-time activities, their loves and hates. I was able to follow some of the happenings behind the outer façade of respectability; to listen to much backbiting; and to observe some of the large scandals which shook the township. I studied a number of social conflicts; how they arose, developed, came into the open, and finally were solved or just faded out. I witnessed the working of public sanctions among the upper-middle and upper classes, the function of gossip and the conflict of values. I saw how social divisions were manipulated and ignorance exploited by personal ambitions; how public occasions and other social gatherings were bent to serve private rivalries and jealousies; how European connections were used to further one's own cause and to eliminate one's opponents; how friendships were cemented and new groupings were formed. I learned how people rose and fell in public esteem and why; how many a promising career was destroyed overnight; and how prestige was built up slowly and laboriously. In sum, I saw how social status worked in the actual living reality of the social life of the community. The values verbally expressed in my interviews became visible reasons for action, or they appeared irrelevant to daily life.

In order to be able to do all this I made myself useful. I was asked to make a speech at next Saturday's get-together; to address a cultural club; to talk to a class; to demonstrate a recipe; to give a sex talk to a youth club; to show how you pack a suitcase and prune a peach tree. I gave lectures on etiquette, on furnishing a lounge, on how to start a woman's journal, on costume jewellery, and on a mad array of diverse subjects. I brought European lecturers to the township.

More and more people became used to seeing me about, and I gradually became, not only accepted, but, much better, forgotten. In this way I learned not only something about black–white relationships, but, what is more inaccessible, something of black–black relationships. What people say and do when among themselves in the ordinary situations of their daily lives and particularly how they treat each other, affords more significant information than any replies to direct questions. Moreover, and this should be stressed once more, much interviewing was done without the interviewees being aware of it.

In such a situation, for an investigator to be without social status or academic eminence, to be alone and not connected with any important body, to be a woman, and even better, a foreigner untouched by local and national politics, and whose bilingualness in English and

Afrikaans was moreover as ungrammatical and foreign-accented as that of the subjects of her study, was a very great advantage.

Behind these human preoccupations, there was much solid work. A day-to-day diary was kept in which people and events were fully described and conversations recorded. Analyses were made of meetings and conferences, of organizations and their membership, of speeches made, of the ritual and procedure followed by the various strata of the population. In all this I was ably assisted by Miss Mabombo. Where and whenever I could not be present myself, she wrote essays on the public and family occasions: who had attended and with whom they had come; what they had said and done.

Collecting facts in this manner is, however, not only difficult but also time-consuming and, as most of these facts will never appear in print, the most generous fellowship giver must become impatient of results. Yet, it is my firm belief that it is upon this basis, and upon this basis alone, that verbal statements can be interpreted.

To guide the conversations the so-called 'Schedules' were evolved. These were not questionnaires but more like blind geographical maps upon which the names of the mountains and rivers have to be filled in. For the life and family histories to serve not only to explain the individual but to identify the group, the material of the stories had to be divided up into a number of specific events, facts, persons and situations, and for these open spaces or 'cells' were reserved on the Schedules. These cells served to establish cross-correspondences between similar themes in the stories, and thus lead us from the single 'long-sectional' view of the individual to the 'cross-sectional' view of the group, i.e. to sociological findings. It was unimportant how the questions were asked as long as it was clearly understood what kind of information had to be written in each cell. The main aim was to let the topics flow naturally out of the conversations and to induce respondents to tell their stories freely. It was agreed between the two investigators that at first nothing was to be taken for granted or considered as irrelevant or contradictory, and that we would always ask: 'Why?' or 'Can you give an example?'

Of the five double-sheeted schedules, the first two have been used for this book; they covered the educational and occupational histories. To these were added some data from Schedules III and IV concerning the parents and siblings. But the bulk of the material from Schedules III, IV and V, which deals with the family histories, will form the subject of a further book.

Our respondents were generally quite willing and able to talk on some, if not on all topics. Where in the world is the human being who can resist the temptation to tell his life story to a sympathetic and attentive listener?

In spite of the closest collaboration between the two investigators,

300

there were some differences in the responses evoked. To the African, respondents would stress their wealth, to the European their poverty. To the African they would mention that education does not pay, that money is more important. To me they would extol the wonders of education and their thirst for enlightenment. The African had to listen to long stories about the jealousy of colleagues, the exploitation by senior fellowmen, the inter-African cut-throat competition. To me complaints were voiced about the lack of consideration on the part of the European supervisor or employer, too little pay, etc. But these are the two sides of the same medal.

A number of individual and collective ranking tests were done with altogether some 100 rankers, leading gentlemen, upper-class ladies, middle-class young men and women. In these tests Reeftown residents known to me were ranked by name by rankers known to me. Though unsuited for quantitative analysis these tests were very revealing, mainly because of the explanations by the rankers given either at once or in follow-up interviews. It will not be easy to repeat such tests in a more structured form, as, for their full effectiveness, they need considerable prior field-work, and most researchers have not enough time.

Explanation of Educational Qualifications

Explanation of Educational Qualifications[1]
(as at present)

No. of years of education	Average age normal promotion	Primary education	Secondary education	University education (full-time)	Teacher training	Nursing training
1	8	Sub A				
2	9	Sub B				
3	10	Std. I				
4	11	Std. II				
5	12	Std. III				
6	13	Std. IV				
7	14	Std. V				
8	15	Std. VI				
9	16		Form 1		1st year	
10	17		Form 2		2nd year	
11	18		Form 3*		3rd year§	
12	19		Form 4		1st year	1st year
13	20		Form 5†		2nd year¶	2nd year
14	21			1st year	1	3rd year
15	22			2nd year	2**	6 months‡‡
16	23			3rd year‡		
17	24				1st year††	

[1] With acknowledgements to Mr K. B. Hartshorne.
* Junior Certificate.
† Senior Certificate or Matriculation.
‡ Bachelor of Arts or Bachelor of Science.
§ Bantu Teacher's Lower Certificate (the old N.P.L., Native Primary Lower).
¶ Bantu Teacher's Higher Certificate (the old N.P.H., Native Primary Higher).
** Bantu Teacher's Diploma.
†† University Education Diploma.
‡‡ S.R.N.

Notes

Introduction

1 E.g. Kuper, 1960, 14; *Intern. Soc. Sc. Bull.*, vii, 2 (1955), 474.
2 Cf. by contrast Ngcobo, 1956, 435–40.
3 See Nadel, 1956, 116–17.
4 *Op. cit.*, 420.
5 Cf. Ogburn, 1960, 122; also Epstein, 1961, 52–3.
6 In all these appellations there is studious avoidance of any reference to the origin and prototype of this characteristic. Respecting this avoidance, we have chosen therefore the word 'educated', which is the one most frequently used by them. It does not denote a particular level of education.
7 The implication that it did, was one of the main criticisms of the Warner approach to social stratification, e.g. Kornhauser, 1954, 247–8.
8 This is what they are called in South Africa.
9 This was also found by Davis, 1941, 72.
10 In Gosforth (Williams, 1956, 86 ff.), the local upper-middle class did not correspond to the national upper-middle class and in Little-Town-in-Overspill (Whitely, 1953, 223) the local upper class was the British middle class.
11 Also the Smythes (1960, 102) distinguished a more select upper level from the broad general category of persons they designated as the national elite.
12 Cf. Mitchell (*Kalela*, 1956, 28): ' . . . the more distant a group of people is from another both socially and geographically, the greater the tendency to regard them as an undifferentiated category and to place them under a general rubric.'
13 Rosenberg, 1953, 22–7.
14 In Epstein's terminology, prestige as one of the categories of inter-action cedes its primary importance to 'nationality', 'tribe', 'language', 'race', 'skin colour' (Epstein, 1961, 51–2).

15 The UNESCO publication, *The South African Way of Life*, recognized three different so-called European ways of life in South Africa, besides some non-European ones. Moreover, the behaviour patterns and styles of life of the different classes in Europe have undergone some changes in the twentieth century.

16 Smythe, 1960, 5.

17 The term 'emergent African middle class' is even more inappropriate, and a contradiction in terms; for surely at the beginning of social class differentiation in a new and emergent society is, as Schumpeter established, the rise of an upper stratum (Schumpeter, 1955). But it must never be forgotten that in South Africa the choice and use of terms by social scientists and non-scientists is frequently guided by politico-ideological attitudes.

18 See further, Chapter 1, 'The Rise of an Entrepreneurial Elite'.

19 The two methods have been conveniently summarized by Baltzell, 1954. All quotations here have been taken from his essay.

20 *Op. cit.*, 174.

21 See further, 'The Fieldwork'.

22 The Smythes had to make the same reservation about the selection of their sample of a social, though in their case a national, elite (Smythe, 1960).

23 See further, 'The Fieldwork'.

24 Cf. Miller, 1966.

25 Thus, for instance, Schwab (1961, 127) writes about 'the high rate of mobility and the discontinuities in residence and occupation ...'; Epstein (1961, 30) writes: 'Ndola's African population is not only mixed, it is also highly mobile. There is a constant coming and going of people ...'; Reader (1961, 73) writes about 'an intensification of job mobility' and (76) about 'a restlessly high work mobility'.

26 Mayer (1961, xv) calls urbanization a 'form of social mobility'.

27 Cf. Pareto's circulation of elites, paragraphs 2178–9, 2485.

28 Reissman, 1959, 302 ff.

29 As studied by Schumpeter, 1951, for instance.

30 As studied, for instance, by Kurt Mayer, 'Recent Changes in the Class Structure of the United States', *Transactions of the Third World Congress of Sociology*, 1956, with special reference to shifts in occupation and employment status.

31 Such as, for instance, Natalie Rogoff, 1953, or Davidson and Anderson, 1937.

32 Merrill (1957, 323) lists four different senses of social mobility with regard to occupation on the individual level.

33 Reissman, 1959, 302 ff.

34 Clements, 1958; Richards, 1960; Smythe, 1960; Tardits, 1958; Goldthorpe, 1955; Lately, Kuper, 1965, also used some life histories.

35 Dollard, 1937, 485.

36 E.g. Winter, 1959, 2.

37 Dollard, 1935, 5.

38 Mitchell, 1957, 13.

39 According to Winter (1959, 2) the life history can 'give the reader some understanding of what it means to be an Amba', while Dollard

(1935, 287) calls this 'an understanding how it feels to carry a culture'.

40 Kluckhohn in Gottschalk, 1945, 136.
41 Winter, 1959, 2.
42 Dollard, 1935, 5.
43 Andrieux and Lignon, 1961.
44 *Times Literary Supplement*, 26 May 1961. The anonymous reviewer talks of 'this exemplary piece of field anthropology'.
45 Gottschalk, 1945, 110.
46 This was successfully done by Lipton, 1960.
47 Kuper, 1965.

Chapter 1

1 See, e.g. Durant, 1939; Form, 1945; Orlans, 1952; Birch, 1959; Jennings, 1962; Stacey, 1961; Young and Willmott, 1957. Also Whitely, 1953; Williams, 1956; Vidich, 1958; Frankenberg, 1957. The former deal with new settlements, the latter with changes in old settlements.
2 Professor N. J. J. Olivier, 'Ons Stedelike Naturelle Bevolking', brochure published by the SABC based on a series of five broadcasts, during November, December, 1958, 7.
3 Ibid.
4 Literature on the subject is growing daily. A rather complete statement of these changes in Great Britain (and England is, after all, South Africa's reference group) is Anthony Sampson's *Anatomy of Britain*, Hodder & Stoughton, 1962.
5 For instance, Hoggart, 'Mass Communication in Britain', in *The Modern Age*, 1961.
6 In sociological writing, for example, Birch, 1959, 184–5. About the conflicting national and local interests, for example, Orlans, 1952, 289.
7 An interesting historical analysis of how this happened in Cheshire, England, is Lee, 1964.
8 The change from political activity as a result of status to political activity conferring status and even livelihood, as this could be observed in England, was one of the principal themes of Guttsman, 1963.
9 Birch, 1959, 184.
10 Whyte, 1961.
11 See, e.g., Riesman, 1954.
12 See, e.g., Newcomer, 1955; Bendix, 1956; Bendix and Howton, 1957 and 1958.
13 For instance, according to the *Sunday Times*, Johannesburg, 16 February 1964, two M.P.'s would introduce private members' motions, seeking protection for the small merchant and trader

against the chain stores. One of these M.P.'s had said that 'in many suburbs and smaller towns the small businessman, grocer and butcher, was becoming a thing of the past.'

14 In Weber's definition: the notables stem from a time when 'existing social, material and honorific preferences and ranks are connected with administrative functions and duties.' (Weber, 1952, 224–5.)

15 As the old location had not given Africans freehold rights, these individuals were actually home-owners. They had built or bought their houses on rented municipal stands. But the name was adopted from other areas on the Reef where Africans did enjoy freehold rights. Most residents did not know the difference, and the prestige of these home-owners was the same as that of stand-owners.

16 For instance, the slum-dwellers of Glasgow, well described by Brennan, 1961.

17 The history of the changes in political leadership in Reeftown is very similar to that of the changes on the Copperbelt, described in great detail by Epstein, 1958, particularly Chapter III, and to the political history of East London, described by Mayer, 1961, 52–3.

18 It often seemed to us that there were great similarities between the relationships of the white parent cities with their black townships and the relationship of the Federal Government in America with its housing estates in the various states (see, e.g., Form, 1945).

19 This will be further dealt with in a later book.

20 Marjorie Perham in a paper read at the S.A. Institute of Race Relations in February 1958, described the main characteristics of African resistance politics.

21 Weber, 1952, 224.

22 *Op. cit.*, 225.

23 Liebenow, 1961, 33–52.

24 Peter Worsley in 'One-Party Democracy', *The Listener*, 4 August 1960.

25 For instance, Nimrod Mkele, 'The Emergent African Middle Class' in *Optima*, December 1960. The extraordinary observation to be made from this article is that the writer himself, at that time one of the managers as described by us in the previous section, did not belong to the middle class as defined by him in terms of 'those who work on their own', and more particularly 'men with capital' and 'men of independent means' (220).

26 For instance, Julius Lewin in an article 'The Missing Class' (occasioned by Leo Kuper's *The African Bourgeoisie*), R.D.M., 25 September 1965.

27 Expression used by Julius Lewin, see note 26.

28 Most recently and fully by Leo Kuper, *op. cit.*, Chapters 17, 18, and, with particular reference to the Durban conditions, Chapter 19.

29 David Riesman, 'New Standards for Old: From Conspicuous Consumption to Conspicuous Production', in *Individualism Reconsidered*, Anchor Books, 148–63, and particularly 151–2.

30 Compensation was given on the basis of a valuation by the municipal evaluator and by an evaluator appointed by the stand-owner himself. Where these differed, the management, as a principle and

rule, always paid according to the highest valuation. In addition, there was a *Solatium*, according to length of residence. This amounted to 10 per cent of the value and 1 per cent for each two years' residence up to a maximum of 25 per cent. As the location was old and many people had lived up to thirty years in their houses, this added a not inconsiderable 'solace' to their already high compensation. In 1958, on 503 stands, which was about half the total number, the municipality had already offered no less than R435,788 to the residents.

31 As in Watling, an LCC housing estate (Durant, 1939), Reeftown did not allow lodgers, as a rule. But, unlike Watling, an exception was made for single persons, especially if they were related to the core family, so that they could 'help pay the rent'.

32 On 31 May 1957, the population was 48,381. A breakdown showed the following distribution. Adults: male 8,912; female 10,539. Youths (16–18 years): male 2,124; female 2,049. Children: male 12,069; female 12,688.

33 Again, Reeftown showed more consideration for its residents than the LCC housing estate, or the new estate 'Mossdene', to which the population of Bristol's Barton Hill was moved in 1945 (Jennings, 1962). In both these places only persons working in the area were eligible for residence, and old people who no longer worked could not be accommodated.

34 For instance, in Watling, which was founded in 1927, it was not before 1939, i.e. twelve years later, that the new railway providing the essential transport was completed. Before that, 'those who got a seat were lucky'. (Durant, 1939, 10.)

35 Form, 1945, 607–8.

36 Durant, 1939, 37.

37 'Stockfel' is the most usual generic name (origin unknown) for the most popular kind of organization among present-day Africans, whether urban or rural. Its main aim is to provide mutual assistance based on the strictest reciprocity (reciprocity is the most binding code of tribal life). It occurs in an almost unlimited number of different forms and variations, but a large Stockfel generally includes two kinds of activities. The first is the regular pooling of money, goods and/or services by small closed groups of members, generally not more than four; the pool goes to each member in rotation or in need. The second is the giving of a party by each member in his or her turn. At this party the other members and any guests come and consume against payment the drinks and food provided, the profits accruing to the hostess of the week. In Reeftown there were some thirty to forty such Stockfel parties every week-end. A popular hostess could make a profit up to some R300 on one single Sunday. She was then expected in her turn to patronize the parties of other members. The patterns of the Stockfel and the reciprocity on which they were based pervaded all other forms of even the most 'European' types of organizations and all forms of entertaining and hospitality.

38 Whitely, 1953, 229.

39 Form, 1945, 608.

40 Durant, 1939, 59. In Watling functions were also divided: the LCC

controlled housing; Middlesex provided higher education, public assistance and health; whereas Hendon supplied the remaining social services. In Little-Town-in-Overspill (Whitely, 1953, 208–10) the gas supply was so inadequate that, 'There were days on which it was useless to light the gas ring, and baking and grilling were never possible.' But nothing could be done about it, because gas was provided by a private company.

41 Information kindly given by the librarian.

42 N. Mkele, 'Advertising to the African', a paper read to the Advertising Convention, Durham, September 1959, includes the 12,000 policemen in the same class as the 25,800 teachers, the 4,000 nurses, the 6,000 businessmen and the 60,000 civil servants.

43 Epstein, 1958, 234.

44 Harris, 1936, 182–4.

45 Frazier, 1957, 167.

46 About the importance of the founder, Brandel-Syrier, 1962, 65–6.

47 About the Bantu belief that the dead are not dead as long as they are remembered, see, e.g., Brandel-Syrier, 1962, 112.

48 Cf. note 37; Kuper, 1944; Brandel-Syrier, 1962, 17–18 and 98–9.

49 See Brandel-Syrier, 1962.

50 *Op. cit.*, 62–3 and 103–4. This organization, relatively so immune from the customary violent leadership quarrels and secessions, would merit a close and more specialized study of its organizational and political patterns.

51 For instance, Whitely, 1953, 230; Frankenberg, 1957, 52–3.

52 Durant, 1939, 61.

53 Riesman, 1954, 130.

54 Williams, 1956, 126.

55 In this respect, they are similar to Gosforth's lower-upper class, Williams (1956, 125 ff.) explained this by saying that very probably they might find themselves in positions inferior to, say, a chairman of upper-middle class. In Reeftown there were other reasons, see pp. 109–10.

56 Form, 1945, 608.

57 Lewin, 1948, Chapter 12, esp. 189, 193.

58 Frankenberg, 1957, 157.

59 Frankenberg, 1957, 152.

60 Epstein, 1958, 227.

61 Sprott, 1958, 81.

62 Tumin, 1957, 32–7.

63 Professor A. van Selms, with whom I discussed this, drew my attention to this similarity.

64 Halkin, 1950, 71–2.

65 Riesman, 1954, 129, 134.

Chapter 2

1 See pp. 96–7.
2 We shall usually abbreviate privately employed to private (clerk).
3 See *The Explanation of Educational Qualifications*.
4 See the Educational Chart, p. 156.
5 Between 1960 and 1970, the salary of the Senior Social Worker increased by 81 per cent, and that of the Senior Clerk by 61·7 per cent. In addition there are pension benefits, leave bonuses, etc.
6 See Introduction, pp. xxv, xxvi.
7 See further on this topic, 'The Influence of the Missionaries', pp. 259 ff.
8 Cf. pp. 94 ff.
9 For instance, the Irish assimilate less thoroughly than many other immigrants in London, and this is sometimes ascribed to the fact that Ireland is so near and continues to exert a strong influence.
10 'Xhosa country constitutes one of the oldest areas of white settlement south of the Sahara – white and black having both claimed it as home since the 1820s. . . . The 'school' section of the Xhosa people (as against the conservative 'Reds') have received mission and school teaching over a period of five generations.' Mayer, 1961, 586.
11 The Amahlubi are one of three big tribes (the others being the Zizi and the Bhele) that eventually settled in the Ciskei and the Transkei after being driven from their original habitat in Natal by the rise of the Zulu. All these different refugees and immigrants who thus settled among the Mpondo population of the Eastern Cape early in the nineteenth century are collectively known as Fingo.
12 Cf. Mphahlele, 1962, 147–8.
13 This word had no precise meaning. The 'farm' stood for a great variety of types of farm, tenure or labour. It could be a piece of land allocated by a chief, a European mission or a white farmer; it could mean no more than some head of cattle grazing on communal land. The 'farmer' could be a humble squatter, a prosperous share-cropper, a manager or foreman working almost independently, a tribesman or an independent farm owner. 'Farming' could refer to mere subsistence farming but also to cash-crop farming. Furthermore, the occupation of 'farming' did not even imply a fixed residence.
14 Oral information from Mr K. B. Hartshorne.
15 In a sample survey, for instance, made in 1951 in Soweto by the Non-European Affairs Department in Johannesburg (information from Miss Giesela Feldman) it was found that as one would expect, the younger age groups contain progressively more urban-borns: 81 per cent of those aged 0–9; 56 per cent of those aged 10–19; 27 per cent of those aged 20–29; and only 4 per cent of those aged 30–39 were urban-born.
16 Cf. Chapter 5.
17 Cf. Chapter 4, 'The boy'.
18 Tumin and Feldman (1957), calculated by means of what they called GOMS (Generational Occupational Mobility Score), that in Puerto Rico the structure of opportunity was such that 'in its present condition of development some literacy makes a big difference; added

amounts of literacy make less difference in terms of available jobs; educational training does not make a big difference again until one has some college training.' It might be worthwhile to do a similar investigation on the Reef.

19 In an unpublished report, 'The Bantu Civil Servant', Rae Sherwood noted with apparent surprise that 'the total extent of urbanization (here defined in number of years spent in a large urban centre or city and expressed as a proportion of the individual's life) is no indication whatever of educational achievements.'

20 Sorokin, 1932, Vol. III, 527–30.

21 *Op. cit.*, 531.

22 *Op. cit.*, 530.

23 In her sample, Rae Sherwood (see note 19) found that as many as 28·7 per cent were born and bred in a city. The sample was educationally and occupationally less select but younger than ours.

24 Cf. Chapter 4, 'First Jobs in Town'.

25 See Chapter 1, p. 25.

26 See Chapter 1, p. 19.

27 E.g. Knupfer, 1954.

28 Riesman, 1954, 130.

29 'The African still cannot appreciate classical music, modern art, or serious drama . . . these values just do not sell, because they have no meaning for him in terms of his goals and experience' (N. Mkele, in a paper 'Advertising to the African', read to the Advertising Convention, Durban, September 1959, 9).

30 Whitely also writes about the 'distinct cleavage' in Little-Town-in-Overspill between 'natives or locals' and 'immigrants' (Whitely, 1953, 217). Frankenberg found the same in his village (Frankenberg, 1957, 40–1). Also of Banbury, Stacey, 1961, reported the existence of two societies.

31 Birch, 1959, 184.

32 Kuper, 1947, 223.

33 For instance, after many a European-attended township wedding, so well described by Kuper, 1965, 106–9, and particularly after the grandiose wedding described by Kuper on p. 118, there was strongest criticism and disapproval: 'Africans were apparently not good enough for Edith', it was murmured, because many an upper-class African had found himself 'displaced' by European guests.

34 Drake and Cayton, 1945, Chapter 19; Frazier, 1957, Chapters II–VI.

35 Lipton, 1960, 272–9. Lipton explains these vices, 'not petty vices, but the big juicy vices': 'supporting a kept woman; fathering a bastard child . . . destroying private property with relative immunity, say, in a rowdy hotel party; going on wild joy-rides in the country; sneaking off for a lost week-end to a love-nest at a mountain hide-away or a seaside resort; or on a "moral holiday" to Paris . . .' as well as what he calls 'the larger but less conspicuous vices', such as: 'plundering the natural resources, raiding the stock-market in private behind-the-scenes deals, bribing public officials, floating fraudulent stock issues, or ruining competitors by financial mayhem or legal murder . . .'. All such vices 'belong exclusively to the upper classes, if only because

they were expensive ones that only the rich could afford' and get away with.

36 Frazier (1957, 126–7) found various reasons to explain this development. The secularization of religion which had become divorced from any real religious sentiment (129); the influence on the morals and manners in the Negro community coming from the successful members of the show and sports worlds; and, probably most important, the fact that money had become the chief requirement for social acceptance. All these conditions were already becoming noticeable in the African community of Reeftown.

37 Kuper, 1965, 73–6.

38 Kuper, 1965, 281, n. 3.

Chapter 3

1 On Schedule I we had a complete record of every stage in the educational history of fifty-nine of our sample (of one individual the data were incomplete). We knew the years and ages of starting and completing the various standards and forms, any further academic and professional studies, and all degrees and diplomas attempted, the period of time taken, the institution and district where they studied, who paid and how much, etc. We knew the reasons for starting or abandoning any course of studies, as well as whatever and whoever acted as obstacles or encouragements. We also had information about what they liked and disliked in their education and why.

2 Ellen Hellmann, 'Early School-leaving and Occupations of Native Juveniles in Johannesburg', Thesis submitted to the University of the Witwatersrand for Ph.D., May 1939.

3 J. M. Smithen, 'Departmental Education Agencies at Work in the Transkeian Territories and the Problem of the better Co-ordination of Native School Education with them', A dissertation presented for the degree of M.Ed., University of South Africa, 1953. In this thesis various reports from the Superintendent General of Education in the Cape Province, as well as a Survey by Circuit Inspectors, 'Retardation of Native Schools', Cape Education Department, February 1951, have been included.

4 Cf. Hellmann, 58.

5 Cf. Hellmann, 79.

6 Hellmann, 79.

7 Hellmann, 72, 74.

8 The old habit persists. In Reeftown we found one day three boys laying the lino in their principal's kitchen, and upon enquiry we were told: 'Such things are part of their manual . . .' No wonder the parents believe that the new curriculum contains too much manual labour.

9 Hellmann, 71.

10 Hellmann, 126–7.

11 In a paper 'Manpower resources of Africa' delivered to the Council Meeting of the South African Institute of Race Relations, January 1963.
12 Smithen, 49.
13 Smithen, 47–51.
14 Smithen, 44.
15 The average age of 251 children who entered the Pimville Government School in 1937 was 8 years, 11 months (E. Hellmann, *op. cit.*, 574).
16 Age of starting school: Earlier than normal: 29; Normal: 12; Later than normal: 19.
17 The fathers' attitudes towards education: Against, 15; Indifferent, 13; Inactive (father died or deserted or gave the child to a rearer), 11; For, 21.
18 The children's attitudes to school: Positive, 18; Neutral, 24; Negative, 18.
19 See Chapter 5, pp. 254 ff.
20 See e.g., Mr N. G., 'Three lucky boys', pp. 137–8.
21 See further, p. 241 ff.
22 Cf. the movement of the English children in the survey by J. W. B. Douglas, *The Home and the School*, MacGibbon & Kee, 1963.
23 This was one of the important findings also in the survey mentioned in the previous note. In England this was true to a large extent because of the competition for the few grammar school places available. In South Africa it was true because of the lack of compulsory education which threw the full responsibility on the parents.
24 Smithen (1953, 47–51) shows how nearly half of the pupils in Sub A took two years or more over Sub A; more than half of the pupils of Sub B took two years or more over Sub B; three-quarters of the pupils of Std. III took two years or more over Std. III, and so on, increasingly up to Std. VI.
25 Kuper (1965, 236–45) gives the history of African lawyers and doctors with particular reference to Durban and his own emphasis on race-relational factors.
26 Shepherd, 1941, 90.
27 *Op. cit.*, 291–2.
28 *Op. cit.*, 291.
29 *Op. cit.*, 293 ff.
30 *Race Relations Survey*, 1961, 257–8.
31 *Op. cit.*, 261.
32 *Op. cit.*, 220.
33 *Op. cit.*, 241.
34 Ibid.
35 Oral information, Professor M. G. Marwick.
36 These data were derived from Schedule I and, in order to avoid the usual stereotyped replies, such as 'because I wanted to serve my own people', and to keep contact with the actual situation as it occurred at the time, the question 'Why did you go to a teacher-training college?' was asked in connection with schools and studies and not when talking about jobs. Replies were: 'The thing to do', 15; 'I was told to', 7; 'To help other siblings', 3; 'I wanted to teach but after higher

academic qualifications', 8; 'Something which I actually wanted to do fell through', 7; unreliable reply, 1.

37 See the Educational Chart, p. 156.

38 Mphahlele, 1962, 57.

39 Oral information from Mr K. B. Hartshorne.

40 In 1962, 98 per cent of all teachers employed in Bantu education had become African (*Bantu,* September 1962), and the African Teachers' Association never ceased to demand all the teaching jobs for their own qualified teachers. According to Mr K. B. Hartshorne, there were in 1967 still some 500 Europeans employed by the Bantu Education Department, and working in the old 'colleges' such as Adam's, Lovedale, Healdtown, etc. Only four out of the twenty-eight teacher-training colleges have only Bantu staff. The European teachers are, however, no longer 'missionary' in the old sense, but 'career' teachers in the same way as their colleagues in European education.

41 At present in South Africa there are, besides many government, provincial and municipal funds, numerous private bursary funds to assist non-white students. The largest private bursary fund, which helps Africans mainly from the Witwatersrand, is housed in the Johannesburg offices of the South African Institute of Race Relations, and becomes inevitably identified in the public mind with the Institute itself. Since 1955, when the fund started to operate, 478 loans or grants have been made, to a total of nearly R60,000. (Horrell, *Race Relations Survey*, 1962, 200.)

Chapter 4

1 On Schedule II we had a complete record of all successive jobs, their dates and duration, the type of jobs and employers, the place of employment and the wages received, the reasons for taking and leaving the jobs, etc. We also knew how the job had been obtained, and any other general observations a spokesman wanted to make, as well as what he had liked and disliked about it, had learned from it, etc.

2 See, e.g., G. M. E. Leistner, 1964, where other recent researches on similar topics are also mentioned.

3 Lipton, 1960, 276.

4 Herskovits, 1963, 158.

5 All this and the following derives mainly from Hellmann (ed.), *Handbook on Race Relations*, 1949, Chapter XII, 'The Pass Laws', by Ellison Kahn, 275–91.

6 Horrell, *Race Relations Survey*, 1961, 82.

7 In a survey made in 1961 by the Council for Scientific and Industrial Research it was found that '16 per cent of a sample of industrial workers had an early history of mining, probably having used the mines as a jumping-off point' (*Race Relations Survey*, 1962, 112). But this figure says little, as, although the sample (presumably) consisted

of non-professionals, it is not known how many were born and/or reared in town and already had their residence permits.

8 About the security of mine employment see Biesheuvel, 1958, 175.
9 Cf. Lipset, 1954, 457.
10 Cf. Lipset, 1954, 458.
11 L. H. Samuels as quoted by Kuper, 1965, 78.
12 See, e.g., Birch, 1959, 25, 37, 104. Explaining that managers and public servants were newcomers in Glossop, Birch writes, 'Most of them secure advancement either by moving from one post to another, which may well be in quite a different area, or by promotion within an organization which has branches in several places' (p. 37).
13 Lipset, 1954, 456.
14 Cf. also Doxey, 1961, 38.
15 Jabavu, 1960, 188–90.
16 The policy of Job Reservation, 'if it comes to be widely implemented [which it has never been yet] . . . will constitute an extension into the fields of secondary and tertiary industry of a system of racial stratification akin to the colour-bar restrictions which have been a feature of the mining industry since the enactment of the 1926 Mines and Works Act.' (Doxey, 1961, 140–7.) See also *Race Relations Survey*, 1963, 192–6, and 1962, 153.
17 'F. H. Cresswell, leader of the Labour Party (which in the General Election of June 1924 held the balance of power between the Nationalists and the South African Party] was . . . convinced that white labour could obtain the protection it needed through a rigid application of the "rate for the job" principle.' (Doxey, 1961, 126.) This principle is based on the (erroneous) assumption that if the wage rates are fixed at a level sufficiently high to attract whites, then the white man's superior knowledge will retain the job for white against non-white competition.

Chapter 5

1 Brandel-Syrier, 1962, 127.
2 Tardits, 1958, 75.
3 We anticipated (and, it turned out, rightly so) strong reluctance to single out one parent to the possible detriment of the other, which would have sounded like criticism of persons to whom traditional respect was due. We had, besides the direct question: 'Who was (were) the most important person(s) for you?', several opportunities to test the role of the mother unobtrusively; when talking about the actual persons responsible for the upbringing, when discussing the parents' attitude to education and enquiring separately after father's and mother's attitude, and, in the educational story, when dealing with specific instances of encouragement received or obstacles encountered. Data obtained on all these occasions have been used.
4 Gist and Bennett, 1963, 45–8.
5 *Op. cit.*, 46–7.

6 Jabavu, 1960, 194.

7 Also Gluckman, 1934, 22; and Hellmann, 1939, 23, 25 note 1.

8 Complete information about the siblings, their age, education, present occupation, marital status, social status in relation to that of *Ego*, the relations between Ego and sibling(s), the assistance received from and given by *Ego* to the sibling(s), as well as any other particulars respondents would venture to give us either without being asked or in reply to questions, was recorded in the relevant cells of Schedule IV.

9 In this context the ill-defined word 'family' is used to denote the siblings or the sibling group.

10 Feelings about the achievements of the siblings: Satisfied: 28; Disappointed: 11; Partly satisfied and partly disappointed: 21.

11 Pauw (1963, 197) mentions that there is an emotional need for tradition, for something old and established, in all those situations in which the new western patterns cause uncertainty and insecurity.

12 Information about assistance given and received between the siblings was generally broached after each and every sibling had been passed in review. A certain fatigue may have come over our respondents by that time, for the information was not as complete or detailed as had been hoped. There was also, and quite understandably, a greater readiness to talk about assistance given than about assistance received. The data may, therefore, not be entirely reliable.

13 Some information was obtained by means of the question: 'Any other person related to you, who was of importance to you?'

14 Jabavu, 1960, 61–2, 129–30.

15 Mphahlele, 1962, 58.

16 Cf. Little, 1957.

17 MacCrone, 1947; Cryns, 1959; Brett, 1963.

18 Cf. Eysenck, 1948, 35–6.

19 Kuper also found that his sample contrasted the frankness of the Afrikaner with the hypocrisy of the English (1965, 397). He was, however, so astonished about this that he blamed his 'confusing' questions (ibid., note 2), and devoted a whole Appendix (Appendix C, 427–8) to an attempt at explanation, relating this stereotype exclusively to the matter of *apartheid*. But not only is there the historical, and well-known ascription of *Perfide Albion* to Great Britain, but on the continent of western Europe 'hypocrisy' is one of the most common, if not the most common, stereotype about the English people, and it was, therefore, no surprise for the present investigator. It has been expressed in numerous journalistic and literary writings in French and Italian, Dutch and German. One recent example was an article called 'I am a bloody foreigner' (*New Statesman*, 19 November 1965); the author, Willi Frischauer, explains that, in his opinion, the English, 'who are reluctant to accept a foreigner on equal terms, have recently acquired many foreign traits. They are less restrained (or politely hypocritical), ruder and more outspoken.'

20 Mphahlele, 1962, 72; see also Jabavu, 1960, 62.

21 Bogardus, 1932 and 1938.

22 De Kiewiet, 1941, 24, 48.

23 Dollard, 1935, 279–80.

Bibliography

ALLPORT, GORDON W., 'The Use of Personal Documents in Psychological Science', New York: *Social Science Research Council Bulletin*, 49 (1942).

ALLPORT, GORDON W., *The Nature of Prejudice*, New York: Doubleday, Anchor Books, 1958.

ANDRIEUX, ANDRÉE, and LIGNON, JEAN, *L'Ouvrier d'Aujourd'hui*, Paris: Marcel Rivière, 1961.

ARON, RAYMOND, 'Social Structure and the Ruling Class', *Brit. Jour. of Soc.*, i (1950), Part I, 1–16; Part II, 126–43.

BALANDIER, GEORGES, *Sociologie des Brazzaville Noires*, Paris: Librairie Armand Colin, 1955.

BALANDIER, G., *Afrique Ambiguë*, Paris: Librairie Plon, 1957.

BALTZELL, E. DIGBY, 'Who's Who in America and The Social Register: Elite and Upper Class Indexes in Metropolitan America', 172–85, in Bendix and Lipset, *Class, Status and Power*, 1954.

BANTON, MICHAEL P., *White and Coloured: the Behaviour of British People Towards Coloured Immigrants*, London: Jonathan Cape, 1959.

BANTON, MICHAEL P., *West African City*, London: Oxford University Press, 1960.

BANTON, MICHAEL P., 'The Re-structuring of Social Relationships', 113–25, in Southall, 1961.

BENDIX, REINHARDT, *Work and Authority in Industry*, Cambridge: Harvard University Press, 1956.

BENDIX, REINHARDT, and HOWTON, FRANK W., 'Social Mobility and the American Business Elite', *Brit. Jour. of Soc.*, Part I (December 1957), 357–69; Part II (March 1958), 1–14.

BENDIX, REINHARDT, and LIPSET, SEYMOUR M., *Class, Status and Power: A Reader in Social Stratification*, London: Routledge & Kegan Paul Ltd., 1954.

BIESHEUVEL, S., 'The Influence of Social Circumstances in the Attitudes of Educated Africans', *S.A. Jour. of Science*, 53 (1957), 309–14.

BIESHEUVEL, S., 'Methodology in the Study of Attitudes of Africans', *Jour. of Soc. Psych.*, xxxxvii (1958), 169–84.

BIBLIOGRAPHY

BIRCH, A. H., *Small-town Politics: A Study of Political Life in Glossop*, Oxford University Press, 1959.

BLUMER, HERBERT, 'An Appraisal of Thomas and Znaniecki's "The Polish Peasant in Europe and America"', Critiques of Research in the Social Sciences, I, New York: *Social Science Research Council Bulletin*, 1939.

BOGARDUS, EMORY S., 'A Social Distance Scale', *Sociology and Social Research*, xvii, 33 (1932) 265–71.

BOGARDUS, EMORY S., 'Social Distance and its Practical Implications', *Sociology and Social Research*, xxii (1938), 462–76.

BOTT, ELIZABETH, 'Class as Reference Group', *Human Relations*, vii (1954), 259–85.

BRANDEL-SYRIER, MIA, *Black Woman in Search of God*, London: Lutterworth Press, 1962.

BRENNAN, T., *Reshaping a City*, Glasgow: The House of Grant, 1961.

BRETT, E. A., *African Attitudes: A Study of the Social, Racial and Political Attitudes of some Middle-class Africans*, Johannesburg: S.A. Institute of Race Relations, 14, 1963.

BUSIA, K. A., *Report on a Social Survey of Sekondi-Takoradi*, London: Accra, 1950.

CLEMENTS, R. V., *Managers: A Study of Their Careers in Industry*, London: George Allen & Unwin, 1958.

CRYNS, A. G. J., *Race Relations and Race Attitudes in South Africa*, Nijmegen: Janssen, 1959.

DAVIDSON, PERRY E., and ANDERSON, HOBSON D., *Occupational Mobility in an American Community*, Stanford University: Stanford University Press, 1937.

DAVIS, ALLISON, and DOLLARD, J., *Children of Bondage: the Personality Development of Negro Youth in the Urban South*, Washington, D.C.: American Council on Education, 1940.

DAVIS, ALLISON, GARDNER, B. B., and GARDNER, M. R., *Deep South; a Social Anthropological Study of Caste and Class*, Chicago: University of Chicago Press, 1941.

DE KIEWIET, C. W., *A History of South Africa: Social and Economic*, Oxford University Press, 1941.

DOLLARD, JOHN, *Criteria for the Life History with Analyses of Six Notable Documents*, New Haven: Yale University Press, 1935.

DOLLARD, J., *Caste and Class in a Southern Town*, New Haven: Yale University Press, 1937.

DOXEY, G. V., *The Industrial Colour Bar in South Africa*, Oxford University Press, 1961.

DRAKE, ST CLAIR, and CAYTON, HORACE R., *Black Metropolis: A Study of Negro Life in a Northern City*, New York: Harcourt, Brace & Co., 1945.

DUBB, A. A. (ed.), *The Multitribal Society: Proceedings of the Sixteenth Conference of the Rhodes–Livingstone Institute*, with an Introduction by Philip Mayer, Lusaka, Zambia: 1962.

DURANT, RUTH, *Watling: A Survey of Social Life on a New Housing Estate*, London: P. S. King & Sons, 1939.

318

DURKHEIM, EMILE, *The Rules of Sociological Method*, 8th edn., translated by Sarah A. Soloway and John H. Muller and edited by George E. G. Catlin, Chicago: University of Chicago Press, 1938.

DURKHEIM, EMILE, *Sociology and Philosophy*, translated by D. F. Pocock, with an Introduction by J. G. Peristiany, London: Cohen & West Ltd., 1953.

EPSTEIN, A. L., *Politics in an Urban African Community*, Manchester: Manchester University Press, 1958.

EPSTEIN, A. L., 'The Network and Urban Social Organization, Human Problems in British Central Africa', *The Rhodes–Livingstone Jour.*, xxix (June 1961), 29–62.

EYSENCK, H. J., and CROWN, S., 'National Stereotypes: An Experimental and Methodological Study', *Int. Jour. of Opin. and Att. Res.*, ii, 1 (1958), 26–39.

FORM, WILLIAM H., 'Status Stratification in a Planned Community', *Am. Soc. Review*, x, 1–6 (1945), 605–13.

FORM, WILLIAM H., 'Towards an Occupational Social Psychology', *Jour. of Soc. Psych.*, xxiv (1946), 85–99.

FORM, WILLIAM H., and MILLER, DELBERT C., 'Occupational Career Patterns as a Sociological Instrument', *Am. Jour. of Soc.*, liv (January 1949), 317–29.

FRANKENBERG, RONALD, *Village on the Border: A Social Study of Religion, Politics and Football in a North Wales Community*, London: Cohen & West Ltd., 1957.

FRAZIER, E. FRANKLIN, *Black Bourgeoisie: The Rise of a New Middle Class in the United States*, Glencoe: The Free Press, 1957.

FRAZIER, E. FRANKLIN, *Race and Culture Contacts in the Modern World*, New York: Alfred A. Knopf, Inc., 1957.

GIST, NOEL P., and BENNETT, WILLIAM S., 'Aspirations of Negro and White Students', *Social Forces*, xxxxii (1963), 40–48.

GLUCKMAN, MAX, 'The Realm of the Supernatural Among the South-Eastern Bantu: A Study of the Practical Working of Religion and Magic', thesis presented for the degree of Bachelor of Arts with Honours in Social Anthropology, University of the Witwatersrand, June 1934.

GLUCKMAN, MAX, 'Analysis of a Social Situation in Zululand', *Bantu Studies*, xiv (March 1940), 1–30; (June 1940), 147–74.

GOLDTHORPE, J. E., 'An African Elite', *Brit. Jour. of Soc.*, vi (1955), 33–47.

GOLDTHORPE, J. E., 'Educated Africans: Some Conceptual and Terminological Problems', 145–58 in Southall, 1961.

GOTTSCHALK, L., KLUCKHOLN, CLYDE, ANGELI, ROBERT, 'The Use of Personal Documents in History, Anthropology and Sociology', New York: *Social Science Research Council Bulletin*, 53, 1945.

GUTTSMANN, W. L., *The British Political Elite*, London: MacGibbon & Kee, 1963.

HALKIN, SIMON, *Modern Hebrew: Trends and Values, a comprehensive analysis of modern Hebrew creative writing – prose and poetry – and a discussion of the main representatives of that literature*, New York: Schocken Books, 1950.

319

HARRIS, ABRAM L., *The Negro as Capitalist: A Study of Banking and Business Among American Negroes*, Philadelphia: The American Academy of Political and Social Science, 1936.

HELLMANN, ELLEN, 'Early School-leaving and Occupations of Native Juveniles in Johannesburg', thesis submitted for Ph.D., May 1939.

HELLMANN, ELLEN, (ed.), *Handbook on Race Relations in South Africa*, Oxford University Press, 1949.

HERSKOVITS, MELVILLE J., *The Human Factor in Changing Africa*, London: Routledge & Kegan Paul Ltd., 1963.

HOGGART, RICHARD, 'Mass Communication in Britain', *The Modern Age*, ed. Boris Ford, Harmondsworth: Penguin Books, 1961.

HORRELL, MURIEL (comp.), *A Survey of Race Relations in South Africa*, Johannesburg: S.A. Institute of Race Relations, 1959, 1960, 1961, 1962, 1963.

JABAVU, NONI, *Drawn in Colour: African Contrasts*, London: Murray, 1960.

JENNINGS, HILDA, *Societies in the Making*, London: Routledge & Kegan Paul Ltd., 1962.

KNUPFER, GENEVIEVE, 'Portrait of the Underdog', 255–63 in Bendix and Lipset, 1954.

KORNHAUSER, RUTH ROSSNER, 'The Warner Approach to Social Stratification', 224–55, in Bendix and Lipset, 1954.

KUPER, HILDA, and KAPLAN, SELMA, 'Voluntary Associations in an Urban Township', *African Studies*, iii (1944), 178–85.

KUPER, HILDA, *An African Aristocracy: Rank Among the Swazi*, Oxford University Press, 1947.

KUPER, HILDA, *The Uniform of Colour; A Study of White–Black Relationships in Swaziland*, Johannesburg: Witwatersrand University Press, 1947.

KUPER, HILDA, *Indians in Natal*, Natal University Press, 1960.

KUPER, LEO (ed.), *Living in Towns*, Selected Research Papers in Urban Sociology of the Faculty of Commerce and Social Science, University of Birmingham, London: The Cresset Press, 1953,

KUPER, LEO, *An African Bourgeoisie: Race, Class and Politics in South Africa*, New Haven and London: Yale University Press, 1965.

LEE, J. H., *Social Leaders and Public Persons: A Study of County Government in Cheshire since 1888*, Clarendon Press: Oxford University Press, 1964.

LEISTNER, G. M. E., 'Patterns of Urban Bantu Labour', *S.A. Jour. of Economics*, 32, 4 (December 1964), 253–5.

LEWIN, KURT, *Resolving Social Conflicts*: Selected Papers on Group Dynamics, New York: Harper Bros., 1948.

LIEBENOW, J. GUS, 'The Establishment of Legitimacy in a Dependency Situation: A Case Study of the Nyaturu of Tanganyika', *African Studies*, xx, i (1961), 33–52.

LIPSET, SEYMOUR M., and BENDIX, REINHARD, 'Social Mobility and Occupational Career Patterns, II, Social Mobility', 454–64 in Bendix and Lipset, 1954.

LIPTON, LAWRENCE, *The Holy Barbarians*, London: W. H. Allen, 1960 (1st British edn.).

LITTLE, KENNETH, 'The Role of Voluntary Associations in West African Urbanization', *Am. Anthrop.*, xxxix (1957), 581–91.

LLOYD, P. C. (ed.), *The New Elites of Tropical Africa:* Studies presented and discussed at the Sixth International African Seminar at the University of Ibadan, Nigeria, July 1964, Oxford University Press, 1966.

MACCRONE, I. D., 'Reaction to Domination in a Colour-Caste Society: A preliminary Study of the Race Attitudes of a Dominated Group', *Jour. of Soc. Psychol.*, xxvi (1947), 69–98.

MADGE, JANET H., 'Some Aspects of Social Mixing in Worcester', in Kuper, 1953.

MADGE, JOHN, *The Tools of Social Science*, London: Longmans Green, 1953.

MAYER, PHILIP, *Townsmen or Tribesmen: Conservatism and the Process of Urbanization in a South African City*, Cape Town: Oxford University Press, 1961.

MAYER, PHILIP, Introduction to Dubb, 1962 (ed.), pp. v–x.

MAYER, PHILIP, 'Migrancy and the Study of Africans in Towns', *Am. Anthrop.*, 643, Part I (1962), 576–92.

MERCIER, P., 'The Evolution of Senegalese Elites', *International Social Science Bulletin*, viii, 3 (1956).

MERRILL, FRANCIS E., *Society and Culture: An Introduction to Sociology*, New Jersey: Prentice Hall Inc., Englewood Cliffs, 1957.

MILLER, S. F., 'The Concept of Mobility', *Social Problems*, 3 (October 1966).

MITCHELL, J. C., 'Factors in Urban Growth in Bantu Africa with Special Reference to the Federation of the Rhodesias and Nyasaland' (stencilled paper).

MITCHELL, J. C., *The Yao Village, A Study in the Social Structure of a Nyasaland Tribe*, published on behalf of the Rhodes–Livingstone Institute, Manchester, 1956.

MITCHELL, J. C., *The Kalela Dance*, Rhodes–Livingstone Papers, No. 27, Manchester University Press, 1956.

MITCHELL, J. C., 'Urbanization, detribalization and stabilization in Southern Africa', *Social Implications of Industrialization and Urbanization in Africa, South of the Sahara*, UNESCO (1956), 693–711.

MITCHELL, J. C., and EPSTEIN, A. L., 'Power and Prestige among Africans in Northern Rhodesia: An Experiment', *Proceedings and Transactions of the Rhodesia Scientific Association*, xlv (1957), 13–26.

MITCHELL, J. C., *Tribalism and the Plural Society*. An inaugural lecture given in the University College of Rhodesia and Nyasaland. London: Oxford University Press, 1960.

MOSCA, GAETANO, *The Ruling Class* (*Elementi di Scienza Politica*), translated by Hannah D. Kahn. Edited and revised with an Introduction by Arthur Livingstone, New York and London, 1939.

MPHAHLELE, EZAKIEL, *The African Image*, London: Faber & Faber, 1962.

NADEL, S. F., 'The Concept of Social Elites', UNESCO, *International Social Science Bulletin*, viii, 3 (1956), 413–24.

NADEL, S. F., *The Theory of Social Structure*, London: Cohen & West Ltd., 1957.

NEWCOMER, MABEL, *The Big Business Executive*, New York: Columbia University Press, 1955.

NGCOBO, S. BANGANI, 'African Elite in South Africa', UNESCO *International Social Science Bulletin*, viii, 3 (1956), 431–40.

OGBURN, WILLIAM F., and NIMHOFF, MEYER F., *A Handbook of Sociology*, London: Routledge & Kegan Paul Ltd., 4th edn. (revised), 1960.

ORLANS, HAROLD, *Stevenage: A Sociological Study of a New Town*, London: Routledge & Kegan Paul Ltd., 1952.

PARETO, WILFREDO, *The Mind and Society*, ed. Arthur Livingstone, New York: Harcourt Brace & Co., 1935.

PARSONS, TALCOTT, 'An Analytical Approach to the Theory of Social Stratification, *Am. Jour. of Soc.*, xlv, 6 (May 1940).

PAUW, B. A., *The Second Generation: A Study of the Family among urbanized Bantu in East London*, Cape Town: Oxford University Press, 1963.

PFAUTZ, H. W., 'The Current Literature on Social Stratification: Critique and Bibliography', *Am. Jour. of Soc.*, lviii (1953), 391–418.

PFAUTZ, H. W., and DUNCAN, OTIS D., 'A Critical Evaluation of Warner's Work in Community Stratification', *Am. Soc. Review*, xv (April 1950), 205–15.

READER, D. H., *The Black Man's Portion: History, Demography and Living Conditions in the Native Locations of East London, Cape Province*, Cape Town: Oxford University Press, 1961.

REISSMAN, LEONARD, *Class in American Society*, London: Routledge & Kegan Paul Ltd., 1959.

REYBURN, LAWRENCE, *African Traders, Their Position and Problems in Johannesburg's South Western Townships*, Johannesburg: S.A. Institute of Race Relations, 83, 1960.

RICHARDS, AUDREY I. (ed.), *East African Chiefs, A Study of Political Development in Some Uganda and Tanganyika Tribes*, London: Faber & Faber Ltd., 1960.

RIESMAN, DAVID, *The Lonely Crowd: A Study of the Changing American Character*, New York: Doubleday, Anchor Books, 1950.

RIESMAN, DAVID, *Individualism Reconsidered, Selected Essays from*, New York: Doubleday, Anchor Books, 1954.

RIESMAN, DAVID, *Abundance for What?*, London: Chatto & Windus, 1964.

ROGOFF, NATALIE, *Recent Trends in Occupational Mobility*, Glencoe: The Free Press, 1953.

ROSENBERG, MORRIS, 'Perceptual Obstacles to Class Consciousness', *Social Forces*, xxxii (October 1953), 22–7.

SACHS, WULF, *Black Hamlet: The Mind of an African Negro Revealed by Psychoanalysis*. London: Geoffrey Bles, 1937.

SAMPSON, ANTHONY, *Anatomy of Britain*, London: Hodder & Stoughton, 1962.

SCHAPERA, I. (ed.), *The Bantu-speaking Tribes of South Africa: An Ethnographical Survey*, London: George Routledge & Sons Ltd., 1937.

SCHUMPETER, JOSEPH A., *Imperialism and Social Classes*, Oxford: Basil Blackwell, 1951.

SCHWAB, W. B., 'Social Stratification in Gwelo', 126–44 in Southall, 1961.

SHEPHERD, ROBERT, H. W., *The Story of a Century, 1841–1941*, Lovedale, South Africa: The Lovedale Press, 1941.

SHERWOOD, RAE, 'Job Satisfactions Among White American and African Professional Workers', paper read at Congress of S.A. Psychol. Ass., July 1957.

SHERWOOD, R., 'The Bantu Clerk, a Study of Role Expectations', *Jour. of Soc. Psychol.*, xxxxvii (1958), 285–316.

SMITHEN, J. M., 'Departmental Education Agencies at Work in the Transkeian Territories and the Problem of the better Co-ordination of Native School Education with them': a dissertation presented for the Degree of M.Ed., University of South Africa, 1935.

SMYTHE, HUGH H., and MABEL M., *The New Nigerian Elite*, Stanford, California: Stanford University Press, 1960.

SOROKIN, PITTIRIM A., ZIMMERMAN, CARLE C., and GALPIN, CHARLES J. (eds.), *A Systematic Source Book in Rural Sociology*, 3 vols., Minneapolis: University of Minnesota Press, 1932.

SOUTHALL, AIDAN (ed.), *Social Change in Modern Africa*, studies presented and discussed at the First International African Seminar, Makerere College, Kampala, January 1959. Published for the Intern. African Institute by the Oxford University Press, 1961.

SOUTHALL, AIDAN, 'Small Groups and Social Networks', in Southall, 1961.

SPROTT, W. J. H., *Human Groups, A Study of How Men and Women behave in the Family, the Village, the Crowd, and many other Forms of Association*, Penguin Books, 1958.

STACEY, MARGARET, *Tradition and Change: A Study of Banbury*, Oxford University Press, 1961.

TARDITS, CLAUDE, 'The Notion of the Elite and the Urban Social Survey in Africa', UNESCO, *International Social Science Bulletin*, viii, 3 (1956), 492–795.

TARDITS, CLAUDE, *Porto-Novo: Les Nouvelles Generations Africaines entre leurs Traditions et l'Occident*, Paris: Mouton & Co., 1958.

THOMAS, W. I., and ZNANIECKI, FLORIAN, *The Polish Peasant in Europe and America*, 2 vols., New York: Alfred A. Knopf, 1927.

TUMIN, MELVIN M., 'Some Unapplauded Consequences of Social Mobility in a Mass Society', *Social Forces*, xxxvi (October 1957), 32–7.

TUMIN, MELVIN, M., and FELDMAN, ARNOLD S., 'Theory and Measurement of Occupational Mobility', *Am. Soc. Rev.*, xxii, 3 (June 1957), 281–8.

VIDICH, ARTHUR J., and BENSON, JOSEPH, *Small Town in Mass Society: Class, Power and Religion in a Rural Community*, Princeton University Press, 1958.

VAN WARMELO, N. J., *A Preliminary Survey of the Bantu Tribes in South Africa*, Pretoria: The Government Printer, 1935.

WARNER, W., LLOYD, and LUNT, PAUL S., *The Social Life of a Modern Community*, Vol. 1, Yankee City Series, Yale University Press, 1941, 1946.

WEBER, MAX, *Essays in Sociology*, translated, edited and with an Introduction by H. H. Gerth and C. Wright Mills, London: Routledge & Kegal Paul Ltd., 2nd impression, 1952.

WHITELY, WINIFRED M., 'Little Town in Overspill', in Kuper, 1953, 205–83.

WHYTE, WILLIAM H., JNR., *The Organization Man*, Penguin Books, 1961.

WILLIAMS, W. M., *The Sociology of an English Village: Gosforth*, London: Routledge & Kegan Paul Ltd., 1956.

z

WILSON, MONICA, and MAFEJI, ARCHIE, *Langa: A Study of Social Groups in an African Township*, Cape Town: Oxford University Press, 1963.

WINTER, EDWARD H., *Beyond the Mountains of the Moon: The Lives of Four Africans*, London: Routledge & Kegan Paul Ltd., 1959.

WRIGHT MILLS, C., 'Review of W. Lloyd Warner and Paul S. Lunt, *The Social Life of a Modern Community*', *Am. Soc. Rev.*, vii (1942), 264–6.

WRIGHT MILLS, C., *The Power Elite*, New York: Oxford University Press, 1956.

YOUNG, MICHAEL, and WILLMOTT, PETER, *Family and Kinship in East London*, London: Routledge & Kegan Paul Ltd., 1957.

324

Index

325

INDEX

Eiselen, W. W. M., 145, 209–10
Elite, xxix–xxxi, xxxiii, 99; average age, 72, 112, 294; disappearance of older, 19–20, 25–6, 31; emergence of new, 7, 19–20, 23, 25–6, 31, 287; Western, xxxff., 15, 90, 92–3, 105–6
'Emergency', 5
England, 3, 44, 315 n. 19; English, 80, 145, 149, 167, 170, 209
Englishmen, 150, 315 n. 19, 292; see also Europeans, English-speaking
Entertaining, see Hospitality
Entrepreneurs, 7, 8, 17, 42, 108, 112, 204, 287; prestige, 15–18, 66
Epstein, A. L., 55
Etiquette, 51, 99–100, 104
Europe, 36, 53, 59, 145; pre-20th century, 15, 17; western, xxix
European Mission churches, 40, 68, 75, 91, 130, 173
Europeans, Westerners, Whites, 12, 13, 15, 19, 51, 104–5, 127, 172, 288, 292; Afrikaans-speaking, 79–80, 101, 267–85 passim; attitude towards, 16, 42, 53, 80, 225, 264ff., 284, 292; dependence on, 53, 105, 149–50, 266, 292; English-speaking, 79–80, 101, 267–85 passim; influence, 234, 258, 281; receding, 8, 11ff., 17, 51, 97; role, 259ff., 283–4
Exclusiveness: residential, 24, 25; social, 19, 114, 118ff., 295

Factory workers, 44, 48, 50, 86, 96, 195, 249
'Factotum', 185
Failures, 152, 155, 158, 159, 162–3, 166, 174, 198
Family, 178, 182, 244–5; circumstances, 143, 172, 287, 290, 291; commitments, 146, 152, 162, 174; considerations, 178, 180, 228, 229, 288; council, 247; obligations, 164, 178
Fanakalo, 80
Farms, 76–7, 131, 309 n. 13; Bantu- or African-owned, 77, 133, 168, 225; communal, 77, 133, 168; Dutch, 122; European- or white-owned, 76, 113, 122, 124, 131, 211; 'family farm', 186, 244; labour, 148; Native Trust, 168
Farmers, 309 n. 13; Bantu, 185; elite parents, 76; white, 76, 122
Fashions, 100, 104

328

Fathers, 75–8, 120, 121–3, 124, 128–9, 147, 154, 262, 281–2, 290–1
Father's people, 242–3
Fingoes, 73–4, 113, 135, 309 n. 11
Finland, xxviii
First-born (female), 243, 247–8, 248, 249, 251, 282–3
First-born (male), 225, 246, 247–8, 249, 250, 282–3
'Followers', 105, 109; status, 97
Football, see Soccer
'Foreign Natives', 189
Fort Hare, 118, 135, 137, 138, 139, 140, 141, 142, 167–9, 171–2, 183–4, 210, 238
Founders, 46, 49
Frankenberg, Ronald, 54, 55
Frazier, E. Franklin, 108
Freehold, 122, 207; rights, 69, 70, 306 n. 15

General Hospital, Johannesburg, 200
Ghana, 13
Ghetto, 53, 62
Girl Guide organizations, 46
Gist, Noel P. and Bennett, William S., 238
Glasgow Missionary Society, 138
Glossop, 95
Goals, Aims, 180, 182, 230; lack, 164
Golf caddy, 149
Golf clubs, courses, 27, 48
Gossip, 106
Government Service, 198–9, 200
Greenbelt, 28
Greig, Doreen, 101ff.

Halkin, Simon, 55
Harris, Abram L., 43
Hartshorne, K. B., 313 nn. 39, 40
Healdtown, 261
Health Inspectors, 25, 72, 86, 95, 107, 112, 154, 167, 213–14, 253; Association, 49; Chief, 41, 214, 253; educational history, 165–6; prestige, 41
Herding, 121, 122, 124, 127, 132, 134, 148, 176, 237, 240; interruption to schooling, 124, 132
Hlonipa, 96
Hlubi, 73–4, 309 n. 11, 113
Homelands (Bantu, African), Bantustans, 16, 42, 71, 199, 296
Home-owners, 21, 87, 102, 114, 294; earliest bourgeoisie, 22